Gordon J. Bolt, president of the Bristol branch of the Institute of Marketing, is head of the School of Business Studies at Bristol Polytechnic. Since Mr. Bolt entered business education and consultancy practice, he has successfully completed many management, marketing, and sales training assignments in industrial and consumer products and service areas. He is a member of the Market Research Society and the International Market Marketing Institute.

Gordon J. Bolt

Market and Sales Forecasting Manual

A SPECTRUM BOOK

Prentice-Hall, Inc., Englewood Cliffs, New Jersey 07632

Library of Congress Cataloging in Publication Data

Bolt, Gordon J.
   Market and sales forecasting manual.

     Rev. ed. of: Market and sales forecasting—a total
   approach. 1972.
   "A Spectrum Book."
   Includes index.
   1. Sales forecasting.   I. Title.
HF5415.2.B59 1982   658.8'18   81-17693
                                         AACR2

ISBN 0-13-558189-3

ISBN 0-13-558171-0 {PBK.}

This Spectrum Book can be made available to businesses and organizations at a special discount when ordered in large quantities. For information, contact Prentice-Hall, Inc., General Publishing Division, Special Sales, Englewood Cliffs, N.J. 07632.

© 1982 by Prentice-Hall, Inc., Englewood Cliffs, New Jersey 07632.
All rights reserved. No part of this book may be reproduced in any form or by any means without permission in writing from the publisher.
A Spectrum Book. Printed in the United States of America.

10 9 8 7 6 5 4 3 2 1

First published by Kogan Page Limited, 116a Pentonville Road, London NI 9JN.
Copyright © 1971 by Gordon J. Bolt. Second edition May 1973.

Prentice-Hall International, Inc., *London*
Prentice-Hall of Australia Pty. Limited, *Sydney*
Prentice-Hall of Canada, Ltd., *Toronto*
Prentice-Hall of India Private Limited, *New Delhi*
Prentice-Hall of Japan, Inc., *Tokyo*
Prentice-Hall of Southeast Asia Pte. Ltd., *Singapore*
Whitehall Books Limited, *Wellington, New Zealand*

Contents

Preface to the First Edition 9
Preface to the Second Edition 11

Part One: The Forecasting Environment

Chapter 1. Marketing, Its Scope and Effect on Forecasting 17
The market economy, *18*; Profit – the success criterion, *18*; Value satisfactions, *19*; Market orientation v production orientation, *19*; Company resources and competitive elements, *20*; The marketing mix, *21*; External influences, *21*; Internal influences, *22*; The marketing mix analyzed, *22*; The marketing mix and management, *28*; The role of the marketing executive, *29*; Brand or product group management, *31*; Consumer markets v industrial markets, *33*; Conclusion, *34*.

Chapter 2. The Product Life Cycle — a Conceptual Framework Approach 36
The product life cycle analyzed, *37*; Production economy implications of the life cycle, *46*; The life cycle as a planning and forecasting unit, *53*; Summary, *63*.

Part Two: The Market and Sales Forecasting Plan

Chapter 3. Market and Sales Forecasting 67
The forecast's planning role, *67*; The forecast as target, *67*; The need for continuity and system, *68*; Pre-forecasting considerations, *68*; Profit gap analysis, *70*; A comprehensive forecasting approach, *70*; Environmental considerations, *71*; The effect of market forces, *73*; Short- , medium- and long-term forecasts, *74*; The impact of medium- and long-term factors on short-term forecasting, *77*; Sales forecasting definitions, *79*; Setting forecasting objectives, *81*; Company-wide uses of forecasts, *88*; Why, what, how, who, where and when, *88*.

Chapter 4. The Collection of Data for Forecasting   90

Scope, *90*; Desk research into internal records, *91*; Desk research into secondary sources of information, *95*; Gathering forecasting information by original field research, *103*; Types of field research, *103*; Methods of collection, *105*; Sales and technical staff as information sources, *105*; Field surveys, *106*; Telephone surveys, *107*; Postal surveys, *107*; Panel or audit methods, *107*; Observational methods, *108*; Motivation research, *108*; Experimental marketing, *108*; Use of field research in forecasting, *109*.

Chapter 5. Basic Forecasting Considerations   111

Assessment terms, *111*; Units of measurement, *112*; Demand analysis, elasticity and price, *116*; The multi-technique approach, *120*.

Chapter 6. The Measurement of Change   122

The use of indicators, *122*; Economic change, *122*; Distribution system change, *123;* Sociological and consumer behavior change, *130*; Industrial change, *135*; International change, *139*; Technological change, *141*.

Chapter 7. Objective Methods of Forecasting   150

Tied indicators and derived demand, *151*; Lead and lag techniques, *151*; Correlation and regression analysis, *154*; Market correlation with economic indicators, *155*; Least squares method — a regression line technique, *171*; Least squares method — even number of items, *175*; Least squares method with confidence limits, *176*; Least squares method using non-time-constrained data, *184*; Regression – summary, *187*; The use of probability in forecasting, *188*; Time series analysis and historical analogy, *210*; More effective forecasting through segmentation, *215*; Forecasting by percentage change, *216*; Forecasting using index numbers, *217*; Simple trend projection allowing for seasonal factors, *217*; Forecasting market share and competitor activity, *218*; Percentage take-off graphs, *223*; Moving Annual Totals and Moving Quarterly Totals, *226*; Conclusion, *232*; The Z chart, *232*; Moving averages, *237*; Other decomposition methods, *246*; Weighted moving averages, *248*; Exponential smoothing, *250*; Exponential smoothing forecast using deseasonalized data, *253*; Forecasting sales by the assessment of advertising, *259*; Model building and forecasting, *261*; Decision models, *264*; Linear models, *265*; Models based on learned behavior, *265*; Market share models, *265*; Brand-switching models, *266*; Preference analysis, *267*; Product life cycle models, *268*; Other models, *268*; Simulation models, *269*; Computers and forecasting, *269*; Which method to use? *271*.

Chapter 8. Subjective Methods of Forecasting   272

Indicator assessment method, *272*; Subjective factor assessment, *275*; The Delphi method, *275*; Survey of consumer/user purchasing intentions, *277*; Panels of executive opinion, *278*; 'Prudent manager' forecasting, *278*; Composite forecasts of the sales force, *279*; Surveys of expert opinion, *280*; Uncertainty and probability in subjective forecasting, *281*; Making uncertainty visible, *282*; Probability and forecasting by composite opinion, *284*; Probability and expected values, *286*; A forecasting application of Bayesian decision theory, *287*; Probability forecasting with large contracts, *290*; Success forecasting in a competitive bidding situation, *291*; Major customer forecasting, *296*.

Chapter 9. Sales Forecasting for New Products 298

The historical analogy approach, *298*; The marketing research approach, *299*; The test market approach, *299*; The life cycle approach, *300*; The substitute approach, *300*; The composite forecasts of salesmen and sales executives, *300*.

Chapter 10. The Application of the Forecast 301

The forecast as a decision-making tool, *301*; Break-even analysis, *302*; Committed and managed costs, *303*; Product mix and ratio analysis, *305*; Application of forecasts to profit centers, to sales territories, in industrial markets, in consumer goods markets, *306*; Application of the forecast by distribution channels, *307*; The forecast as a basis for budgeting and control, *309*; Combined objective/subjective forecast plan, *310*.

Chapter 11. Controlling Forecasting and the Forecast 312

Scope of control, *312*; Forecasts v actual sales, *313*; Variance analysis, *313*; Ranking variances, *314*; Ratios, *314*; The sum of forecasting errors, *314*; The standard error as a monitoring device, *314*; Investigation of variances, *315*; Levels of accuracy, *315*; Formats for comparative assessment, *318*; The Z chart as an auditing device, *318*; The management accounting approach to auditing the forecast, *322*; Using probability in control of the forecast, *326*; Quantitative assessments and measurement values, *328*; Auditing the 'machinery' of forecasting, *330*; Accuracy of forecasting methods, *330*; The life-cycle approach to choice of techniques, *331*; The forecasting control cycle, *331*; Taking remedial action, *333*; Re-forecasting, *333*.

Index 335

Preface
to the First Edition

'If you can look into the seeds of time, and say which grain will grow and which will not, speak then to me.'
Banquo to the three weird sisters in *Macbeth*

On occasions, when visiting a company either as a consultant or as an educationalist, I am astounded to find quite sizeable organizations that claim either that they do no forecasting or merely 'add 10% to last year's sales figures' without reference to the market. I usually ask these executives, 'When are you leaving?' for the odds that they can go on obtaining effective forecasts using this 'head in the sand' approach with impunity are very much against them. If the market declines by 10% the company will have heavily overproduced, and tied-up capital in the shape of stocks will fill the 20% gap. Alternatively, if the market increases by 25%, the company will have missed a marketing opportunity and lost part of its share of the market that may be hard to regain in a highly competitive field. In many cases very elementary prediction techniques will take a lot of the guesswork out of forecasting.

In other companies I find that naive extrapolation of historic sales data is used as a forecast without reference to the changing market or the environments in which the companies operate.

In the vast majority of companies I visit I find a range of forecasting methods being used that produce predictions varying in their effectiveness.

Most books on forecasting treat the subject from a narrow, specialized or partial-subject point of view. Some briefly examine forecasting as a part of overall marketing activity, others are collections of statistical techniques that ignore subjective, non-statistical methods and the overall forecasting/marketing process. Some books ignore the environments in which companies operate and sales performance takes place, others examine the problems of forecasting the economy and certain markets but avoid the problems of company sales forecasting. Approaches are many: statistical, non-statistical, behavioral, subjective, objective, etc. This book seeks to bring together all of these approaches, examining the market environment and marketing influences, and suggests an effective plan of forecasting that can be used as a framework of operations.

The material in this book has emerged over a long period, with systems, methods and techniques obtained from many sources including simple experience. Their development and application comes from the sheer necessity of evolving tailor-made forecasting systems to operate in ever-changing market and company situations.

While this book presents a total approach to marketing and sales forecasting in the sense that it suggests a complete philosophy and an effective overall framework, it would not be possible to list every forecasting technique. But it does suggest a range of methods that show the principles of most forecasting categories and examines a number in detail that have practical applications or implications for all engaged in market and sales prediction.

The book is intended for marketing and other company executives in small/medium sized companies, but also for marketing researchers, forecasters, and management trainees in large organizations. Academically it is aimed at management and business studies students at universities, business schools, and other colleges of further education.

Just as forecasts are affected by the environment in which a company operates, so the author has been influenced by the environment in which the book has been written. I would therefore like to thank the wide range of people who have helped me, some personally and some through their writings. Their names would be too many to list, ranging as they do from executives of client companies, other business acquaintances, fellow members of the Institute of Marketing, to colleagues.

However, I would particularly like to thank Richard Carless who reviewed the manuscript at the later stages of its development, making valuable suggestions with regard to sequence and layout. I would also like to thank Gordon Brand who reviewed Chapter 4 and made a number of useful observations as to content; also Arthur Mugridge who reviewed Chapter 5 and who made a number of suggestions including the multiple correlation example.

Preface
to the Second Edition

In this revised edition some earlier techniques have been further developed and 'new' ones have been added. The problem is what to leave out rather than what to put in. I have tried to continue the earlier practical approach to the subject and I would like to thank everyone who has helped me, especially colleagues at Bristol Polytechnic and numerous friends in industry and commerce. I would also like to thank my wife for her continued support and patience and for indulging me in one of my hobbies, this fascinating subject of forecasting.

In researching and/or applying these methods in company situations it is noticeable that many organizations rely on 'part-time' forecasters. It is significant that the approach in this book (and therefore appropriate techniques) is particularly of use to the 'part-time' forecaster.

Some companies appoint specialist forecasters or market analysts to make market and sales forecasts, but in many organizations the forecasting (particularly short-term) task is treated as an adjunct to the main role of such personnel as salesmen, sales managers, management accountants, brand or product group managers, depot managers, etc. Some companies use these 'operations personnel' to develop a short term forecast (eg a six to 12 months ahead operations forecast) but use centralized marketing specialists or others to develop a short-term forecast (eg a six to 12 months ahead operations plan. Many of the former group of operations personnel have little experience of formal forecasting techniques or know how to develop a forecast objectively. Consequently in some cases highly suspect 'guesstimates' are added into the cumulative forecast.

Sometimes the forecasting function conflicts with the main role of a job/position, perhaps because of time constraints, the nature of the job, the nature of the person, etc.

Although all budgets in an organization are ultimately dependent upon forecasts of how many products and/or services an organization should or could sell or provide, in various companies the forecasting activity is given different degrees of priority depending on how its importance is perceived by an individual, his or her manager, and management generally.

The result is often an effort by the 'operations personnel' to 'make the forecast happen' rather than to take advantage of changing market conditions and do what is best for an organization 'in the market place'. For example, if during the forecasting period sales are down, pressure is put on the sales force to increase sales. The sales force tends to sell what is easiest to sell, which may not be what is in stock, or which causes problems of an unanticipated out of stock situation on some lines. In industries with relatively fast changing technology some not-so-easy-to-sell lines may be left in stock and they may have to be heavily price discounted or risk becoming obsolete. This in turn may affect the profit forecast. In some cases, to ensure that forecasts happen, over-ordering takes place, resulting in a disproportionate amount of capital being tied up in stock at the year end, cash flow problems and, possibly, price discounting.

It would appear that if organizations are to depend particularly in the short term on 'part-time' forecasters, some training in elementary forecasting is necessary to obtain more meaningful forecasts in the first place.

Very rarely does one see sessions on forecasting in a training program for salesmen, sales managers or brand or product group managers. Sometimes this is because it is not the prime part of the job, (eg a salesman must be able to sell or he will not have anything to forecast) or because it is considered that one has to have an advanced qualification in mathematics to do 'formal' forecasting. It is possible, however, by using appropriate examples, to develop so called non-numerate operations personnel into more credible forecasters. Also it is possible to show methods which develop a rolling forecast that is easily updated so that the forecast for the next period is not such a formidable task to obtain.

The fact that these 'operations personnel' are closer to the customer/market place than others within an organization means that they already have, to some degree, one of the essential forecasting abilities, ie 'understanding the forces at work in the market place'. Giving them guidance in forecasting methods may mean that they can produce more viable forecasts.

Conclusion

Somewhere, sometime, the author read:

> Market and sales forecasting is too crucial to an organization to be reduced to simple guesswork, prayer, or the toss of a coin. The 'inspired amateur' is still with us and the question is how much longer can organizations afford him; on the other hand his activities should not be confused with real subjective forecasting, or the application of

human experience and judgement to 'mechanical' forecasting methods.

Forecasting has many skeletons in organizational cupboards and these need to be brought out into the open because forecasting accuracy has a direct effect on an organization's strategy, tactics and performance. A poor forecast today can haunt a company tomorrow in the form of insufficient or excessive capacity and/or inventory, the cost of which will eventually be reflected on the profit line of the balance sheet.

This must be more true today than the day it was written.

Part One: The Forecasting Environment

CHAPTER 1

Marketing, Its Scope and Effect on Forecasting

'A good data base and detailed market surveillance are crucial to good forecasting'
                                                                A Wilson

Marketing has been defined as 'the management process responsible for identifying, anticipating and satisfying customer requirements profitably.'[1] Earlier Kotler used the term *metamarketing* 'to describe the processes involved in attempting to develop or maintain exchange relations involving products/services, organizations, persons, places or causes.'[2]

He expanded this definition as follows:

> Although marketing is traditionally associated with business products and services, the concept of marketing is highly relevant to other types of 'products' as well. Metamarketing describes the application of marketing concepts and tools to the marketing of organizations, persons, places and causes, as well as business products and services.
>
> Product/service marketing is only one of five types of marketing. It can be subdivided into durable goods marketing, nondurable goods marketing, and service marketing. Organization marketing represents efforts to increase response and exchange between an organization and target audiences. It is carried on by business organizations, government agencies, cultural organizations, and service organizations. Persons, too, are marketed as is evident in political-candidate and celebrity marketing, as well as in credential marketing and affect marketing. Place marketing consists of efforts to influence attitudes and bring about exchanges concerning domiciles, business sites, land investments, travel, and national images. Social marketing attempts to influence the acceptance of ideas, such as social causes or social programs.
>
> The marketing concept would call upon the marketer to choose products, prices, distribution, and promotion that meet the needs and wants of his markets and audiences, rather than trying to persuade

1. Institute of Marketing, 1976.
2. P Kotler, 'Metamarketing', *Marketing Forum,* July/Aug 1971.

them to want what he offers. Good marketing practice will always contain elements of both selling and serving. If the marketing concept works, it will provide the link so necessary in making private action serve the public interest.[1]

Although this book is mainly concerned with market and sales forecasting related to business products and services, the basic concepts and prediction techniques can be adapted to most of the aspects of metamarketing listed above.

The market economy

The British and North American economies, like other developed economies, are *market* economies, that is, they are geared to the production of industrial and consumer goods and services for profitable sale, often in distant markets, rather than for personal consumption by the individual producer and his dependants.

Quite early in the development of the North American economy, production in many fields became specialized, first by product and later by process. As the speed of this development increased, producers and consumers, as well as the centers of production and consumption, became more separate and complex. This development has continued: markets have become highly specialized and segmented, and it is no longer possible to consider the total population as the market for any particular product. It is necessary to define highly specialized markets by their characteristics, ie in various combinations of age, sex, occupation, location, income, socio-economic groups, psycho-social groups, industry, etc, so that products may be developed by the specialized producer for the specialized market segment of an economy. Even in situations of relative monopoly, and other non-competitive situations, marketing now influences all phases of business activity. It has therefore become necessary for specialist producers to influence specialist consumers to prevent the substitution of products of other industries by them.

Profit — the success criterion

The criterion by which the success of a business organization is measured is the level (or absence) of its profits; no business unit can remain in existence in the long run without external support unless its activities are profitable. However, many companies would make a profit by closing down immediately and setting their liabilities against their assets. Alternatively, by taking certain short-term measures, large profits one year could be followed by bankruptcy the next; neither course would foster the long-term prosperity of a company. So the company aim must be continuous and long-term profit.

1. Ibid.

Value satisfactions

But the making of profits is not normally possible without selling something to a customer. Therefore, while the aim of a company is normally its profitable operation, to achieve this the company's immediate objective must be the discovery, creation, attraction and satisfaction of customers. But what is this 'something' that is sold to customers? It is *not* a product. It is true that at the end of a sale a physical product may have changed hands, but that is only part of the selling proposition. No one has ever sold a product or service; what buyers buy, and consequently what companies must sell, are groups or combinations of consumer/user *value satisfactions*. These satisfactions include logical benefits (actual product differences or product performance), psychological benefits (prestige, snob value, appeal of aesthetic design, etc), added subjective values, price/value relationships, and even the satisfaction of dealing with a particular company (the attraction of the corporate image), or buying from a particular salesman. To complicate matters, different consumer types will be motivated by different priorities and combinations of the benefits and satisfactions at different stages during the life of a product.

Effective marketing, therefore, can be defined as providing consumer/user satisfactions at a profit.

Market orientation versus production orientation

But not all companies are market-orientated in this way. The rationale of the marketing concept implies that the executives of companies make all decisions in terms of market orientation which begins with the consumer. The concept recognizes that the dictator of marketing success or failure is the *customer*, who is also the key concern in determining company policies and actions. All other company activities are integrated and balanced in terms of what is good for the company in the market. Marketing rather than production should dominate business thinking. In some companies forward plans are still being founded almost entirely on production or financial considerations instead of what is good for the company in the market place. In production-orientated companies they manufacture what it is technically convenient to make, rather than what the consumer needs. As long as easy market conditions make it possible for such companies to operate, there is no pressure on them to establish effective marketing practices; but rarely do they achieve optimum profitability until they do so.

Differences of orientation can be recognized in complete industries as well as in the individual member companies. The terms *production-orientated industries* (or companies) or *marketing-orientated industries* (or companies) indicate quite accurately the relative weight which the sum total of all companies in an industry place on either their production or marketing functions in order to succeed competitively.

However, no industry (or company) producing and marketing goods or services could ever be entirely production or entirely marketing-orientated. There is always a blend of production (cost performance) and marketing (sales performance) resulting in the company's profit performance.

Company resources and competitive elements

Maximization of profit is achieved by making the fullest use of company resources and by seizing marketing opportunities in the current period and by making adequate provisions and profit plans for the future. Market and sales forecasts are vital both in the present and in the future. In the present so that results can be compared with the forecast as a yardstick of performance and as a means of control, and in the future so that the dynamic, changing marketing environment may be anticipated and appropriate action taken. Also market and sales forecasting is a key factor in establishing an effective profit forecast.

To operate a business successfully involves integrating a number of component functions: production, marketing, finance, purchasing, design, personnel, etc. While the latter four functions are important, they wait upon, and are subsidiary to, the strategies of the first two, ie production and marketing. This is because they cannot exist in the long term unless the company finds the correct product(s) and the correct market(s). In fact, marketing sandwiches production between two parts of its operations. Within the laid-down marketing plan, marketing research should be carried out to discover and determine consumer needs, to assess company resources in relation to them, develop products to satisfy them, set up pricing and financial studies, forecast sales and market-test prototypes. If management approval is given to the project, production is carried out and is followed by the communication (advertising, sales promotion, public relations, etc) and direct selling (before-sales service, selling, distribution, and after-sales service) operations of marketing.

It follows therefore that it is essential to analyze the competitive elements of both production and marketing. This will discover strengths, weaknesses and the true company potential, and enable advantage to be taken of them in the marketing plan, and indeed to determine whether a company should be in a particular industry or market at all. The selection of new markets and/or products and the operation of existing marketing operations need to be appraised in the light of competition and potential competition.

By determining the markets in which a company's resources and potential resources have an advantage and potentially a greater chance of success, a company is laying a firm foundation for continued long-term prosperity.

It follows therefore that in the same way as a company needs to analyze and determine its competitive elements in relation to production and marketing resources, and potential resources, thus determining its most advantageous industry, it also needs to develop new products and services that will attain profitable commercialization, by a similar analytical method. Such an approach will reduce new or revitalized product failures and enable the company to influence and extend existing markets and create new ones.

The marketing mix

The way in which the various component parts and techniques of the marketing effort are combined and emphasized determines a company's marketing *mix*. Market-orientated organizations are constantly striving to discover the optimum marketing mix under existing and potential marketing circumstances, ie the marketing mix that will produce the maximum profit in the long run.

Further, the composition of the marketing mix will be influenced by the expectation that the market situation will be different during each stage of the life of a product. The pattern of the progressive life of a product and its implications has caused the concept of the *product life cycle* to evolve. It is necessary to recognize at this point that the market mix needs to be different, because its task is different, during each stage of the life of a product.

External influences

The profitable success of a business unit will also depend upon the appreciation of the external (and largely uncontrollable) factors that bear upon its particular market and industry situation.

External uncontrollable factors lay down the broad environmental limits within which the company will operate. They include such forces as the general economic and political environment, technological factors, climatic factors, cultural forces, population factors, standard of living factors, ethical and social forces and appropriate international considerations, both as they exist and as they may develop in the future. The total environment also includes government controls, influence and intervention over the product, over competitive and restrictive practices, over pricing, over advertising and sales promotion, over other company activities, and over business generally; all normally enforced by legal instrument or government pressure. A part of the external business environment will be molded by the general legal system of the country such as common and statute law, and the attitude of the courts. The attitudes and habits of consumers and potential customers (used in the widest sense), and the component parts of the trade channels of distribution, trade structure, practices, and procedures, will be an important part of the broad business environment affecting a company's marketing mix. Competition (home and international) in its many forms (price, non-price, product, choice, service, direct and indirect, etc) and its relationships (size, market share, etc) is a further aspect of the business atmosphere within which the business unit must operate.

Internal influences

Among the many internal controllable factors are a number that do not come within the company's marketing program but about which decisions must be made in terms of what is good for the company in the market. These would include such factors as the company's financial strength generally, particularly with regard to money available or obtainable for expenditure upon product research and development, and for financing the marketing program. Especially important are those parts of the marketing plan that require investment. These are sometimes without an immediate or apparent return in the short period (eg marketing research or public relations) or are cumulative in effect over a period of time (advertising). The company's financial strength is also a vital factor where new products or new ventures introduce the possibility of operating losses in the early stages of the life of the product. Other internal business factors that will have an impact upon the company's marketing effectiveness are its specialized experience or know-how (in manufacturing, marketing, scientific research, or managerial techniques), its plant capacity, its material resources and skilled personnel available, its image and reputation, its position in the market. Also important are its location with regard to markets, raw material sources or transport links, labor and basic utilities. Lastly, the ownership or control of a technical monopoly through patents, copyrights, or trademarks is a powerful internally controlled factor.

The marketing mix analyzed

Internal controllable factors coming within the scope of the marketing program can be classified into the eight broad categories shown in Figure 1.

Figure 1 shows functions of marketing rather than departments of a company, in the sense that someone within the organization, whether it is large or small, must be responsible for them, otherwise the marketing effort will be weakened. The emphasis and the degree to which each function is employed should depend upon the needs of the market situation in which the organization finds (or purposely locates) itself. In each of the stages of the life of a product, the emphasis or 'mix' of these functions needs to be adjusted to obtain the optimum marketing effort.

The eight functions shown in Figure 1 are:

1. Marketing research and market intelligence

This means research into every aspect of marketing as well as into a particular market. As a marketing function it serves as professional and/or technical expertise in collecting, classifying and storing relevant information. It should also recommend, execute, interpret, and present marketing research studies to marketing management. It is a management tool for reducing managerial risk-taking by providing facts that enable judgements and decisions made by management to be more soundly based. As such it should be a systematic, continuing study and evaluation of all factors bearing on any business operation which involves management decisions to be made in terms of what is good for the company in the market.

2. Product/service planning

This function will vary from company to company depending upon resources, market situation, objectives, etc. It has been suggested[1] that there are four product/service strategy approaches open to most companies in an industry based on changing technology:

(a) *First to market*, based on strong research and development, technical leadership and risk taking.
(b) *Follow the leader,* based on strong development resources and an ability to react quickly when the market starts its growth phase.
(c) *Applications engineering,* based on product modifications to fit the needs of particular customer segments in mature markets.
(d) *Me-too,* based on superior manufacturing efficiency and/or cost control.

It is important to identify the strategy being adopted by the company because the particular choice can affect sales performance and consequently the sales forecast.

While it is possible for an organization to market a service without a product (eg dry cleaning, design consultancy, travel agency services, maintenance contracts, etc) it is rarely possible to market a product without some aspect of service (eg repair and/or spares service, convenience of location, technical advice, demonstration,

---

1. Ansoff H I & Stewart J M 'Strategies for technology based business' *Harvard Business Review,* March/April 1967 pp 71-83.

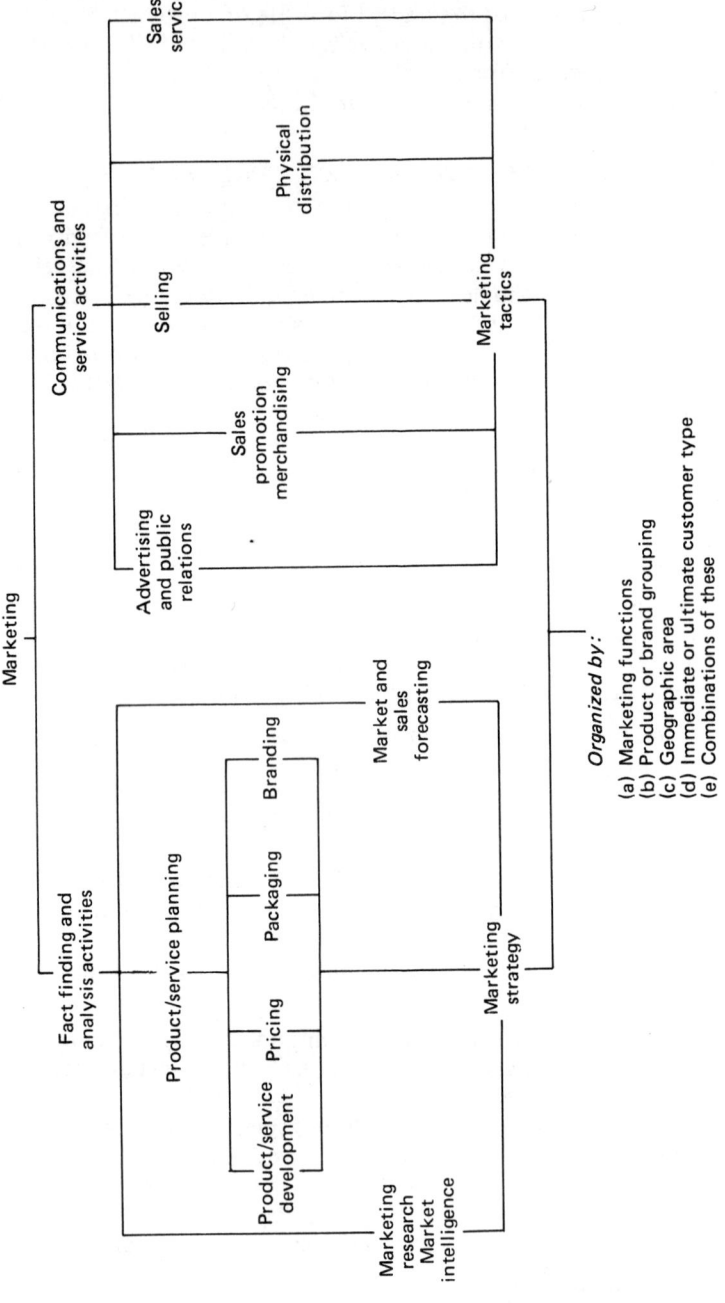

Figure 1. *The component parts of the marketing mix*

etc). The balance between the product/service ratio offered to customers is often crucial in competitive markets and can affect the numbers of products sold in changing market situations.

The broad function of product/service planning can be sub-divided into four parts:

(i) *Product/service development*. This covers the revitalization and development of existing products/services, products/services new to the company, and new generic products/services both for existing and new markets. It should also cover the phasing out of products/services when they no longer contribute to the profit or other objectives of a company.

(ii) *Pricing policy*. Prices will affect the number of units purchased by customers and changes in the general level of prices in a market and the individual product/service price in particular can cause changes in demand patterns. The pricing plan should, during planning phase, outline the policy to be adopted, price levels to adopt on launching a new product/service and price levels considered desirable in later stages of the product/service life cycle, eg skimming, penetration or premium price policy adoption. Trade discount structure, quantity discounts, status pricing, etc, would all be included in the pricing plan. The effects of planned and other price changes need to be anticipated in the market and sales forecast.

(iii) *Packaging policy*. The three aspects of packaging, protection in transit, protection in storage, and its marketing role, all play an important role in the marketing mix effectiveness, and the original pack and any later changes in its design may have a direct effect on sales and consequently on the ability to forecast.

(iv) *Branding*. Branding of products/services is a fundamental necessity in highly competitive markets to ensure customer recognition and the projection of company/product/service images. The branding plan should include objectives, policies and procedures regarding the selection of brand name(s) and trade mark(s), individualized or 'family' brand for the product/service range, branding related to quality, geographical areas, or markets, and the degree of emphasis on own brand, 'private' label or unbranded products. The impact of the 'brand' is an important consideration in market and sales forecasting.

3. Market and sales forecasting

The importance of market and sales forecasting is derived not only from its function as part of the marketing mix. In market-orientated companies it also forms the basis of all financial budgets of departments throughout the company — production, purchasing, finance, personnel, etc. All budgets in these areas depend to some extent upon an estimate of the number of products the company expects to sell, the spread of fixed costs over this volume, the revenue the company will receive, and expected profits. Even company policy decisions will be influenced by the sales forecast. This is because in both single and multi-product companies quantity decisions have to be made regarding the attainment of company objectives and marketing strategy.

Market and sales forecasting concerns the potential and prospective sales volume or market trend for the individual product (company), and sets a sales goal in an anticipated market within the overall economy.

4. Advertising and public relations

Advertising is a prime factor in the marketing mix; it has been defined as 'the preparation of visual and oral messages and their dissemination through paid media for the purpose of making people aware of, and favorably inclined towards, a product, brand, service, institution, idea, or point of view'.[1]

The public relations task has been defined as 'the deliberate, planned and sustained effort to establish and maintain mutual understanding between an organization and its publics'.[2] Although in this case the term 'publics' is used to mean more than the marketing public, if no formal PR department is looking after this special marketing area then the marketing function must 'acquire' it. Advertising and marketing PR are complementary; one promotes the products and their benefits, the other promotes the company image.

Just as the objectives, theme, and media of advertising change as the life of a product progresses, so will the objectives, theme and media of PR change as it seeks to achieve the right 'public' climate and attitude, and to present the corporate image in the most favorable light.

---

1. Albert Frey 'Promotion', *Marketing in Business Management,* p 351. Macmillan, New York, 1963.
2. Definition of the Institute of Public Relations.

5. Sales promotion, packaging and merchandising

Sales promotion is concerned with a variety of activities (exhibitions, demonstrations, dealer and consumer education, competitions, deals, offers, samples, etc) that 'push' the product towards the customer. It acts as a bridge between advertising and direct selling, making both more effective by inducing salesmen to sell more, wholesalers and retailers to stock and promote more and the ultimate customer to buy.

Packaging, today produced from a variety of materials, was originally conceived as a simple vehicle, branded to facilitate repeat sales, for carrying a premeasured quantity from the manufacturer to the ultimate consumer or user, suitably protecting the contents. It has become a most powerful visual symbol, the handle by which to promote and sell the product. But the protective function of packaging still performs a vital role, because unless the product and package arrive at their destination in first class condition, sales appeal will be greatly diminished.

Merchandising is directly applicable to consumer goods marketing. It has been defined as psychological persuasion of consumers at the point of purchase without the aid of personal salesmanship. Alternatively it has been described as all those non-personal aids and activities that make sure that goods 'sold in' are 'sold out' by retailers at the anticipated rate.

Merchandising has a vital sales promotional part to play in those highly competitive consumer goods fields where manufacturers and marketing organizations realize that to maximize sales they cannot afford to leave all the activities at the point of purchase in the hands of the retailers.

6. Selling

The activities of the field sales force represent another aspect of a company's customer communications. The nature of the selling task is to sell through distributors, wholesalers, and/or retailers, or to the ultimate consumer or user, by means of planned selling techniques.

In consumer goods marketing, field selling may be supported by a telephone sales organization. In the industrial marketing situation the technically trained sales force is the spearhead of customer communications supported by advertising and sales promotion.

7. Physical distribution

The main responsibility of this function of marketing is that of having the right goods in the right place at the right time and in the right condition. Physical distribution is concerned with the economics and use of various combinations of channels of distribution, with transport and delivery, warehousing, stock control and dispatch, and the placing of strategic stocks at positions in the market to beat competition. The distribution chain balances the output of production, based on the sales forecast, with the anticipated demands of the buying public and with intermediate links such as wholesalers and/or retailers.

8. Sales service

This can be a prior sales function to a retailer to get display space in a retail store (eg merchandising) or before-sales service (eg a demonstration or trial) or during-sales service (eg design work for a planned kitchen) or after-sales service (eg a spares service or maintenance contract). In some cases (such as certain household appliance companies) the servicing is 'franchised out' to independent servicing companies.

In some industrial companies where the product is complex, sales service is underpinned by a product support group which provides information in various ways, eg technical publicity, training notes and materials, workshop manuals, spare parts books, operators' handbooks, etc. It also often carries out service training and product sales training.

Whether the sales service activity is carried out by a department of the company, or a dealers services department, or franchised to an independent maintenance company, it is imperative that the maintenance engineers are trained to the standard of service that customers expect because of price, product image and performance, and company reputation, otherwise company sales performance and the accuracy of the sales forecast will be adversely affected.

The marketing mix and management

Obviously the effectiveness of any of these marketing mix activities or indeed the total marketing effort will depend on how well they are managed, ie planned and controlled.

Planning and control can be divided into five main activities:

(a) Setting objectives, identifying key tasks, setting acceptable performance levels, standards, goals, etc.
(b) Developing a program to achieve these objectives.
(c) Measuring performance against pre-determined goals.
(d) Interpreting trends and results.
(e) Knowing where, when and how to take corrective action.

A further aspect of control is recording performance information for use as a guide in planning and forecasting future operations; it also highlights marketing opportunities.

Special decision areas in this marketing function relate to acceptable profit levels, trade discount structure, credit policy, pricing strategy, branding policy, etc.

A particular planning role is the development of an operational marketing plan with the stages suggested in Figure 2.

Just as the effectiveness of marketing planning depends to a great extent on market and sales forecasting, it must be appreciated that a forecast will be affected by policy decisions made in marketing planning.

The best methods of measurement and control are through the use of a variety of communication devices. These include marketing audits, budgets, performance appraisals, field inspections, ratio analysis, reports, job descriptions, critical path and network scheduling, conferences, the application of the profit center concept, sales and cost analysis, etc.

In practice, effective marketing management control is not used simply to determine how good or bad marketing has been in the past, but also to set effective goals to determine what action to take to obtain optimum results in the future.

The role of the marketing executive

The responsibility of the marketing executive is to implement company policy and to plan, co-ordinate and evaluate the eight functional parts of marketing, even where one of them has been contracted out to an agency or consultant (eg advertising and public relations). He or she must ensure that the right objectives are set and achieved. The marketing executive is not necessarily an expert in each aspect of marketing, but must know enough about each functional part to co-ordinate them effectively to meet the company's aims, objectives and purpose. No one marketing function should be considered separately when thinking in terms of total marketing effort. Each function should always be valued in terms of its relationship to the other functions and the alternatives available.

It is possible in a small company to envisage one person controlling and executing the whole of the eight marketing functions. But, as the size of the enterprise increases, each function tends to be delegated to a specialist who may eventually head a complete department. This follows the basic concept of delegation, and normally it will be found that both the duties retained by the executive and those delegated will tend to be performed more effectively. Thus, as an enterprise continues to grow, a point will be reached where the ability to co-ordinate this complex range of marketing functions will be beyond the scope and capacity of one person. In such a situation a company is faced with the choice of one of two alternatives. Either the company's activities can be arranged into marketing or regional areas (ie the executive position is duplicated) or alternatively they can be divided into product or brand groups.

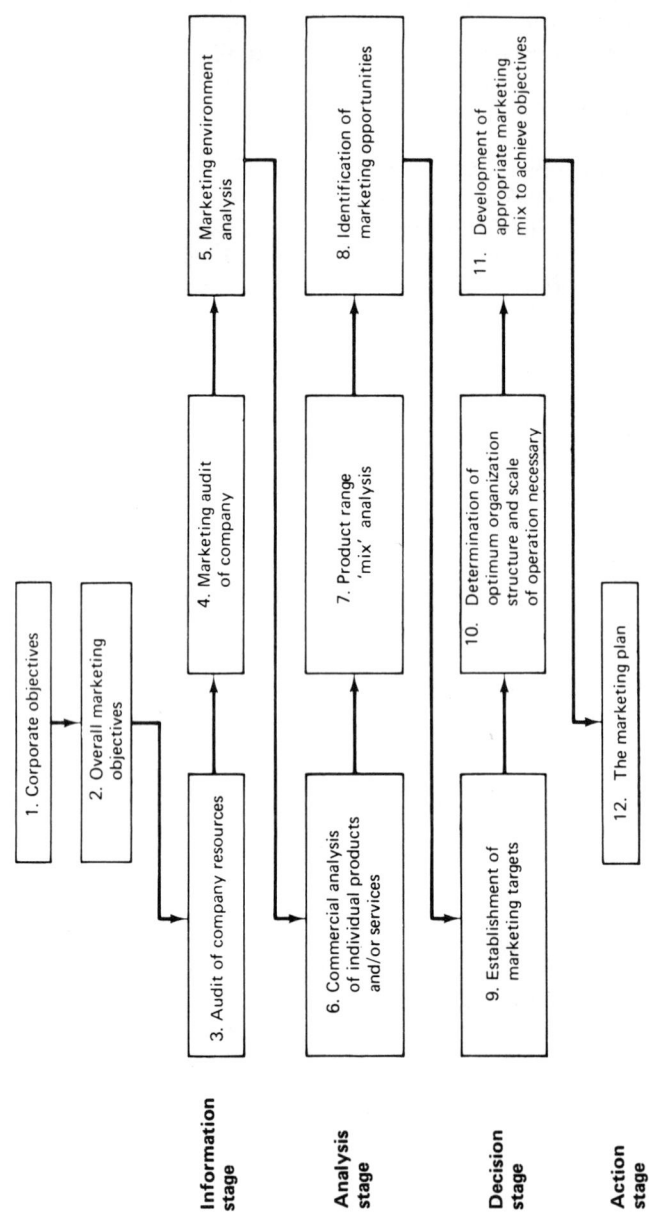

Figure 2. *Stages in the development of an operational marketing plan*

Brand or product group management

The marketing executive is responsible for the profitable marketing of all the company products but if the brand or product range becomes diversified and/or in some areas requires intensive marketing, then it is possible for him or her to delegate product management to brand or product range managers.

The *brand manager* is responsible for the marketing and profitability of a brand or product group. This responsibility includes liaison with production and finance as well as organizing the appropriate amount of activity from the eight functional aspects of marketing. The brand manager's role is to work with these departments and functions, and to co-ordinate their activities on his or her product group to an overall marketing plan within budgetary limitations and to an all-important timetable.

The brand or product group method of organization ensures that no products are neglected. It permits delegation of product responsibility and accountability, and makes possible continuous analysis and evaluation of individual product performance. In most cases the eight marketing functions have to serve all brand or product group managers. This tends to cause organizational problems because the eight marketing activities described assume a functional role by producing a service. No one brand manager has direct control over them. The problem is magnified as the number of brand or product groups within a company is increased. Often, loss of efficiency results because the system is then one of negotiation and persuasion rather than direct mandatory authority. This can be overcome if the services performed by the various marketing functions are organized so that brand or product group managers have to 'buy' them. This is done by the brand manager from the brand budget, within the context of the overall marketing plan and approved by the senior marketing executive. Applying the brand or product group concept, the company's marketing scheme of operation would be as shown in Figure 3.

The concept of brand or product group management purchasing functional department services is widely followed in certain repeat-selling, rapid-turnover consumer goods industries. It is popular because for most departments within an enterprise it is simply a matter of the allocation of resources controlled by budgets. For example, the size of any marketing function's budget will tend to be the sum total of all the individual brand manager's budgets in that specialized field (eg sales promotion, advertising, sales force, etc). Problems arise if all the brand managers press for additional services from one particular function, (eg special sales drives by the field sales force), which then becomes overworked. At the same time problems could arise with regard to the other functional services if they become under-employed, as the brand managers cut back their demand for

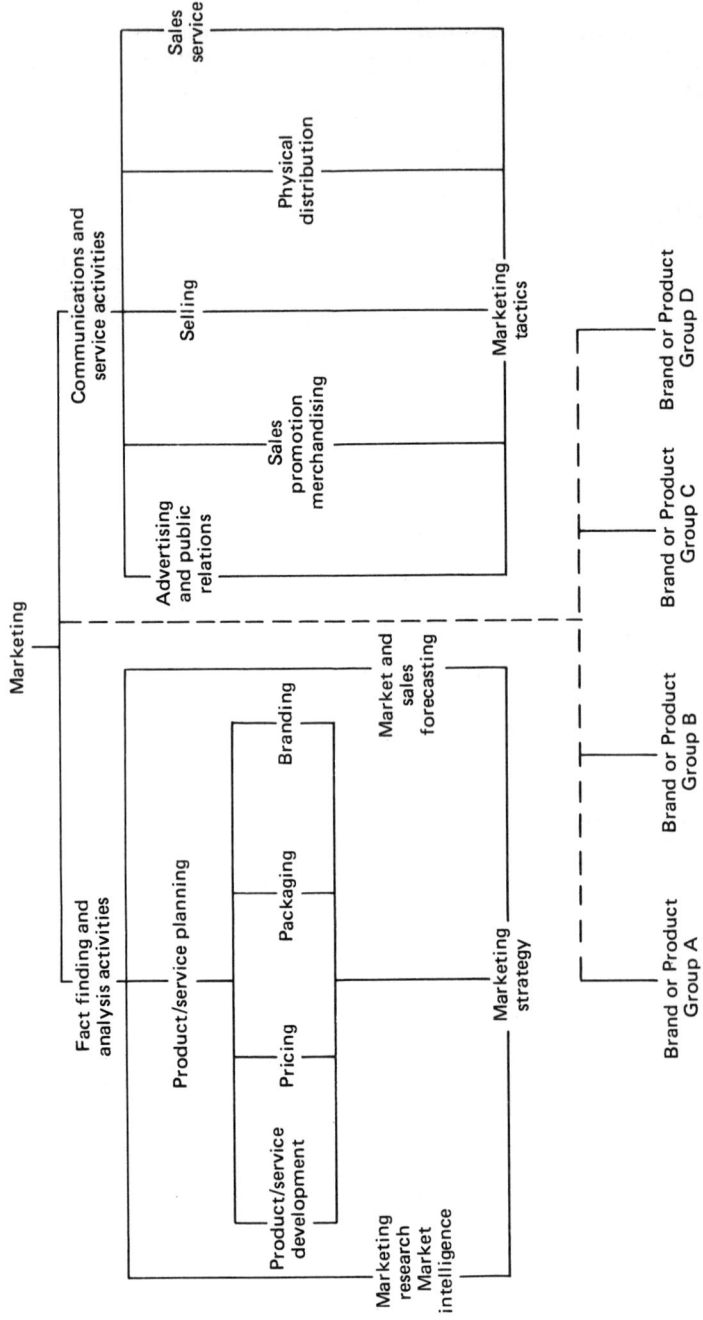

Figure 3. *The brand management concept related to the eight broad categories of the marketing mix*

such services. Under-employment of functional service facilities (such as advertising) means that costs per unit sold will be higher than necessary. Such functional departments have certain fixed costs that have to be met whether their services are used or not.

So far the marketing organization has been considered as being made up of eight separate major functions, but even in large organizations individual functions reflected as departments may not be found. In fact, it may be a matter of necessity in the medium and small company that one department carries out several of these functions. But there is the need for the performance of these functions in the form of the optimum marketing mix, if the company is to be really effective in a competitive market situation.

Consumer markets versus industrial markets

Consumer markets are involved with fast moving perishable products, fast moving non-perishable products, durable items (eg shoes, clothes, etc) consumer capital items (eg cars, houses) — and consumer services (eg hotels, dry cleaners, estate agents, etc).

Industrial markets are concerned with materials and components that are used to make a product, supplies that are used in the manufacturing process (eg machine oil, abrasives, cleaning agents) industrial capital items (eg machine tools, plant and equipment), and industrial market services (eg design services, consultancy, industrial cleaning, waste disposal, etc).

While most of the basic marketing concepts apply to both consumer markets and industrial markets, the latter often have a number of special characteristics that make for a different marketing approach in general and a different market and sales forecasting approach in particular.

These characteristics include:

1. *Rational buying motives.* Industrial purchases are normally made after careful evaluation of the 'need' situation and of alternative products. Rational rather than emotional buying motives tend to prevail.
2. *The decision making unit.* Industrial buying decisions in most companies are made and/or influenced by a group of people, ranging from the purchasing executive to production, design, finance executives, etc, any one of whom can influence a purchasing decision.
3. *The time element.* Long negotiations may take place before an order is placed or a supplier changed. The phasing of a company's budgeting year will influence buying patterns. Also in the case of plant and equipment it may be many years before the purchaser is likely to be 'in the market' again, although technological innovations may cause the calculations regarding

replacement business to be radically revised.
4. *The 'anti-all-eggs-in-one-basket' concept.* Even though there may be a distinct advantage in dealing with one supplier (product, performance, price, etc) many industrial purchasers (particularly relating to components) are loth to depend on a single supplier in case of delivery delays. There is often a problem in forecasting the share of available business possible rather than total potential business. Alternatively, capital equipment purchasers may prefer one supplier (in spite of possible short term advantages) because of 'fleet' discounts, reduced spare parts stocks, etc.
5. *Industrial demand is derived demand.* The demand for industrial products/services depends upon the well-being and future prospects of the industry supplied. Thus the demand for a machine that makes a component product will depend on the demand for that product. Such machines have to be replaced and a situation could arise where a 5% cutback in the consumer product demand could (because the machines which have not worn out can cope with the new, lower level of demand) mean a 100% fall in the demand for machinery.
6. *Channels of distribution.* Unlike consumer markets, most industrial markets have relatively simple channels of distribution of the product. A large majority of industrial producers go direct to the customers, and where wholesalers' factors are used they are usually highly specialized.

All these factors and others tend to make the problems of market and sales forecasting different in industrial markets compared with consumer markets.

Conclusion

Marketing is a dynamic process. As the market situation changes, reflected by the various stages of the life of a product, so the composition and emphasis of the marketing mix must change to keep the company ahead of competitors in the new situation. Companies move forward or slip back; they must grow, not necessarily in size but in effectiveness of operation.

There are three possible growth routes; these are through more effective marketing and/or differentiation of the company's existing product range, through the addition of an existing product or range but one that is new to the particular company, or through marketing a completely new generic product. A fourth strategy is possible, that of reducing the existing product range by eliminating unprofitable lines, or those products that use resources that could be more profitably used elsewhere. This should have the effect of helping the three growth routes already mentioned.

Any of these alternatives can be profitable for a company if an effective marketing plan is evolved and implemented. This must recognize the need for an appropriate marketing mix and appreciate the external environment in which the company operates, as well as internal company resources. Further, it should be one that takes account of the changing marketing needs as the life of a product develops, and one that is based on an effective forecasting system to predict the market in general and company sales in particular.

CHAPTER 2
The Product Life Cycle – a Conceptual Framework Approach

'Rome wasn't built in a day? I wasn't in charge of that job.'
Anon

All products have *life cycles*; the shape of sales curves has been generally understood for a long time and has often been used as the basis for marketing strategy. There is a life cycle for the individual company's product, ie a *brand life cycle*, and there is a life cycle for a whole product category. This is the sum total of all individual company brand life cycles for a grouping of products that are physically very similar or that offer similar customer satisfactions. It will be appreciated that an individual company can influence the shape, speed and size of its own brand life cycle in relation to its market situation and resources. But the extent to which it can affect the whole product category life cycle will be limited, and more difficult (though still possible) to achieve, except under conditions of monopoly and duopoly.

The product life cycle is a concept fundamental to forecasting. It provides a conceptual framework within which the forecaster can analyze the dynamics and the underlying forces which exist in the market segment for the whole product category or the individual brand, the sales of which the forecaster is trying to predict.

Also, the product life cycle permits the identification of the out-of-phase relationship or lag between the sales curve and the profit curve normally experienced by companies in competitive markets. Recognition of this factor is vital, for although the forecasting of sales is necessary for the effective operation of a company, it is more meaningful to relate them to anticipated *profits* in view of the basic company objective.

Further, the concept of the product life cycle is a useful device as a planning and forecasting time unit. Even when the exact timing of a product life cycle cannot be determined, it is often more realistic than the arbitrarily imposed accountancy time units.

Each market situation produces its own pattern for a particular product category life cycle. The various stages of both the whole product category and the brand life cycles tend to have their own particular characteristics in all cases, although the duration of each stage may differ considerably. A product life cycle in a hypothetical case could be as shown in Figure 4.

The product life cycle can be considered in two ways:

1. As a *potential* curve. In this case a prediction of size, shape and speed must be determined by an analysis of the underlying internal and external factors that will mold it. A company can adjust the type and emphasis of its marketing activities to suit the current and future stages of the product life cycle. Or, thinking in terms of a product life cycle stage, it will help a company to pick out the right combination of marketing mix factors, and determine the right timing so that a market will be 'created' for its product.
2. As a *realized* curve. In this case it is the result of marketing policies and strategies operating within the constraints of the underlying internal and external factors. By using retrospective analysis the determining factors that caused the cycle's shape and size can be identified, and can be used to produce more effective forecasts.

The product life cycle analyzed

An appreciation of the various stages of a fully exploited product life cycle, as shown in Figure 4, is vital to the forecaster if he is to allow for the dynamics of marketing in the forecast. The actual stages of a life cycle can be identified by a combination of various characteristics some examples of which are shown immediately below the life cycle in Figure 4.

Just as there are characteristics that identify life cycle stages, so there are ideal strategies and responses appropriate to each stage if the company is to take maximum advantage of the market situation in which it finds itself.

The situation during each stage is briefly described as follows:

1. The research and development stage

The opening stage of the product life cycle commences when the market-orientated company identifies market opportunities, growth markets, and when product/services concepts or ideas are explored, screened, researched, evaluated and developed. It is a period of 'tailoring' a product/service to satisfy the particular needs of an identified group or groups of potential customers in relation to company resources and potential resources, and of assessing the profit potential of a product/service. It is a period of expenditure outwards without revenue inwards (with certain exceptions, such as some forms of test marketing where costs can be offset to a degree by sales

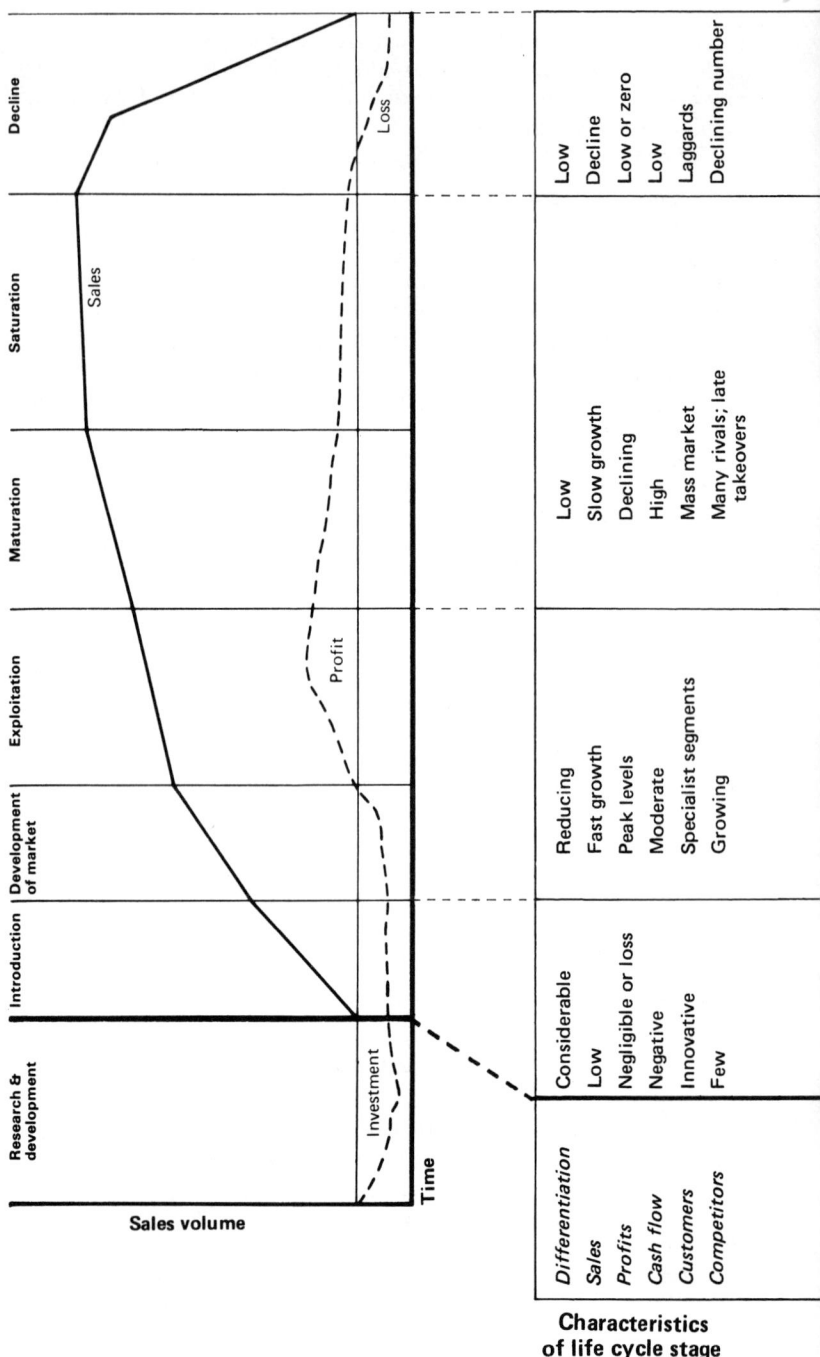

Price character	Differentiation	Differentiation and fluctuation	Stable	Defensive
Number of brands	One or few	Rapid growth	Few new entries	Rapid decline
Strategy	Expand market	Market penetration	Defend share	Increase productivity
Marketing expenditures	High	High (declining %)	Falling	Low
Marketing emphasis	Product awareness	Brand preference	Brand loyalty	Selective
Distribution	Patchy	Intensive	Intensive, later seek others	Selective
Price	High	Lower	Lowest	Rising
Product	Basic	Exploit unique selling proposition	Differentiated	Rationalized
Promotion	High per unit	Growth per unit in total	Stable per unit; develop 'holding campaigns'	Rapid decline
Target group	Trendsetters	Early trend followers	Late trend followers	Specialized group
New product strategy	First in market	Follow the leader	Applications engineering; later 'me-too' product	Reduce range

Effective response to stage situation

Figure 4. *A hypothetical product life cycle applicable to an individual brand or a whole product category; the characteristics of the life cycle stage and the effective responses to each stage situation are shown beneath each stage of the life cycle*

revenue). But it is one that should be viewed as a period of investment in the project rather than as a loss. It is also a period when price must be determined and related to volume at different levels so that a viable forecast can be made.

2. The introduction stage

During the introduction stage, if the product and market have been carefully and extensively researched, if the product has been tested and prepared for the market and is acceptable to potential consumers, and if the emphasis and correct mix of the marketing activities has been properly assessed and the product launch correctly timed, sales will commence and will normally increase throughout this period. However, it is unlikely that overall profits will be made until a later period. Then, sales volume is much higher and has had time to cover the high initial costs incurred in product and marketing research, and research and development, although the latter (R & D) cost is often written off as a historic cost, or applied as a current overhead charge. It is not inevitable that a new product will be accepted by a particular market even when exhaustive research has been carried out. Failure may be caused through the market situation changing between the collecting of research data and using it, or wrongly defining the problem and/or using the wrong data base, or wrongly interpreting data and/or incorrect marketing management decisions.

3. The market development stage

In the market development phase of the product life cycle, if the new product is successful, the rate of sales growth gains momentum as there is a significant increase in consumer/user demand. This increase occurs as information regarding the product is spread by advertising, sales promotion and satisfied customers, and more consumers purchase. It follows either the extension of the geographical area of operations, or the intensification of marketing efforts within the existing area covered, or both. Two factors are responsible for the expansion of demand for the new product; one is the effectiveness of the marketing mix and the other is the market reaction. Market reaction should develop according to the pattern anticipated in the market and sales forecasts. The effectiveness of the earlier research and development of markets and products stage is reflected in the ability of the market-orientated company to expand demand in this current period. The fundamental factor is the whole bundle of consumer/user value satisfactions including the product that is being offered. Often it is relatively easy to create demand initially for a new product, particularly when the uniqueness or novelty factor is high. But a fundamentally good bundle of consumer/user value satisfactions is necessary to foster repeat or recommended sales. The market development stage tends to be a period in which demand is 'created' rather than waiting for it to occur by accident or through the incidence of time. By creating markets, companies can operate at the optimum level of output and, in many cases, achieve economies of scale.

If all consumers were homogeneous, had the same needs and possessed the same ideas about products so that a standardized market existed, then it would be possible to proceed direct from the development of the market stage to the maturation (or maturity) stage. However, because consumers have different needs and wants within the same product group, the limited alternatives offered during the development stage are inadequate to appeal to all potential consumer types.

4. The exploitation stage

The full development of a particular section of the market by a company marketing a particular product does not lead immediately to the maturity of the market as a whole. The product life cycle cannot proceed into its maturation stage until a variety of different product alternatives and marketing options are available to the main market segments that comprise the total potential consumer group. There is, therefore, an intermediate phase, that of the *exploitation* stage. The company exploits its marketing situation, emphasizing the unique features of the product and/or its service and/or other marketing advantages (price, multiple applications, utility satisfaction, convenience packaging, etc).

In the introduction and market development stages, a single generic product type tends to be offered to a main segment of the market. In the exploitation stage, sales propositions are evolved by market-orientated companies that appeal not only to some parts of the existing market but also to completely new segments, thus extending the market further.

5. The maturation stage

Some exponents of the product life cycle concept use the terms maturation (or maturity) and saturation synonymously to describe the stage before the decline of the cycle. However, in the majority of cases, two rather different sets of circumstances, one following the other, normally exist during both the company and overall industry life cycles, between the exploitation stage and that of decline. It is appropriate to describe the first as maturation and the second, saturation.

The life cycle moves into its maturation stage when a variety of different product alternatives have been made available to each of the main market segments that comprise the total potential consumer group.

Maturation is a gradual process. Product improvements and differentiation continue during the early part of the stage but later there tends to be a decline in the rate of new or improved product development. In the early part of the stage also, consumers are faced with an increasing range of brands and need 'educating' as to what satisfactions each brand offers. Later the market settles down as consumers become skilled in the evaluation of brands.

Further, over the period there tends to be a gradual decrease in the number of new entrant companies introducing improved products. However, the degree of competition will tend to increase between companies during the maturation stage as there will be an increased supply of the various versions of the product into a market that is growing only very slowly. Another characteristic of this stage is that price levels decline in real terms, mainly because of the increased competition factor. They also decline in many cases because of the increased scale of production operations and mass production techniques that permit a reduction in fixed cost per unit as overheads are spread over a greater sales volume.

It is a dynamic, transitional period; the early part characterized by many improved and differentiated products, shifting brand loyalties, fluctuating market shares and prices, but later culminating in the maturation of products, markets, competition and prices.

By the time a product moves into its maturation stage the basic product concept has gained general consumer acceptance, but although the demand for it continues to rise slightly, the rate of increase has diminished considerably. This reduced rate of market growth is partly caused by increased competition developing in the market and partly because of the early signs that the market is becoming saturated for the product as it exists. Both the competitive and saturation factors are linked and are significant. The maturation stage is one where supply is catching up with general demand and supplies are freely available to many specialized market segments. This situation has arisen because companies who contemplated entry into the market during the development period made individual company production equipment and marketing policy decisions. Such decisions, made in isolation, and in ignorance of other companies' plans, are based upon early life cycle data and the predicted steepness of the curve in the two previous periods. They often lead to excess production capacity in the industry in the maturation stage.

The marketing mix or emphasis upon the various functions of marketing will need to be changed in each phase of the life cycle. The task of the marketing mix is so different basically in the introduction, development and, to an extent, in the exploitation stages compared with the later stages, that companies who do not recognize the phase change continue to use the marketing mix from an earlier era.

By the time the maturation stage is reached, three distinct types of demand have emerged. Each requires a different approach if a company's marketing effort is to be effective. It is necessary for marketing men to distinguish between expansion demand, replacement demand and repeat demand. *Expansion demand* relates to completely new consumers or users entering the market for this type of product. *Replacement demand* is associated with consumer durable and industrial capital goods, and is caused by consumers or users scrapping existing equipment and replacing it. *Repeat demand* is concerned with frequently purchased consumable products. Thus in consumer durable and industrial goods markets extra sales obtainable in the maturation stage will come by attracting new consumers into the market, and by encouraging users to replace existing equipment. In the same stage, extra sales in consumable product markets come from new customers or by persuading existing consumers to increase their frequency or unit of purchase rather than spend their money on another class of product.

Although present in other stages of the life cycle, the changing relationship between the types of demand is an outstanding characteristic of the maturation stage. The *rate* of market growth decreases throughout this stage although actual volume continues to increase; it becomes increasingly difficult to discover potential expansion demand. Therefore expansion demand will tend to depend upon the quality of the marketing effort and the ability of companies to discover profitable market segments. The fostering of replacement demand will depend upon the ability to project a more efficient performance and up-to-date image together with many plus benefits, logical and psychological, that the potential purchaser is having to forgo with his existing equipment. But the fostering of repeat demand will depend upon such factors as the number of existing customers, the ability of companies to cause and retain brand loyalty, and the frequency of purchase.

6. The saturation stage

In the next stage, the market becomes saturated under existing circumstances. This state is characterized by intense competition with a high level of sales promotion activity, as the main suppliers in the market tend to overproduce and seek to take from their competitors some of their brand share of the market. Expansion demand for the product in the market has almost ceased, as consumers that make up the existing market are satisfied with existing designs or composition of the product. New consumers are offset to a great extent by some existing consumers changing to a 'new' substitute product. Within the overall product category market, individual company market shares and consequently their sales volume, can and do change, depending how competitive the industry is, and the degree to which consumers of one brand can be persuaded to switch their loyalty to a competitor's product. The saturation stage may be indicated in its early phases by a weakening of brand preference, itself indicated by a higher cross-elasticity of demand among leading brands.

In the early part of this stage, price competition is typical and, in many cases, this forcing down of prices towards costs makes economies of scale crucial to survival. In the latter part of the saturation stage this highly competitive situation causes the structure of the industry to change, ie the number of product companies to be reduced but not necessarily the number of product alternatives. The overproduction resulting from planning decisions in earlier life cycle stages leads to the rationalization of products and processes. But, as designs become standardized and the most efficient production methods become established, there will be a tendency for products to begin to look the same or similar within each market segment (eg cars, detergents, petrol, etc).

In the saturation stage, where economies of large scale production are forthcoming, the cost of producing a product that is different to the main types being offered in the market segment is disproportionately so much higher that a number of consumers are not prepared to pay the extra for a special product. The specialist consumers then merge with the main body of the market, making possible even greater economies of scale. Then, some of the specialist product ranges that were profitable in the earlier life cycle stages are no longer so, and are withdrawn.

During the saturation period most companies in the market realize that they must change to the new type of marketing mix appropriate to the latter end of the product life cycle. Survival of companies in the saturation stage will depend upon the objectives and the effectiveness of the marketing policy adopted, and its application to the market situation. This is, in turn, molded by consumers and competitors.

Because all brands of a product type are beginning to look the same, the emphasis will tend to be upon psychological and emotional appeals rather than upon product differences. Further, it may be possible to extend the saturation stage. For example, a new or differentiated product or market fragmentation is often possible, creating a new market situation; alternatively the product will move into the last stage, that of decline.

7. *The decline stage*

Decline cannot be avoided in the long term in the sense that sales will fall eventually as the product concept is superseded. Decline can often be anticipated with fair accuracy by effective market and sales forecasting techniques. A product can then be withdrawn at an appropriate time, or another product introduced to replace the sales volume of the declining product when it is phased out. Anticipation is important to large-scale producers because the replacement product must be at an appropriate level of sales when the declining product is phased out to ensure continued economies of large-scale operation in a volume market.

The decline stage can be caused by a variety of factors, the most important of which are changes in consumer or user tastes or habits, a changed rate of market acceptance, impressive improvements in competitors' or substitute products, and normal product degeneration.

Often, because of intense competition during the saturation stage, companies become less consumer-orientated and more competitor-orientated. The obsession with beating competition at all costs often results in activities that effectively challenge competitors but that are not necessarily ideal for providing the best combination of consumer value satisfactions. Consumers often become dissatisfied and search for substitute products and methods of satisfying their needs. In fact, if more consumer-orientated marketing plans had been operated by the companies in such an industry, the decline stage of the product may have arrived at a later time.

The decline stage is characterized by a pronounced downward trend in sales volume. This indicates, in the case of a company life cycle, that the consumer is buying another brand, or in the case of an overall product category life cycle, that the generic product concept has been superseded by one that has more consumer appeal. It is the result of the consumers' assessment of the advantages of, and the familiarity with, the old product versus the appeal, the extra satisfactions and the attractiveness of the sales proposition of a new product. By this stage in the product category life cycle there appears to be enough familiarity, sophistication and acceptance of the overall product concept to permit consumers to compare not only brands, but also to compare the price/value alternatives of existing and substitute products.

The decreasing demand in the decline stage will tend to be of the repeat purchase or replacement purchase type, with a low level of brand loyalty. Brand loyalty uncertainty is fostered by the disappearance of well-known brands of volume producers no longer finding the contracting market attractive, or by the introduction of improved or replacement products accompanied by different claims in the area of product performance or satisfactions.

Income levels of consumers are important factors during the complete length of the product life cycle. As the incomes of potential consumers increase so does the market potential and opportunity, but it is not inevitable that sales will follow. The extension of a product life cycle will depend in the short term upon the marketing strategies of companies supplying the market. This emphasizes a basic difference in the approach of the economist compared with the marketing man. The economist looks upon demand as something that exists, and income and price as determinants of demand; changes in either having a direct effect upon demand. The marketing approach is that income and price are determinants of marketing potential and opportunity, and for these to be realized as actual consumer demand, marketing effort in the form of the appropriate marketing mix must be expended.

Production economy implications of the life cycle

Production economy, getting the greatest possible output at the lowest possible cost, will have an important influence upon a company's marketing plan. Costs of production are affected by the scale of operations and the extent of capacity utilization; both factors need to be considered in planning and the company brand life cycle should be related to them. Generally, the larger the scale of production the greater the chance of utilization problems arising. This is especially true where production units are large and indivisible (eg a large steel mill), and/or are highly specific in their nature (eg only cotton can be produced on cotton manufacturing machinery whereas a center lathe can be used in many industries).

With each set of productive resources a break-even diagram can be evolved by relating sales revenue to costs. This will show how many units must be sold or the sales revenue needed to cover fixed and variable costs of various levels of production. It also indicates when a project passes its break-even point, moving from a position of loss to that of profit. It can also show when current production capacity is being fully used.

In most cases, the smallest economic business organization that has adequate facilities to perform a given production and marketing task is the most efficient and profitable. The relationship between scale of operation and utilization of plant and equipment can be seen by the comparison of two hypothetical company situations each with the same sales growth rate in Figures 5a and 5b.

It will be noticed that the smaller company (Figure 5a) would tend to break even, and therefore make profits, earlier than the larger company (at $20,000 sales revenue compared with that of $80,000). This is due to the fact that the larger company has greater fixed overhead costs. However, the advantage of the large company would be in mass volume markets where large-scale production is more efficient. This is reflected in lower costs per unit as the total cost is more widely spread, and also in higher profits. It can be seen in Figure 5b that with sales revenue at $180,000 the larger company would make $40,000 profit and this would increase as the volume became larger.

In both cases (5a and 5b) there will be limits to the companies'

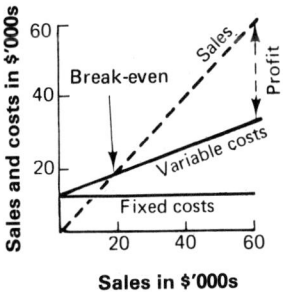

(a) *Small scale operation*

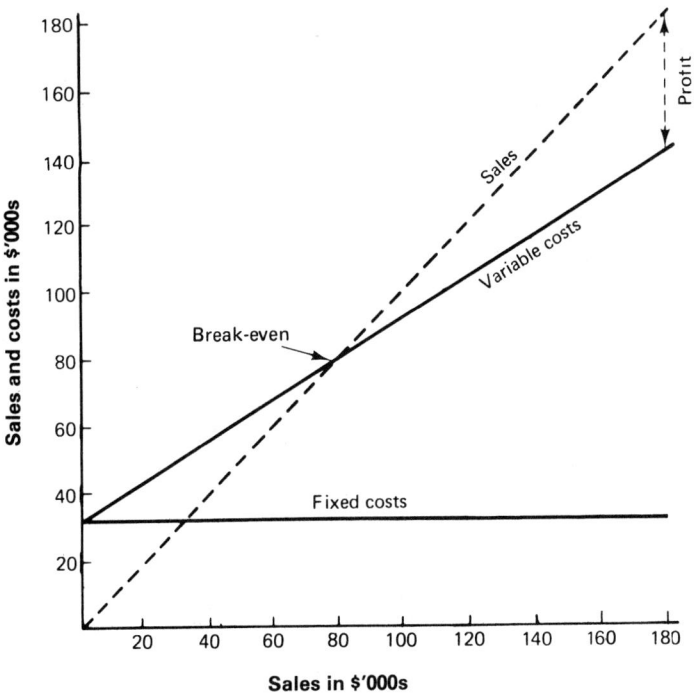

(b) *Large scale operation*

Figure 5. *Relationships between scale of operation and plant comparing (a) a small scale operation with (b) a large scale operation*

ability to extend production and this will be at the point of 100% utilization of plant: unless work is subcontracted to other producers or unless a further production-resources increment is added.

The comparison of the two diagrams (5a and 5b) indicates the need for large companies to find volume markets and why they often run into difficulties when they enter low investment industries that are easily penetrated by small scale producers.

Production 'blocks' and sales 'curves'

The need to exploit current capacity to the full will often force a company to increase the rate of growth of sales volume and consequently force it to enter a new phase of the company brand product life cycle. This is because production capacity increases in 'blocks' as new machines, production lines, and plant increase production potential not by single unit increments but by large multiple unit batches, whereas sales volume moves in curves. This is illustrated in Figure 6.

In Figure 6 when an additional production increment is introduced at point A to meet increasing demand, it follows that in the interest of production economy the target output will then become the volume at point B: ie the level of production where the new plant increment is being fully used, so as to spread its additional fixed cost overheads over as many units as possible to obtain the lowest cost per unit and the highest profit level. If the production capacity forecast is over-optimistic sales will not achieve the anticipated level (as at point C). Overheads will then be spread over insufficient sales volume, the company will find it difficult to compete with large competitors who are selling at relatively low prices only attained through large scale and high level of production capacity utilization. In such a situation, and depending on the position of the break-even point, a major problem arises because of surplus capacity and because overheads are spread over insufficient sales volume. Consequently, profits will be reduced or losses increased. This in turn accentuates price competition in an endeavor to achieve the necessary sales volume.

Therefore, although current production capacity decisions made at the beginning of the development stage are important, those made at the beginning of the maturation stage are crucial. If production capacity goes 'on stream' in the development stage it has a potential growth market to supply. But if large capacity equipment is brought into operation in the maturation stage the results could be financially crippling. As the potential growth for the overall market is slight at this stage, it would be difficult to plan for the spreading of large overheads in the future, unless the company was prepared and could afford to fight for a considerably increased market share.

Alternatively, marginal markets may be used while the main target market is developing. However, care must be taken in choos-

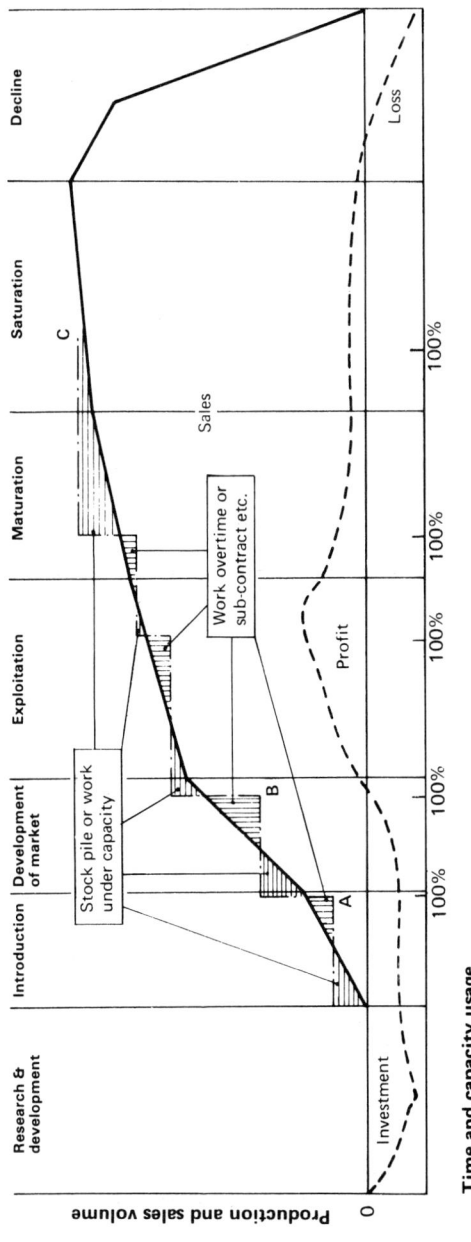

Figure 6. *A hypothetical individual company brand life cycle; production and sales volume comparison*

ing marginal markets if these are to be 'dropped' later, particularly if it is planned that they will eventually form part of the company's total market sometime in the future. A favorable company image may be difficult to regain.

It follows, therefore, that the speed and growth of the product life cycle is logically a further dimension of the use of existing plant and the scale of operation. Further, if productive capacity can be increased in relatively small unit increments its development can be phased with the growth of the market. This is particularly useful if a new and unique product is being launched and is still, in spite of research, an unknown quantity. The degree of investment risk is lowered by establishing a small production unit and expanding it as the project develops.

Economies of scale

However, some manufacturing plants cannot be laid down very quickly, or in some cases the economic optimum of manufacturing plant is of a size that can only be described as large-scale. To emphasize the importance of the size of market and scale of operation factors it would be useful to examine the possible combinations of market growth and production scale as in Figure 7.

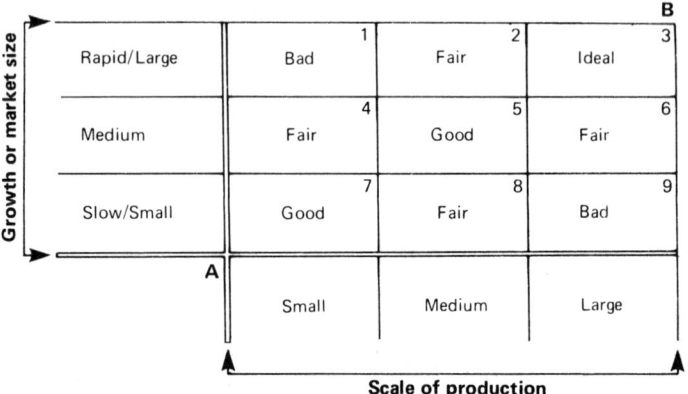

Figure 7. *Effects of various combinations of degrees of growth on market size and scale of production. An ideal progression is diagonally upwards across the matrix from A to B, ie from 7 through 5 to 3*

Assuming that economies of scale are possible, the ideal progression during the build-up of the brand life cycle of a new and unique product that requires time to obtain consumer acceptance would be diagonally upwards across Figure 7 from A to B, through situations

7, 5 and 3. The best possible combination of size and scale as the market develops in Figure 7 is position No 3: a large market and large-scale production facilities to meet demand. A market situation such as No 3 could simply exist, or a future market/profit potential or opportunity may be observed or predicted in an industry currently characterized by position No 7: low market size/growth rate and small-scale production units. In such a case a company could finance large-scale production facilities, and, using marketing techniques, cause a rapid market growth rate to commence. However, if small-scale production is as efficient as large-scale production then situation 1, for example, can be satisfactory. But if economies of scale are feasible then the worst position in Figure 7 is that of No 9, a company having large-scale production facilities but operating in a small market with a low growth rate. The effect of large-scale production overheads spread over low and only slowly increasing sales volume could, if unplanned, cause a considerable financial strain upon a company. This is particularly the case in a highly competitive market situation where the overheads could not be passed on to the customers in the form of higher prices. An effective marketing plan could be used to develop such a market more rapidly.

In situation No 1 in Figure 7, longer delivery delays would result if competitors generally permitted it or unless new companies were attracted into the industry. Alternatively, production work could be placed with sub-contractors in the short and medium term. But, in the long term, in the interests of controlling supplies and quality, if economies of scale are possible then the laying down of a large-scale production unit or the acquisition of one is the only effective way of fully developing the market/profit opportunity.

The other positions shown in Figure 7 not already mentioned are all less than ideal. Positions 1, 2 and 4 tend to be filled with those companies that are predominantly production-orientated; that is companies that do not accept the need for marketing or the marketing concept, often because they can sell all they can make with current production resources in the short term, completely ignoring the long-term market/profit opportunity. Positions 6, 8 and 9 tend to be filled with companies who have surplus capacity. They have either misjudged the size/growth factor of the particular market through poor forecasting, or are in industries where the optimum size of production unit is large. Alternatively, they may not be marketing effectively, or are unable to discover an additional market segment in which to specialize and are typically either making a loss or very low profits. Because of their rather unstable position, such companies are often forced to turn their excess production to the manufacture of products for other companies (sub-contracting or 'private-labelling' for distributors or competitors) at very low prices as a contribution to fixed costs. Also they tend to be ripe for takeover, merger, or acquisition by other companies, particularly if other companies are looking for cheap extra capacity.

From this examination of the relationship of production economy and the company brand life cycle, it is logical to conclude that the effectiveness of the former is dependent upon the latter's speed and rate of growth, its size, its current stage and potential future stages.

If large-scale production is more efficient than small-scale operation, the former will be the only way to operate effectively. Therefore, the marketing plan should take into account the size of operation necessary for technical efficiency and also the desirability of its full utilization at the earliest possible moment. Unless a new entrant company aims to cater for the needs of a small specialized segment of the market, the marketing plan must aim for a rapid build-up of the individual company brand life cycle. This is the reason why some companies are unable to use the techniques of test marketing; if products can only be produced on a full production line, the cost of idle plant or partially used equipment while a test is taking place will be too high.

The importance of production characteristics in product planning

The scale of production may be determined by other suppliers already in the market. If they are operating at the lowest-cost scale of production, and if the resulting production costs are correctly reflected in their profits and prices, this must be the scale of operation for new entrants wishing to compete. However, if they have not achieved the lowest-cost scale of production or have not achieved adequate utilization of that size of production unit, then new entrants may be more effective at a lower size of technical efficiency but with high capacity utilization.

From this it can be appreciated that technical characteristics of manufacture are important determinants of marketing policy, the marketing mix and the size and build-up of the brand life cycle. They are an important part of the basic environment in which the forecast operates. These production characteristics will be a strong argument for trying to produce a particular style and shape of company brand life cycle. There will be a shape of brand life cycle that is the optimum for a particular company.

However, production considerations should not be the dictators of marketing policy. All decisions within a company must be made in terms of what is good for the company in the market and, if production considerations do not fit the ideal marketing plan, then production resources must be reviewed. It may be more economical to have certain parts, sub-assemblies, and even complete products made by sub-contractors. This may obviate the need for increasing the scale of operation in the short and medium term. Alternatively, if the size of plant to achieve technical efficiency is large and the company's market share relatively small, the operation may still be profitable if the marketing plan includes sub-contracting or private labelling for distributors or competitors. Marketing considerations must dominate if the company is to achieve long-term profitability and prosperity.

The life cycle as a planning and forecasting unit

While it is important to plan sales, it is even more important to plan profits, not at one moment in time but over the whole planned life of the product, if the long-term continuity and prosperity of the company is to be ensured. Profits are tomorrow's surplus after today's consumption, and as such are important not only to provide a return in the form of dividends to shareholders for money invested, and to employees as an insurance for continuity of employment, but also as the means of financing research and development for new and existing products to ensure their acceptance in the market.

Before a product is launched, indeed before it is even produced, product ideas, the resulting developed product, and the market, must be researched, and to do this, money must be invested in the overall project. This is essential even with existing products; in a competitive economy few products can remain profitable for long periods unless they are kept up-to-date. Realizing this, many companies make periodic changes in product formulation or presentation to keep their products in a leading position.

The risk factor in this period of research and development (and in the stages of introduction and market development) is one of the justifications for relatively high profits in later stages of the product's life. In some cases profits are made in the early stage, but often, in highly competitive markets, profits are not made until very late in the development-of-the-market stage. Some products may not reach profitable commercialization and are withdrawn from the market. Profits tend to reach their highest level in the exploitation stage because of the company's product or marketing advantage, its brand lead in the market, and its company image. During the maturation and saturation stages, profits tend to decline, although sales may continue to increase slightly. This situation is largely due to the effects of competition requiring the company increasingly to engage in more and more sales promotional activity. Also, to maintain adequate distribution, larger trade discounts have to be given to intermediaries, and/or lower prices need to be offered to consumers. It is in these two latter stages and in the decline stage that the objective of the company may not be the making of profit in the short term but simple survival. Profits will continue to be eroded to the point of disappearance and will eventually turn into loss during the decline stage of the product life cycle if the situation is allowed to deteriorate that far.

The life cycle as a planning unit

The brand life cycle is a useful overall planning unit because profit potential changes in each stage of the cycle. If arbitrary time periods for planning products are chosen, eg five years, a product with a seven years life cycle could be shown to be highly profitable at the end of the five years planning period. In the following years the product could show a considerable loss, and therefore the five years planning unit presents an incomplete picture and is misleading. Alternatively a product with a nine years life cycle might, over a five years period, show relatively poor profit performance, but may commence making high profits in years seven and eight, making the product a highly attractive investment in the long term. It may be necessary to set a five years overall sales and profit horizon for the total product range, but as each product has a different life span, the planning and later assessment of individual products should be carried out on a different basis.

Medium period forecasting, planning and assessment can be carried out by using individual brand life cycle stages as the time base, particularly as a different marketing strategy will be required in each, and these stages can be recognized and joined together in a logical sequence. However, as the criterion would be overall long-term profitability of products, the brand life cycle is the ideal unit for planning and forecasting sales, costs, and profits over the whole life of a product.

Use of ex-factory and consumer sales data

When using the product life cycle as a planning or forecasting unit, or as a method of control where sales performance is compared with it, care must be taken regarding the selection of data. It is possible to measure sales volume by ex-factory delivery movements and/or by ultimate consumer sales (over the counter sales); in some industries these two sets of data could produce two brand life cycles with very different shapes.

Take for example a brand of paint; the ex-factory sales (brand life cycle) could be as shown in Figure 8.

The brand life cycle pattern in Figure 8 is due to the heterogeneous nature of brands of paint. Differences are caused not only because of the need for a range of colors and different sizes of tins, but also because of the need for a range of different finishes, ie undercoat, gloss, matt, emulsion, etc, to be available in retail outlets. The number of combinations is considerable. Thus the high level of sales

The Product Life Cycle

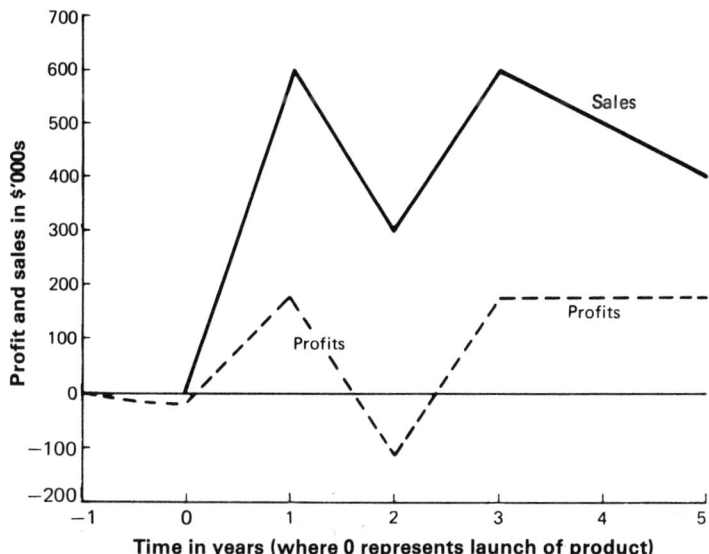

Figure 8. *The ex-factory sales and resulting profits/loss (brand life cycle) for a brand of paint*

in the first year of a new or replacement product could be partly attributed to the need for merchants and retailers to put into stock a complete range so as to be able to offer adequate customer service. In the second year, sales would tend to reflect the normal growth rate, from zero, of true consumer demand, ie to $300,000. In Figure 8 the return to the $600,000 sales peak in year three could come from the normal development of the ultimate consumer product life cycle (ie from the increased consumer brand acceptance and demand) and from the extension of distribution through new wholesale and retail outlets.

It is particularly noticeable in the market development stage that as the rate of consumer/user acceptance increases so trade (wholesale and retail) attitudes tend to soften, and acceptance by parts of the trade, which initially refused to stock the new product, gradually takes place. In some cases the consequent filling of wholesale and retail warehouses causes the ex-factory deliveries to far exceed the 'over the counter sales', often causing a sharp decrease in factory sales in the ensuing periods as the trade 'lives off its stocks'. Yet replacement stock ordering will be less than stock-building unless sales increase further. This situation can also give the overall product category life cycle a twin peak (bi-modal) pattern similar to that shown in Figure 8. In the market development stage, the innovating company may still dominate the market but once it has shown that a definite market exists for the new unique product, it is joined late in this period by a number of competitors, who, observing a potential profit and/or marketing opportunity, enter the market with a slightly different product and/or sales proposition. The apparent profit opportunity is magnified to potential new entrants by the large ex-factory sales of the innovating company whilst the trade channels are stocking up. Thus, new investment in production and marketing facilities takes place often based upon ex-factory sales movements, whereas in fact consumer purchases are moving at a much slower rate. Excess supply over the true market growth rate causes some new entrants to offer abnormal discounts to wholesalers and retailers to ensure channels of distribution, and, in some cases, lower prices derived from production economies or lower gross margins.

It should be noted, however, that the twin peak (bi-modal) pattern of ex-factory data will often form when middlemen are used, merely reflecting the measurement of demand data in a different way. This does not alter the fundamental slope and pattern of the product life cycle when measuring consumer demand. The two ways of measuring sales, ex-factory, and ultimate consumer sales, are important timing indicators for forecasting in many fields of marketing where middlemen are used. For example, in the scheduling of advertising and marketing effort, a Christmas product requiring heavy promotional effort to appeal to consumers in October, November and December will require trade press and trade direct mail advertising, together with personal selling pressure in August, September, October, or even earlier.

Life cycles in multi-product companies

The multi-product company has to contend with a number of brand life cycles and overall product category life cycles. Not only will different products be in various stages of their life cycles but all will be of varying degrees of profitability at a given time. It will be obvious that there will be an optimum combination of sales of the various products if maximum profits are to be achieved. Thus with a range of four products A, B, C and D, in a hypothetical company situation, the greatest profit level may be reached if three of A are sold to seven of B, three of C and one of D — this relationship is referred to as the *product mix*. As each brand life cycle will have a different life span and the stages of each will be of varying duration, it will be necessary to review the profitability of the product mix at frequent intervals. It may be possible to change the emphasis of products within the product mix to ensure a continued high level of profitability.

An appreciation of the product mix concept will also ensure that a company will have continuity of profit balance, ie will not have all its products in the introduction stage or all in the decline stage at one time. Products can be scheduled into the product range to ensure that as one market becomes saturated and eventually begins to decline, another product is already entering the exploitation stage. This is particularly important to large-scale producers who must ensure volume follow-on products to replace former volume products in declining markets.

Market reaction as the life cycle progresses

The overall product category life cycle (the sum total of all individual brand life cycles in a particular product area) begins as the first company makes and markets the first product of a new type. Therefore it is possible in the early stages of the marketing of a new and unique product that the overall product category life cycle will coincide exactly with the company brand life cycle as there is only one supplier in the market. As more companies begin to supply the product, the overall product category life cycle develops its own pattern. Its overall size, shape, and speed will be different from any individual company brand life cycle, but the stages will be the same as already described. The first company's product is introduced and slowly displaces products of other industries or attracts consumers to spend their income upon a new type of consumer satisfaction. More and more consumers purchase the product as the cumulative weight of marketing and advertising effort causes a compound increase in the market size. Later the life cycle moves into its exploitation stage, where, if the individual brand and overall product category life cycles are at the same stage of evolution, companies in this situation will make the highest level of profit. By this time, the rate of increase of the size of market has declined and the life cycle is levelling off as existing design or composition of the product is good enough to attract nearly all consumers who are likely to be attracted; few extra sales can be gained by further product improvement. The few new consumers attracted to the product are offset by some changing to substitute products. This continues from the early part of the maturation stage until the saturation stage, when the demand for the product begins to decline as other and/or new products take the place of the original product.

Competitive patterns during the life cycle

Figure 9 shows that in the *introduction stage* of the overall product category life cycle the innovating company is a monopolist, being the only supplier. In the *market development stage* the innovating company still dominates the market but has been joined by a small number of competitors who enjoy a small share of the market and who can foresee profit and marketing opportunities in the new product.

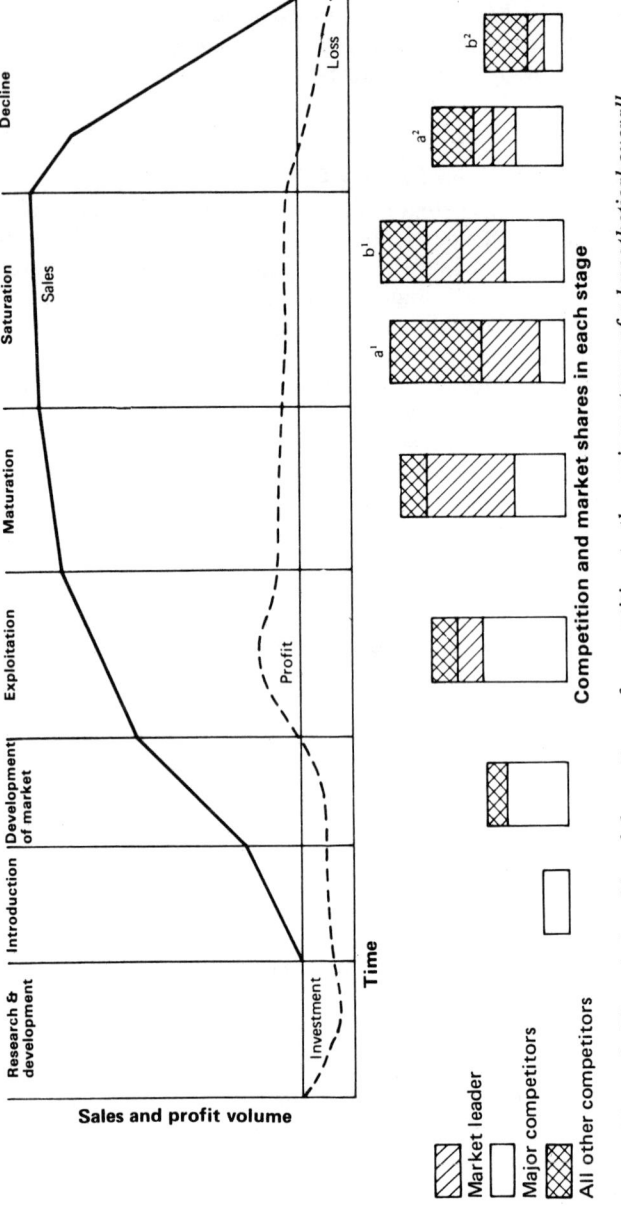

Figure 9. The relationship of the pattern of competition to the various stages of a hypothetical overall product category life cycle; competition and market share is shown beneath each stage of the life cycle

In the *exploitation stage,* while one company has a major share of the market, it may not be the original company; the innovator may have been overtaken by a newcomer exploiting some tangible or intangible asset. Also one or two strong competitors have emerged to challenge the brand leader, and the main body of competitors (numerically) have a relatively small share of the market. Characteristically, because of competition, the leading company's market share will tend to fall during this period, but as total industry sales continue to increase, it will be generally a smaller percentage of a larger sales volume. Thus company sales will tend to continue to increase, and this is an important forecasting factor. However, the overall product category sales volume will not continue to increase at the same rate of growth as in the market development stage, and this will be reflected in the slope of the life cycle line.

In the *maturation stage* the innovating company, or the one that became the brand leader in the earlier stages, still has the greatest individual share of the market but this share is smaller in comparison with the total share of all other competitors; other strong challengers to the brand leadership have emerged.

In the *saturation stage* two situations develop, one emanating from the other. Initially (a^1) in Figure 9 the major share of the market is dominated (numerically) by brands other than the brand leader and the next major brands. There are many relatively small suppliers all trying to find a special niche in the market that they can control, by offering a differentiated product or marketing service. Towards the end of the stage, because of the supremacy of large-scale production in mass market segments, over-production and non-profitable operation, mergers and acquisitions occur and rationalization of the industry takes place. This second situation (b^1) evolves as a natural consequence of the first, and tends to follow it towards the end of this saturation period. In the second type of situation, two, three, or four large groups dominate the mass market, maintaining their position mainly with advanced marketing techniques, using the high cost of advertising and marketing activities as a deterrent to potential entrants. An example of this type of situation is the US soap and detergent industry where in one year 62% of soap and detergent was shipped by the four largest companies in the industry.[1]

In the *decline stage* the leading brand company of the saturation era may be superseded as brand leader by a company whose scale of operations is more appropriate to a smaller, contracting market. In the first part of the decline stage (a^2 in Figure 9) the leading brand company plus its major rivals usually dominates the market with between 50% and 75% market share. However, as specialized market segments gradually become smaller and no longer economical for

1. *Statistical Abstract of the United States*, 1979, National Data Book and Guide to Sources, p 814, published by US Dept of Commerce.

large scale producers to cover, market shares also tend to diminish as more companies market a general product.

Life cycle stage recognition

Recognition of the current stage of the overall product category product life cycle is important to a company contemplating the launch of a new product. For example, it will be easier to enter a market that is at present experiencing a period of growth. Competition will be easier, and existing brands will be less concerned about losing some share of their market if their volume of sales is stable or continues to expand. But in a relatively static (the maturation or saturation stages of the overall product category life cycle) or declining market, any new product will tend to take all of its sales from established brands, thus decreasing their market share and causing a sharp reaction from their manufacturers. Launching a product under such extremely competitive conditions will probably be slow and costly, and is likely to generate price wars and the use of other retaliatory techniques from established brands.

Consumer/user behavior during the life cycle

The nature of the consumer (used in the broadest sense to include industrial purchasers) changes at each stage of the overall product category life cycle, and so therefore the marketing mix and the company marketing strategy must also change if the approach to the consumer is to be effective. When marketing a new and revolutionary product the prime strategy in the introduction and development of the market periods will be to get consumer acceptance of the generic product. If the product is marketed correctly there will always be some consumers who will purchase the product to try it.

This 'trendsetting' or 'innovators' group is usually characterized by such factors as high social status (maintained by the psychological image of being first or being different), relatively high incomes (necessary in most cases, as often in the introduction stage of a new unique product, prices are high), intense need, snob appeal, above average educational level, younger and family people, those with a tendency to high mobility and personality leadership types. Even in the marketing of industrial products there are companies, known as leaders and trendsetters in purchasing patterns, who must obviously be reached in the introduction and development of the market stages.

Later in the product category life cycle, the 'trendsetters' are joined by consumers who follow the fashions, the social behavior, and the trends set by the former group. These 'early followers' have many of the innovator group's characteristics in a diluted form. They are slightly more conservative, they delay buying because they are not certain initially that the new product will satisfy their needs. They are more concerned with performance and about the continuity of supplies, lower prices, spare parts and/or service, and often reject or do not believe some of the earlier claims made for the performance of the product.

In the later stages of the product category life cycle the 'trendsetters' are changing to even newer products but the market has now become a mass market as existing consumers are joined by the main body of the potential consumers who have been more resistant to change, or who have just been made aware of the product and its consumer satisfactions. One of the major causes of this movement of 'late followers' towards the product is that of competition and the ensuing reduction of prices, as each new supplier competes with others for a share of the market, thereby appealing to an increasing number of potential consumers further down the income scale.

Buying motives during life cycles

Many psychologists have listed what they consider to be primary and secondary human needs which are conversely human buying motives. If these needs are recognized and the marketing and advertising appeal based upon them, consumers are more likely to react in the way desired by the marketer.

Just as there are general characteristics of consumers to be found in the various stages of the overall product category life cycle, there are specific consumer buying motives that can be attributed to particular groups of products. In each stage the needs of the particular groups of consumers must be recognized, their buying motives analyzed, and a special approach made to them by exposing them to logical and psychological buying benefits that appeal.

Here are some of the many buying motives:

1. *General buying motives.* Approval of others; thrift, saving, profit; freedom from fear; dependability; economy of operation; convenience, ease, comfort; insurance, security, safety; pride; simplicity of operation; ease of financing; esteem, snobbery, prestige; novelty, curiosity, 'up-to-dateness'; appearance; love, affection, sympathy; durability; imitation of others; to obtain status; to gain recognition; to satisfy sensibilities; to satisfy sex motives; stylishness and fashions.
2. *Industrial buying motives.* Lower price; advantageous incentive offered; faster working speed; lower maintenance costs; reduced labor required; cheaper labor required; reduced material stockholding; safer operations; better working conditions; reduced working space required; reduced overheads; additional flexibility; customer preference; reliability; custom made (utility); security,

quality; complementary advantage; economy; service advantages.

It is possible with the minimum of marketing research to compile a list of buying motives appropriate to the life cycle stage and the 'typical' consumer profile in any marketing situation.

However, in framing the buying motive appeal it must be remembered that the purchaser is not necessarily the consumer. For example, a considerable number of men's shirts are purchased by women; the motives of both women (as purchasers) and men (as consumers) must be included in the marketing appeal. The satisfaction of a mother purchasing a packet of heavily advertised breakfast cereal (together with its 'free enclosed gift'), will be very different from the satisfactions of her young son who demanded that particular brand, and the motives of both should be reflected in the marketing appeal.

But even when marketing industrial products, the buying motives of all who can influence a purchasing decision (ie plant superintendents, personnel managers, foremen, etc — even the titular purchasing agent or buyer) should be assessed and the marketing appeal weighted accordingly.

These buying motives in the form of viable purchasing benefits must be shown to consumers and users through the marketing communications channels of advertising, public relations, sales promotion, personal selling, and, if it is a consumer product, through the window and interior displays of shops. How well they are identified and communicated will have a direct effect on sales and therefore on the forecast. An effect on sales may also be felt if there is a change in communications strategy, eg if more money is to be spent on advertising the benefits.

Yet if the individual company is introducing a 'new' product into an already mature market (on the overall product category life cycle) it will tend to find that throughout the individual company's brand life cycle, the type of consumer will remain the same. It becomes merely a matter of appealing to the same type of consumer in the mass market, but the marketing strategy used needs partially to convert sufficient numbers from existing brands and needs partially to be directed towards new customers who have never tried the generic product. In the saturation stage it becomes mainly a matter of converting customers from existing brands, as completely new consumers are joining the market at a greatly diminished rate. Thus, at this stage, the aim will be to obtain a share of the existing market and/or appeal to a specialized but fragmented part of the overall market.

Life cycle effect on marketing strategy

During each stage of the overall product category life cycle a different marketing strategy will be necessary to meet the changing situation. Recognition of the product life cycle concept indicates that market situations and their functions, ie demand, supply, and price environments, are dynamic and constantly changing at three levels: that of the company, of the market and industry and of the economy. Thus the innovating company introducing a revolutionary, new, or unique product will enter the introduction stage of the brand life cycle at the same time as the commencement of the whole product category life cycle, because they start it. Later entrants will find that although they launch their own brand at its own introduction stage, they are also entering an overall product category life cycle that can be at varying degrees of evolution.

The main difficulty in the successful marketing of new products, including forecasting the anticipated volume, is the reconciliation of the different stages of the two types of life cycles. Even with products already on the market, optimum results will be obtained only if the brand cycle moves on together with the product category life cycle. The product category life cycle is the dominant factor although it can be influenced by an individual brand, particularly that of the brand leader. These reconciliation difficulties need to be appreciated and allowed for if a company is to carry out effective market and sales forecasting.

Summary

In production-orientated companies (those in which all or most decisions are made in terms of production or technical convenience), product life cycles and their accompanying profit life cycles are matters of historic fact, the existence of which is discovered and considered only in retrospect. In market-orientated companies (those in which all or most decisions are made in terms of what is best for the company in the market), product life cycle stage recognition is an important preoccupation of management (both at the policy-making level and at the operational level) so that they may use the appropriate marketing strategy at the right time. Life cycle stage recognition in combination with the optimum marketing mix enables a company to shape a product's destiny. However, not only is stage recognition of the product category life cycle important, but, as in many market-orientated companies, the brand life cycle is planned together with profits over the anticipated 'life' of the product, and an attempt is made to ensure that the ensuing strategies are adhered to.

The acceptance of the concepts and recognition of individual company brand and the overall product category life cycles enables companies to seize market/profit opportunities. The typical pattern of introduction, development, exploitation, maturation, saturation, and decline, with each reflecting differences (inherent or created) in demand, supply, and price patterns, makes the life cycle approach a necessity for effective market analysis and prediction.

However, a most important task of market and sales forecasting is that of determining changes in the slope and speed of brand and product category life cycles, ie to predict their course. Also important is establishing whether a decline or increase in sales is due to short-term seasonal effects, medium-term business cycle factors, long-term changes in the company brand cycle, or the overall product category life cycle as well as to external (possibly competitive or economic) factors. Further, the concept of the product life cycle, if applied, will help a company make better forecasts and will suggest ways of interpreting and evaluating the data upon which the forecast is based.

Part Two: The Market and Sales Forecasting Plan

CHAPTER 3
Market and Sales Forecasting

'It is bad enough to know the past; it would be intolerable to know the future'.
W Somerset Maugham

The forecast's planning role

Market and sales forecasts are important tools of company management and decision-making as they assist in the appraisal of investment projects, in the analysis, measurement and improvement of current marketing strategy, and in the identification and/or development of new products and new markets. Further, they promote and facilitate the proper functioning of the many aspects of company activity, ie production, marketing, finance, research and development, purchasing, etc.

The scale of operation of a company will depend upon the sales and potential sales available in a particular market and/or its ability to find and enter new markets. The sales forecast will therefore have a vital role to play in company planning in general and marketing planning in particular. An effective market and sales forecast enables management to plan fundamental marketing strategies and tactics, and compile an overall marketing plan to achieve realistic as well as desirable predetermined profit targets or other objectives in the short, medium and long term. In this marketing planning role it enables management to integrate a company's general objectives and its operating plans and schedules with marketing opportunities in existing and/or potential markets or market segments.

The forecast as a target

The ideals of various company functions can be crystallized at the optimum profit level through an effective sales forecast in its role as a target. The production function's ideal is simplification, standardization, long planning periods and absence of time pressures, no under-utilization of plant, and long, even production runs. The marketing function's desire is for innovation, diversification, a wide variety of products and high levels of stock. The demand by the finance function is for low stocks, low costs, high turnover, high return on capital invested, predictive cash flow, and low credit risk. These ideals often conflict, but the best possible combination of them can be built into the company plan based upon effective market and sales forecast information. In fact the sales forecast should form the basis of all budgets throughout a company. This is because, in the last analysis, all budgets depend upon, or are limited by, how many units a company can sell and/or the level of sales revenue. The sales forecast therefore plays the role of regulator of company resources as there is little point in using technical, financial, marketing or managerial resources unless the resulting goods and/or services can be sold.

Forecasting targets are set in some companies at an artificially higher level than 'realistic' forecasts. This is rationalized on the basis that sometimes the forecast becomes a maximum rather than a minimum aim.

The need for continuity and system

The overall process of forecasting should be continuous and systematic. It should be continuous to enable the assembly of adequate information and possibly the updating of forecasts to allow for changing environmental patterns or freshly revealed information. It should be systematic to be effective; the assumptions made, the logical processes and the methods used, must be explicit and well-defined. Systematic forecasting provides the managers of a company with an effective method of control and measurement of performance, and indicates the various limitations within markets. It will be possible to compare forecasts with actual sales both within time periods and between time periods, thereby permitting the analysis of the difference between the two and enabling the overall forecasting process to be improved. Furthermore, it keeps management informed of sales progress and trends, and results can be interpreted indicating where and when to take remedial action.

The cost of having a continuous detailed forecasting system for a large number of product variations or markets can be high in terms of money and time. Bearing in mind the widely quoted 80/20 rule, ie 80% of profits comes from 20% of products, one approach is to forecast individually and in detail those products/services that make the greatest profit contribution. The growth factors or other indicators that are discovered can then be applied to the remainder in several appropriate groupings. It may be necessary to supplement this 'secondary' type of forecasting with ad hoc, periodic forecasts.

Pre-forecasting considerations

Before forecasting can be considered, however, an overall assessment of company activities must be made; for example:

1. What business is the company in? This must be defined broadly in terms of consumer or user requirements rather than in terms of products or immediate services: the home laundry business rather than detergents; the public transportation business rather than railways; the food preservation business rather than refrigerators; home-heating rather than oil-fired boilers.
2. What products will the company be making in the future to meet the anticipated needs of customers and potential customers, and how will these products be related to the current product range?
3. In which markets is the company operating and how are they defined, eg in terms of size, region, age groups, location, socio-economic groups of consumers or industrial grouping? Is the total size of each of these markets likely to grow or decline?
4. What are the factors that affect demand in the various market segments that make up the total markets? Are there any gaps in these markets that could be filled by other products?
5. What is the company's present and desired future market share? Without market share knowledge it is not possible to measure true progress in relation to market opportunity. In a growth market it is possible to have rising company sales volume but a declining market share.
6. What are competitors doing and how effective are they in particular markets? As far as possible a profile of competitors should be prepared showing their production capacity, resources, investment, level of sales, level of advertising, degree of competition in specific product or market areas, etc.
7. What is the price/value relationship between the existing and planned product ranges? What is the value of company products to customers in terms of logical and psychological function and performance?
8. What profit levels are desirable in the short, medium and long term? It was shown in Chapter 2 that in various phases of the company brand and/or product category life cycles the company aims and consequently profit objectives will vary. However, for effective forecasting it will be necessary to recognize and anticipate the results of these future profit aims by profit gap analysis. One way of looking at future profit goals is by using a profit gap analysis diagram.

All these and other factors will help the forecaster to understand what he is trying to forecast.

Profit gap analysis

This is shown in Figure 10 where the company's past profit performance is plotted, a straight line trend is fitted (see, later, least squares method) and is projected to some appropriate medium- or long-term point in time (perhaps four to 10 years ahead). This assumes that the present trend will continue, and if for any reason (perhaps the anticipated decline of a product) it can be seen that this will not be the case, an adjustment to the trend will be necessary. If the level of anticipated profits at the future point is acceptable then no further action is necessary. But if the desired level of profits (A in Figure 10) and the projected level (B) do not coincide, an analysis of this gap is necessary. Management must then plan strategies and tactics to ensure that profits are lifted to the desired level over the period, and these will affect the volume of sales and must therefore be allowed for in sales forecasting calculations. In some cases three levels of profits are considered; the level that *must* be reached if the company is to continue, the level that *should* be reached, and the level that *could* be reached in certain defined circumstances.

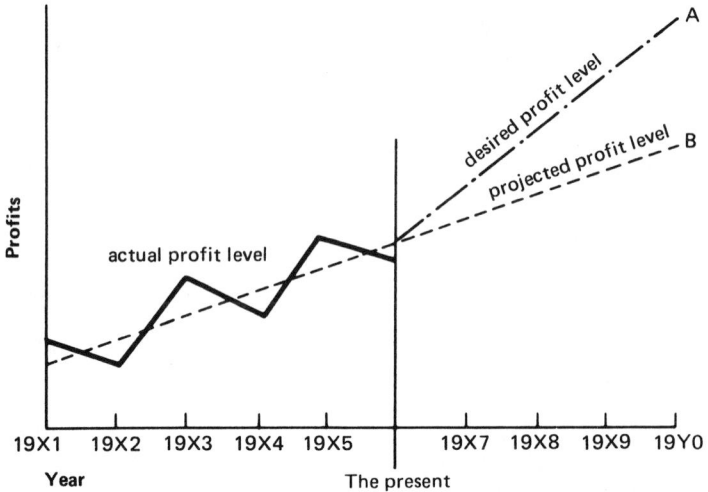

Figure 10. *A hypothetical profit gap analysis diagram indicating actual profits, trend, projection and profit objective*

In fact it is necessary to make an appraisal of markets, potential markets and marketing activities.

A comprehensive forecasting approach

The modern approach to market and sales forecasting is to remove as much of the guesswork and as many of the hunches as possible, and to substitute scientifically processed facts to enable predictions to be made. The wide range of variable factors involved in predicting market or company sales makes exact forecasting impossible; a forecast merely provides a means of assessing future probabilities so as to reduce the uncertainty that is always associated with the future. In fact, analysis of the differences between actual sales and forecasts will often indicate the beginning of new trends and cause management to take appropriate action. Any forecast is made with a number of qualifications, eg that the prediction will be within certain limits (for example ± 5%), or that basic economic factors such as demand, real income, relative price, habits and attitudes, etc do not change radically or else change on a predetermined or anticipated course. As far as possible market and sales forecasts should be expressed in terms of probabilities, with the forecaster putting forward the market or sales prediction with the highest probability, but at the same time showing other less probable but nevertheless important possibilities.

Furthermore, the use of statistical information and forecasting methods does not rule out the need for intelligent human judgement and discretion in anticipating future market and sales activity. In fact, the forecaster must avoid attaching too much importance to naive and mechanical extrapolation. There must be a combination of statistical analysis and human judgement to determine and define the variables at work in any forecasting situation. After any purely statistical analysis and prediction it is necessary to apply intelligent human judgement to validate such a forecast.

Forecasting does imply the ability to determine the primary and secondary underlying forces at work in the international and national economies and the market, and also implies the ability to predict the future importance, growth and trend of these forces. A fundamental premise in predicting the future course of economies, markets and sales is that factors that operated in the past, producing certain situations and sales volume, will continue to be associated to a greater or lesser extent with these situations and sales in the future.

Environmental considerations

All companies operate in, and therefore are affected by, four interdependent environments: those of the international economy, the national economy, the broadly defined consumer satisfactions market and the immediate market. Their relationship is indicated in Figure 11. They are basically non-controllable and their effects must be determined and reflected in the forecasting operation.

The extent of the effect on company operations of the international environment will depend upon whether or not the company considers the entire world (or parts of it) as its potential market, or the extent to which it is open to foreign competition in its home markets. The international marketing concept is that world-wide trading should be carried out not simply by exporting products but also product parts, exporting research know-how, arranging for products to be made under licences abroad, setting up companies and/or

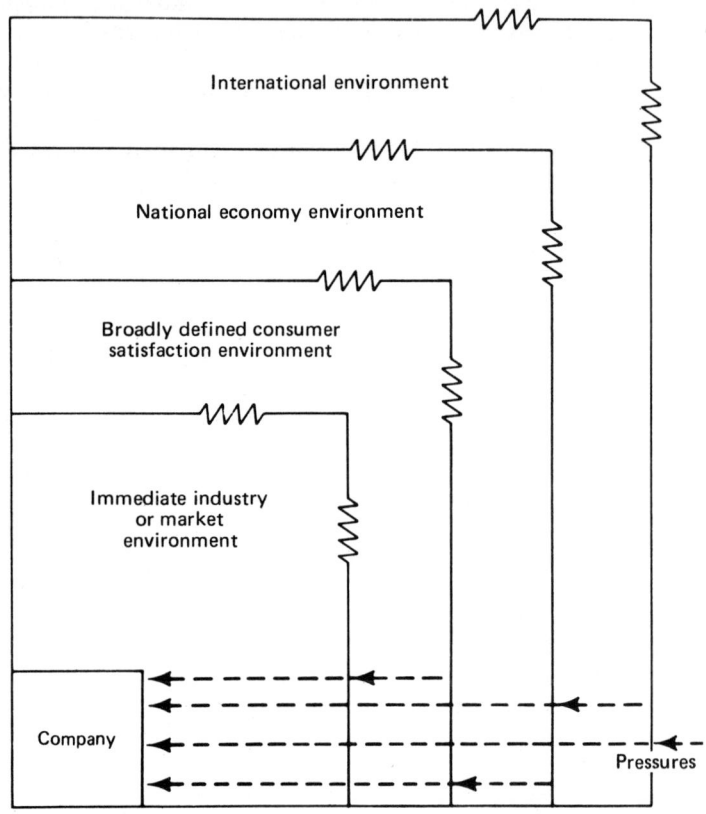

Figure 11. *Environments within which companies operate*

investing in other countries and also importing products or parts that are cheaper or better to incorporate in home products. The nature of the product and the number and location of potential customers will also indicate the importance of the international environment; for example it will affect a large-scale aircraft or space vehicle components manufacturer to a greater extent than an ice-cream manufacturer.

The second interdependent environment is the national economy and one way of looking at the economy of a country is as the sum total of all industries within it, the gross national product being an economic indicator that measures the economy. External and internal pressures upon the economy will cause pressures upon industries and consequently upon companies as shown in Figure 11. For example, external balance of payments problems may cause a government to restrict credit and place restrictions on hire purchase thereby directly affecting sales in a number of consumer durable industries (television receivers, washing machines, etc).

Consumers can often obtain similar groups of satisfactions from alternative products in different industries. For example they can obtain home heating from coal, oil, gas, electricity and from different applications within these groups. These substitute products form the third environment in which the company, and consequently the forecaster, must operate. Companies in any of these very different industries are in fact in competition and are in the broadly defined consumer satisfaction market of home heating.

The fourth interdependent environment is that of the immediate market where companies are in direct product competition with each other, eg one type of oil-fired boiler against another. But even so, pressures can come from companies in other industries infiltrating a particular market, eg in recent years companies making metal components have lost ground to manufacturers of plastic components. When the marketing researcher or forecaster discovers the beginning of such a trend, the company has the alternatives of maintaining sales by buying new plant and manufacturing plastic components, or of doing nothing and suffering declining sales, or of withdrawing from the particular components market and extending its production of other metal products. Pressures may also come from industries in no way, or only remotely, connected with an industry, eg companies in the tobacco industry under social and medical pressure in their own markets have diversified into many other product fields. In such circumstances the sales forecaster will have to consider how attractive his industry is to outside companies wishing to diversify.

The effect of market forces

Market and sales forecasting will depend upon how effectively the forecaster can unearth the primary and secondary forces at work in a particular market, and discover from past experience how they combine and connect, and how their relationship will be modified by the general economic and market climate. He must decide how much weight should be given to one factor as opposed to another. It is important not to overlook the influence of new developments and situations, as they may be powerful enough to negate or at least modify a conclusion based merely upon past experience. Such new developments and situations may indicate the commencement of minute changes in trends that may gain momentum and directly affect sales in a later period.

Thus the effective forecaster will need to have the ability to identify and understand the forces at work in a particular economy and/or market place. This includes being aware of the ideal data (although the company may not be able to afford its cost in terms of money and/or time to obtain), the sources of relevant data, and the changing importance or momentum of the various market factors, either singly or in combination.

Only after examining the various interdependent environments that have an effect upon company operations will the forecaster be able to consider the detailed activity of forecasting. Initially this implies the ability to predict the future course of market forces. In turn this means being aware of the various techniques available, the ability to identify the techniques most appropriate to the existing and anticipated situation, understanding the strengths and weaknesses of the various techniques and the need to weigh and/or change the combination of techniques in a dynamic market situation.

Short-, medium- and long-term forecasts

The need for, and the distinction between, short-, medium- and long-term forecasts must be recognized. Obviously to different companies in different industries, these terms mean very different things. For example, the short term in an industry such as shipbuilding would obviously be much longer than the short term in the manufacture of such a consumer product as a packaged cake mix, not only because it takes longer to design and produce the article, but also because consumer demand, habits and fashions change more rapidly in the consumer goods industries than in the capital goods industries.

Short-term forecasts

However, despite the differences in various industries, it is often possible to link the seasonal pattern of demand within an industry with its short-term period. In economics, the short term is a period which is long enough to allow the variable factors of production (direct labor, direct materials, existing machinery and buildings, etc) to be used in different combinations and amounts, to ensure that the maximum profits are obtained. Further, it is a characteristic of such a period that it is too short for new fixed capital (new plant, new equipment, production lines, factories, etc) to be planned, purchased and brought into operation. These are important considerations, as any short-term operational sales forecast for a company should not exceed the total product capacity of its present equipment unless it is prepared to sub-contract or purchase outside the company. If an inflated sales forecast figure is achieved in book orders but the production function is unable to meet these orders, the ensuing customer frustration and ill-will caused by delivery delays will only serve as an obstacle to future sales by the company. In certain capital goods industries during a period of boom, this situation does occur and is characterized by 'longer order books'. But these industries remain in this fortunate position only as long as demand remains high, as long as new suppliers do not enter the industry, and as long as competitors (home or overseas) do not introduce other products that can be substituted for the original and which can be delivered more quickly. Further, in such circumstances a mistaken picture of true demand, reflected in forecasts, can be built up by buyers placing orders with several suppliers merely to ensure delivery of part of these orders.

The fact that demand in the short term is influenced by seasonal factors is emphasized more in some industries than in others. The fact that it can be linked with certain periods, such as any of the four seasons, Christmas or the summer holiday seasons, tends to make this factor regular. Consequently, in many industries it is possible to allow for peak sales periods, by manufacturing and stocking in off-peak periods. If seasonal factors are important, it is necessary to make a forecast with a seasonally adjusted estimate of sales rather than a straight line trend. Because of the regularity of seasonal factors and the relatively short time element involved, it is usually easier to obtain a more accurate forecast for the short term than for the medium and long term. Short-term forecasting is necessary for immediate planning and the scheduling of existing resources.

As soon as the time period under review moves beyond the short term, the forecasting time periods (medium- and long-term), in addition to marketing considerations, tend to be dependent upon the time it takes to plan, purchase and bring into operation new fixed capital and assets (new plant, equipment, production lines, factories, etc) and upon the potential operating life of such assets.

Medium-term forecasts

In most industries there is a recognized business cycle in which, although the actual volume of business is either higher or lower than in the past, the pattern of business is characterized by a fairly even cyclical movement. In various industries (particularly capital and industrial goods) this 'business' cycle ranges from two to five years and tends to be more difficult to forecast than the seasonal pattern because of the longer time span involved.

Also, although on such a cycle it is possible to anticipate an increase or decrease in sales in any one period, the magnitude of fluctuations experienced tends to be much greater. However, because of a medium-term recurring business cycle, it is possible in many industries to anticipate future movements of demand in a number of markets. Some companies in the machine tool industries, for example, use such business cycles as one of their techniques to forecast sales, making the necessary adjustments to allow for the disappearance or lessening of some factors that operated in the past and the presence of new influences in the current situation. Medium-term forecasts are required to enable realistic detailed budgeting to be carried out, and to ensure the best possible use of company resources. This type of forecast affects marketing planning and policy; it has the effect of either adapting company resources to match the market situation and/or of adjusting the marketing mix to match company resources in the medium term.

Long-term forecasts

The long-term forecast is the most difficult type of forecast to make with any degree of accuracy. This is mainly because of the time factor; obviously the longer the time period the greater the opportunity for new situations to arise and new variable factors to emerge. It is also due to the long-term influences of much wider economic factors such as world trade, international competition, population trends, the general trade cycle, the product life cycle, income trends, changes in standards of living, productivity changes, technological developments, a country's ability to attract and foster growth industries, and many others. But even though such difficulties prevail, a long-range forecast is an essential tool of business activity. It is necessary for the future planning of resources such as finance, buildings, plant and equipment, labor, research and development, raw materials and marketing facilities, etc. It is necessary for long-term consideration of entry into new markets, or for deciding on matters of product diversification as well as for determining the overall direction of a company's policy. Long-term forecasts of between five and 20 years are best approached by considering them as trends rather than highly detailed forecasts. As such predictions are influenced by long-term patterns in the national and world economies, they should be based upon national and international economic and political indicators rather than recent sales experience by a company in a particular market or industry. Long-term forecasts will also be influenced by the progress of the overall product category life cycle. The application of all these factors can be seen in current world energy markets.

Long-term forecasts are made to ensure the availability of resources. In fact the importance of this type of forecast is in direct proportion to the specialization of the resources to be made available or acquired. Buildings, equipment, materials, skills, etc to be used in company operations that are so specialized that they cannot be used for other than their originally intended purpose need a more accurate sales forecast. For any group of products, the different resources required have different lead times, ie for a factory the necessary lead time could be two to four years, for plant and equipment one to three years, components and materials a month to 18 months. Even specially trained labor may require a lead time of one to 12 months. These points indicate that the term (ie the time unit) of the forecast should be related to the purpose for which it is to be used. Long-term forecasts need updating from time to time, sometimes revealing a substantial change to be made in the allocation of resources. This is particularly true when a need is indicated to convert fixed resources to some other use, eg buildings, plant and equipment, etc, that have been planned, or partially completed.

It will be appreciated that in long-term forecasting precise timing matters much less than with short- or medium-term predictions. This is because the aim of long-term forecasting is to get a picture of the probable level of demand in five to 20 years' time, assuming, of course, that situations have developed according to the anticipated pattern. Generally, it is important to realize that in long-range forecasting it is the general sweep of the economy and the market that is important, not actual and detailed prediction of sales in the twentieth year.

The impact of medium- and long-term factors on short-term forecasting

Because of the differing time horizons of short-, medium- and long-term forecasts and their different uses by various functional areas within an organization, it is often the case that they are each calculated by different people with different roles within that organization. Thus product/brand managers, sales managers and salesmen may be directly involved in making short-term forecasts and the corporate planning group in making a five to seven year corporate plan.

There is a tendency for the short-term forecaster to leave the medium- and long-term considerations to other people. However, Figure 12 shows, in a hypothetical situation, the cumulative effect that medium- and long-term business cycles have on the short-term sales patterns.

The seasonal pattern will continue at a higher or lower level depending on the influences of the medium- and long-term cycles. The diagram illustrates why a seasonal recession can be sometimes very minor and sometimes more severe. This is also one of the commonest faults in forecasting: the forecaster gets the pattern right but the level wrong. If the data appears in tabular form this may never be realized and a fundamentally effective method of forecasting may be re-

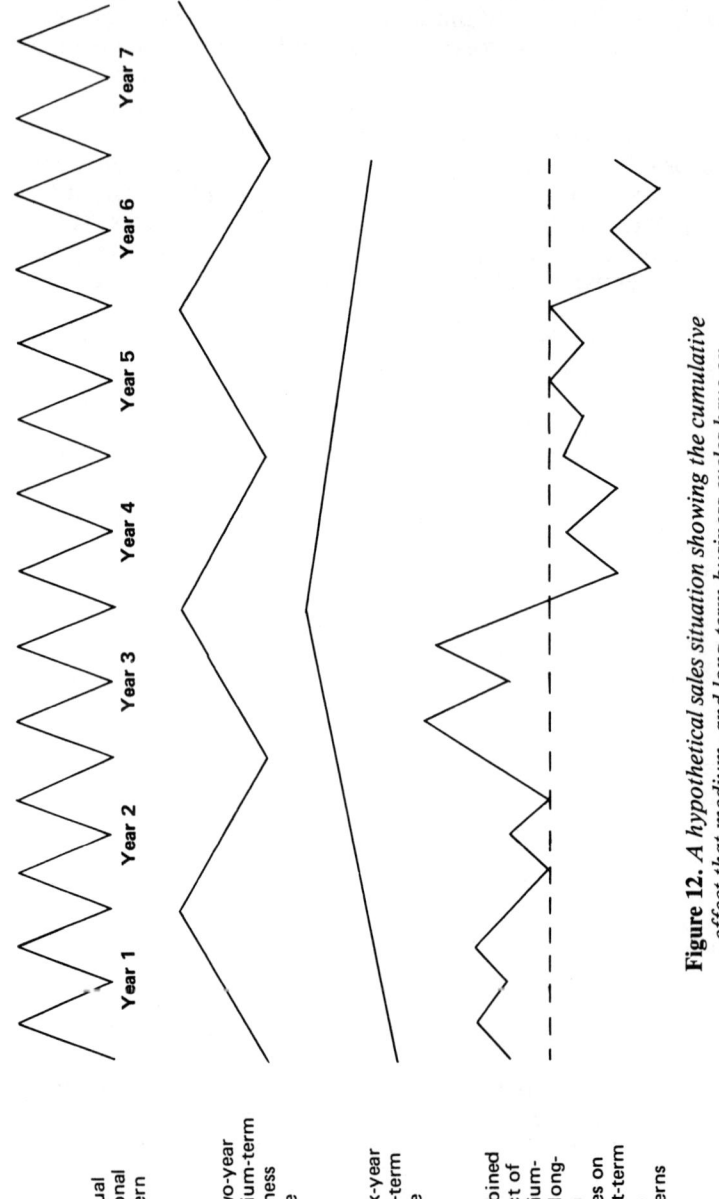

Figure 12. *A hypothetical sales situation showing the cumulative effect that medium- and long-term business cycles have on short-term sales patterns*

jected. By always showing forecasts and sales performances on graphs, patterns that are vertically wrong can be identified, as well as sales patterns and forecasts that have a lead/lag relationship, ie where the pattern of sales leads or lags horizontally. In both cases, the cause may well be the pressure of medium- and long-term cycles and influences upon short-term forecasts or sales performance.

The main problem in either very short-, short-, medium- or long-range forecasting is to determine when a change is about to take place and when a new situation is about to present itself. As minor influences can start new trends, the forecaster must use all the forecasting tools appropriate to his particular company and industry, and get as many opinions as possible about the full meaning of the current data and trends. The magnitude of the problem then lessens because it becomes one of discerning an average trend from a variety of trends and reliable opinions. The multi-technique approach to forecasting is essential.

Sales forecasting definitions

In Chapter 1 it was stated that sales forecasting concerns the potential and prospective sales volume or market trend for the individual product (company) and sets a sales target in an anticipated market within the overall economy. It is concerned with the potential sales volume because this implies the possible extent of the market at a particular time and it is important to determine the market share of the company to use it as a measuring device. If company sales are increasing but its market share decreasing, it could mean that the company is not taking full advantage of the existing market situation and its market opportunity. On the other hand, market share must be related to profitability and the cost of maintaining existing, or obtaining a higher, market share. For example, a company in a highly competitive consumer goods field had at one period of time a 23% share of a market and was making a huge loss. After re-assessing its resources and the market, and changing its marketing plan, it had a 12% share of the market but was making a good profit.

The above definition mentions the prospective sales volume and this refers to the volume a company could sell by seizing market opportunities. For example, it would contrast the company opportunity to sell 500 units during a period with the current production capacity of 350 units. Such a prediction could be of use to the marketing planning function and should cause management to consider a number of alternatives so as to maximize marketing opportunity. Alternatives could be to sub-contract, to purchase from another source, to change the emphasis in the product range, or to obtain production facilities by the acquisition of another company etc, all of which would eventually affect the forecast.

The definition also distinguishes between sales volume and market trend, the need for which can be seen when considering the different time periods of short, medium, and long terms. The relative preciseness of the sales forecast in the short term would be out of place and indeed be unbelievable in the long term where the prediction of the general trends is the best that the forecaster can hope to achieve. Further, it should be appreciated that the longer the time span the greater the chance of increasing error in the forecast.

The last part of the definition suggests that the company sales forecast simply sets a company sales goal in an anticipated market and again emphasizes the underlying interrelationships between the product, the company, the industry (or market), and the economy (national and/or international). The importance of appreciating these interrelationships and the market share concept is illustrated in the case of a multi-product company marketing five product groups; the forecast and achieved sales figures of two are considered here:

Product group	Company sales forecast	Actual sales achieved
A	$800,000	$900,000
B	$600,000	$560,000

From the data shown it would appear that a better marketing job has been carried out on group A by increasing sales by $100,000, than on group B where sales were $40,000 down on forecast. But if the size of the market involved and the company's share of the individual market or industry are considered, a totally different picture is revealed.

Forecast:

Product group	Industry or market forecast	Company sales forecast	Forecast share of market
A	$10,000,000	$800,000	8%
B	$12,000,000	$600,000	5%

Achieved:

Product group	Industry or market sales	Company's actual sales	Actual market share
A	$15,000,000	$900,000	6%
B	$8,000,000	$560,000	7%

If the above data is considered, the former assessment of the marketing performance with these two product groups will be reversed. In the case of A the fullest advantage has not been taken of a tremendously expanding market, and the company's market share has dropped from 8% to 6%. On the other hand, the initial assessment of a bad marketing performance for group B must be reconsidered because this market has in fact contracted, and although the product group is down on forecast, the market share has increased from 5% to 7%. It is therefore very important when comparing forecast sales with actual sales to consider (a) whether the market upon which the forecast was based has expanded or contracted, and (b) what was the size of the market share.

The above example also emphasizes the need for effective market forecasts as well as company sales forecasts. It also raises some questions as to the effectiveness and adequacy of the company's market forecasting techniques; these need an urgent, critical reappraisal. Further, if the sales forecasts were the basis of budgets throughout the company, the circumstances in which the purchasing department could make available extra raw materials, and the production function could make available extra capacity for an additional $100,000 of A to be manufactured, would be worthy of investigation.

Another approach to defining a sales forecast could be: 'an estimate of future product/service sales in volume/value over a given period of time regarding current and prospective customers'.

It could be argued in management terms that the forecast is merely the first step and that the sales forecast becomes a budget once it has been costed and accepted. When this happens the budget could be defined as: 'a financial statement of forecast revenue and expenditure over a given period of time'.

It could be further argued that once the original forecast becomes a budget and resources have been committed, then the predicted targets must be achieved. However, the implications of forcibly achieving a forecast/budget must be understood. By various means it is nearly always possible to achieve a sales forecast, eg prices may be cut, trade discounts increased, more money can be spent on advertising and sales promotion, more salesmen can be employed, etc. But all these methods incur increased costs and therefore although the sales forecast/budget may be achieved the profit target may not.

A widely accepted practice is that of updating the forecast or re-forecasting at appropriate intervals during the year in the light of the market situation then prevailing.

Setting forecasting objectives

In any form of planned activity it is necessary initially to lay down the objectives, the purpose and the desired achievement. Market and sales forecasting is no exception, and it is essential to lay down individual company objectives because each organization represents a different combination of policies, resources, products and market aims.

One objective could relate to the degree of accuracy; it could indicate what is desirable and what is considered realistic. A company forecasting objective could be to forecast within ± 3% of the monthly sales figure and within ± 5% of the total sales for the year. In complex market situations it may not be possible to obtain a high degree of accuracy because of the influence of a great number of independent variable factors, and the level of accuracy attainable in one industry may not be acceptable in another. In some cases a trend rather than a highly detailed forecast may be adequate in a particular range or market. In other situations 'flexible' forecasting may be appropriate. In a complex market situation or where fundamental changes are likely to take place, a range of forecasts may be made in an effort to cover all eventualities. This could lead to a 'worst' situation forecast, a static situation forecast, an improved situation forecast, and a best situation forecast. Such a sales forecasting exercise provides a fringe benefit for the company as it forces executives to examine possible alternatives and plan accordingly. The accuracy factor, within the feasible levels accepted by a company, can be improved by using a multi-technique approach to forecasting. This is especially so where variations between the forecasts of various techniques can be investigated or where a forecast is built up empirically as in the case of forecasts by salesmen, area managers and regional managers, in addition to statistical techniques.

Forecasting objectives need to be set in relation to costs; a forecast must be obtained around a budgeted cost figure. The cost of obtaining a forecast and the expected profit contribution as a result of using it need to be balanced. But the cost of making a wrong forecast and causing an expansion of company resources or causing them not to be available when needed should be considered; it often follows that a more effective forecasting system is set up.

Other objectives will concern time; a weekly, monthly, quarterly, yearly, five yearly forecast may be needed, but forecasts are required in time to take effective action. If the degree of sophistication of the forecasting system is such that by the time the forecast is ready it is too late to be used, then something less sophisticated must be accepted; the ideal forecasting system must be modified to circumstances.

Because companies have different policies, different sets of resources and operate in different markets they need to emphasize certain aspects of the various company functions (production, finance, marketing, etc) in order to optimize their profits. The objectives of any forecast should reflect the relative importance of various aspects of company activity. But even within the various company

1. Forecasting objectives and research and development

Market and sales forecasting objectives in the field of research and development are numerous but in the main are concerned with obtaining longer design and development lead times, assessing how functional features of products will affect sales, providing forecasts in segments rather than total markets and forecasts for product sizes, colors, models, etc.

Such forecasts center around the questions: is there a market for a product? How big is it? Is it intensive or extensive? How many products can be sold and at what prices? Where is the market located? What are the shares of the market held by competitors? What are the short-, medium- and long-term prospects? What are the implications of the results of product tests and test markets when interpreted into sales in regional, national or international markets? In this area potential profit levels can be anticipated, for there is an obvious link between the range of unit volumes that can be sold at a range of various prices, which in turn is linked to costs.

2. Purchasing

The objectives of a forecast related to the purchasing function are concerned with future material requirements in types, materials, sizes, colors, quantities, qualities and the timing of their purchase. Effective forecasting enables the purchasing function to (a) deal in standard parts or materials, bulk quantities or grouping of orders related to special discounts, (b) purchase at times geared to seasonal price changes, (c) reduce the number of buying occasions, and (d) lower raw material stock levels. It also permits the planning of financial requirements for purchasing and the procurement of special or non-standard material. Depending on individual company needs, objectives should be set giving due consideration to the needs of the purchasing function.

3. Production

The main objectives of forecasting as an aid to the production function concern the scale of operation and the degree of use of existing and future production resources. In industries where economies of scale are possible, volume predictions as the life cycle progresses are of extreme importance in planning for future production resources. But with any scale of operation, sales forecasts indicate the degree of potential use of existing plant and equipment. This gives management the opportunity to consider new product development projects and to ensure more economical working of production resources in the future. Effective production and product line scheduling, long order lead times, long runs of one product, size or color, are factors that affect production economy and the forecasting objectives should reflect them. Sales forecasts in this area are therefore likely to take the form of an analysis by brand or product groups, sizes, models, etc.

Stocks have to be financed and in most cases inventory costs are high and the aim of a forecast could be to enable a company to carry economic levels of finished and partly finished stock.

4. Personnel

Manpower budgets as well as materials budgets must be planned, and the sales forecast forms the basis of planning for future increased, decreased or static personnel requirements. The objective of forecasts in this company activity area is to give the personnel department the greatest possible lead time, not only to obtain suitable personnel but also, ideally, to permit proper training to take place. Effective market and sales forecasting can also foster good employer/employee/trade union relationships as it gives advanced warning of future changes in the numbers and types of staff the company will be requiring in the future.

5. Finance

The objectives of the sales forecast with regard to the financial function of the company will be to provide appropriate data upon which to forecast stock turn, cash flow, return on capital invested, desired profit margins, profits, and dividends. In many companies the balance between the inflow of cash and the outflow of expenditure is very fine and month by month predictions of volume by product type, price, and market segment will assist financial management. In different markets, and sometimes in different segments of the same markets, accepted credit limits will be different, and the identification of these different credit areas can be carried out by analysis of a forecast by consumer group, type of outlet, or industrial classification.

Further, as the sales forecast should form the basis of all budgets in a company, it therefore assists financial management to determine the company master budget, and also to plan that money will be available at the correct times during the short, medium and long term for working and fixed capital and capital projects.

6. Marketing

Although it forms one of the sub-functional activities of marketing, market and sales forecasting will have a number of uses for other parts of marketing, and in consequence will have a variety of objectives in each marketing area.

The sales forecast will be either the input or the output of various marketing research activities. Its role in the function of the marketing effort has already been examined under the heading of general research and development. In advertising and sales promotion the prediction objective might be to indicate the volume markets which in turn will help to determine the appropriate levels of advertising expenditure. Forecasts of the size, location, type of market and consumer, with forecasts of product models, help to determine which media and advertising theme is appropriate to reach such a market.

In the area of packaging the aim of the forecast will be to provide information regarding volume, size and type of pack etc, to enable the economic purchase of unit packs, display outers, and shipment cases.

The sales forecast objective in relation to the sales force is to provide a basis for area, branch, and salesmen's sales target. However, it is essential to ensure that the target does not become an implied maximum to the salesman so that opportunities are missed because the target has been reached. It is better to have a quota that *must* be achieved, together with a target that *could* be reached with considerable extra effort, both being part of the overall potential of the territory. The forecast could form the basis for a remuneration plan for the sales force.

Sales forecasting objectives in the area of physical distribution relate to information for transport, warehousing, location of strategic stocks, and channels of distribution (wholesalers, retailers, etc). In the case of transport, the number of items that will be sold, size of order and geographic spread in various areas will help to determine such factors as whether to use the company's own or external transport services, size of fleet and size of individual vehicle, frequency of delivery, etc. Volume, seasonal factors and a breakdown of size and type of product are important factors when considering warehousing and the placing of strategic stocks. Forecasts help to determine the channels of distribution to be used by a company. When volume is small and/or the geographic spread is wide, manufacturers' agents or wholesalers may be more economic to use than when volume is relatively large, in which case the increased overheads of dealing direct with the retailer or consumer can be spread over a greater sales volume. The forecast may have to allow for longer production lead time if wholesalers are used. For example, it may be that products purchased by consumers in November and December have to be sold into retailers in September and October, but sold into wholesalers in July and August. Further, in forecasting the initial sales of a new product range, the forecaster will need to dif-

Time horizon	Marketing	Production	Inventory	Finance	Purchasing	R & D	Top management
Short-term (up to 3 months)	Sales of each product type Sales by geographical area Sales by customer Competition prices Sales force targets	Demand of each product Plant loading	Demand of each product Demand for material Demand for semi-finished products Weather conditions	Sales revenue Production costs Inventory costs Leading indicators Cash in-flows Cash out-flows	Production Cash availability Purchasing of supplies and material		Competition evaluation
	Total sales Product categories Major products Product groups Stock levels	Total demand Demand of product categories and product groups Scheduling employment levels Costs	Demand for material	Total demand Inventory levels Cash-flows Short-term borrowing Prices	Demand for products Demand for material Lead time for purchasing		Total sales Sales breakdowns Pricing

	Marketing	Production	Facilities	Finance	Purchasing	R&D	Top Management
Medium-term (3 months to less than 2 years)	Total sales Product categories Prices General economic conditions Promotional emphasis	Costs Budget allocations Buying or ordering equipment and machinery Employment level		Budget allocations Cash-flows	Demand for products Demand for raw and other materials	New product introduction	Demand for sales other other expenses Cash-position General economic conditions Controls Objectives
Long-term (2 years or more)	Total sales Major product categories New product introduction Saturation points Market research emphasis	Costs Investments selection Expansion of plant and equipment Ordering of heavy equipment	Total sales Expansion of warehouses	Total sales Investment selections Capital expenditure Allocations Cash-flows	Contracts for buying of raw material	Total sales Technological social political and economic conditions of future New product development	Total sales Costs and other expenses Social and economic trends Goals and objectives and strategies establishment New products

Figure 13. Uses of forecasting in organization function areas

ferentiate between ex-factory deliveries to wholesalers and retailers and the actual over-the-counter purchases by consumers. Initial ex-factory sales may be high as middlemen purchase a variety of the whole range to give consumers a choice and possibly an adequate service; a new range of household paint with a variety of different sizes, finishes and colors is an example quoted in Chapter 2.

Company-wide uses of forecasts

Because all budgets in a company ultimately come back to the question of how many units the organization will sell, all functional parts of a company will be interested in a forecast. In some cases a functional department will make its own individual forecast for use in a particular way.

Figure 13 indicates the various forecasts needed by functional areas of a company, and it will be seen that needs differ in the short, medium and long term. The purpose of Figure 13 is to highlight forecasting needs and to indicate where forecasting may be in operation. Any forecaster needs to research his organization to determine whether other personnel have made or are making a similar forecast to the one he needs. Such research can avoid duplication of effort and save valuable time.

If the marketing department is not responsible for all forecasts, the management implications are that all forecasting activity should be integrated and ideally a composite forecast should be made.

Why, what, how, who, where and when

Setting objectives is in effect giving the answers to a series of questions commencing with the words Why, What, How, Who, Where and When.

Why do we need a forecast? Is it for short-term production scheduling, for financial planning, or to buy advantageously in a seasonal market? The most important primary and secondary reasons should be determined and the forecasting system built around them.

What are we trying to achieve, in terms of accuracy, scope, and effectiveness; do we need a trend or a detailed forecast? What are the particular problems involved in obtaining short-, medium- and long-term forecasts. What are the costs involved in terms of time and money, and what is the forecasting system's contribution to company profits? What sources of information are we going to tap?

How are the forecasts to be compiled and how many techniques are to be used? Is it to be calculated as a total forecast and broken down into product forecasts or started as product forecasts and built up to a total company forecast, or both? How can the forecasting system's adequacy be determined and what checks can be built in to ensure that it is working properly?

Who is going to do the forecasting? Is it to be done at executive level, or by specialist forecasters, or are the routine parts to be delegated to others; or a combination of these? Who will be involved in forecasting: company executives, specialist sales forecasters, marketing researchers, customers, potential customers, key people, salesmen, consultants, etc?

Where will the forecasting be done: in the marketing research section, in the marketing statistics or budgetary control section, in a specialized forecasting section, or in a combination of these?

When will forecasting be done? Will it be done on a weekly, monthly, quarterly, or yearly basis? When and how often will the forecast be reviewed? When and under what circumstances will the forecast be amended, if it is wrong by 5%, 10%, 25% etc of actual sales? When and for what reasons will certain forecasting techniques be dropped and others introduced?

For effective control, objectives must be set so that the success of each forecasting technique is measured by comparing each component forecast with actual sales and any variances analyzed. It is the analysis of these variances, however small, that indicates the beginning of a new up-turn or down-turn in sales.

CHAPTER 4
The Collection of Data for Forecasting

'Knowledge is of two kinds. We know a subject ourselves or we know where we can find information upon it.'
Dr Johnson

Scope

The next stage in market and sales forecasting is the collection of relevant and market-related information. This information is usually one of four types: *historic and factual data* referring to the past or present, *assumptive information* that makes rational assumptions for the future, data based upon the *statistical probability of an event taking place* and information regarding *future plans and policies*.

There are three main classifications of sources of information for marketing research in general and for market and sales forecasting in particular:

1. Desk research into internal records, which is the analysis of available, or potentially available company statistics and historic information. It also involves the collection of information regarding activities planned for the future (viz the marketing plan, etc), and details of company policy and an analysis of their possible effects on the sales forecast.
2. Desk research into secondary sources of information in published or existing material such as government statistics, economic data, trade information, published surveys, etc.
3. Original external field research ranging from informal approaches to key people and customers, regional or national surveys and experiments (ie controlled test marketing, pilot launches, etc).

Within these three areas data can be obtained covering the external (and largely uncontrollable) factors and the internal (and largely controllable) factors examined in Chapter 1. Unless an adequate picture of the relevant market environment is obtained, even the most sophisticated predictive methods will fail to produce an effective forecast.

Desk research into internal records

This is the most useful, economic and logical starting point for market and sales forecasting. The continuous analysis of sales should be a normal everyday activity of any efficient marketing organization. Facts discovered by such an analysis often provide the solutions to many research and forecasting problems and are found within the company files. It is merely a matter of extracting and processing them into a usable form. The methods and types of internal records analyses are numerous, and their pattern and range will depend upon the problems facing the company, or indeed what information it requires.

However, there are a number of basic groups of data that can be used, improved upon, or rejected, and an analysis of their recent, past and current performance can make market and sales forecasting more effective.

Sales volume

One of the most important is sales volume. Total sales volume, and sales volume by product or product group, or service, is necessary. Such information would indicate the relative importance of each product or service in the company's product mix and in terms of income added to total company revenue or number of units sold. This data and the other groups that follow are extremely useful for statistical extrapolation.

Area sales volume

Area sales volume statistics involve a breakdown of past sales into geographical areas, salesmen's territories, television area coverage, or evening newspaper area coverage. Such data is necessary to relate the actual sales of an area to its potential.

Time sales volume

The analysis of sales over a period of time allows the progress of a company to be assessed, but it should cover not only sales in terms of money, but also sales in terms of units sold. Otherwise, fluctuations in price or (in the long term) the fall in the value of money may seriously restrict the usefulness of this data for forecasting purposes. Analysis of sales over a period of time allows seasonal fluctuations to be isolated and allowed for, as these are often hidden in yearly total figures.

Price/sales volume

Price/sales volume analysis indicating the effect on past sales of changes in price and discount levels is another key area of internal desk research.

Channels sales volume

The sales performance of the various channels of distribution being used by a company makes possible assessment of the contribution that each group, or type of outlet, makes to total revenue and is an indicator in establishing outlet profitability. It highlights current trends in channels of distribution and acts as a guide to a really effective advertising policy which in turn will affect sales.

When the policy of a company is to sell through retail outlets, analysis of the size and number of such outlets, as well as the distribution coverage (ie the number dealt with in relation to all outlets), produces essential forecasting information. Further, analysis of the type of outlets being used and a comparison made with the current trend in the pattern of distribution will enable a company to forecast and adjust to changes. Examples might be the growth of 'giant' retailing, of self-service and self-selection, of composite trading (widening of product ranges available in formerly specialist outlets) and of voluntary chains and groups.

Recognition of these changes will make possible more realistic forecasting of sales by allowing for the current distribution trend and by placing less reliance upon historic data obtained from an 'old' distribution pattern. Such analysis will enable a company to determine the minimum size of dealer or user with whom it is economical to deal direct, and will act as a guide as to whether an increased or decreased use of wholesale channels is indicated. Likewise, when a company is selling through agents, wholesalers, factors or distributors, or selling direct to industrial users, analysis of this kind will allow the forecaster to predict potential and permit marketing management to choose the most profitable method. Often this type of analysis will reveal a pattern of purchasing that can be used in forecasting. Also it may indicate the greater profitability of one type of outlet in one part of the country compared with the same type in another part.

When marketing industrial products, sales by SIC (Standard Industrial Classification) group will reveal the equivalent information regarding sales by types of industry. The Standard Industrial Classification Manual is published in the USA by the Executive Office of the President — Office of Management and Budget, and prepared by the Statistical Policy Division. It classifies industries by broad categories (eg Manufacturing, Division D), then by major group (eg Electrical and Electronic Machinery, equipment and supplies, Major Group 36) and then by specific industry group (eg Electric Lamps, Group 364, Industry No 3641). The Standard Industrial

Classification approach not only allows an industrial marketing company to analyze its sales by user industry type, but also permits a comparison with official statistics and data from other sources using the SIC. As a consequence it may be possible to derive the company's percentage share of the industry market. Internal company data based on the SIC can be linked also with input/output analysis described in Chapter 6.

Order size statistics
The minimum and average size of order statistics are important forecasting indicators, as the size and value of an order must be related to the cost of preparation, handling, administration, and delivery. Such overhead costs have an obvious and direct influence upon sales and profit, and there is a minimum size of order below which it is unprofitable to do business. If the company is in a strong position it can dictate what business it will handle direct and what it will pass through wholesalers. The minimum and average size of order decision will obviously affect sales and therefore forecasting.

Cost data
The actual cost of marketing is a further group of data that can be obtained from company records, and the sales and marketing cost per $ of sales obtained is a useful indicator for period-to-period comparison. It is particularly important in the case of the field sales force, and the sales cost per $ of sales obtained should be broken down into cost per salesman's territory. Marketing cost analysis will indicate particular problem spots in total marketing expenses. Such expenses should be broken down and attributed to all the sub-functions of marketing, from marketing research, product planning, publicity and promotional costs, to direct selling, physical distribution and administration, etc. By comparisons *within* sub-functions, for example, it may be found to be more profitable to have more door-to-door couponing and less television advertising. From comparisons *between* sub-functions (ie more spent upon advertising and less upon the sales force), it will be possible for marketing management to determine which is the best mix of the various marketing factors and enable predictions to be made that are more realistic. This type of analysis often leads to decisions by marketing management to change the use of company resources. Therefore, forecasters must follow through the consequences of their earlier analysis.

Sales potential
Sometimes potentials have been calculated for the sales force, ie total market potential by area, the number of customers and/or potential

customers per area, etc. If they have been calculated carefully the comparison of increases or decreases in actual sales with potential at regular time intervals is a useful indicator to the forecaster.

Sales force statistics

Data regarding the sales force, ie length of journey cycle and frequency of call, differing time allocation to various classes of customers, changes in the numbers of calls and the effect in different time periods, the number of calls in relation to the orders obtained, and even the effect on turnover of sales training etc, can all be obtained from internal records and in some cases are fundamental to the making of a realistic forecast.

Stock control data

The analysis of stock and the calculation of maximum and minimum stocks that it is economic to carry, both within the firm and in wholesalers and retailers, will bring to light stock control data. However, an economically low inventory must be reconciled with the level of stocks necessary to give adequate customer service or to meet competition and this in turn will have an effect on sales. Closely linked with stock control is the discovery and calculation of stock turn data during various periods of the year. Increasing stock turn will make a product more attractive for wholesalers and retailers to stock and sell actively.

Further, the availability of stock, where it is located and in what variety, will be a further influence upon sales and consequently upon sales forecasting. If stocks are not available, then the demand created by company advertising may be satisfied by competitors.

Accounting ratios

Statistics and facts regarding any aspect of company activity, especially those concerning marketing that are relevant to forecasting, should be extracted from internal records. In fact, the effectiveness of both marketing and general management can be calculated by using appropriate management accounting ratios comparing one period with another, or, if the facility exists, one company with another (eg inter-firm comparisons operated by private firms or trade associations). A statistical picture of company progress can be obtained when such ratios are calculated on a continuous basis.

Historic information

All types of historic marketing data must also be taken into account in forecasting: past marketing research information, the progress of both new and existing products (including product/process/service life cycle data), the expenditure, pattern and emphasis of advertising and sales promotion, and the relationship of sales volume and market share to these expenditures. Also pertinent would be information regarding size and type of sales force, the channels of distribution, methods of physical distribution and information regarding past pricing, branding, and credit policies. Between various time periods, comparison of changes in any of these factors would indicate their effect upon sales and therefore upon future predictions.

Predictable future data
Just as historic information regarding the eight sub-functions of marketing is important, so too are the planned future levels of these factors, particularly if they are to be different from the recent past. Therefore part of internal research will be concerned with the potential repercussions of future plans. For example, what effect will a proposed increase in the advertising budget have upon sales and why is it contemplated? In a growth market a particular increase in advertising expenditure may cause a disproportionate increase in sales. Alternatively, in highly competitive markets such an increase may merely be intended to hold sales at the level attained in the previous period. But where a new company enters a relatively static market, its sales can only come from customers of existing companies, therefore these companies may have to increase advertising expenditure as sales fall rapidly, merely to try to retain a reduced share of a market (a holding campaign). Company plans for the future in all activities (marketing, production, finance, etc) must be considered if forecasting is to be effective. Even a plan to commence, improve, or increase training for salesmen must be taken into account, as this will have an obvious effect upon sales performance.

These examples do not exhaust the range of possible headings under which past and proposed future data can be obtained from within a company, and therefore the individual forecaster must tailor the company's own internal research to suit its particular resources and market situation.

Desk research into secondary sources of information in published or existing material

Effective market and sales forecasting also uses basic economic and industrial data, government or official statistics, data from institutions and trade associations, national and trade press information, data from international bodies, previous surveys covering similar or analogous subjects and markets, and published information regarding competitors' strategy and tactics. To obtain optimum results from this type of desk research, existing information should be regularly updated.

Government sources
Principal social and economic statistical programs

A. *Criminal justice statistics:*
   Criminal justice system-wide statistical programs
   Crime statistics
   Judicial statistics
   Correctional statistics
   State statistical programs

B. *Education statistics*

C. *Energy and energy-related statistics:*
   Exploration and reserves of energy fuels
   Production, supply, and distribution of energy
   Use and consumption of energy
   Financial information

D. *Environmental statistics:*
   Air quality and emissions data
   Water quality and supply
   Radiation data
   Pesticides
   Noise pollution
   Toxic substances
   Solid wastes
   Geologic hazards and other geologic environmental data
   Pollution abatement and control expenditures

E. *Health and vital statistics:*
   Health statistics
   Medicare
   Vital statistics

F. *Income maintenance and welfare:*
   Social insurance and related programs
   Social and rehabilitation services
   Child welfare
   Vocational rehabilitation
   Other assistance programs
   Poverty statistics

G. *Labor statistics:*
   Labor force
   Nonagricultural employment, hours, and earnings
   Agricultural employment
   Current and projected industry and occupational employment
   Wages and related practices
   Scientific and technical manpower
   Manpower employment and training

Productivity estimates
Labor turnover
Occupational safety and health
Work stoppages and collective bargaining
Health manpower
Foreign labor statistics

H. *National economic and business financial accounts:*
Financial reports of business
Capital spending and capacity utilization
Income
Expenditures
Saving
Government transactions
Export and import statistics
Money, credit, and the securities markets
National economic accounts

I. *Construction and housing statistics:*
Construction
Housing

J. *Population statistics:*
Population counts
Immigration and naturalization
Travel statistics

K. *Price statistics and price indexes:*
Wholesale prices
Retail prices
Prices paid by farmers
Prices received by farmers
GNP price indexes
International price competitiveness measures

L. *Production, distribution, and service statistics:*
Manufacturing production
Mineral production
Agricultural production
Index of industrial production
Wholesale and retail trade and selected service industries
Marketing of agricultural products
Transportation
Communications
Research and development

Principal statistical publications of federal agencies

Executive Office of the President
Office of Management and Budget
Council of Economic Advisers

Department of Agriculture
Agricultural Marketing Service

Agricultural Research Service
Economic Research Service
Farmer Cooperative Service
Foreign Agricultural Service
Forest Service
Statistical Reporting Service

Department of Commerce
Domestic and International Business Administration
Bureau of the Census
Bureau of Economic Analysis
Maritime Administration
National Bureau of Standards
National Oceanic and Atmospheric Administration
United States Travel Service

Department of Defense

Department of Health, Education and Welfare
Office of Human Development
Public Health Service
National Center for Education Statistics
Social and Rehabilitation Service
Social Security Administration

Department of Housing and Urban Development
Administration
Policy Development and Research
Housing Production and Mortgage Credit
Community Planning and Development

Department of the Interior
Bureau of Mines
Mining Enforcement and Safety Administration
Bureau of Reclamation
Bureau of Land Management
National Park Service
US Fish and Wildlife Service
US Geological Survey

Department of Justice
Immigration and Naturalization Service
Federal Bureau of Investigation
Law Enforcement Assistance Administration
Drug Enforcement Administration
Bureau of Prisons
Antitrust Division

Department of Labor
Bureau of Labor Statistics
Employment Standards Administration
Labor-Management Services Administration
Manpower Administration

Department of Transportation
   Office of the Secretary
   Federal Aviation Administration
   Federal Highway Administration
   Federal Railroad Administration
   National Highway Traffice Safety Administration
   US Coast Guard

Department of the Treasury
   Office of the Comptroller of the Currency
   Bureau of the Mint
   Office of the Assistant Secretary for International Affairs
   Bureau of Government Financial Operations
   Internal Revenue Service

Independent Agencies
   Board of Governors of the Federal Reserve System
   Civil Aeronautics Board
   Environmental Protection Agency
   Equal Employment Opportunity Commission
   Federal Communications Commission
   Federal Deposit Insurance Corporation
   Federal Energy Administration
   Federal Home Loan Bank Board
   Federal Power Commission
   Federal Trade Commission
   General Services Administration
   Interstate Commerce Commission
   National Science Foundation
   National Transportation Safety Board
   Railroad Retirement Board
   Securities and Exchange Commission
   Selective Service System
   US Civil Service Commission
   United States Commission on Civil Rights
   United States International Trade Commission
   US Water Resources Council
   Veterans Administration

Every major governmental body and commission generates statistics and special reports of many kinds, all of them listed in the cumulative catalog of government documents available in every major library. However, the basic information source will be *The Statistical Abstract of the United States* published every September by the Bureau of the Census.

Non-government sources

Many private organizations also generate primary statistics. Most trade associations conduct statistical operations on subjects important to their members and some of their findings are published, others are available on request. Some organizations compile and digest various official data, converting them into more convenient forms. Examples of these private compilations are:

- *Rand McNally Commercial Atlas and Marketing Guide*
- *Sales Management Survey of Buying Power*
- *Editor and Publisher Market Guide*
- *Advertising Age Market Data Issue*
- *American Marketing Associations Research Bibliographies*

Press sources

The world, national and local press and specialized trade magazines provide valuable current data for the forecaster in general and specific fields. The usefulness of the highly specialized trade press varies from industry to industry with overlapping of information in some areas (much of it calculated on different information bases) and a great number of information gaps in others. Trade publications gather and publish many series of considerable value in conjunction with their news and promotional series.

Additionally, the following publications will be of use to the forecaster:

- *Business Periodical Index*
- *Index to the New York Times*
- *Wall Street Journal Index*
- *Directory of Newspapers and Periodicals*
- *Ulrich's Periodical Directory*
- *Executives' Guide to Information Sources*
- *Standard Rate and Data Service* (media information)

Directories

A wide range of directories form an invaluable group of information sources giving details of companies, type of product, company structure, number of employees, addresses of parent companies and subsidiaries, etc. Examples of these are:

- *The Directory of Directories* (annotated guide to business and trade directories)
- *Thomas Register of American Manufacturers*
- *Thomas Register Catalog File*
- *Sweets Catalog File*
- Dun and Bradstreet — *Reference Book*
- Dun and Bradstreet — *State Sales Guide*
- *Directory of National Trade and Professional Associations in the United States*
- *Encyclopedia of Associations*

Published surveys
Published surveys also represent another category of information source for the forecaster.

Competitors
Competitors' catalogs, obtained either direct or through customers or from trade fairs and exhibitions, are possible sources of data, as well as competitors' advertisements, public relations announcements and financial reports.

Subscription and consultancy services
There are many sources of published information in the USA operated by marketing research, advertising agencies, and consultants from which specialized information may be purchased.

1. *Early intelligence system.* A combination of services from a broad reliable information base to serve the planning, forecasting and decision-making needs of both the new product marketer and corporate management.
2. *Product pickup service.* National facility for economically providing actual shelf samples of products currently on the market for either marketing, forecasting or quality assurance needs.
3. *Store observation service.* A fast method of evaluating key conditions for forecasting at the point of purchase in retail outlets. It also provides observations on shelf location, facings, price, availability, etc, reporting to clients as quickly as seven days after completed field work.
4. *Local area services.* Major market service with comprehensive research reports from large syndicated samples in any of 38 diversified metropolitan areas for testing or regional monitoring of clients' brands.
5. *Custom audit service.* Permits selecting virtually any US city or area for exclusive product testing at retail level. A complete projected report designed to the client's statistical, geographic and brand format specifications, enabling adjustments to be made to current forecasts.
6. *Data market service.* Minimizes the administrative problems of testing by providing warehouse and distribution services, as well as comprehensive store audits in widely dispersed, smaller test cities which enable necessary re-forecasting of current predictions or adjustment of future forecasts to take place.
7. *Retail index services.* Continuous national and regional measurements of consumer sales and sales influencing

factors at the retail outlet for manufacturers of consumer packaged goods enabling future forecasts to be more soundly based on directly relevant market information.
8. *Alcoholic beverage service.* Liquor, wine and malt beverage reports detailing consumer sales, retailer purchases, inventories, distribution and the like in selected markets.

A C Neilsen also produce promotional literature which summarizes market data, eg *Neilsen Review of Retail Grocery Trends.* Other companies operate subscription information services in a number of industries (consumer and industrial) on the basis of panels, audits, interviews, ad hoc reports, etc. Information regarding companies, TV ratings (viewing), radio listening, readership, etc are also available. A number of agencies specialize in particular markets, eg the operation of panel audits of farmers, doctors, etc.

International sources

In the international field a wide range of information can be found in the various publications of the United Nations. These include data on agriculture, atomic energy, cartography, computers, demography, economics (eg world economy, trade statistics, manufacturers, commodities, finance, industrial development, fertilizers, food, natural mineral resources, small industry, economy of regional areas of the world, steel-engineering, coal, chemicals and timber), environment, housing, international statistics, narcotics, petroleum, social questions, transport and communications, and many others.

International data is also available from many US government agencies, eg the Department of Commerce checklist of international business publications. Information is available from such agencies as the International Monetary Fund, the International Wool Secretariat, the European Economic Community, the International Labor Office, Organization for European Co-operation of Development, special reports and overseas market studies by US and foreign banks etc. International data is also available from a number of private sources, a good example being the annual worldwide review of the grocery marketing scene published by A C Neilsen Company, Northbrook, Illinois.

Availability of information

The examples of published information sources mentioned above are merely a few from each potential group. The sources chosen by any forecaster will depend upon the objective of the survey, the type of product, the market, the industry, and the company with which he is concerned. It is obvious that a combination of sources would be used if possible, both for cross-checking data and to obtain a comprehensive overall picture.

Gathering forecasting information by original field research

This means direct contact with past, present and potential customers and with any other person able to give relevant market and sales forecasting information.

Whether original field research needs to be used by a company in forecasting the market and sales will depend upon the availability of information from internal or published sources. For example, if the subject of a forecast is a completely new product concept or a unique improved product, original field research may be the only source of forecasting information. If competitive factors in a market have changed greatly in recent periods, historic data from desk research may no longer be a reliable source upon which to base a forecast. Further, depending upon cost, time, and accuracy factors, original field research may be the only method of obtaining realistic demand and supply forecasts. Statistically based forecasts often omit vital factors in human behavior which drastically affect market (demand and supply) patterns. Direct field research provides the opportunity to assess the possible effects of such behavior on forecasts. It can also fill in gaps in published data.

Types of field research

The types of market and sales forecasting research that can be carried out 'in the field' are numerous, and a company has the choice of doing the work within its own organization, obtaining the services of specialist market research agencies or of using the market research facilities often offered by advertising agencies.

Some of the main areas in which original field research can be useful in market and sales forecasting are classified as follows:

1. Product

It is possible to investigate product acceptance by the market of new, improved, or existing products, as well as examining the reception of a basic product concept. It is also possible to discover the market segmentation pattern and the corporate image associated with a product. The reactions of a representative sample of consumers/users can be studied and it becomes possible to forecast the size of the various parts of the market in advance, subject to other forecasting factors.

2. Market

The geographical location of a market and its size in terms of market segments can be found by field research if they are not available through published data. This also applies to market share analysis. Potential trends, user characteristics (and consequently ideal profile) and user/purchaser attitude research are also possibilities in this area.

3. Packaging

Unit sales volume can be affected by reaction to the packaging of a product and research into product acceptance through the pack, its protection performance in transit and in storage, its marketing performance, its convenience and after-use function. All these factors can help when considering the effect a pack will have on sales volume in the future.

4. Pricing

Price is a function of demand and therefore should be a prime consideration of the forecaster. Price confrontation studies, in which a sample of consumers is asked what price they think a product (either a general group or specific product) should be, and how much they actually paid the last time they purchased such a product, will give important forecasting data. Other pricing data can be obtained through price/value/quality relationship research of the complete sales proposition (not just the product) and through the determination of psychological and 'bargain' prices.

5. Sales and distribution

This area of forecasting research is concerned with the methods and channels of distribution, activities in retail stores, distribution coverage, the activities of the field sales force, before and after sales services, availability of stocks and the effect of transport facilities.

6. Advertising, sales promotion, and merchandising

Media research, pre- and post-testing of copy and artwork, research into sales promotional techniques, can produce data of importance to the forecaster. It can also broadly indicate the effect the communication media will have on the sales of a new product or the effect that a change in emphasis in the promotional mix will have upon the sales of the existing product range.

7. Industrial

The special problems of industrial marketing require additional research to be carried out. This would include research into market structure, characteristics, and growth as well as end-use analysis of products that are vertically integrated into a chain of manufacturing processes, analysis of customers and potential customers by 'trade use' or SIC (Standard Industrial Classification). It should also include an examination of specific industry buying policies and research into the 'originating' industries, if a company's product enters at some stage in the chain of manufacture. An example of the latter point is the metal container industry's concern with current crops of fruit and vegetables for forecasting purposes. These and other research areas appropriate to particular industries provide vital information for the special needs of the industrial forecaster.

8. Competition

An analysis of competitors' and potential competitors' profiles (production capacities, prices, corporate images, product development, promotional expenditure, future development plans, etc) in the light of a company's own future policies, can help the forecaster to make a more realistic prediction of market conditions and consequently of sales volume.

Methods of collection

The collection of data under these various headings is largely based upon sampling techniques, where a representative sample of consumers or users is surveyed. The main exceptions to this are in the case of competition (where competitors are relatively few) and where the number of consumers or users in a market is small, as in some industrial situations where the data can be collected about all competitors and from all users. Alternatively, data may be collected from key customers only, especially where they purchase a large proportion of a company's or industry's products. However, even with key customers, it can be dangerous to draw wide conclusions from data from small samples. Other key people who can provide information that can affect forecasts are to be found in most government departments.

Sales and technical staff as information sources

Within a company both sales and technical staff can provide market information, although often their contribution is subject to certain limitations, due primarily to inherent bias and lack of market research training.

This tactical information, which should be the easiest to obtain, is usually the most difficult. Every salesman should be trained to pass information back to headquarters. In fact, this intelligence-gathering quality should be developed to a high degree.

If it is important that salesmen are trained to note and report back information, it is equally important that someone is trained in the collation and interpretation of this information. Continuous study and analysis of salesmen's reports can produce profitable information results.

Examples of customer 'grass-roots' forecasting information that salesmen can find out are:

— Manufacturing methods.
— Rate of production.
— Testing procedures.
— Need for finance.
— Quality requirements.
— Name of present supplier.
— Purchasing procedures.
— Competitive equipment in use or product stocked.
— Decision patterns.
— Budget period.
— Stockholding policy.
— Is the company a trendsetting or following company?
— Need for technical advice.
— Does the customer rely on demand derived from another industry?
— Seasonal demand.
— Has the customer a new, unusual or different application for your products?
— Investment plans.
— In which industry or consumer goods market does the customer operate?
— Product development plans.
— Competitive situation of customer.

This information from a particular company is important if a forecast of whether a large contract will or will not be obtained is required.

Field surveys

Surveys can involve the use of the personal interview, where the individual consumer/user is taken through a formal questionnaire, or the focused interview in which guide questions are asked to get the consumer to speak freely about a specific topic giving facts, opinions, feelings, etc. The success of these techniques depends on having a skilled interviewer, a sound questionnaire or adequate guide question list and a good response from a properly selected representative sample of consumers/users.

Telephone surveys

Another method is the telephone interview which relies upon asking consumers/users to recall some recent action (purchase, visits, viewing, etc) or where the consumer/user is asked about something that is happening or something that he is doing at that time (viewing television, listening to the radio, etc).

Postal surveys

Postal or mail surveys can be used to gather data, either based upon a mailing list where a questionnaire is sent to consumers/users, or upon 'mail in' questionnaires in newspapers and magazines, or upon replies to questionnaires included in the packaging of products. These postal methods often require the use of incentives to motivate consumers/users to provide the information.

Panel or audit methods

There is a series of data-gathering techniques that can be classified as panel or audit methods. Product testing panels are used where the comments of a group of consumers/users are sought in relation to products and product acceptance. They can be used also to gauge the impact of packaging, design, brand names and advertising. The panel can operate as a group meeting at a central point or as individuals being interviewed on a continuous basis. Another type of continuous panel deals with consumer purchasing habits and patterns, and requires panel members to record in diaries details of purchases. Alternatively, pantry or 'dustbin' checks are made to obtain purchasing and usage data from a panel of consumers. Although panels are widely used in consumer goods fields they can also be used to obtain data for industrial marketing. The panel technique can be used directly for sales forecasting purposes. Some companies use a panel of experts or specialists, some from within the company (various executives) but mainly from outside the company (economists, statisticians, key customers and business consultants) to meet, discuss and come to an agreed forecast.

Audit services on a subscription basis have already been mentioned in the section dealing with desk research into published data. Occasionally, the retail audit method is used by single manufacturers on an ad hoc basis.

The laboratory shop is a further audit device where a shop or series of shops operating in normal market conditions and owned by a manufacturing company or agency is used to examine the purchasing patterns and movements of all manufacturers' products together with their point of sale material, price and discount offers, etc. Audit methods are particularly useful in obtaining 'over-the-counter' sales data where distribution lines are long and ex-factory deliveries to wholesalers do not reflect immediately the changes in consumer purchasing patterns.

Although panel and audit techniques could be described as 'pure' marketing research the data obtained from them can have a direct bearing upon future sales and therefore should be used by the forecaster if the results are available or warrant the cost.

Observational methods

There are also observational methods of gathering information. These include observing additional information during a personal interview, observation by consent (stock audits and pantry checks are examples), observation of behavior where the people concerned are not aware that they are being observed (eg observing the effectiveness of point-of-purchase promotional advertising material), observational counts of customers (purchasers of a product group or brand, passers-by, etc), and participant observation such as cookery, gardening, operating a machine, driving, or any other such activity.

Motivation research

In the appropriate market situation, consumer research as described above can be of direct use to the market and sales forecaster by indicating who buys what, where, how, when and how often, but it may be less successful in discovering why consumers behave in the way they do and what motivates them. This has in recent years given rise to the use of indirect methods that probe beneath the surface of consumer or user behavior to analyze those factors that influence the choice and attitude of the consumer. This is known as motivation research. Social psychologists and others have helped market researchers to evolve such techniques as group discussion interviews, depth interviews (in which persons interviewed are encouraged to 'talk themselves out' on a particular topic), perception tests, shopping list tests, picture or situation completion tests, word association tests, sentence completion tests, etc. All these techniques are designed to provide data and results that are expressed in qualitative terms as opposed to the quantitative results of conventional marketing and forecasting research.

Experimental marketing

Another method of gathering forecasting information externally is through marketing experiments. Test towns and/or test areas or industries are examples of obtaining information by controlled experiments. For example, a test town may be used to discover consumers' acceptance of product features (flavor, color, design, performance, packaging, etc) and to measure the level of repeat purchases. A test area (perhaps a television region) may be used to study sales under realistic marketing conditions using the same weight of advertising and sales promotion per capita that the company intends to use during a national launch. The experiment becomes 'controlled' when two test towns or areas are used; one with certain features of the marketing proposition included and one without. Perhaps one is provided with special packaging, or special point of purchase display material, or special advertising, and the other is not. A comparison of the sales results of the two areas is then made and the effects on sales are assessed.

But test marketing forewarns competitors, and therefore in industries where security and surprise impact upon a market is important the pilot launch technique may be used. With this method the company may research a market segment regarding particular consumer needs and develop a product in its laboratories to meet these needs. They then introduce the product using the data obtained from this stage of the product life cycle to make adjustments to the product, the overall sales proposition and the marketing mix as they proceed; this would include adjustments to the original forecast and possibly to forecasting methods.

Experimentation also includes split run advertisements in newspapers or magazines where different advertisements are run in national or regional media to gauge the effect of particular advertisements on sales in different areas.

The effect on sales of changes in factors relating to the sales force is another area for experiments. The comparison is made of results in one area using salesmen plus a display team and in another using merchandisers; or in one area using the normal sales force and another using a special task force to obtain distribution coverage. Experiments using variations of call frequency and journey cycles, differing time allocation to various classes of customer, etc can also be used to study potential sales volume changes.

Use of field research in forecasting

Whether the sales forecaster will use any or all of these techniques of original external field research will depend upon how important the forecast is to the company, whether this type of research is to be carried out for other purposes and the results will be available anyway, and whether or not adequate information is available from desk research into internal records or published data. It will also depend upon the cost of obtaining the data through original field research in relation to the money available or the profit contribution such research findings will make. Lastly, it will depend upon the time available, the degree of accuracy required, and the type, size, and geographical spread of the markets to be surveyed.

CHAPTER 5
Basic Forecasting Considerations

'It is a capital mistake to theorize before one has data'
                                        Arthur Conan Doyle

Assessment terms

It has already been acknowledged that forecasting is affected by the various environments in which a company operates. Broadly, these are the international economy, the national economy, and the individual market. Forecasts can therefore relate to these various market environments in addition to the particular company's sales forecast.

More specifically, there are quantifying terms that should be clearly defined before a forecast is made or compared, eg is the forecast relating to the market potential or to the actual market volume? The range of quantifying terms include the following:

1. *The overall market capacity* — this is the amount of product and/or service that could be absorbed in an overall market *irrespective of price* or market segmentation considerations. For example, the future potential overall market for cars of all types would include consumers who would like to own a car but are not able or willing to pay the existing price as well as those who are.
2. *Market segment capacity* is the amount of a product and/or service that could be absorbed in the future by a specialized segment of a market *irrespective of price* considerations.
3. *Market potential* — this quantifies the effective demand for a product and/or service *at a given price* within a specific market segment.
4. *The actual market volume* is the sum total of suppliers' sales made *at a given price* or price range to a specific market segment.
5. *The market prospective* is the quantity a company could sell in a particular market segment irrespective of company resources, eg a company could have a marketing opportunity to sell 500

111

units but has current production or financial resources to produce 350 units. It was indicated earlier that this situation requires management to consider alternatives (sub-contracting, acquisition, etc) to maximize the company's market opportunities.
6. *Actual company market share or sales* — a company's sales in a particular market segment are obviously an integral part of the actual market volume, of which they are often expressed as a percentage.

The relationship between the various assessment terms can be seen in Figure 14.

Units of measurement

To get a really comprehensive prediction of the future, forecasts should be based on three types of data with an appreciation that a fourth type of data can affect market and sales forecast.

1. *Current price sales volume data*, ie sales volume valued by the prices *currently* prevailing during each time period. The main disadvantage of this approach is that rising/inflationary current prices can give a misleading picture of sales. See Table 1.
2. *Constant or base year price sales volume data*, ie sales volume values that have been adjusted by relating them to the prices

Year	Personal consumption expenditures at current prices ($ billion)	Personal consumption expenditures at 1972 price ($ billion)
1970	618.8	668.9
1971	668.2	691.9
1972	733.0	733.0
1973	809.9	767.7
1974	889.6	760.7
1975	979.1	774.6
1976	1089.9	820.6
1977	1210.0	861.7
1978	1350.8	900.8
1979	1509.8	924.5
1980	1669.2	931.8

Source: *Economic Indicators* published by Joint Economic Committee of Congress

Table 1. *Comparison of personal consumption expenditures at current prices and at base year (1972) prices in USA*

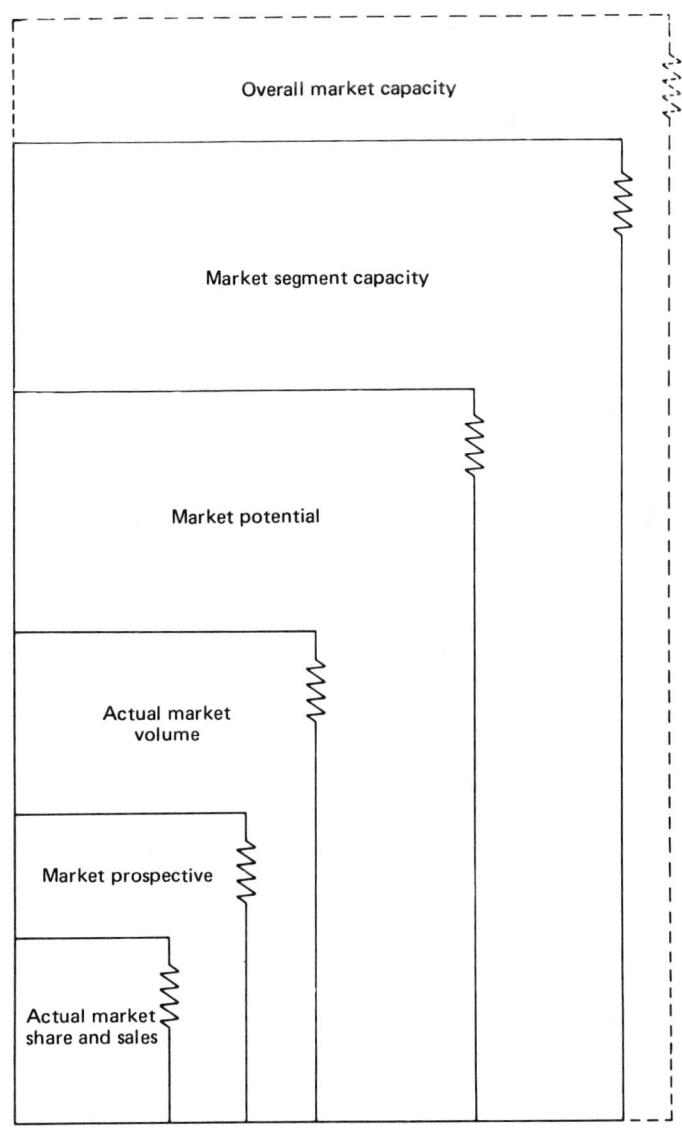

Figure 14. *A diagram showing the relationship between various assessment terms*

prevailing during a *particular* sales period. The particular period chosen is known as the base period and all the sales volume figures of other sales periods in the series being considered are calculated at base year prices/values. The main advantage of this method is that it removes much of the inflationary influence on the forecast of increasing (or decreasing) prices over a span of time and gives a 'real' or 'true' picture of the market measured in terms of value (money). See Table 1 which has been constructed from 'economic' data, although it is possible to obtain this type of information regarding particular industries and/or markets.

The two series represent the same data presented in two different ways; the only common item in both series being 1972. Although projected predictions are often needed for sales volume, sales targets, cash flow forecasts, etc, the adjusted base year figures (and their projection) are likely to give a more realistic 'real' or 'true' projection in money (value) terms.

3. *Commodity units*, ie sales measured by the number of units sold: tons, yards, gallons or any particular unit. This method removes any problems of rising or falling prices, inflation, etc, but can only be used for total company/market forecasts where the measured units are fairly uniform throughout, or where companies sell only a few product types. The actual unit sales can be compared with sales at current prices to determine

Year	Personal consumption expenditure of alcoholic beverages in $ billion	Per capita consumption of alcoholic beverages			
		Beer in gallons	Distilled spirits in wine gallons	Still wines in wine gallons	Effervescent wines in wine gallons
1960	10.6	24.0	1.87	1.36	0.04
1965	13.1	25.5	2.13	1.44	0.06
1970	17.7	28.6	2.61	1.70	0.15
1973	21.3	29.7	2.81	2.31	0.15
1974	23.0	31.0	2.89	2.26	0.14
1975	24.9	32.8	2.49	2.20	0.13
1976	26.7	31.2	2.11	2.40	0.14
1977	28.2	32.3	2.67	2.45	0.16
1978	29.3	32.9	2.88	2.59	0.17

Table 2. *Personal consumption expenditures of alcoholic beverages in billions of dollars compared with per capita consumption of alcoholic beverages in gallons by sub-product group in the USA*

whether or not the market is price sensitive; both can be used to forecast the future. Table 2 is an example of current price/unit comparison.

A number of interesting relationships for the forecaster can be derived from Table 2; for example, when the personal consumption expenditure of all alcoholic beverages increased in $ terms by 4%, the unit consumption for beer increased by only 1.8%, but distilled spirits increased by 7.8%, still wines by 5.7% and effervescent wines by 6.25%; at the time beer was price sensitive and any future expected price increase should influence the forecast. The other three areas do not appear to be price sensitive and again this must be considered in the next forecast.

4. The fourth type of data that can influence market and sales forecasts may be considered where appropriate: it is that of local, state or federal sales taxes. As changes in this factor will result from arbitrary decisions based on government policy to gather more revenue and/or to reduce or encourage demand, it will be more difficult to forecast.

It will be necessary to exclude any element of taxation from (1) and (2) above to determine trends, but it should be included when considering overall demand for a product/service because changes in indirect taxation will affect price, and as a general economic rule, the higher the price the less will be demanded (and vice versa) if the product/service is price sensitive.

A historic comparison of the three (or four) groups of data will highlight various sensitive relationships, eg what happened to demand and the other variables when one variable changed at a different speed from the others. Such analysis will produce useful facts that will influence future forecasts.

A further technique is to plot the percentage increase/decrease values between the years and endeavor to project such data into the future, thereby predicting the next period percentage increase/decrease value.

The type of analysis using expenditure at current prices, at constant prices, indirect taxation and unit volume data may highlight a much more serious situation. It could be possible for a company experiencing increasing sales revenue to discover that this has come about possibly from an increased price per unit (or even taxation), whereas unit sales volume could be steadily declining.

Chapters 6, 7, 8 and 9 examine a range of basic methods of market and sales forecasting: so, for simplicity, only forecasting methods using one of the above types have been used. But with each example given, it should be remembered that all three types of data (and, if appropriate, the fourth concerning taxation) should be considered and projected for effective market and sales forecasting. Further, it will be useful to calculate a forecast based upon the above-mentioned methods for each different type of market segment to get a true picture of the sales in different geographic or socio-economic groups. This means, where appropriate, separating the home market sales from the export, the teenage market from the 'more mature', urban dwellers from rural dwellers, etc.

Demand analysis, elasticity and price

Demand analysis discovers and measures the factors at work in the market place that affect sales. It is therefore a fundamental factor in forecasting. But effective demand (which is another way of considering sales) has certain implications when viewed from the point of marketing. Not only does effective demand mean that the potential customer has the money to pay for the product, but also that he has the power to make buying decisions and that he is a person who can receive satisfaction from the total sales proposition. Even in industrial marketing where the buying decision may rest with a group of people (the decision-making unit), a company can be said to receive satisfaction from the product or service.

The relationship of the amount demanded to the price of a product or service is a prime consideration of the forecaster because it is upon potential sales as well as on costs that prices are set.

In fact in economics the term elasticity is used to describe this relationship, and has been defined as the responsiveness of demand (sales) to relatively small changes in price. For example in Figure 15a, demand for the product is said to be relatively inelastic, a slight change in price making little difference to sales. Where this market situation prevails, a price increase (from B to A) will cause only a slight decline in sales (from Y to X). Conversely, it is not a good market situation for using price reductions as a sales promotion tool, because a price reduction must be considerable to increase sales slightly.

In Figure 15b, demand for the product is said to be relatively elastic, a slight change in price making a disproportionately larger difference to sales. Where this market situation exists a price increase (from D to C) will cause a considerable decline in sales (from Q to P). Conversely, it is a good market situation for using price reductions as a sales promotional tool, since a slight decrease in price (from C to D) will cause a disproportionately large increase in sales. Knowledge of the effect that price changes will have on sales is vital to the forecaster.

The slope of any demand curve (ie its elasticity) will change over a whole range of prices and in practice it is difficult to set up demand schedules over a very large range of prices. However, the elasticity of

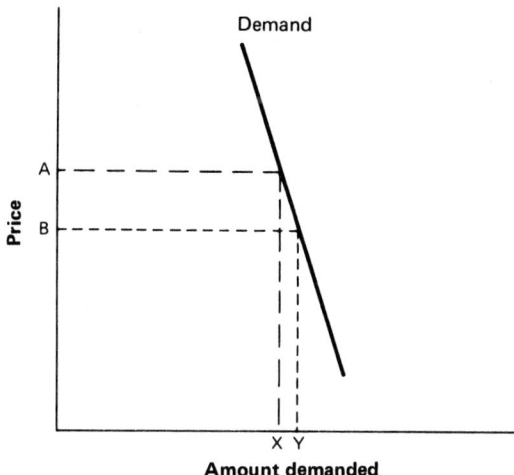

Figure 15a. *A relatively inelastic demand curve — a price increase from B to A causes only a small decline in sales (from Y to Z)*

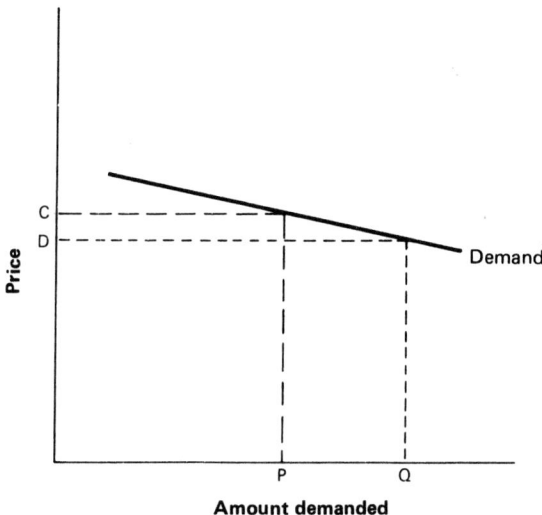

Figure 15b. *A relatively elastic demand curve — a price increase from D to C causes a considerable decline in sales (from Q to P)*

Market and Sales Forecasting

demand can be determined by two arithmetical methods:

1. Percentage change method where

$$\text{Elasticity of demand} = \frac{\text{Proportionate change in amount demanded}}{\text{Proportionate change in price}}$$

For example, if on a demand schedule (or from marketing research) the following two items occurred:

@ $9 per unit   4,000 units were sold
@ $8 per unit   5,000 units were sold

then using the above formula, elasticity could be expressed as:

$$\frac{\frac{1000}{4000}}{\frac{1}{9}} = \frac{\frac{1}{4}}{\frac{1}{9}} = \frac{1}{4} \times \frac{9}{1} = 2\frac{1}{4}$$

Where the result is more than 1, demand is relatively elastic; a fall of 1/9th in price causes an increase in sales of 1/4. Alternatively, if the two items from a demand schedule were:

@ $9 per unit   300 units were sold
@ $6 per unit   330 units were sold

then using the above formula, elasticity could be expressed as:

$$\frac{\frac{30}{300}}{\frac{3}{9}} = \frac{\frac{1}{10}}{\frac{1}{3}} = \frac{1}{10} \times \frac{3}{1} = \frac{3}{10}$$

Demand is relatively inelastic as the result is less than 1. A price reduction of 1/3rd causes only a 1/10th increase in sales.

2. The outlay method of determining elasticity: this involves the examination of the outlay that customers are willing to make for a product, ie price × volume. For example:

@ $9 per unit   300 units are sold = $2,700 consumer outlay
@ $6 per unit   330 units are sold = $1,980 consumer outlay

By reducing price, the outlay (sales revenue) is less, even though the number of units sold has increased. This indicates that demand is relatively inelastic.

When considering the effect of a price change on sales revenue it is necessary to recognize that because of market circumstances it is possible for the demand curve to slope the opposite way for part of its length, ie an exceptional or backward bending demand curve. This implies that at the current stage of the market, as price increases so will sales.

Between points A and B in Figure 16 sales increase as prices go up. This can happen in situations of shortage, or where further price increases are anticipated, or where consumers associate a range of prices with an expected quality or image. In the last case, if prices are increased, the product becomes associated with a different 'quality group', and if the demand is greater than in the former group, sales will tend to increase. Sales of many luxury and semi-luxury consumer products react in this way.

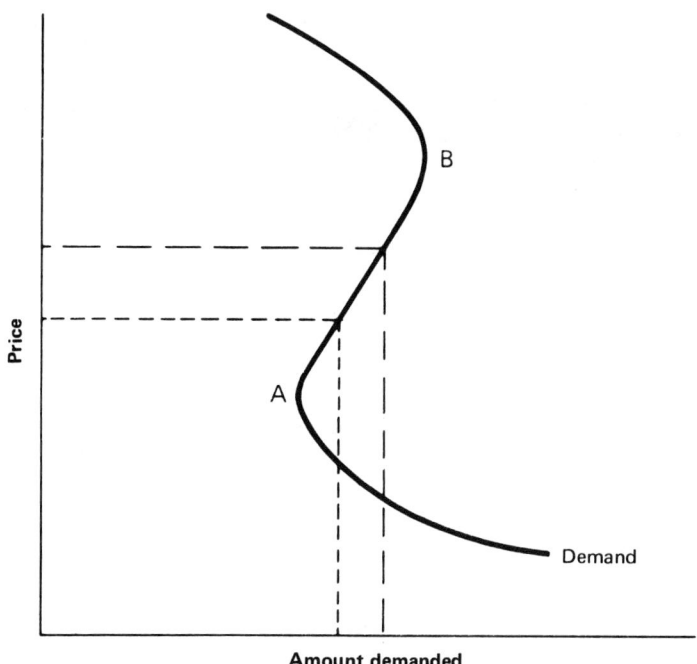

Figure 16. *An exceptional demand curve*

Pricing studies and income

Many products are either over-priced or under-priced, and in either case this has a direct effect on sales and therefore on sales forecasting. In fact, incorrect pricing has caused the failure of many new products. The under-priced product is not only losing sales revenue and profit, but it could also be losing sales because the price does not project the image expected by consumers. Alternatively, the over-priced product, by restricting demand, is not only causing a loss of sales and perhaps a loss of sales revenue, but also a loss of profit by preventing fixed overhead costs from being spread over a greater sales volume.

The market-orientated approach to pricing is to charge what the market will bear in relation to the type and size of market, customers' needs and priorities, and the scale of the marketing company's operation. Price confrontation studies can be used in marketing research to help determine an effective pricing policy. A sample of potential buyers is confronted with a product and their reactions to a series of prices at which products of this nature could be sold are assessed. The reasons for willingness or unwillingness to buy at certain prices are analyzed and an optimum price, related to potential sales revenue and profit, is established.

Pricing policy and consumer/user reaction to price has a direct effect on sales and therefore is a prime consideration in sales forecasting.

But price is not the only factor that will affect demand. The consumer's demand for a product will be positively related to his income. If his income increases, he will tend to buy more of a number of products, although there are exceptions to this. Income elasticity can be seen by relating the proportionate change in income to the proportionate change in the amount demanded.

Information regarding demand can be obtained through published data and from marketing research. Information concerning prices can be obtained from official statistics and observation in the market; and details of consumer incomes analyzed by various groups can be gathered from official statistics and observation.

The market forecaster can relate present or projected price and income data to market demand, and can carry out statistical analysis of the effects of changes in price and consumer income on market demand. For example, it may be found that a 2% increase in price caused a 1% fall in demand and a 2% increase in income resulted in a ½% increase in demand.

The multi-technique approach

Although a number of forecasting techniques are mentioned in Chapters 6, 7, 8 and 9, it is not suggested that any one technique should be used in isolation. Within the company constraints of acceptable costs, the limits of time, and the company's needs in the market, as many forecasting techniques as possible should be used. Each forecast obtained will be different but investigation of the variances between them will bring to the surface factors contained in one and not in another, that are increasing or declining in forecasting importance. In fact, analysis of such variances, horizontally across the board, will often bring to light new trends or the up-turn or down-turn in market or sales values.

In some cases it is possible to establish a vertical check by one forecast on a group of others. For example, the sum total of all salesmen's forecasts can be compared with area managers' forecasts. Why do they differ? Can one of the parties identify a factor that will influence the forecast, which has not been appreciated by the other party? A further stage is possible by comparing the sum total of all area managers' forecasts with regional or national sales managers' forecasts.

Finally a total forecast is obtained by assessing all the component forecasts; it is useful to have a forecasting committee, a panel of experts, or jury of executive opinion to do this. Complete agreement may not always be possible but this approach ensures that every aspect is critically examined.

The forecast may be a total forecast figure or be broken down into product, size, model, etc. Also it may take the form of a single figure or of maximum and minimum values, together with a percentage probability of achieving them.

At the final level of assessment of the component forecasts, techniques need not be highly sophisticated, for if the best possible methods and data have been used to obtain the component forecasts, the final assessment is often a matter of enlightened averaging out.

CHAPTER 6

The Measurement of Change

'Economic forecasting, like weather forecasting in England, is only valid for the next six hours or so, beyond that it is sheer guesswork'
M J Moroney

The measurement of change

It is necessary to measure the changes in certain general factors outside a company's control which could affect the marketing environment in which it operates. In fact, these external factors were mentioned in Chapter 1, the major groupings being shown as the general economic and political environment, technological factors, climatic factors, cultural forces, population factors, standard of living factors, ethical and social forces, and appropriate international considerations.

The use of indicators

When statistics regarding one or part of these areas signal broad movements in them, they are indicators in the forecasting sense. Before using indicators the forecaster must consider what precisely the indicator measures, what type of base period it uses, how it was constructed, what unit of measure it uses, how valid it is, and whether it could contain an element of bias. He must also consider whether it shows a provisional or final figure, whether it is seasonally adjusted, and the degree of relevance to the forecasting problem.

Economic change

Economic indicators measuring economic change are very good examples of this method of forecasting and to explain their use will show the application of indicators generally.

To qualify as an economic indicator, the data concerned should provide a yardstick against which periodic movements in the cost or volume of the economic factor concerned can be measured.

A good starting point for making a market forecast for various product groups is to use an indicator relating to the total economy, eg the gross national product. If this is linked with the percentage attributable to total consumer expenditure and the percentage of consumer expenditure attributable to the particular product and service, a very precise picture of the market is obtained. Forecasts of such economic indicators are often made by government and private agencies.

Economic indicators refer to a wide range of economic and financial information showing changes and movement in various fields. For example, there are indicators of industrial production, employment and unemployment, machine tool orders, retail sales, wages rates, raw material prices, and many more. Such indicators can be presented either in absolute figures or values (eg the value of exports shown in dollars), or presented as an index number where increases or decreases are shown as a percentage of the base year figure of 100. Whether actual values or index values are used, data can be further presented either on a period basis (eg the level of industrial production over the last three months), or on a basis of a particular moment in time (eg the total hire-purchase debt as at 31st December 19X3).

Examples from *Economic Indicators* published by the Joint Economic Committee of Congress and the Council of Economic Advisers, which indicate recent economic business history, permit comparison with industry or company sales and possibly allow a degree of projection, are shown in Figure 17.

Since most economic indicators are, by their nature, general, they often have to be interpreted and evaluated to determine how changes in them will affect a particular company, industry, or market. Further, some indicators will be more appropriate for certain markets than others, and in most cases a combination of such indicators will be necessary to provide data to set up an effective composite indicator forecast for a particular company.

Various facets of the economy and the economic climate can be examined through economic indicators and often trends in them can be anticipated, permitting more realistic industry or market forecasts to be made.

Distribution system change

A channel of distribution can be described as a vertical sequence of levels of trading activities that bridge the overall gap between the manufacturer and the consumer. Thus the wholesaler is one level and the retailer another.

The choice of the channels of distribution is the prerogative of the individual company, but the channels available or acceptable will develop as part of the economic structure of a country. The freedom of choice by the individual company may not be as real as it appears,

PRICES

Producer Prices

In September the producer price index for all finished goods fell 0.2 percent, seasonally adjusted. Prices of finished consumer foods fell 0.2 percent and prices of other finished consumer goods fell 0.1 percent. Prices of capital equipment declined 0.1 percent.

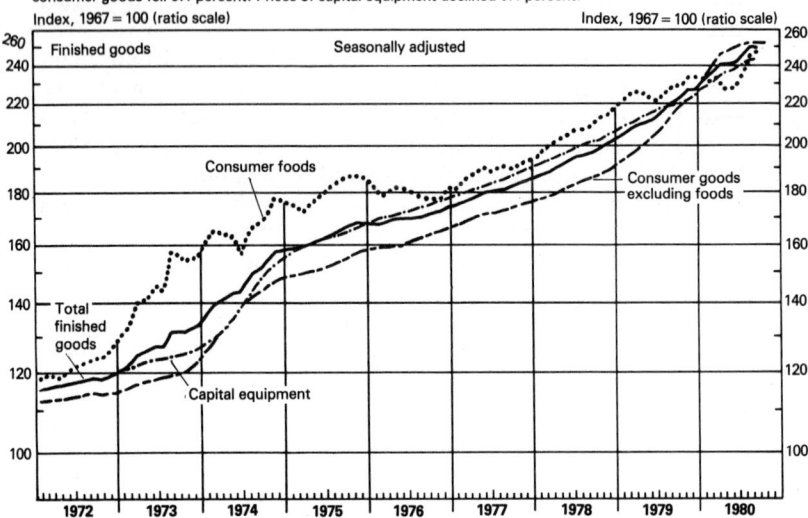

Source: Department of Labor

Consumer Prices

In September the consumer price index for all urban consumers rose 1.0 percent seasonally adjusted (0.9 percent unadjusted). Food prices rose 1.6 percent (0.9 percent unadjusted) and nonfood commodity prices were up 1.1 percent (also 1.1 percent unadjusted). Services prices were up 0.7 percent (0.8 percent unadjusted).

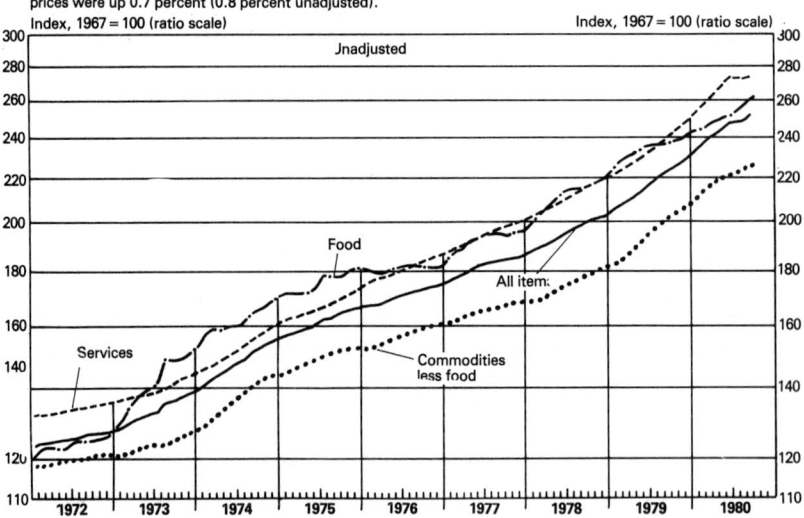

Source: Department of Labor

124

TOTAL OUTPUT, INCOME, AND SPENDING

Gross National Product

According to preliminary estimates for the third quarter, gross national product rose $61.7 billion or 10.2 percent both at annual rates. Real output (GNP adjusted for price changes) rose 1.0 percent from the second quarter level and the implicit price deflator rose at a 9.1 percent annual rate.

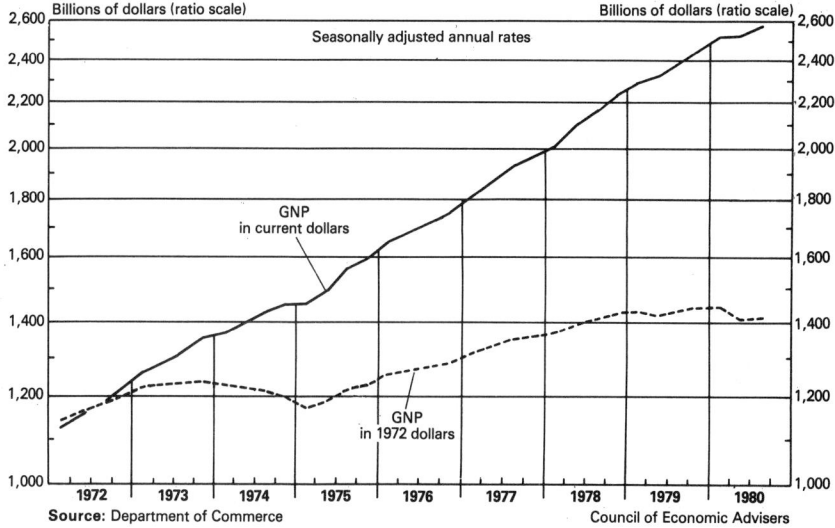

Source: Department of Commerce

Council of Economic Advisers

PRODUCTION AND BUSINESS ACTIVITY

Industrial Production and Capacity Utilization

Industrial production rose 1 percent in September, following a ½ percent rise in August. From January to July output had fallen nearly 8½ percent.

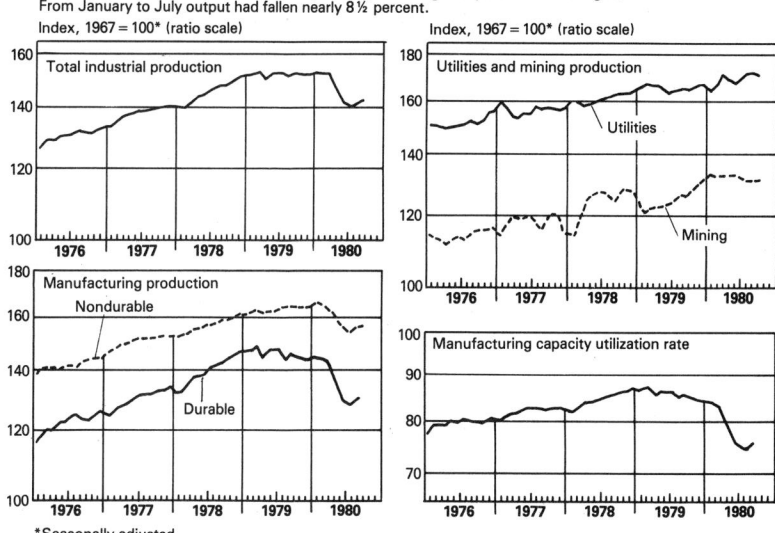

*Seasonally adjusted
Source: Board of Governors of the Federal Reserve System

Council of Economic Advisers

EMPLOYMENT, UNEMPLOYMENT, AND WAGES

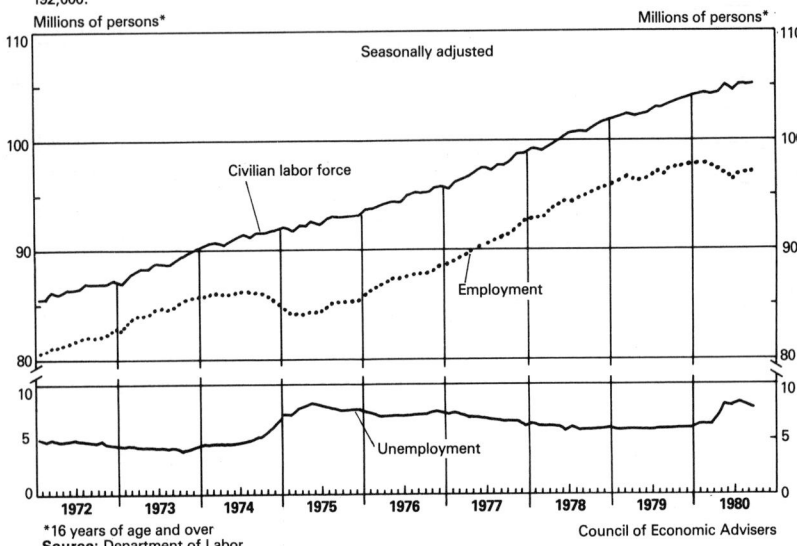

Status of the Labor Force
Seasonally adjusted employment rose 201,000 in September while unemployment fell 192,000.

*16 years of age and over
Source: Department of Labor

Council of Economic Advisers

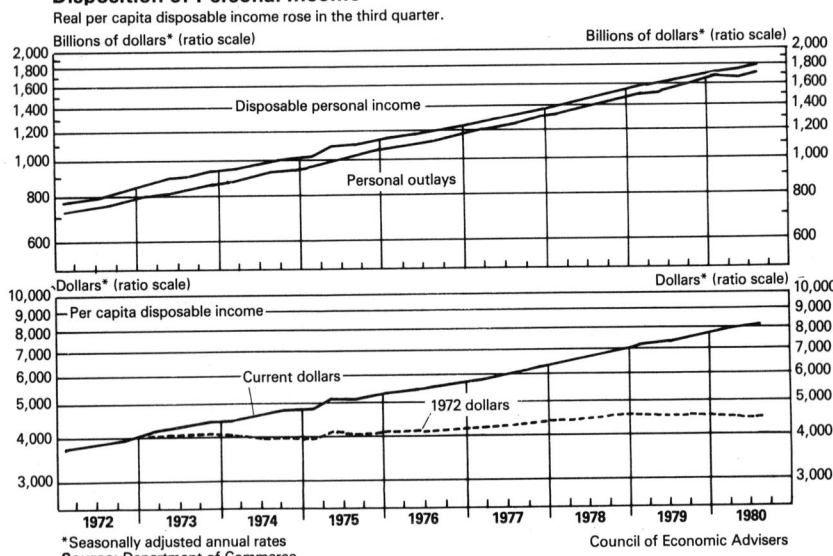

Disposition of Personal Income
Real per capita disposable income rose in the third quarter.

*Seasonally adjusted annual rates
Source: Department of Commerce

Council of Economic Advisers

The Measurement of Change

Expenditures for New Plant and Equipment

Business plans to increase capital spending 8.7 percent in 1980, according to the Commerce Department survey conducted in late July and August. The planned increase in spending is 1.2 percentage points lower than the 9.9 percent reported in June and 2.4 percentage points lower than the 11.1 percent reported in March.

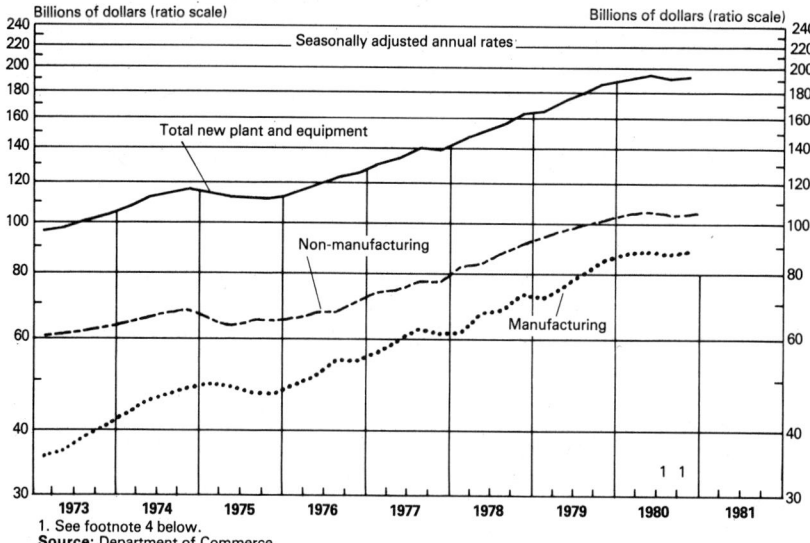

1. See footnote 4 below.
Source: Department of Commerce

Business Sales and Inventories — Total and Trade

Business sales rose 1 percent in August while inventories rose $1¾ billion. According to the advance survey, retail sales rose 1½ percent in September following increases of ½ percent in August and 3 percent in July.

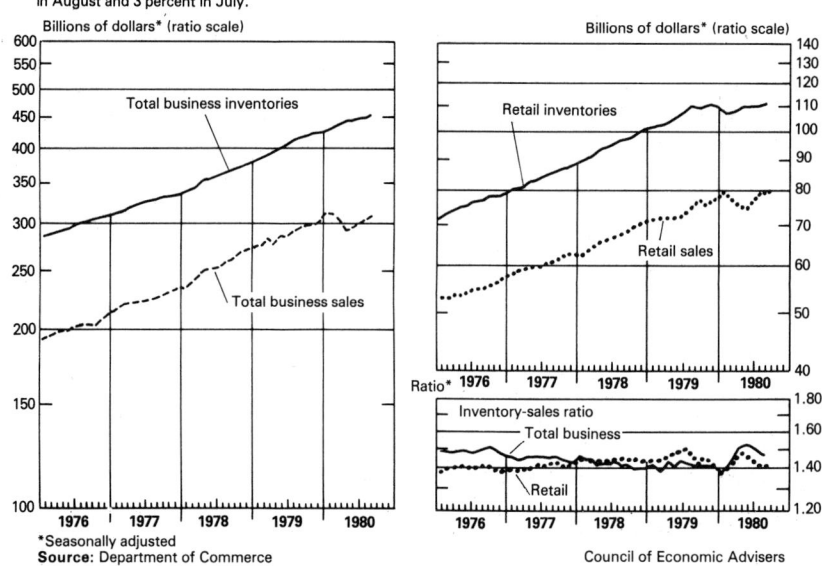

*Seasonally adjusted
Source: Department of Commerce   Council of Economic Advisers

Figure 17. *Examples of economic indicators*

for in the last analysis, the economics of operation, the service offered by competitors and the level of service customers are willing to accept will all be key factors when deciding the choice of channels.

Channels of distribution cannot be considered in isolation; they are interrelated with, and sometimes substituted for, other aspects of physical distribution: for example, if economical, local company warehouses may be substituted for wholesalers, or the appointment of a retail agent (exclusive dealership) may eliminate the need for wholesalers. Alternatively, powerful voluntary chain or group wholesalers, through whom a large number of small retailers can be reached effectively, may be substituted for a company local warehouse.

Changes in distribution systems can occur either through a conscious change of policy within the existing channels structure, or through the emergence of new channels. In actual fact these two alternatives represent the effect of the same factor, ie the dynamic nature of channels systems: they are constantly, though gradually, changing. This change can relate either to the nature of the particular channel level, ie the changing role of the wholesaler, or a change in the relationship of levels, ie the new relationship between retailer and wholesaler through the emergence of voluntary chains and groups.

In consumer goods markets the choice of alternatives of combinations of the various levels and types of channels of distribution available can be seen in Figure 18. In forecasting, the trends in the volume of business done through the various combinations of channels cannot be ignored. The decline of the share of business done by independent retailers reflects the trend towards 'giantism' in retailing in recent years and the reduction in the number of small retailers.

Often trends in distribution channel emphasis are caused by basic considerations such as lower cost or more efficient operation through one channel compared with another. But often factors emerge that have varying effects upon channel decisions; the development of supermarkets, hypermarkets, self-service and self-selection, the concept of one-stop shopping, the abolition of resale price maintenance, and the appearance of voluntary chains and groups, cash and carry warehouses, discount stores and private labelling, would all have an effect on a channel decision.

In some industries highly specialized channels develop, eg in pharmaceuticals some companies own their own outlets (Boots The Chemist) while others use specialist wholesalers. But most ethical drugs must be retailed by a qualified pharmacist. In industrial markets manufacturers mainly distribute direct to the customer, but in some cases specialist wholesalers are used.

The forecaster must consider what effect a change in distribution channel would have on company sales; or perhaps the medium-term effect of the increasing importance of one distribution channel com-

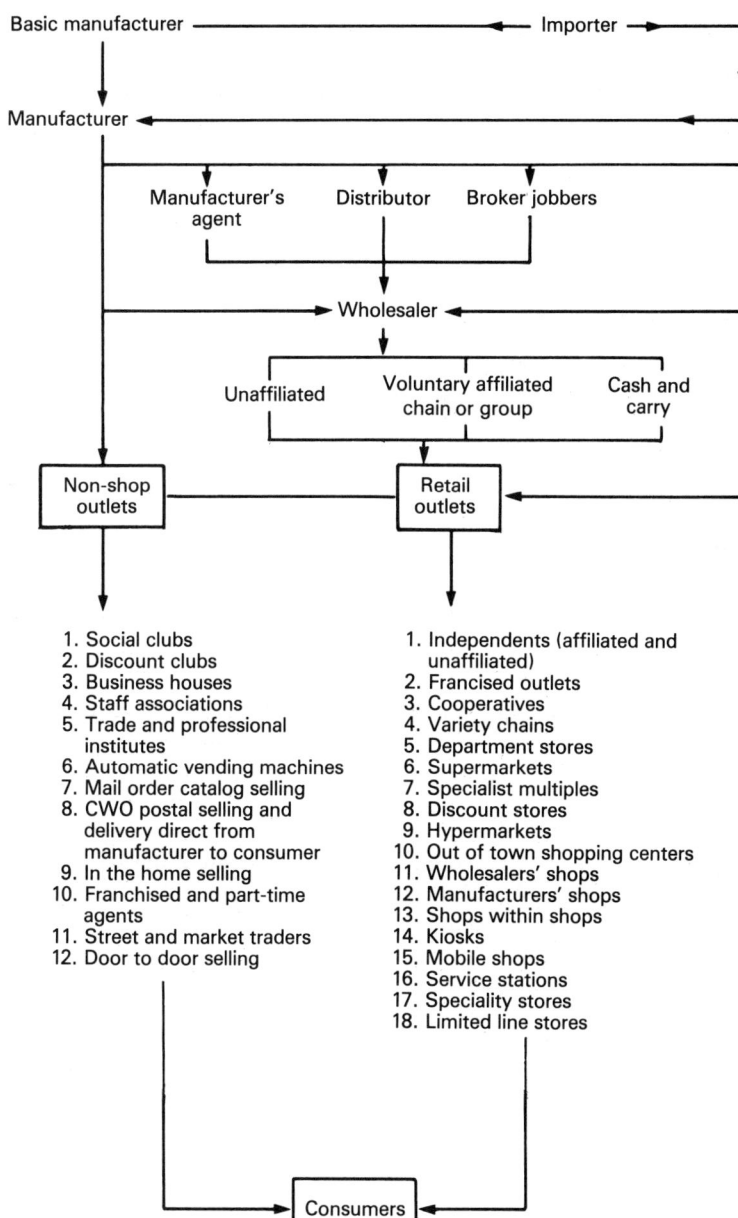

Figure 18. *The various levels and types of channels of distribution possible in consumer goods markets*

pared with other current channels.

Sociological and consumer behavior change

There are two basic approaches to the examination of consumer behavior. One of them deals with the understanding of the behavior of a variety of consumer groups, and the other concentrates on understanding the behavior of the individual consumer. Group and individual behavior will have a direct effect on sales and therefore on the sales forecast. It follows that the market and sales forecaster must be able to identify, measure and allow for sociological and consumer behavior changes.

There are certain well-recognized sociological and psychological groups that are changing at different speeds. The nature of the groups and the speed of change will have varying impacts on different industries and markets. The broad groups are as follows:

1. Population.
2. Cultures and sub-cultures.
3. Social and socio-economic classes.
4. Reference groups, including face-to-face and family groups.
5. The individual.

1. Population

This refers to the degree to which a country or region is populated, usually expressed as the total number of inhabitants. It is a physical state and can be indicated by volume, location, urban or rural, region, sex, age groups, movement, etc. Changes in these and related factors (marriages, births, deaths, etc) affect consumer buying patterns. The main source of population information in the USA is the American Office of Population Censuses and Surveys. More information is given in Chapter 4 under the heading of Government Sources of Statistics.

Demography, the study of population trends, permits comparison of data from period to period, or region to region and identifies patterns that are fundamental, when interpreted, to the forecasting of total markets and company sales.

Markets are people, and effective tracking of population trends and shifts is bound to increase the accuracy of forecasting one dimension of the environment in which a company operates.

2. Cultures and sub-cultures

These refer to particular forms, types, or states of manners, taste and intellectual development at a particular time or place. The whole form is intangible but the effect on consumer behavior is real.

A cultural pattern emerges over a period of time and often through successive generations. It is a way of life developed through common ideals and the solving of common problems. It is often based on religion, race, region, patriotism, politics, or combinations of these.

As the population of a culture increases, the broad common ideals no longer satisfy certain minority groups and sub-cultures emerge. They have different problems and ideals, and place a different emphasis on various cultural factors compared with the majority: for example, a Moslem culture in a basically Christian country, the negro culture in the US, a Communist culture in a capitalist society. Sub-cultures affect consumer behavior by influencing the formation of attitudes and are important indicators of the standards and values of the individuals making up the groups.

A relaxation or change in the 'rules' or basic concept of sub-cultures could be of importance to researchers forecasting human behavior. These changes, and indeed the cultures and sub-cultures, may be difficult to quantify, but even a qualitative assessment is better than no assessment at all.

3. Social and socio-economic classes

Social classes emerge because consumers are brought together through certain common characteristics or states either inherent or acquired. Such social grouping factors include status, occupation, job performance, wealth and ownership, skill, power and identification. Often combinations of these factors fashion particular social groups, eg the linking of status with occupation or wealth.

Indicators of social class change are more equal educational opportunity, greater social mobility, the impact of modern communication and mass media, etc, and they cause some blurring of rigid social divisions and attitudes.

By research it is possible to determine the buying motives and the purchasing and consumption habits of a particular class. The movement upwards in social classes often means that consumers spend more money on what the lower groups consider to be non-essentials. The consumer in the higher class groups will not be motivated by the same basic needs of consumers at subsistence level, but will often be searching for such satisfaction as esteem, convenience, prestige, uniqueness, approval of others, etc. Often the attainment of these satisfactions can be expressed in the purchases of certain types of products such as status cars, large houses, extreme fashions, leisure pursuit products and even in the reading of particular newspapers and magazines.

Leisure pursuit products often indicate a consumer's identification (real or imagined) with a particular social group. As consumers' affluence increases and they have more disposable income, their demand for more sophisticated leisure products increases.

Market and Sales Forecasting

The existence of social classes and the way they express themselves in purchasing and consumption indicates differences in attitudes, values and priorities, and has important implications for the setting of marketing objectives and the forecasting of total markets and company sales.

4. Reference groups

This includes face-to-face and family groups. Consumer buying motives, brand choice, purchasing and consumption patterns are often influenced by what other consumers say or buy, especially those people with whom they compare themselves or whom they use as reference groups. Such groups can be classified as:

(a) *Membership groups.* These are groupings of people to which a person belongs and is recognized as belonging by others. It usually implies identification with the group's ideals, values, tastes, and behavior. Groups such as the family, a club, company, church, college, political party, etc, can all fit into this category.

(b) The opposite to (a) is the *dissociative group* with whom an individual does *not* want to be identified or associated. Reference in this case is to the ideals, values and behavior he finds acceptable. The group types are the same as for (a).

(c) *Aspirational groups.* These refer to groupings of people to which the individual would like or aspires to belong. The individual's buying behavior is influenced by how he thinks the group behaves or purchases. Reference groups of this type are often made up of TV, film or radio stars, sportsmen or women, astronauts, millionaires, or even particular social sets.

(d) *Face-to-face groups.* These are groups of people small enough for the individual to communicate with face-to-face. This type of group has the most direct influence on an individual's ideals, tastes, values, and behavior. This type includes the family, close friends, neighbors, fellow workers or students.

In many cases the greatest influence on the individual in forming and maintaining ideals, attitudes, tastes, values, etc, is the family group. Sometimes the result of the reference is positive, ie the individual does the complete opposite to express himself. The forecaster must be alert to the various behavioral and attitudinal patterns that dominate families in particular market segments and to the current trends and how they are expected to change in the future.

The purchases of certain products are more subject to reference group influence than others. For example, branded beer, cigarettes, clothing, cars, toilet soap, etc, are products that are associated strongly with reference group influence. Customer communication (advertising, etc) in this area will be most successful if it stresses the types of people who buy the product, particularly if it is designed to encourage the learning/educational process of product application or usage and is exhibited in media where those who refer to the group form the main audience.

Where reference group influences are weak, the marketing strategy is to stress product innovations and characteristics, functional advantages and performance, price, etc.

An appreciation of the influence of reference groups on consumer buying behavior is an essential for forecasters in consumer goods markets, or for those carrying out end-use analysis for products being sold into industrial product markets.

5. The individual

A basic approach to the study of consumer buying behavior is at the level of the individual. It has been said that:

> Social influences determine much but not all of the behavioral variations in people. Two individuals subject to the same influences are not likely to have identical attitudes, although their attitudes will probably converge at more points than those of two strangers selected at random. Attitudes are really the product of social forces interacting with the individual's unique temperament and abilities.
>
> Furthermore, attitudes — in buying as in anything else — do not automatically guarantee certain types of behavior. Attitudes are predispositions felt by buyers before they enter the buying process. The buying process itself is a learning experience and can lead to a change in attitudes.[1]

It is necessary to understand why the individual consumer behaves as he does so that changes in ideals, tastes, values, etc, of groups of consumers can be anticipated and predicted.

It was shown in Chapter 1 that individuals do not buy products but groups of satisfactions or benefits to satisfy logical and psychological needs. But the individual will only purchase a product if he can perceive (hence the concept of perception) that it will satisfy his needs. Perception can be aided by physical stimuli including the actual product. But the effect of physical stimuli will be modified and interpreted by the individual's tastes, ideals, temperament, experiences and memory. Often the individual perceives only what he wants to perceive, and therefore the physical stimuli must be ap-

---

[1]. P Kotler *Marketing Management, Analysis, Planning and Control* p 93. Prentice-Hall, NJ, USA.

propriate and appealing to satisfy his logical and psychological needs.

Individual behavior in purchasing and consumption is to a certain extent a learned response and as such can be influenced and changed. For example, the consumption of branded, ready-to-eat breakfast cereals in Britain and North America has been 'learned' over a period of time, in many cases replacing porridge, which needed preparation. Also the type of diet, way of life, etc, acceptable in one society may be repugnant in another, and is a learned response.

There are numerous learning theories that seek to explain consumer buying behavior. They include stimulus response theories that are based on the concept of reward for each correct response; many sales promotional devices are based on this approach.

Other learning theories are based on the concept of cognition. While acknowledging the stimulus response approach, cognitive theories imply that buying behavior is influenced by habit based on memory, achievement, seeking, and insight based on reasoning. Basically, acceptance of the concept of a cognitive decision-making process implies an endeavor by the consumer to reduce risks. By repeat purchasing of a particular brand, or the repeated assessment of available information, the consumer is trying to avoid taking undue risks. Cognitive concepts are founded on habit and consistency, and are fundamental to brand loyalty and repeat purchasing.

Inconsistency in cognitive systems has been described as cognitive dissonance. Thus the person who purchases and consumes fattening foods when he is on a health diet experiences dissonance (ie psychological discomfort) and often tries to reduce the dissonance and achieve consonance by rationalizing his actions.

Some other learning theories are founded on the personality of the individual and on the probability of the repetition of past purchasing behavior. Such theories are based on the premise that if a man's personality can be understood, ie his underlying organization of characteristics and behavior patterns, then it should be possible to understand also why he behaves as he does, and what the reasons are for some of the superficial inconsistencies that occur in his behavior. Based on these assumptions, it should then be possible to predict with greater random success how a given individual is predisposed to respond to given circumstances and suggestions.

A wide range of other factors affect the individual consumer's buying behavior: attitudes, knowledge, faith, opinion, beliefs, economic motivation, rationality, etc. Every sale is a reflection of a decision to buy. This decision will be based on the consumer's perception (influenced by the other factors mentioned above) of the proposal related to value, utility, and ability to satisfy needs. If the initial impression is unfavorable, it will need to undergo a change before a positive buying decision is made. The consumer's perception depends on his attitude to the subject being considered.

All these theories relating to the individual seek to measure and predict the future response and pattern of consumer buying behavior. As such, at least a broad appreciation of them is necessary for effective market and/or company sales forecasting.

This section on sociological and socio-economic factors can be summarized thus:

> The statement 'No man is an island' has empirical support. No man exists who does not reflect interaction with other people. Values, learning patterns, and symbolism are some of the results of the society in which a consumer develops. Sometimes social influences are negative rather than positive influences, but always they are influences. Man evaluates his self against the behavior of others and the values he has learned from others on previous occasions. He depends on others as a source of new information about product decisions and as a reference for evaluating the information.
>
> Organizations seeking to influence consumer behavior should realize that they must communicate not only with an individual but also with a social system.[1]

Industrial change

In industrial marketing one way of measuring change and of discovering the total market potential and the amount of business done by supplying industries with various user industries, is through input/output analysis.

Market forecasting using input/output analysis is based on the concept that in industrial marketing situations the output of one industry is the basic input product/material of another. Input/output tables show the extent to which one segment of industry (defined by a broad Standard Industrial Classification category) obtains its basic materials/products from other segments, and in turn reflects the pattern in which the next stage of industries products are sold to a third set of industries; this has obvious forecasting implications.

Input/Output Structure and Tables of the US Economy are published in the *Survey of Current Business* by the Bureau of Economic Analysis of the US Department of Commerce; they indicate a variety of interrelationships between industrial and/or commodity groups. Amongst many tables providing information for the market forecaster, one provides a classification by commodity group of purchases of domestic products used in current production by each industry group and final buyers. An extract from the tables illustrates the main features in Table 3.

---

1. Engel, Kollat, & Blackwell *Consumer Behavior* p 615. Holt, Rinehart and Winston, New York, USA, 1978.

Survey of Current Business — (Percent distribution)

For the distribution of output of a commodity, read the row for that commodity.

Commodity number / Industry number	1 Livestock and livestock products	2 Other agricultural products	3 Forestry and fishery products	4 Agricultural, forestry, and fishery services	5 Iron and ferroalloy ores mining	6 Nonferrous metal ores mining	7 Coal mining	8 Crude petroleum and natural gas	9 Stone and clay mining and quarrying	10 Chemical and fertilizer mineral mining	11 New construction	12 Maintenance and repair construction	13 Ordnance and accessories
1 Livestock and livestock products	27.8	2.1	—	0.5	—	—	—	—	—	—	—	—	—
2 Other agricultural products	29.5	3.3	—	.2	—	—	—	—	—	—	0.5	—	—
3 Forestry and fishery products	—	—	0.4	.5	—	—	—	—	—	—	*	*	*
4 Agricultural, forestry, and fishery services	29.4	31.0	1.2	2.5	—	—	—	—	—	—	2.4	—	—
5 Iron and ferroalloy ores mining	—	—	—	—	1.9	—	—	—	—	—	—	—	—
6 Nonferrous metal ores mining	—	—	—	—	.1	11.7	—	—	—	—	—	—	—
7 Coal mining	—	—	—	—	.1	*	0.1	—	—	—	—	—	—
8 Crude petroleum and natural gas	—	*	—	—	.2	—	12.1	3.6	—	—	—	—	—
9 Stone and clay mining and quarrying	*	—	*	*	—	—	—	*	2.1	*	35.4	12.9	0.1
10 Chemical and fertilizer mineral mining	—	3.0	—	—	—	—	—	—	—	0.5	—	—	*
11 New construction	—	9.3	—	—	—	—	—	—	—	5.1	—	—	*
12 Maintenance and repair construction	.6	—	—	—	.1	*	.1	2.0	.1	*	—	*	.1
13 Ordnance and accessories	—	.8	*	.2	*	*	*	*	*	*	.1	*	4.2
14 Food and kindred products	4.4	—	—	*	—	—	*	*	*	*	.1	*	*
15 Tobacco manufactures	.*	*	*	*	—	—	.1	—	—	—	*	*	*
16 Broad and narrow fabrics, yarn and thread mills	.2	.1	—	.7	—	—	—	—	—	—	.1	.9	.1
17 Miscellaneous textile goods and floor coverings	—	.9	.9	—	—	—	—	—	—	—	11.6	*	—
18 Apparel	—	—	.4	—	—	—	.2	—	—	—	*	.4	—
19 Miscellaneous fabricated textile products	.2	.3	—	.2	—	—	—	—	—	—	—	3.8	*
20 Lumber and wood products, except containers	—	*	—	—	—	—	—	—	—	—	41.1	—	.1
21 Wood containers	.2	26.4	—	3.6	—	—	—	—	—	—	—	—	7.6

136

Row	1	2	3	4	5	6	7	8	9	10	11	12	13	14
22 Household furniture	—	—	—	—	—	—	—	—	—	—	—	1.2	.1	—
23 Other furniture and fixtures	—	—	—	—	—	—	—	—	—	—	—	7.7	.9	—
24 Paper and allied products, except containers	.4	.1	*	—	—	*	—	—	—	*	*	1.8	.5	*
25 Paperboard containers and boxes	*	—	*	1.5	—	—	—	—	—	—	—	.1	*	.3
26 Printing and publishing	.1	—	—	.1	—	.1	—	—	—	—	.1	—	.1	.1
27 Chemicals and selected chemical products	.4	11.7	.1	.4	—	—	.3	.2	.4	.2	*	1.3	.4	—
28 Plastics and synthetic materials	—	—	*	—	—	—	*	—	.1	—	—	—	—	.1
29 Drugs, cleaning and toilet preparations	.4	—	.2	—	—	—	—	—	.1	—	*	—	—	*
30 Paints and allied products	—	—	—	—	—	—	—	—	—	—	—	15.8	29.8	.1
31 Petroleum refining and related industries	.6	2.9	.2	.2	—	*	.1	.3	.2	.3	*	6.5	3.7	.1
32 Rubber and miscellaneous plastics products	.6	1.0	*	*	—	.1	.2	.2	*	—	—	—	—	—
33 Leather tanning and finishing	—	—	—	—	—	—	—	—	—	—	—	.1	*	*
34 Footwear and other leather products	.3	—	—	.1	—	—	—	—	—	—	—	2.9	1.0	.1
35 Glass and glass products	.1	—	*	*	—	*	*	—	.1	.1	*	60.6	7.6	1.2
36 Stone and clay products	—	.1	—	.1	—	*	.1	.2	.1	.6	*	7.0	.8	1.0
37 Primary iron and steel manufacturing	*	*	—	*	—	*	.1	.2	.3	—	.1	10.8	.5	—
38 Primary nonferrous metals manufacturing	—	—	—	—	—	*	*	.1	—	—	*	—	—	—
39 Metal containers	—	—	.8	—	—	—	—	*	—	—	—	—	—	—
40 Heating, plumbing, and structural metal products	*	*	—	—	—	*	*	.1	.1	*	*	70.0	6.7	—
41 Screw machine products and stampings	.1	—	—	—	*	.1	.6	—	—	*	*	.5	.2	.6
42 Other fabricated metal products	.3	.3	.3	.2	.1	.1	.1	—	.5	.1	*	19.7	2.5	.4
43 Engines and turbines	—	.3	.3	.3	.1	.2	.2	—	.8	.6	*	—	—	.1
44 Farm and garden machinery	—	—	—	—	.3	—	—	—	—	—	—	—	—	—
45 Construction and mining machinery	3.2	5.1	—	—	.1	.6	3.4	1.5	1.4	.2	—	3.6	1.1	—
46 Materials handling machinery and equipment	—	—	—	—	.3	.2	.5	.9	.1	—	—	16.7	8.1	.6
47 Metalworking machinery and equipment	—	—	—	—	.1	*	*	.4	*	—	*	.2	.1	—
48 Special industry machinery and equipment	—	—	.2	*	—	.1	.1	.9	.9	.2	—	5.1	.6	.3
49 General industrial machinery and equipment	*	.1	—	—	—	.2	.1	1.0	1.0	.1	—	.2	.2	.7
50 Miscellaneous machinery, except electrical	.2	.1	—	—	.2	—	—	—	—	—	—	—	—	—
51 Office, computing, and accounting machines	—	—	—	—	—	—	—	—	—	—	—	—	—	—
52 Service industry machines	—	—	—	—	—	—	—	*	—	—	—	*	*	—
53 Electric industrial equipment and apparatus	—	—	*	—	—	*	*	1.2	*	*	*	16.3	8.9	—
54 Household appliances	—	—	—	—	—	—	.2	*	*	—	—	7.9	1.4	.1
55 Electric lighting and wiring equipment	*	*	—	—	*	—	—	.1	—	.1	*	3.5	3.5	*
												32.4	11.6	*

Industry											
56 Radio, TV, and communication equipment	*	*	*	*	—	—	—	*	*	.6	.3	.7
57 Electronic components and accessories	—	—	—	—	—	—	—	—	—	—	—	1.5
58 Misc. electrical machinery and supplies	.3	.7	*	.2	*	—	—	—	—	1.3	.4	*
59 Motor vehicles and equipment	*	*	*	*	*	*	*	*	*	.1	*	*
60 Aircraft and parts	—	—	*	*	—	—	—	—	—	—	—	2.3
61 Other transportation equipment	—	—	.5	*	*	*	—	*	*	*	*	—
62 Scientific and controlling instruments	—	—	.1	*	—	—	.1	*	—	5.9	1.8	.4
63 Optical, ophthalmic, and photographic equipment	*	*	*	*	—	—	*	*	—	.2	*	*
64 Miscellaneous manufacturing	.9	.6	.1	.2	*	—	.1	.1	*	1.5	1.2	.1
65 Transportation and warehousing	.4	.3	*	.1	—	—	*	.2	*	4.3	1.2	.1
66 Communications, except radio and TV	—	*	—	*	*	—	.1	*	*	1.1	.5	—
67 Radio and TV broadcasting	—	—	—	—	—	—	—	—	—	—	—	—
68 Electric, gas, water, and sanitary services	.6	.4	*	.1	.1	.1	.2	.4	.2	.3	.1	.1
69 Wholesale and retail trade	.7	.6	*	.1	*	*	.1	*	*	4.6	1.3	*
70 Finance and insurance	.7	.6	*	.1	*	*	*	.1	*	1.0	.4	*
71 Real estate and rental	.6	2.1	*	.1	.1	*	.1	1.6	.1	.4	.2	*
72 Hotels: personal and repair services exc. auto	*	*	*	.1	*	*	.1	.1	*	*	*	.1
73 Business services	.2	.6	.1	.3	.1	.1	.2	.4	*	8.7	.7	.3
74 Eating and drinking places	*	*	*	.1	*	*	*	.2	*	1.1	.5	.3
75 Automobile repair and services	.5	.4	.1	.3	*	*	*	.1	*	1.8	.7	.1
76 Amusements	*	*	*	*	*	*	*	*	*	.1	*	*
77 Medical, educ. services and nonprofit org	.3	*	*	*	*	*	*	*	*	.1	*	*
78 Federal Government enterprises	.1	*	*	.1	*	*	.1	.1	*	.4	.2	.2
79 State and local government enterprises	—	—	—	*	*	*	.1	.3	*	.2	.1	*
80 Noncomparable imports	*	*	*	*	*	*	*	*	*	.3	.1	*
81 Scrap, used, and secondhand goods	—	—	.2	*	.7	2.8	1.9	.1	.3	1.3	.5	.6
82 Government industry	—	—	—	—	—	—	—	—	—	—	—	—
83 Rest of the world industry	—	—	—	—	—	—	—	—	—	—	—	—
84 Household industry	—	—	—	—	—	—	—	—	—	—	—	—
85 Inventory valuation adjustment	—	—	—	—	—	—	—	—	—	—	—	—
VA Value added	.8	1.7	.1	.1	.1	.1	.3	1.0	.1	4.6	1.8	.3

Table 3. *An extract from Input/Output Tables of the US Economy*

In Table 3 the columns represent commodity group purchases of domestic production from the commodity group shown at the beginning of each row, eg the commodity producers of (No 31) petroleum refining and related industries sold 0.6% of its production to companies producing livestock and livestock products, 2.9% of its production to 'other agricultural products', 0.2% to 'forestry and fishery products' and so on across the whole of the 80 commodity/industry items. Providing the total industry production value is known, it would be possible for segmentation analysis of industry sales to be carried out.

When the data in Table 3 is linked with another table which 'provides an analysis of purchases of imports similarly classified by industry and final demand destination', it provides the forecaster with 'a complete analysis of the total purchases by each industry of goods and services used in current production and by each form of final demand, cross-classified by commodity group'. By analysis, products and services (and therefore markets for them) can be traced and qualified from original producer to ultimate end-user.

Input/output tables therefore permit the forecaster to make more accurate forecasts of a market or segments of it, by making comparisons with existing market forecasts obtained from other sources. Investigation of differences between two market forecasts often reveals unexploited marketing opportunities and new potential segments not previously apparent.

Input/output tables establish a user industry pattern that can be used on total industry data. Comparison between the data in several publications of official input/output tables would also indicate emergent trends. The effects of changes in one industry can be traced backwards through any chain of inter-industry relationships and forecasts made of variations in demand that will result.

International change

The indicators (and methods of using them) shown in the previous sections will apply also in this section; in essence the international environment is the sum total of all economies, cultures and social classes in the world.

Obviously some of these indicators are more relevant to forecasters in particular companies than others. Just as there are market segments in the home country which a company would not contemplate entering, so there are total markets or market segments abroad in which a company would not be interested, either from the viewpoint of profits or some other factor. Alternatively, there may be markets abroad where a company could make more profits than in the home market. The problem is finding such markets, measuring them and forecasting their future.

One initial stage could be to place countries into certain broad categories, and decide with which groups it is desirable to trade. By noting changes in these countries and their gradual movement from one category to the next, international change can be measured.

Indicators that can be used as a basis for measuring change in the international environment are many. They include: the gross national product; income per capita; population change; urban/rural structure; analysis of socio-economic groups; size of market; levels of unemployment; availability of raw materials; sufficiency of food supply; availability and cost of energy; foreign trade and balance of payments position; the home country share of total country imports; the home country share of total country exports; type and stability of government; degree of state ownership; degree of industrial concentration; transportation services and facilities; recent attitude to the home country; exchange control and restrictions; facilities for the transfer of profits, royalties, interest, etc; the ratio of industry to agriculture.

Many of these are expressed as a statistic, eg, the home country share of total country imports is 15%. Others are qualitative, eg recent attitude to the home country, but can be partially quantified by expressing them in degrees of intensity, eg openly friendly, tolerant, critical, bitter.

Change can be measured by comparing the value of an indicator in one period against its value in another.

Another method of measuring international change is by the comparison of a series of appropriate indicators in different countries. From such analysis has emerged the concept of *comparative marketing* which can be defined as the identification, analysis, and measurement of common factors and differences in structure, systems and techniques among various countries and regions.

This approach can help companies to decide which are the most advantageous and favorable international markets to enter. But it is of particular use to market forecasters through the technique of historical analogy. This is based on the concept that in like circumstances similar market situations and sales volumes could emerge, often with a time lag between them. For example, certain similarities in market situations observed in the USA have been seen to happen in Britain five years later. If the right combination of indicators can be found to indicate an appropriate market situation, a certain size of market volume can be anticipated in various countries.

Problems in measuring international change arise from the difficulty of obtaining reliable measurable data to form indicators and from the problems of effectively quantifying intangible national characteristics and traditions. Some sources of international data are listed on page 102.

To summarize, the use of indicators and their projection through extrapolation, historical analogy, lead and lag techniques, or assessment methods can all help the forecaster to assess changes in the international environment.

Technological change

Just as there is a need to examine the conditions in a market and to give an overall forecast before attempting to make an individual company forecast, there is also a need to examine existing technology used in an industry and to forecast the future development of sales of a product, but in the long term a fundamental factor will be the range and type of products technology generally has evolved.

Many companies attempt to forecast future developments in technology because of their obvious effect on the development of new products, and also because of their impact on market forecasting in general and on individual company product forecasting in particular.

It is not only the innovating type of company that needs to forecast technological developments, but also the company that follows the lead set by the innovators. Further, it is needed by the company that modifies a basic product concept to the needs of a specific market segment, and also by the company with the same product as others but which offers a different overall combination of customer satisfactions. All operate in the technological environment and will be affected by it.

Technological forecasting can be highly sophisticated or very elementary in its methods: but the fact that it is considered at all will cause executives to examine, consider and plan their own product range more effectively.

Generally, technological forecasting is concerned mainly with trends, not precise predictions. For example, it would be extremely useful for some companies to know how power sources such as engines will develop over the next 20/30 years. Technological forecasting would be able to produce predictions about the general trends and concepts in various power source areas but would not expect to establish the precise design specification likely to be used.

Some of the most popular methods of technological forecasting are as follows:

1. Morphological research

This is an exploratory approach which seeks to divide the problem into its basic areas through a detailed analysis of the parameters relating to an existing product. An example of this technique was featured by Erich Jantath[1]: 'It is possible to show that a simple,

---

1. *Science Journal,* October 1967, London.

chemical jet engine characterized by 11 basic parameters can be constructed in 25,344 combinations of these 11 parameters. Some of these represent quite novel devices which might not have been conceived without the kind of rigorous analysis which morphological research provides.'

By considering each component of a product in terms of all the possible alternatives (chemical formulations, design, materials, etc) it is possible to examine the assembly of various combinations of alternatives so that suggestions as to the future development of a product, concept, or technology are evolved.

2. Systems analysis
This approach makes a highly detailed examination of the components and factors of existing systems. From the current operations areas of potential growth, development or innovation are suggested when existing technology from other fields is applied: for example, the application of plastics in a situation where metal was formerly used, or the application of computerization to complex machinery that had previously been manually controlled.

3. Normative relevance tree techniques
Techniques in this area are based on establishing desirable goals and objectives in products, concepts, technology, etc. This is followed by a detailed evaluation of the alternative actions, resources, developments or ways by which the target objective can be reached. The term 'tree' is derived from the pattern of the model (see Figure 19). The main trunk is the objective or goal, the alternatives are the branches and these are extended to the twigs, the ends of which represent the shortcomings and deficiencies in existing technology that prevent or discourage the alternatives being used to reach the objective.

One major approach is to consider systematically the possible impact of any probable developments in technological knowledge, or the probable evolution of new concepts, on future developments.

Another major normative approach is to identify a range of potential problems in a technology, product, or concept that is likely to be met in the short, medium and long term. The various technologies and developments to resolve these problems are then identified either objectively or subjectively.

The major advantages of the normative method are that it forces a company to set objectives, recognize future technological problem areas and carry out effective planning for the future. Further, it can help to forecast future demand in relevant product areas and can also indicate to a company opportunities for new product development. Normative relevance tree techniques linked with cost/benefit

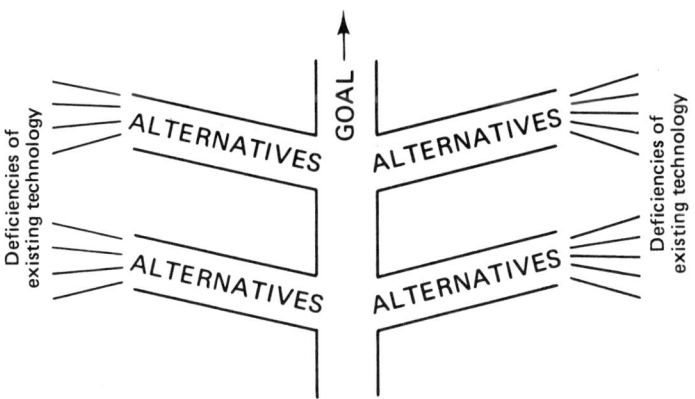

Figure 19. *A diagram giving a broad description of the normative relevance tree concept*

analysis, critical path analysis and PERT (program evaluation and review techniques) can be very effective in causing a more efficient application of capital expenditure, in establishing more appropriate priorities in company programs, in reducing costs and in keeping a company ahead of competitors in appropriate technological areas.

4. Brainstorming

This technique is not strictly a technological forecasting device, but can be used in such a way as to have a useful role in technological prediction. It is a group technique for stimulating and developing creative ideas in a company: it has been said that, with brainstorming, high caliber ideas can be deliberately brought to the surface.

The method is to get together a small group of 10 to 15 persons who are appropriate to the technology/new product area, such as research and development engineers, designers, marketing researchers, consultants, high-level salesmen, etc, then start them thinking about the development of new technology or products in a specific area, eg power sources. As ideas are put forward rapidly they are written down, preferably where they can be seen by the group so that, by combining them with other ideas and improving them, new ideas are sparked off. It is necessary to develop a momentum and not to interfere with the 'ideas-getting' process by discussion or criticism at this stage. Quantity is required as this increases the probability of obtaining non-standard ideas and the 'ideas period' goes on until the group dries up, although care must be taken not to end prematurely.

The ideas are then discussed one by one, some eliminated, others retained and some improved upon.

The next stage should be carried out after a break in the meeting, to give participants a rest and time for ideas to germinate. This final stage is another brainstorming session on how the barriers to the development of technology in specific areas can be overcome, and then a discussion of how long it will take to achieve these breakthroughs. Usually, range time periods, eg 1988-95, are agreed upon.

5. The Delphi approach

A panel of experts from immediate and associated scientific and technological areas is set up. Although they never meet, the effect is an advanced version of the brainstorming technique. A number of rounds are played. First, the members of the panel are asked individually to predict the future course of a technology or product development. The results are analyzed and this initial survey is followed by another which is based on the distilled results of the first, perhaps on the first 10 predicted technological revolutions. The second survey questionnaire may ask the experts to state specifically levels of probability of achieving the first 10 new concepts and/or technology. They may also be asked to rank their individual expertise or competence to deal with a particular concept area. The resulting list would show potential technology breakthroughs in order of probability. This list would again be circulated to the panel of experts and they would be asked to indicate both the time and probability of the distilled list of potential developments.

The Delphi technique does not make a precise forecast or explicit assumptions, but it does produce a suggested time period during which a potential breakthrough could take place, eg 'automated interpretation of medical symptoms, 1985-1990' and 'remote facsimile newspapers and magazines printed at home, 1995-2025.'[1]

The Delphi approach is founded on the intuitive thinking of experts based, after the first round, on information that is the distilled result of the panel as a whole. While it may not be precise, it has a very definite effect on company goal-setting in the research and development area.

6. Scenario writing approach

This method also depends on intuitive thinking, describing in a logical sequence of events how, starting from the present day, technology in a specific area will develop step by step. From this sequence, problems are listed that are associated with the required breakthroughs needed to achieve the ultimate objective.

This method of forecasting identifies areas of difficult development but also systematically examines the branches or direction of

1. *Science Journal*, October 1967, London.

potential technological change or development and the possible courses of action at each key decision point in the future.

7. Technological trend extrapolation

This method is based on the collection of historic and present data regarding a technology, product, or product concept, which is then projected into the future.

It is a useful exploratory approach, but the high degree of uncertainty surrounding the range of parameters that can be chosen and the possible number of interpretations of the resulting trends tend to reduce the forecasters' level of confidence in it.

Technological trend extrapolation is particularly applicable to pace-setting data, speed, efficiency, strength, performance, etc, but becomes less effective and accurate in highly complex, fast-moving situations of high reaction or interaction. Further, in situations where the normative approach (starting at some point in the future and working back to the present) forces the pace of development, trends based on historic data are less likely to be relevant.

Direct extrapolation. This is merely a case of taking an existing trend and projecting it to some future point in time. It ignores the possibility of radical breakthroughs in technology and its findings may have to be modified by some other approach such as the Delphi technique.

The vector approach. Where a total concept, product, set of resources, etc, is being considered it is possible to calculate average growth or development rates over the recent past and show them on a

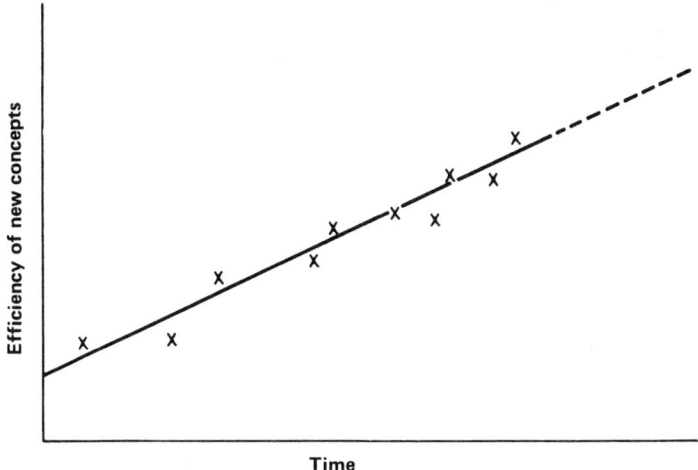

Figure 20. *The line of best fit approach*

vector diagram. This has the effect of ranking the average growth rates. Consideration can then be given to the effect of extrapolating these average growth rates into the future.

The line of best fit approach (Figure 20). By this method the various stages of the development of a total concept or product are plotted on a time scale at the point where they were introduced, in relation to the increase in efficiency or performance they cause. For example, the diagram could show the pattern of discovery of computer technology measured in terms of speed of handling data or decision-making. The historic development pattern could be plotted and a line of best fit added and projected into the future. This projection would indicate the speeds of handling data or decision-making that could be expected in the year 2000.

Envelope curve extrapolation (Figure 21). This is a development of the last method, of considering new developments in a technology. Not only is the initial point in time plotted together with the efficiency or performance level, but also the whole pattern of development of each aspect of the overall concept. For example, if the development of the efficiency of power sources, ie engines and motors of different types were considered, a curve of development related to time would evolve from plotting the efficiency development and improvement pattern of each type, ie the steam engine, petrol engine, electric motor, diesel, turbine, diesel electric, jet engine, rocket motor, etc.

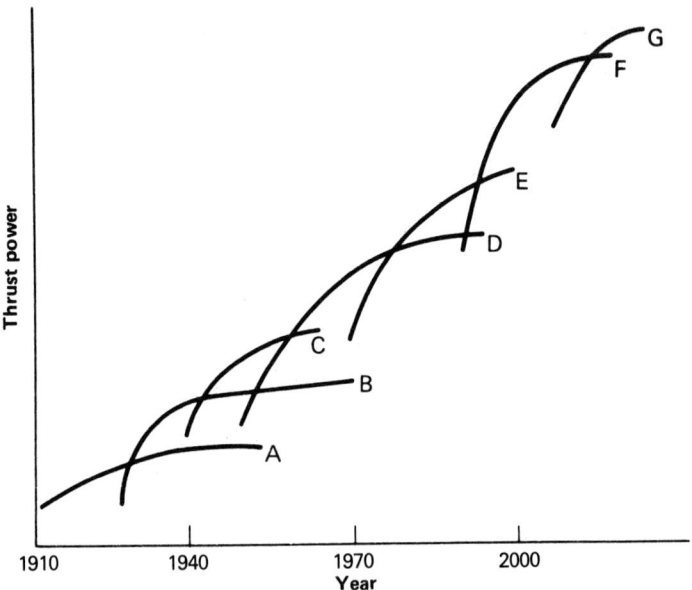

Figure 21. *Envelope curve extrapolation — the hypothetical development of aero engine types*

The current pattern, plus the known discoveries that have yet to be fully exploited, can be projected into the future. It is a means of forecasting the impact of anticipated developments without specifically determining the technology by which it will be reached.

'S' curve trend comparison (Figure 22). In many technologies, their developments in terms of improved efficiency, speed, performance, etc takes the shape of a misshapen letter S. There is the discovery, followed by the gradual improvement in efficiency as time passes, which in turn is followed by a 'take off' period where the technology suddenly develops and performance increases rapidly over a relatively short period of time. This is later followed by a lower development growth rate. Later still, at saturation level a plateau can develop where it becomes impossible to develop the technology further. Extrapolation in this case means completing the S shape pattern for existing technology. Also when existing S curves are tending to level out it suggests that a new development in technology will emerge to take the overall concept forward. It might also indicate to innovating companies areas ready for technological development.

The long-/short-term performance graph (Figure 23). This is not so much another technique as a variation on the S curve trend comparison above. It recognizes the S shape development, but poses a

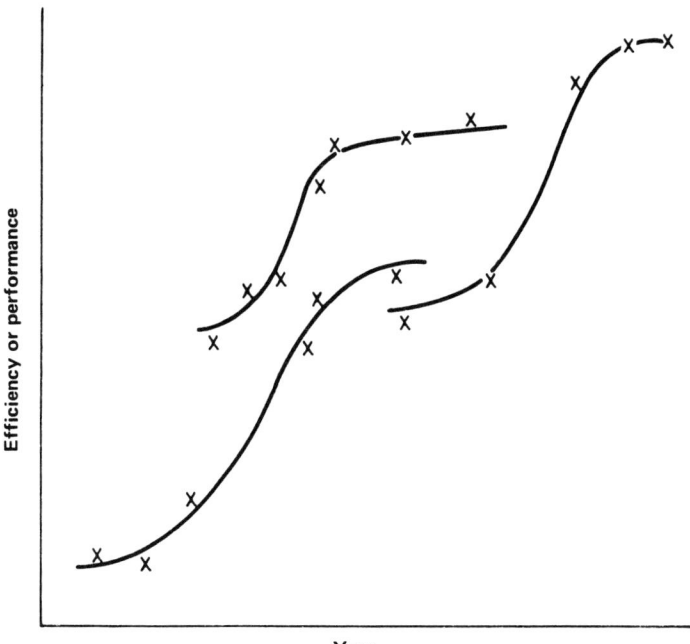

Figure 22. *S Curve trend comparison*

situation where two technologies have developed to perform the same or similar functions. Consider an area in the technology of pneumatics, the compression of air as a power source.

There are two main ways of efficiently compressing air. Expressed simply, one is the *reciprocating method* where air is compressed by means of cylinders and pistons. The *rotary vane method* is the second approach, where a vaned rotor is rotated at speed, forcing air up through a tube. The reciprocating method came first and the S pattern developed as improvements to design improved efficiency. In 1949 the rotary vane method was introduced, commencing another S pattern, particularly in the area of the mobile compressor unit. Both methods perform the same task and, as developments in each of the two methods emerge, a comparison of efficiencies is possible. Also by the long-/short-term performance graph it is possible to extrapolate the S pattern into the future. This might indicate, as in the graph, that the method that is giving the greatest level of performance in the short term may be overtaken in the long term by the other method, when remotely possible developments occur.

It will be seen that the technological forecasting methods listed tend to be rather more subjective than objective, and as such may tend to be less precise than some others. The methods shown are either attempting to link the development of technology with its effect on the market, or are information feedback systems. The information derived makes it possible to anticipate and identify possible future technological developments and assess the various alternatives.

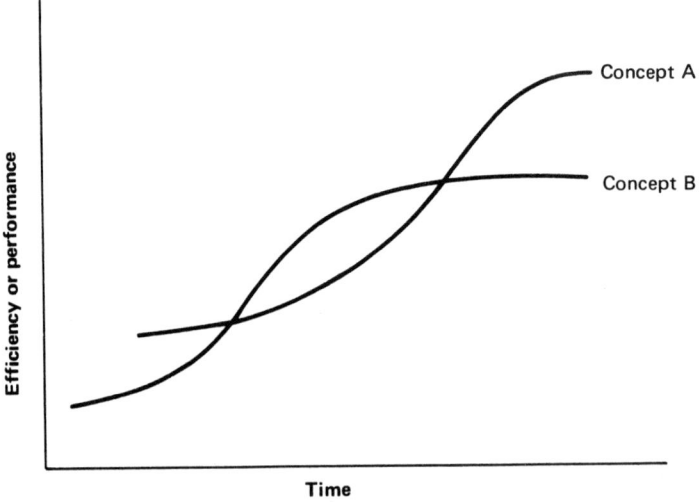

Figure 23. *Long-/short-term performance*

Technology is one of the market environments in which a company operates and will have a direct effect therefore on sales forecasting. While not all companies have the resources to embark upon highly sophisticated technological forecasting, any attempt, no matter how elementary, is better than no prediction of future technology at all.

In fact, the techniques of technological forecasting fall into two categories, *exploratory* and *normative*. These have been defined thus: 'exploratory forecasting consists in using our present knowledge of science potentialities and technical trends for projection purposes under a *ceteris paribus* assumption which generally neglects all other possible structure changes. On the contrary, normative forecasting works backwards from the future to the present; it implies a coherent examination of future needs in a future society, which helps define first socio-economic objectives and then purely technical research objectives and the best way to achieve them.'

CHAPTER 7
Objective Methods of Forecasting

'Statistics must be as the lamp post is to a drunken man, one of support rather than illumination'

Anon

Objective methods of forecasting

Forecasting methods can be either objective (predictions and projections), subjective (conclusions) or a combination of both. Objective forecasts tend to be of a statistical/mathematical nature and subjective forecasts tend to be intuitive, based on the application of experience, intelligence and judgement.

The ideal forecast is a combination of both types. It is made up of a number of individual forecasts, some objective and some subjective. The degree of emphasis on either type will depend on a number of factors. These include the type of industry. A composite forecast in a fashion industry will tend to need a higher subjective content than a forecast in a basic raw materials industry. The absence of appropriate quantitative data may force a company to rely more heavily on subjective methods. Further, the cost in terms of time and money of obtaining a sophisticated statistical forecast may cause a company to use mainly intuitive techniques. In some cases (perhaps with a product completely new to the company) the appropriate experience and the informed intuition may not be available and emphasis will tend to be on statistical techniques.

But even with the individual objective statistical forecast there is a case for subjecting it to the appraisal, judgement and intuition of practical marketing men. Mechanical forecasting by statistical researchers who are far removed from, or out of touch with, the market place can often result in naive projections of future sales. In some companies the results of statistical projections are referred to as forecasts and after they have been subjected to informed intuition they become predictions. Although perhaps apparently pedantic, such an approach does emphasize the importance of the dual forecasting approach.

Objective Methods of Forecasting

Not all techniques can be precisely defined as objective or subjective; therefore, they have been assigned either to this chapter (objective methods) or to the next chapter (subjective methods), on the basis that their nature is predominantly one or the other.

Tied indicators and derived demand

For some products published statistics upon which to base a market forecast are scarce. In such a case there may be other products which sell in an identifiable relationship, and which are better documented, with readily available data.

Where sales of one product may be related to the sales of other products the latter would be termed a *tied indicator* and demand is derived. This relationship can be seen where products are incorporated into others, eg the demand for fractional horsepower motors might be linked with the sales of washing machines, vacuum cleaners, dish washers, and refrigerators. Forecasts of the latter products would be useful to forecast the sales of specific motor types.

Sometimes a 'double tie' can be identified and used. For example, if a company manufacturing metal cans identifies a specific end-product market it may forecast the sales of its own product by using the tied indicator of the demand for tinned peas. But also the forecast of the market for the sales of cans for that specific product could be ascertained by considering the acreage of peas which are contracted for sowing by the leading canning companies.

End-use analyses of the ultimate market, together with tied indicators, make useful forecasting devices where a company's products are merely one stage in a line of product stages for ultimate consumer or user purchase.

Lead and lag techniques

One of the most popular approaches for the use of independent variables such as economic indicators is the *lead/lag method*. This method involves finding one or more economic indicators that tend to assume a similar pattern to the data being forecast, but which increase or decrease ahead of it. By observing movements in the leading indicator, forecasts can be made, as these movements will repeat themselves later in the lagging data. This is done ideally by the use of graphs as well as tables of figures, for although the units of measurement of the indicators compared may be different (eg $s, index numbers, tons, etc), directional changes, upwards or downwards, will be clearly indicated. An example is shown in Figure 24. There, the wholesale price index (the leading indicator) is three months ahead of the cost of living index (the lagging indicator).

There are many types of independent variables, such as economic indicators, that have a direct lead/lag effect on sales; it is necessary

Market and Sales Forecasting 152

for forecasters to discover those most appropriate to a particular company's needs and situations.

In some cases it is possible to establish a more long-term lead/lag relationship: movements in the birth rate will affect the demand for school clothing five years later. This lead/lag relationship can be useful not only in forecasting but also in indicating marketing opportunities.

The main advantage of the lead/lag technique is in determining potential directional increases or decreases in market situations or sales, eg a turn down or turn up on a total consumer expenditure graph. But it is unlikely to provide information regarding the extent of the directional change.

Lead/coincident and lag method

A refinement of this method is the introduction of midway or coincident indicators. The indicators used, although only indirectly related to the lead and lag indicators, tend to coincide, and therefore help to reinforce or modify conclusions arrived at from the leading indicators. Some examples will illustrate this method:

Leading	Coincident	Lagging
Average hours worked	employment position	retail sales
Government 'below the line' expenditure	gross national product	employment position
Industrial production	retail stocks	retail sales
Raw material prices	wholesale prices	cost of living
New orders for durable goods	machine tool orders	level of industrial production
Bank advances	home building starts	building society advances
Wage rates	new orders for durable goods	hire purchase debt
Machine tool orders	level of industrial production	corporate profits
Factory building approvals	machine tool orders	index of industrial production

The coincident indicator is useful in checking the validity of using a pair of indicators as one leading another. Consider item one in the above list where average hours worked lead retail sales. The use of the employment position indicator will show how retail sales will be affected. If average hours worked increases and the employment posi-

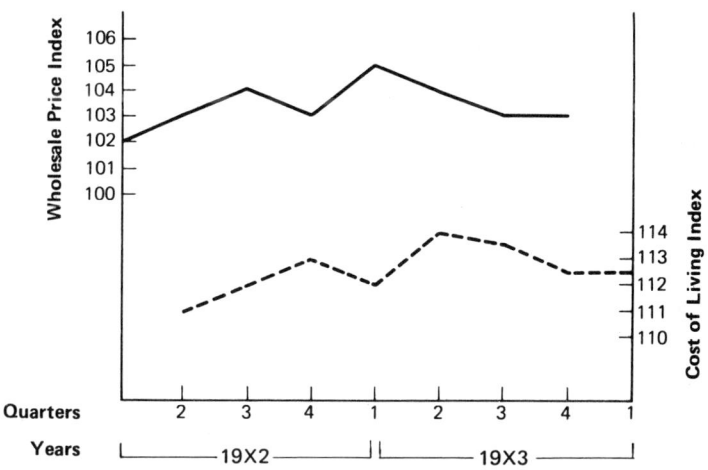

Figure 24. *An example of lead/lag indicators; wholesale prices leading the cost of living*

tion remains unchanged, then this will reflect overtime working by the existing labor force. This in turn will affect the retail sales of luxury or semi-luxury products or services as more disposable income is available above the basic required for general living. But if average hours worked increases and the employment position improves during a period of medium or high unemployment then the tendency will be for retail sales to increase in sectors dealing with basic items of food and clothing.

Where both leading and coincident factors increase or decrease and the lagging one does not move or moves in the opposite direction, investigation will often show the emergence of a new factor. For example, in the above case, if average hours worked increased together with an improvement in the employment situation, retail sales did not increase or increased only slightly, a new factor such as increased saving might be found.

When using lead and lag techniques it is advisable to use a number of pairs of indicators as some can be used to check the validity of others. It will be noticed that in the above list of indicators the same indicator can appear in different columns depending on what information is needed. Lists of appropriate lead and lag indicators can be evolved for various market situations.

Chain reaction in lead and lag methods

Occasionally, a chain reaction will develop throughout the market segments served by a company, and the time lags can often be measured over a period and used on future occasions. For example, companies marketing portable compressors have basically four market segments: government departments, local authority and service authorities (gas, water, etc), contractors of all types (civil engineering, builders, etc) and plant hire. When an economic squeeze is imposed and is seen by the indicator of the minimum lending rate and restriction of credit facilities, etc, the first market to be affected will be that of government departments. Within a few months the effect of central government financing and influence will affect the local and service authorities' market segments. The market segments covering contractors of all types will be affected within six to nine months, as new construction projects are postponed or curtailed. However, some projects must go on and when, because of the economic squeeze, capital for equipment is either unobtainable or too costly, there tends to be a considerable increase in business in the plant hire sector from three months after imposition of restrictions.

Economic lead and lag indicators can be used not only to forecast sales but also to indicate in advance the segments of the market upon which the company should be concentrating its sales promotional efforts.

Sometimes the lagging effect can be measured relatively accurately. In many areas of the capital goods market the effect of an economic indicator, the minimum lending rate, has a direct lagging correlation, ie a 1% increase in the minimum lending rate will cause a 3% to 4% decrease in sales in six months' time. Conversely, when the minimum lending rate decreases by 1%, sales tend to increase 3% to 4% in six months' time as the new minimum lending rate permeates the economic system. Relationships such as these are extremely useful in forecasting and individual companies will need to develop their own lead/lag values, as economic changes affect different companies in different ways.

Correlation and regression analysis

Two widely used forecasting techniques are regression analysis and correlation. In the former, a function is developed mathematically which expresses the relationship between a dependent variable (sales) and one or more independent variables. Correlation, on the other hand, is designed to measure the direction and intensity of this relationship. Normally, only those variables showing a significant level of correlation are subjected to regression analysis.

If two or more quantities or factors vary in sympathy, so that movements or changes upwards or downwards in one tend to be accompanied by movements of a corresponding nature in the other, they are said to be correlated. But the forecaster must ensure that the correlation is not spurious, as it is possible to get a high numerical correlation where two series have increased continuously, without there being any necessary cause and effect relationship at all.

Correlation can be direct or positive with both series of data moving in the same direction, increasing or decreasing, or it can be inverse or negative with the two series moving in opposite directions, ie as one increases the other decreases and vice versa.

Correlation between two series of data can be completely absent, in which case it could be said that the two series were completely independent of each other.

There are degrees of correlation, where data is partially correlated, and although care must be taken when using such data to forecast, it can still be used with qualification as a very useful method of prediction.

Market correlation with economic indicators

Taking two economic indicators from the Joint Economic Committee of Congress and Council of Economic Advisers' publication *Economic Indicators,* ie total personal consumption expenditure and personal expenditure on jewelry and watches, a very definite positive correlation between the two indicators can be seen over a period of time in Table 4. That is, as total personal consumption expenditure increases, the amount spent on jewelry and watches increases almost proportionately.

Year	(a) Total personal consumption expenditure ($ billion)	(b) Personal expenditure on jewelry and watches ($ billion)	Percentage (b) of (a)
1970	618.8	4.1	0.66
1973	809.9	5.4	0.66
1974	889.6	5.8	0.65
1975	979.1	6.3	0.64
1976	1090.2	7.1	0.65
1977	1206.5	7.6	0.64

Source: No 723 Personal Consumption Expenditures, by Product, based on US Bureau of Economic Analysis, *The National Income and Product Accounts of the United States, 1929-74,* and *Survey of Current Business, July 1977, July 1978 and March 1979.*

Table 4. *The relationship of personal expenditure on jewelry and watches to total personal consumption expenditure*

It can be seen in Table 4 that the total spent on jewelry and watches as a percentage of total personal consumption expenditure varies relatively little from year to year, although there is a tendency to a slight overall decline. The reason for this would need to be identified; for example, it could be the result of inflation affecting the spending power of lower income groups. On the other hand, in times of high inflation this percentage would tend to increase as higher income groups endeavor to purchase more jewelry as a hedge against inflation.

Total personal consumption expenditures in the USA are forecast regularly by government economists, and if a relationship can be established such as the one in the jewelry and watches industry shown in Table 4, a forecast for both the industry and a company within the industry could be made. Alternatively, the forecaster could project a trend from total personal consumption expenditure to obtain a forecast for the next year or sales period. Assuming that the 0.64% share of total personal consumption expenditures continued, a prediction of the sale of jewelry and watches could be obtained.

Further, there would be a relationship between the sales of a company in the jewelry and watches industry and the size of the market measured by personal expenditure on jewelry and watches, ie market share. This relationship is reflected in the hypothetical situation shown in Table 5.

Suppose a forecast of total personal consumption expenditures was made either by government economists or by in-company projection and this prediction was $1327.1 billion. A company sales forecast could be made as follows:

(i) $1327.1 billion × 0.64% = $8.49 billion forecast expenditure on jewelry and watches
(ii) $8.49 billion × 5% = $424.5 million predicted company sales.

The validity of such a forecast would depend upon market factor relationships remaining fairly stable or at least changing at the existing rate.

The company may hope to increase its share of the market, or competition being experienced at the present time may be such that the company may have to make a great effort to maintain its 5% share of the market. In both cases marketing, advertising and other promotional expenditure may have to be expanded considerably to increase or maintain market share.

In the above example, total personal consumption expenditures have been taken as the economic indicator, but others may be chosen that are more appropriate to a market or a company. For companies in the consumer durables market, disposable personal income might be more appropriate as it takes account of the amount consumers may be inclined to save as well as spend. Total new plant and equipment would be an indicator appropriate to companies in industrial machinery markets; and there are many other examples.

Year	Personal expenditure on jewelry and watches ($m)	Company sales ($m)	Market share %
1970	4100	123	3.0
1973	5400	189	3.5
1974	5800	232	4.0
1975	6300	299	4.75
1976	7100	355	5.0
1977	7600	380	5.0

Table 5. *The relationship of personal expenditure on jewelry and watches to a company's sales*

Correlation and company sales

One of the most important stages of the correlation technique is to determine the degree of correlation, and this can be done graphically, or, more precisely, by statistical methods. Supposing research has shown, or it has been noticed over a period of time, that movements in the size of a particular economic indicator (although it could be any independent variable) tend to coincide with the sales of (and consequently the demand for) a particular product — product A. The two series of data could be listed as in Table 6.

Year	Economic indicator ($m)	Sales of product A ($000s)
19X3	322	25.7
19X4	320	27.7
19X5	311	30.0
19X6	329	33.6
19X7	358	36.9
19X8	363	38.2
19X9	379	39.6
19Y0	390	38.6
19Y1	430	42.7
19Y2	446	43.7
19Y3	466	48.1
	11)4114	11)404.8
	374 average	36.8 average

Table 6. *Two series of data which are to be examined for correlation*

Market and Sales Forecasting

If the data in Table 6 is plotted on a graph with the economic indicator on one vertical axis, the sales of product A on the other, and time along the horizontal axis, the result would be as shown in Figure 25.

It will be noticed that although the lines on the diagram are not in exact unison, they tend to have a similar basic pattern.

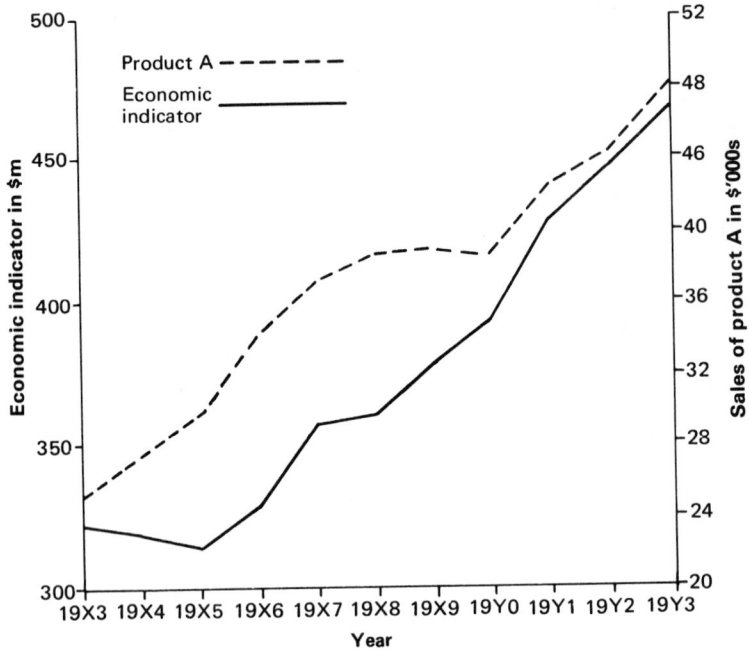

Figure 25. *The values of the economic indicator in $m and the sales of product A in $'000s plotted on a time series diagram*

If the two series of data were shown in a different way, with the economic indicator on the horizontal axis and the sales of product A on the vertical axis and the pairs plotted, a scatter of plot marks will be obtained as in Figure 26.

The first plot mark in Figure 26 will be found by observing 322 on the horizontal and 25.7 on the vertical axis, and marking where these two values intersect on the graph; and so on for all the pairs of data. In the foregoing table both columns were totalled and then divided by 11 to give the average in both cases. The average pair can be plotted (marked 0 in Figure 26) and a trend line inserted through the average mark and as near the center of the scatter of all the other marks as possible.

This method of fixing a regression line is rather rough, as a slight movement of the line on the pivot of the average plot mark will alter

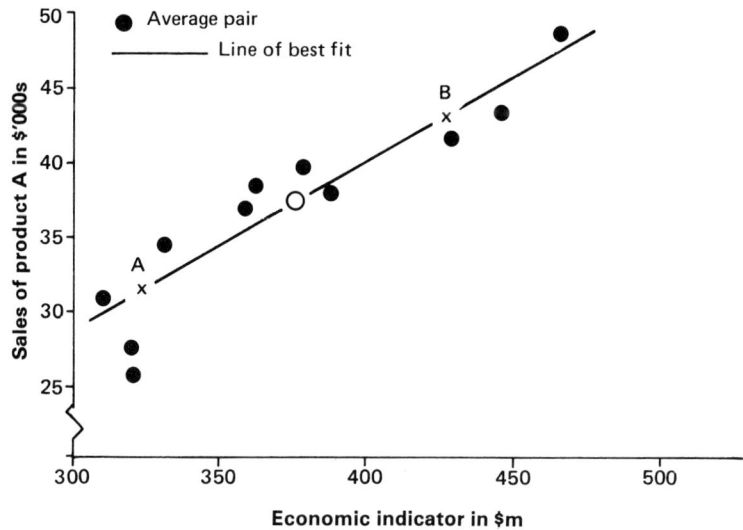

Figure 26. *A graph of two sets of data plotted in pairs and indicating a high degree of correlation*

the reading considerably at the ends of the line. It is a guide to the degree of correlation, but if the regression line is intended as a basis for forecasting other anticipated values, it would be advisable to adopt a more precise way of fitting a regression line, perhaps by the least squares method shown later in this chapter. In fact the line of best fit has been added to the data, between points A and B as calculated on page 186.

It will be noticed that there is a tendency for the plot marks to form an irregular pattern from low left to high right. This indicates that there exists a degree of positive or direct correlation. The nearer the slope of the line to 45 degrees, the greater the degree of correlation; a line with a slope of 45 degrees indicates that the two series are perfectly correlated. If the scatter was so wide that no overall trend could be distinguished, this would indicate the absence of correlation, and the fact that after change in the value of one set of data, a sympathetic change could not be anticipated in the other series. The implication in the above example is that if the value of the independent variable, ie the indicator, moved upwards, the sales of product A would tend to do the same.

If it is easier to obtain a forecast of an independent variable such as an economic indicator than to project the sales level itself, or if a lead/lag relationship exists, then forecasting by this method is relatively easy. The forecast of the appropriate economic indicator is used and the forecast of the other value is read from the regression

Market and Sales Forecasting

line on the scatter diagram. In the last example, if the forecast of the economic indicator was $450m, reading from the diagram, the sales of product A could be expected to be around $46,000; perhaps in x months' time if there was a lagging effect.

The degree of correlation is very important when using a linear regression line in sales forecasting. It is possible to take the data from the previous example (Table 6) and, using statistical methods, determine how closely correlated these two sets of data really are. Further, it can be calculated just how much confidence can be placed in concluding that a movement in one series of data would anticipate a movement in the other series.

The data in Table 6, showing values of the economic indicator and the sales of product A, can be listed and, using the symbols x and y respectively, a table can be evolved to provide data leading to a co-efficient of correlation (Table 7). Columns 3 (x_{dev}) and 6 (y_{dev}) in Table 7 show the deviation each value is away from the appropriate average (bottom of columns 2 and 5). These figures are then squared in columns 4 (x_{dev}^2) and 7 (y_{dev}^2). Column 8 represents column 3 (x_{dev}) multiplied by column 6 (y_{dev}).

The question is whether the two series of data move in sympathy and to what degree. To answer this the following formula is used.

$$r = \frac{\Sigma(x_{dev}\,y_{dev})}{\sqrt{[\Sigma(x_{dev}^2\,y_{dev}^2)]}}$$

where r is the co-efficient of correlation.

Σ is a summation sign (the sum of),
(so Σx_{dev}^2 is sum of all the x_{dev}^2 values, ie 29,056)

The other values are taken from the table. Therefore:

$$r = \frac{3533.6}{\sqrt{(29056 \times 485.66)}} = 0.9542$$

To visualize the implications of this value (0.9452 co-efficient of correlation), consider the following scale:

```
        Perfect                           Perfect
        direct                            inverse
        correlation      Independence     correlation
Value  +1 —— +0.75 —— +0.5 —— 0 —— -0.5 —— -0.75 —— -1
```

The nearer the correlation co-efficient is to unity (±1) the better the degree of correlation, and a zero (0) co-efficient indicates that there is

1	2 Economic indicator ($m) x	3 x_{dev}	4 x_{dev}^2	5 Sales of product A ($000s) y	6 y_{dev}	7 y_{dev}^2	8 $x_{dev} \times y_{dev}$
19X3	322	−52	2,704	25.7	−11.1	123.20	+577.2
19X4	320	−54	2,916	27.7	−9.1	82.81	+491.4
19X5	311	−63	3,969	30.0	−6.8	46.24	+428.4
19X6	329	−45	2,025	33.6	−3.2	10.24	+144.0
19X7	358	−16	256	36.9	+0.1	0.01	− 1.6
19X8	363	−11	121	38.2	+1.4	1.96	− 15.4
19X9	379	+5	25	39.6	+2.8	7.84	+ 14.0
19Y0	390	+16	256	38.6	+1.8	3.24	+ 28.8
19Y1	430	+56	3,136	42.7	+5.9	34.81	+330.4
19Y2	446	+72	5,184	43.7	+6.9	47.61	+496.8
19Y3	466	+92	8,464	48.1	+11.3	127.70	+1,039.6
	11)4,114	−241	29,056	11)404.8	−30.2	485.66	+3,550.6 −17
	374	+241		36.8	+30.2		+3,533.6

Table 7. An analysis of the values of the economic indicator and sales of product A to permit the calculation of the co-efficient of correlation

no correlation between the two series. Values falling between these limits suggest degrees of dependence and correlation between any two series of data being considered. Thus, in the example where $r = 0.9452$ (a positive figure) it could be concluded that there is a considerable correlation or connection in changes and movements between the two sets of data. The nearer the co-efficient (r) falls to the independence value of 0, the lower will be the degree of reliability that can be placed on using one series of data to anticipate or forecast the movements of the other. A value of less than 0.5 would not be considered reliable but a value over 0.75 would be taken to indicate a highly reliable correlation.

Testing the significance of the co-efficient of correlation

It would be quite wrong, however, to take the co-efficient of correlation without some qualification. It does not necessarily provide conclusive evidence that there is correlation to the degree that future predictions for the movement of one variable factor can be based upon the movements of another. In the last example a sample of 11 years was taken, and the size of the values for these 11 years may, or may not, have been caused by sheer chance, or may not be representative of values that could be normally expected. The fewer observations made, or the shorter the range of time over which they are made, the greater will be the chance of obtaining non-typical values by sheer chance. In order to accept the co-efficient of correlation without qualification it is necessary to check its significance or reliability, and to take into account the number of observations (n) made. Further, it is generally assumed that the degree of correlation is not satisfactory unless the odds against a particular correlation co-efficient being obtained by chance alone are less than 5 in 100. That is, in only 5 cases out of 100 could the observed value for r have been obtained accidentally in the absence of correlation. Any probability value between 0.05 (5 cases in 100) and 0.01 (one case in 100) is significant and reliable. Any value less than 0.01 is highly significant or reliable. Thus, 0.0001 (1 case in 1,000) is a highly significant value, as such a value would occur by chance or accident only once in 1,000 cases. The significance of the correlation co-efficient can be checked by using a table of the type shown in Table 8.

The number of *degrees of freedom* to be used to check the significance of a co-efficient of correlation is determined by deducting 2 from the number, n, of items used (ie $n-2$). In Table 7, 11 items were used, therefore

$$n - 2 = 11 - 2 = 9 \text{ degrees of freedom.}$$

Having determined the degrees of freedom (9), it is necessary to read across Table 8 until the value of the co-efficient of correlation being examined is found, or at least a value close to it. At the top of columns 2, 3 and 4, the measures of significance are shown. Column 2, headed 0.05, indicates 5 chances in 100. Column 3, headed 0.01, indicates 1 chance in 100. Column 4, headed 0.001, indicates 1 chance in 1,000: additional measures of significance columns are given in books of statistical tables.

The co-efficient of correlation in the last example was 0.9452 with 9 degrees of freedom. Reading across Table 8 at 9 degrees of freedom it can be seen that such a value (0.9452) is beyond the last column, ie is more than 0.847, which represents the probability of 1 chance in 1,000. Thus, it can be said that the co-efficient of correlation of 0.9452 with 9 degrees of freedom is highly significant and reliable, as the chance of it being obtained accidentally is less than 1 in 1,000 times.

1 Degrees of freedom	2 Co-efficient 0.05	3 of correlation 0.01	4 0.0001
1	0.997	1.000	1.000
2	0.950	0.990	0.999
3	0.878	0.959	0.992
4	0.811	0.917	0.974
5	0.754	0.874	0.951
6	0.707	0.834	0.925
7	0.666	0.798	0.898
8	0.632	0.765	0.872
9	0.602	0.735	0.847
10	0.576	0.708	0.823
11	0.553	0.684	0.801
12	0.532	0.661	0.780
13	0.514	0.641	0.760
14	0.497	0.623	0.742
15	0.482	0.606	0.725
16	0.468	0.590	0.708
17	0.456	0.575	0.693
18	0.444	0.561	0.679
19	0.433	0.549	0.665
20	0.423	0.537	0.652

Table 8. *A table for checking the significance of the co-efficient of correlation*

The importance of taking an adequate number of observations, that is, an adequate size of sample, can be seen if the co-efficient of correlation of the last example (Table 7), 0.9452, is examined under different circumstances. If this value was obtained using only three observations, the degrees of freedom would be $3 - 2 = 1$ degree of freedom (ie $n - 2$). Referring to the table, it can be seen that the chance of such a value being obtained by accident is much higher; in fact more than 5 in 100. That is, at 1 degree of freedom it is not high enough to enter column 2 (0.05) which has a value of 0.997. As the chance of such a value occurring by accident should be less than 5% (ie 5 in 100) for the value to be significant, that is for the two series of data to be correlated to a reliable degree, it could be said that where $r = 0.9452$ with one degree of freedom, it is not significant. The implication is that the values of the two sets of data being tested for correlation could, based on three observations, have been freak values obtained purely by accident. The obvious thing to do in such circumstances would be to increase the number of observations, thereby increasing the degrees of freedom, and again calculate the chances of such a value occurring by accident.

Inverse or negative correlation

So far, circumstances have been considered where movements in one series of data tend to be accompanied by *sympathetic* movements *in the same direction* in another series of data, ie direct or positive correlation. However, in some cases it will be found that *inverse* or *negative correlation* will permit forecasts to be made; ie where the values contained in one series of data increase, the values in the other

Observation	Outdoor temperature in degrees Centigrade	Demand for electricity in MWatts
1	14	20
2	13	3
3	17	26
4	9	48
5	8	35
6	6	80
7	5	60
8	4	50
9	1	98
10	3	90
	10)80	10)510
	8 Average	51 Average

Table 9. *Two series of data that are to be examined for an inverse relationship*

series tend to decrease, and vice versa. Consider as an example an increase in the demand for, and consequently the sales of, electricity as the outdoor temperature changes. By taking an imaginary part of the country and making 10 random observations, the two series could be evolved as in Table 12.

If the values in Table 12 are shown in a graph with the demand for electricity on the vertical axis, and the outdoor temperature on the horizontal axis, a scatter diagram would be obtained. By determining the average plot mark, ie plotting the averages of the two series of data, 8°C and 51 MWatts, it would be possible to draw a line through the centre of the plot marks thereby adding a regression (see Figure 27). Alternatively, a more precise way of fitting a regression line would be by the least squares method (see page 171).

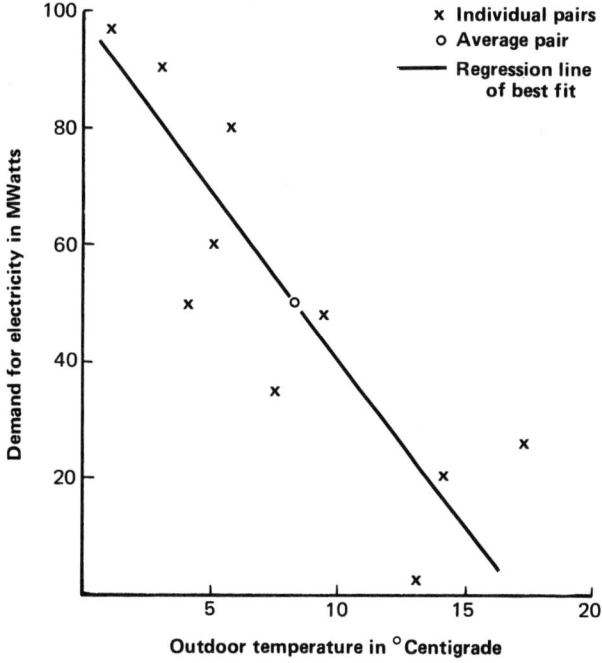

Figure 27. *An inverse correlation diagram showing that as one variable increases in value the other decreases*

Notice how the pattern of the scatter diagram tends to fall from high left to low right, indicating the presence of a degree of inverse correlation. Whether the regression line is roughly fitted by pivoting a ruler on the 'average' pair or whether it is more precisely fitted statistically, perhaps by the least squares method, the diagram can be used for forecasting.

1	2	3	4	5	6	7	8
Observation	Outdoor temperature in degrees Centigrade x	x_{dev}	x_{dev}^2	Demand for electricity in MWatts y	y_{dev}	y_{dev}^2	$x_{dev} \times y_{dev}$
1	14	+6	36	20	−31	961	−186
2	13	+5	25	3	−48	2,304	−240
3	17	+9	81	26	−25	625	−225
4	9	+1	1	48	−3	9	−3
5	8	0	0	35	−16	256	0
6	6	−2	4	80	+29	841	−58
7	5	−3	9	60	+9	81	−27
8	4	−4	16	50	−1	1	+4
9	1	−7	49	98	+47	2,209	−329
10	3	−5	25	90	+39	1,521	−195
	10)80		246	10)510		8,808	−1,263 +4
	8 average			51 average			−1,259

Table 10. *An analysis of the values of the demand for (sales of) electricity and the outdoor temperature to permit the calculation of the co-efficient of correlation*

Again, if it is easier to forecast an independent variable, such as a climatic factor in the last example, than to project the demand level itself, or if a lead/lag relationship exists, then forecasting by the inverse correlation method is relatively easy. Using Figure 27, when a weather forecast is made indicating the outdoor temperature, eg 10 degrees Centigrade, the forecast of demand for electricity can be read from the regression line, ie 40 MWatts.

Weather forecasts are usually readily available, so although the relationship is contemporary, ie changes in both series happen at the same time, a forecast of demand for electricity can be made. But where forecasts of the independent variable are not readily available, forecasting is easier when the independent variable has a lead/lag relationship to the demand to be forecast.

It is possible to determine the degree of inverse correlation precisely by using the statistical techniques shown in Table 10.

Using data from Table 10, the co-efficient of correlation can be calculated:

$$r = \frac{\Sigma (x_{dev}\, y_{dev})}{\sqrt{[(\Sigma x_{dev}^2)(\Sigma y_{dev}^2)]}} = \frac{-1259}{\sqrt{(246 \times 8808)}} = -0.86$$

The negative value (-0.86) indicates inverse correlation; that is, as the outdoor temperature falls, demand for electricity increases. The nearer the co-efficient of correlation (r) is to -1, the greater the degree of inverse correlation. However, as seen previously with positive correlation, the negative co-efficient of correlation $r = -0.86$ should not be accepted without checking its significance. Therefore, examining the probability table used to check positive correlation (Table 8) and reading across the line, degrees of freedom 8 (ie the number of observations $10 - 2 = 8$), the value 0.86 is not reached until the last column, ie 0.0001, indicating that it could be expected to occur by accident slightly more than once in 1,000 observations. Under these circumstances, $r = 0.86$ is highly significant, and movements in outdoor temperature are very good indicators of potential demand for electricity in the opposite direction. Linked with official weather forecasts, fairly accurate forecasts for the sale of electricity could be made. There are many cases where economic indicators can be found that tend to move in the opposite direction to industry or company sales, ie where some degree of inverse correlation exists.

Correlation and regression analysis techniques are useful in market and sales forecasting not only with economic and industry indicators but with any type of independent variable that appears to be linked with the sales of a product, although the two unit values may not be the same, eg in the last example demand for electricity in MWatts and the outdoor temperature in degrees Centigrade. Small or medium sized companies that have a negligible or relatively small market share could establish a correlation series with independent variables outside their immediate industry, thus making their forecasting more effective.

Multiple correlation or multivariate analysis

The last section considered the situation where movements in one set of data are accompanied by 'sympathetic' movements in another series. Sometimes a number of variable factors are correlated to the particular series under consideration, eg market or company sales. This is known as *multiple correlation*.

Obviously, the greater the number of variables, the more complex is the calculation, and it becomes the ideal problem to be handled by a computer. As the number of variables increases, the exercise becomes one of market simulation and model building and this is discussed later.

The basic principle of multiple regression and correlation can be illustrated by an elementary example:

There are three commodities, X, Y and Z, and it is believed that the demand for Z is partly dependent upon the demand for X and Y.

The relationship can be examined by using a multiple regression equation:

$$\hat{Z} = A + BX + CY$$

where $\hat{Z}$ is the predicted or best estimated number of units demanded of the dependent variable; X and Y are the respective units demanded of the independent variables, and A, B and C are constants to be determined from the data in Table 11.

Period	Units demanded			Deviations from mean							
	X	Y	Z	x	y	z	x^2	y^2	xz	xy	yz
1	4	6	12	−2	−4	3	4	16	−6	8	−12
2	5	8	11	−1	−2	2	1	4	−2	2	−4
3	5	9	8	0	−1	−1		1			1
4	7	12	8	1	2	−1	1	4	−1	2	−2
5	8	15	6	2	5	−3	4	25	−6	10	−15
Totals	30	50	45	0	0	0	10	50	−15	22	−32
Means	6	10	9								

There are five sets of items ∴ $n = 5$

Table 11. *An analysis of data to permit the calculation of the degrees of multiple correlation between variables*

After the analysis in Table 11, 'normal' equations can be set up, in terms of deviations from the arithmetic means instead of from zero origin:

(i) $\Sigma z = nA + B\Sigma x + C\Sigma y$
(ii) $\Sigma xz = A\Sigma x + B\Sigma x^2 + C\Sigma xy$
(iii) $\Sigma yz = A\Sigma y + B\Sigma xy + C\Sigma y^2$

Where Σ = sigma, the sum of, ie a summation sign.

Therefore:

(i) $0 = 5A + B0 + C0$
(ii) $-15 = A0 + 10B + 22C$
(iii) $-32 = A0 + 22B + 50C$

Notice how the use of deviations from the arithmetic means of the variables eliminates many expressions in the 'normal' equation, eg $A\Sigma x$ = zero.

Solving these equations in the conventional way, ie by the use of determinants or simple substitution

$$B = -2.875 \text{ and } C = 0.625$$

The above calculations were based on deviations from the arithmetic means, and it is necessary to restore them to zero as the origin, therefore

$Z - \bar{Z}$ (mean) = $-2.875(X-\bar{X}) + 0.625(Y-\bar{Y})$
$Z - 9$ (mean) = $-2.875(X-6) + 0.625(Y-10)$
$Z = 9 - 2.875X + 17.250 + 0.625Y - 6.25$
$Z = +\ 9$
$\ + 17.25$
$\ \overline{+ 26.25}$
$\ \underline{-\ 6.25}$
$\ 20 - 2.875X + 0.625Y$

This gives the required multiple regression of Z on X and Y, as

$$\hat{Z} = 20 - 2.875X + 0.625Y$$

The 'fit' is as follows:

	Actual values of Z	Predicted values of Z
	12	12.25
	11	10.625
	8	8.375
	8	7.375
	6	6.375
Totals	45	45

1	2	3	4	5	6	7
Year & quarter	Sales in $000s	Deviation of each quarter from assumed mean quarter	Dev²	Sales × deviation	Trend ordinates	Trend
19X3 2	34	−4	16	−136	35.3 − (4 × 0.86) =	31.86
3	29	−3	9	−87	35.3 − (3 × 0.86) =	32.72
4	35	−2	4	−70	35.3 − (2 × 0.86) =	33.58
19X4 1	36	−1	1	−36	35.3 − (1 × 0.86) =	34.44
2	37	0	0	0		35.30
3	31	1	1	31	35.3 + (1 × 0.86) =	36.16
4	37	2	4	74	35.3 + (2 × 0.86) =	37.02
19X5 1	40	3	9	120	35.3 + (3 × 0.86) =	37.88
2	39	4	16	156	35.3 + (4 × 0.86) =	38.74
n =	9)318		60	+381 −329		
	35.3 = arithmetic average			52 ÷ 60 = 0.86		

Table 12. Analysis of sales data to calculate a trend by the method of least squares

It may be verified that

regression sum of squares $(\hat{Z}-\overline{Z})^2$ = 23.125
and error sum of squares $(Z-\hat{Z})^2$ = 0.875
and total sum of squares $(Z-\overline{Z})^2$ = 24.000

The multiple correlation co-efficient is accordingly

$$\sqrt{\left[\frac{23.125}{24.00}\right]}$$

approximately perfect negative correlations, ie $r = -1$.

The example shows that the demand for commodity Z decreases as the demand for commodities X and Y increases. Conversely, the demand for Z increases as the demand for X and Y decreases.

The above formula can be proved by using the arithmetic means, ie where $X = 6$ and $Y = 10$, therefore the predicted or best estimate of Z:

$$20 - 2.875 \times 6 + 0.625 \times 10 = 9$$

(which is, in fact, the arithmetic mean of Z)

Using this formula, a forecast can be made for Z; for example, where $X = 8$ and $Y = 12$:

$$Z = 20 - 2.875 \times 8 + 0.625 \times 12$$
$$20 - 23 + 7.5 = 4.5 \text{ forecast for } Z$$

Least squares method — a regression line technique

The least squares method is a relatively simple mathematical technique that ensures that the calculated functional linear equation is the one with the best fit of the data. A line is said to be the best fit line when it minimizes, in relation to all other possible lines, the vertical deviations of the observations from that line. Its drawback is that if the sales data used is too erratic, the straight line will only represent a broad directional trend, and if the data is very smooth there will be no need for a trend line. If a series of quarterly sales is taken, a simple way to find the trend by the least squares method is shown in Table 12.

In Table 12 columns 1 and 2 represent the sales volume in the various quarters; the quarterly sales are totalled and the arithmetic mean is found (35.3).

As quarter 2 of 19X4 is the middle quarter of the nine quarters considered, this quarter has been chosen as the assumed mean or middle quarter and column 3 shows the deviation + or − away from the assumed mean.

In column 4 the deviations have been squared (thereby eliminating the minus signs) and then totalled. In column 5 sales (column 2) are multiplied by the unsquared deviations (column 3); the minus total is subtracted from the plus total and the answer is divided by the total of

Year & quarter	Sales in $000s	Deviation of each quarter from assumed mean quarter	Dev²	Sales × deviation	Trend ordinates	Trend
19X4 2	37	−2	4	−74		34.2
3	31	−1	1	−31		35.5
4	37	0				36.8
19X5 1	40	1	1	40	36.8−(2 × 1.3) =	38.1
2	39	2	4	78	36.8−(1 × 1.3) =	39.4
n =	5)184		10	118 −105	36.8+(1 × 1.3) =	
	36.8 = arithmetic average			13 ÷ 10 = 1.3	36.8+(2 × 1.3) =	

Table 13. *An analysis of sales data from recent periods giving a short-term picture of current trends*

the deviations squared, ie the total of column 4. The resultant figure (ie 0.86) will show by how much the trend line will change in each quarter: in fact, it represents the slope of the line and is the increment by which the trend line increases. In column 6 the arithmetic mean of the sum of the quarterly sales figures (ie 35.3) is used, and by adding or subtracting according to the item's position either side of the assumed mean, the number of quarters (column 3) is multiplied by 0.86. The answer in each case is the plot mark for the trend line and is shown in column 7. In practice, as it is a straight line trend, it is necessary only to calculate the top and bottom values in column 6 and join them, checking that the line runs through the arithmetic mean. The original sales data and the trend line are shown in Figure 28.

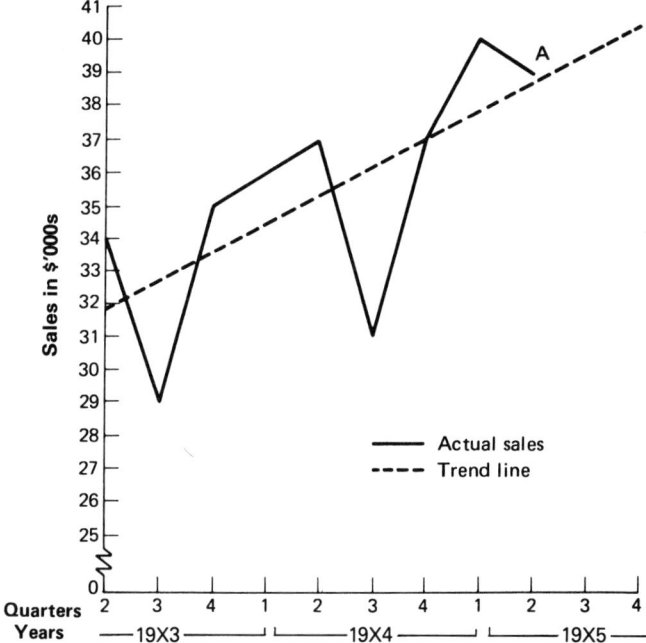

Figure 28. *Quarterly sales volume curve with least squares trend line superimposed*

It will be seen in Figure 28 that the trend line can be projected into the future (from point A) with sales forecasts being obtained from the projection. This projection will be of use for medium- or long-term forecasting but not for short-term prediction as it does not allow for the seasonal pattern clearly indicated on the graph.

Short- and long-term comparisons

Later in this section a method of seasonally adjusting this straight line projection will be considered. However, it has a short-term use, as it is often advantageous to observe a change in trend in a recent, relatively short period, compared with a longer period. Figure 28 showed the sales curve for nine quarters and a trend line fixed accordingly. However, if the data for the last five quarters is taken, and a trend line obtained, as in Table 13, it would give a short-term picture of current trends.

This process of comparison (Table 12 with Table 13) could be used over any time span series, eg nine years (compared with the nine quarters in the example) indicating a long-/medium-term business cycle pattern. Superimposed on the previous graph, the trend line just obtained in Table 13 would indicate the presence of new short-term influences that were either not present throughout the period covered by the long-term data or were hidden or modified by other influences in the opposite direction (see Figure 29).

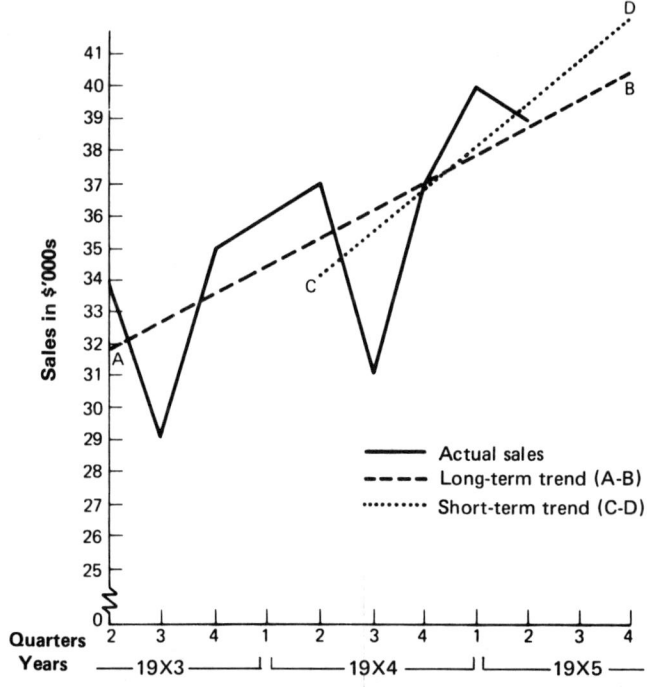

Figure 29. *Quarterly sales volume curve with two least squares trend lines — A-B long-term, and C-D short-term*

Figure 29 shows that the conditions being experienced in the short-term are causing the trend of sales to be higher (C to D) than the long-term sales trend (A to B). It is the analysis of the differences in these predictions that will warn the forecaster of fundamental changes in conditions in the market. Then it must be decided whether such differences are only temporary, in which case there may be a reversion to the long-term trend, and there might be a case for removing the causal item from the sales total. Alternatively, if the conditions are likely to recur, allowance must be made for them in future predictions. Where the short-term trend line fits the long-term line exactly, it is wise to suspect the apparent confirmation that things are the same in the short and long periods; there are often compensatory factors outweighing each other, thereby giving the same trend line as before.

Least squares method — even number of items

In the previous two examples, series containing an odd number of items were used and the 'assumed mean quarter' in column three was not difficult to identify, ie item five in the first series and item three in the second series. However, occasions arise when only an even number of items are to be considered (eg 12 months) and/or where a

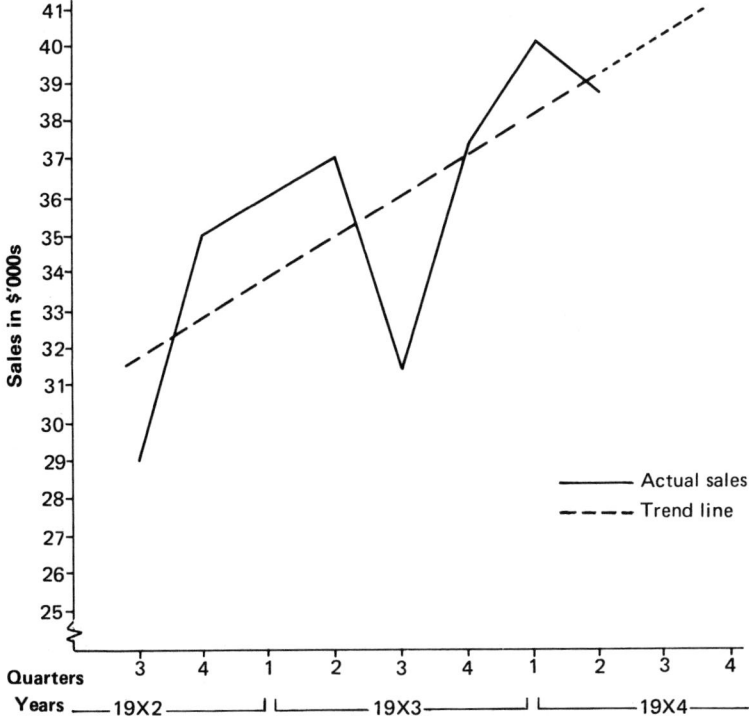

Figure 30. *A quarterly sales volume curve with least squares trend line based on an even number of lines*

better indicator of trend is obtained by using an even number, eg where quarters are considered it is obviously more accurate to work in units of four (four, eight, 12, etc).

When an odd number of items is considered it is possible not only to identify the middle year or quarter but also the middle point in that item, eg midnight 30 June for a year, or in the case of a series of quarters, midday of the middle day or midnight between the middle two days. Therefore with an even number of items in a series the method is to work in half years or half quarters. Thus if a series was as follows (eight items) the former least squares method would be adapted as in Table 14 and Figure 30.

1 x Year Quarter	2 y Sales in $000s	3 x dev in ½ quarters	4 x dev^2	5 Sales y × x dev	
19X2 3	29	−7	49	−203	35 − (7 × 0.55) = 31.65
4	35	−5	25	−175	
19X3 1	36	−3	9	−108	
2	37	−1	1	−37	
3	31	+1	1	31	
4	37	+3	9	111	
19X4 1	40	+5	25	200	
2	39	+7	49	273	35.5 + (7 × 0.55) = 39.35
$n =$	8)284		168	+615 −523	
$\bar{x} =$	35.5			92 ÷ 168 = 0.55	

Table 14. *The calculation of the highest and lowest trend points using the least squares method with an even number of items*

Least squares method with confidence limits

There is a slightly different method of obtaining a line of best fit by the least squares technique. This alternative method permits the forecaster to exploit the available data further by calculating probability control limits within which the *actual* sales will tend to be located in ensuing periods. All this assumes that the basic factors underlying business conditions do not radically change. An example of this method is shown in Table 15.

The least squares method is based upon an equation. The equation of the trend line is expressed so:

$$\hat{y} = a + bx$$

where $\hat{y}$ is the estimated value, given the value of an independent variable, x
where a is the intercept of the trend line on the vertical axis and is, therefore, a constant
where b is the slope of the trend line indicating the mean increment of sales and is, therefore, a constant.

Therefore, the mean quarterly increment of sales will give the slope of the trend line:

$$b = \frac{\Sigma (x_{dev} y_{dev})}{\Sigma x_{dev}^2} = \frac{1560}{28} = 55.71$$

(where Σ is the sum total or summation sign)

Therefore 55.71 represents the value by which the slope of the trend line will increase in each time period.

The bottom value of the trend is found by taking the average and the appropriate number of increments.

$$243 - (3 \times 55.71) = 75.87$$

The upper position of the trend line is fixed by calculating:

$$243 + (3 \times 55.71) = 410.13$$

These two points can then be joined by a line and this will give a line of best fit to the data.

Probability control limits can now be calculated to discover the extent of error that the estimated trend could experience. This is done by using the formula:

$$\text{standard error} = \sqrt{\left[\frac{\Sigma y_{dev}^2 - b(\Sigma x_{dev} y_{dev})}{n - 2}\right]}$$

where n is the number of items, ie 7

$$\sqrt{\left[\frac{93143 - 55.71 (1560)}{7 - 2}\right]} = \sqrt{\left[\frac{93143 - 86907.6}{5}\right]}$$

$$= \sqrt{(1247)} = 35.31$$

1	2	3	4	5	6	7
X Months	y Sales in $000s	x dev of each quarter from assumed mean quarter	y dev from rounded sales average	x dev^2 col 3 squared	y dev^2 col 4 squared	x dev $\times$ y dev (col 3 $\times$ 4)
Jan	50	−3	−193	9	37,249	579
Feb	190	−2	−53	4	2,809	106
March	180	−1	−63	1	3,969	63
April	200	0	−43	0	1,849	0
May	300	1	+57	1	3,249	57
June	370	2	+127	4	16,129	254
July	410	3	+167	9	27,889	501
	7) 1700			28	93,143	1560
	242.8 Rounded to 243					

Table 15. *Analysis of monthly sales data to establish a trend line and to set probability confidence limits*

Later, in the section dealing with probability (page 188), measures of dispersion or the scatter of data about an arithmetic mean are considered. It is stated that one standard error either side of the arithmetic mean, on data having a normal frequency distribution, would include 68.3% of the values (see page 191). Further, two standard errors either side of the arithmetic mean would include 95.4% of the values. Considering the trend line in the last example, as the arithmetic mean and by calculating two standard errors ($2 \times 35.31 = 70.62$) either side of the trend line, it could be confidently predicted that in approximately 95 cases out of 100 the future sales will fall between these two limits when they are projected into the future. By taking actual sales and the trend shown in Table 15, confidence control limits of the trend can be fixed by taking the trend reading for January as 75.87 ± 70.62. Therefore,

$75.87 - 70.62 = 5.25$ is the lower limit line
$75.87 + 70.62 = 146.49$ is the upper limit line

Similarly, if the value of the line of best fit at July is taken, the control lines can be fixed accordingly:

$$410.13 \pm 70.62.$$

Therefore,

$410.13 - 70.62 = 339.51$ is the position of the lower limit
$410.13 + 70.62 = 480.75$ is the position of the upper limit

Probability confidence lines could then be drawn, superimposed on the sales curve and line of best fit and projected into the future as shown in Figure 31.

When setting probability confidence limits it would be possible to use three standard errors ± the trend line, but such limits are generally too wide to be of use. It is a question of balancing usefulness and convenience with the degree of accuracy required. The control limits of two standard errors are usually used in this type of calculation, because a 95% degree of accuracy is adequate: ie in only five cases in 100 is there the possibility that the actual sales volume achieved will fall outside these limits. The probability control lines will become further apart as the degree of fluctuation of sales increases.

In some forecasting situations the control lines are used as maximum and minimum levels for production scheduling, purchasing levels etc.

In Figure 31 the actual sales figures for August, September, October, November and December have been inserted and show that with the exception of November they are contained within the projected probability control limits. The November sales figure is marginally below the lower limit line (sales $550,000 as opposed to limit line value of $555,000), but based on past figures such an exception would be expected to occur only in five cases in 100, ie 95% probability of inclusion within the limits.

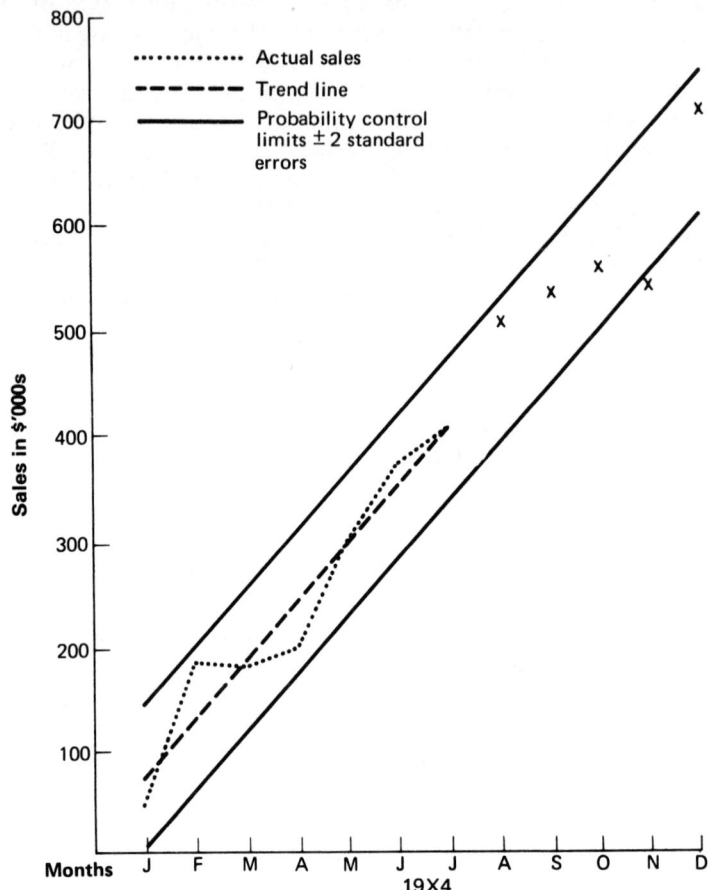

Figure 31. *A graph of monthly sales, a least squares trend line and confidence limits set 2 standard errors either side of the trend and projected into the future. The actual sales figures for later months are marked as X*

Seasonal adjustments to straight line trends

Seasonal adjustments of the projected trend line would be useful in the former case (Figure 29) and would make it a more effective forecasting tool. Sometimes when the probability confidence limits are set at only ± 1 standard error (that is with 68.3% confidence) they will be so wide apart, because of seasonal influences and non-

Objective Methods of Forecasting

1	2	3	4	5	6	7
Year and quarter	Sales in $000s	Trend	Sales away from the trend	Sales dev (as a % approx)	Mean quarterly seasonal dev as a % approx	Other random factors (as a %) (5 – 6)
19X3 2	34	31.86	+2.14	+6%	+4%	+2%
3	29	32.72	–3.72	–11%	–13%	+2%
4	35	33.58	+1.42	+4%	+2%	+2%
19X4 1	36	34.44	+1.56	+5%	+5.5%	–0.5%
2	37	35.3	+1.7	+5%	+4%	+1%
3	31	36.16	–5.16	–15%	–13%	–2%
4	37	37.02	–0.02	0%	+2%	–2%
19X5 1	40	37.88	+2.12	+6%	+5.5%	+0.5%
2	39	38.74	+0.26	+1%	+4%	–3%

Table 16. *Analysis of sales data by trend, mean seasonal deviation and random factors*

typical residual factors, that they will be of little use in making a sales forecast within *reasonable* probability limits. Therefore, it will be of great use to the forecaster when considering historic data to determine actual sales deviations away from the trend and then to analyze these deviations, determining how much is due to average seasonal factors, and how much is due to non-typical factors. Thus, it is possible to draw up a table indicating by how much, plus or minus, the actual sales figures are away from the trend. This is shown in Table 16.

In Table 16 columns 1, 2 and 3 show the quarterly sales figures, and also the trend line values as calculated in the previous example (Table 12). Column 4 denotes *actual* deviation values of sales away from the *appropriate trend* value. In column 5 these values have been converted into percentages *of the trend*. Column 6 shows mean quarterly seasonal deviation, the values of which were found by gathering all the percentage values for each quarter and finding the mean quarterly seasonal average, as in Table 17.

Year	Quarters			
	1st	2nd	3rd	4th
19X4	–	+ 6%	– 11%	+ 4%
19X4	+ 5%	+ 5%	– 15%	0%
19X5	+ 6%	+ 1%	–	–
	2) + 11%	3) + 12%	2) – 26%	2) + 4%
	+ 5.5%	+ 4%	– 13%	+ 2%

Table 17. *Showing the method for obtaining the mean quarterly seasonal average*

By repeating the averages shown in Table 17 for the appropriate quarters (column 6), they can be subtracted from the percentage sales deviation (column 5 in Table 16) to establish how much was due to average seasonal factors and how much was due to other random causes (column 7 in Table 16). It is particularly useful to establish these values as percentages rather than absolute values (although this could be done as well), because it permits more effective proportionate comparisons between periods. Although actual sales volume in one quarter might be down, the seasonal percentage value could still be correct in relation to other quarters' seasonal percentage values in the rest of the year. This is particularly so of luxury or semi-luxury items for which consumers may reduce their purchases if incomes fall, rather than staple or necessity items which will be the last to suffer a cut in demand. Further, there is often a need for a company to maintain its share of a market. Therefore, if the market is contracting, it is obviously wise to consider the percentage the company holds in two different periods rather than absolute amounts. The same applies to the percentage sales deviation, percentage mean quarterly average and other random factors as a percentage. It becomes possible to compare these values *of the trend* no matter what the basic absolute values happen to be.

The quarterly seasonal percentage values are also of use in further predictions of sales where the probability control limits (± 2 seasonal deviations) are rather wide because of seasonal fluctuations. For example, it is possible to convert the mean quarterly percentages, + 5.5%, +4%, −13%, +2% (Table 17) into their relationship to the trend. If the trend line is considered as 100%, then the 1st quarter seasonal percentage being + 5.5% can be read as 105.5% of the trend line value. The 2nd quarter seasonal percentage being +4% can, therefore, be read as 104%; the 3rd quarter seasonal percentage being − 13% can be read as 87% of the trend line (ie 100% − 13%); and the 4th quarter seasonal percentage being +2% can be read as 102% the trend line. This is shown graphically in Figure 32. Notice here that

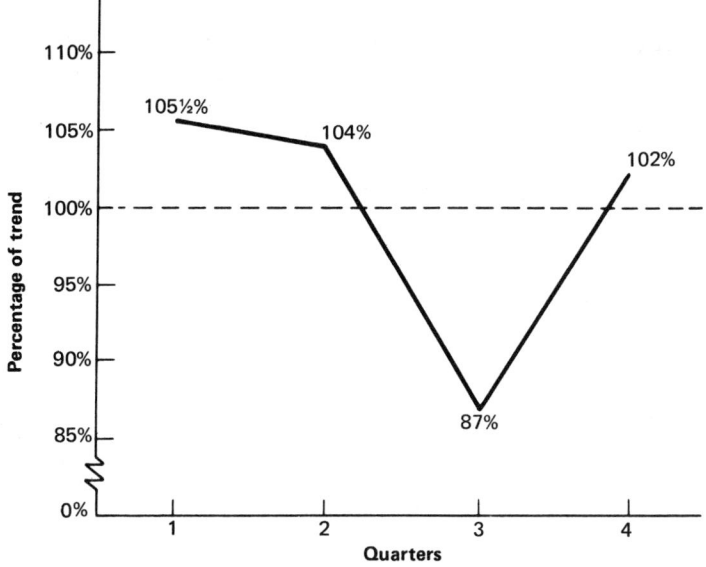

Figure 32. *Mean quarterly seasonal averages shown as percentages of a trend line*

the vertical axis is a percentage of trend; the trend being shown horizontally at 100%.

Taking the trend line as shown in Figure 28 and projecting it into the 3rd and 4th quarters of 19X5 and on to the 1st and 2nd quarters of 19X6, it is then possible to seasonally adjust and plot estimated sales by multiplying by the appropriate quarter seasonal percentages shown in Figure 32. The relationship of the actual sales, actual and projected trend line and the estimated seasonally adjusted sales is shown in Figure 33.

The seasonally adjusted projected sales trend is calculated as shown in Table 18.

This method of seasonal adjustment can be applied to any method of straight line projection, eg moving averages shown later in Figures 55 and 56.

1 Year	2 Quarter	3 Projected trend reading	4 Quarterly seasonal percentage	5 Seasonally adjusted sales trend (3 × 4)
19X5	3	38.75	87	33.7
	4	40.6	102	41.4
19X6	1	41.5	105.5	43.8
	2	42.5	104	44.2
	3	43.25	87	37.6

Table 18. *Calculation of seasonally adjusted trend line*

Least squares method using non-time-constrained data

In the section on correlation and regression analysis (page 154), a least squares regression line was fitted to a scatter diagram (Figure 26, Line A-B). On the vertical axis was the dependent variable, ie 'Sales of Product A' and on the horizontal axis was the independent variable 'Economic Indicator'; thus the data was not of the time series type as in the examples of the least squares method used so far. The absence of the time factor means that the device of the 'assumed mean quarter' or other time period used to calculate the regression line in the examples so far cannot be used.

The method that should be used in such a situation could be described as 'fitting a line of best fit' to a scatter diagram or the linear regression of Sales (y) on Economic Indicator (x) and could be calculated as follows (the data used is from Table 6).

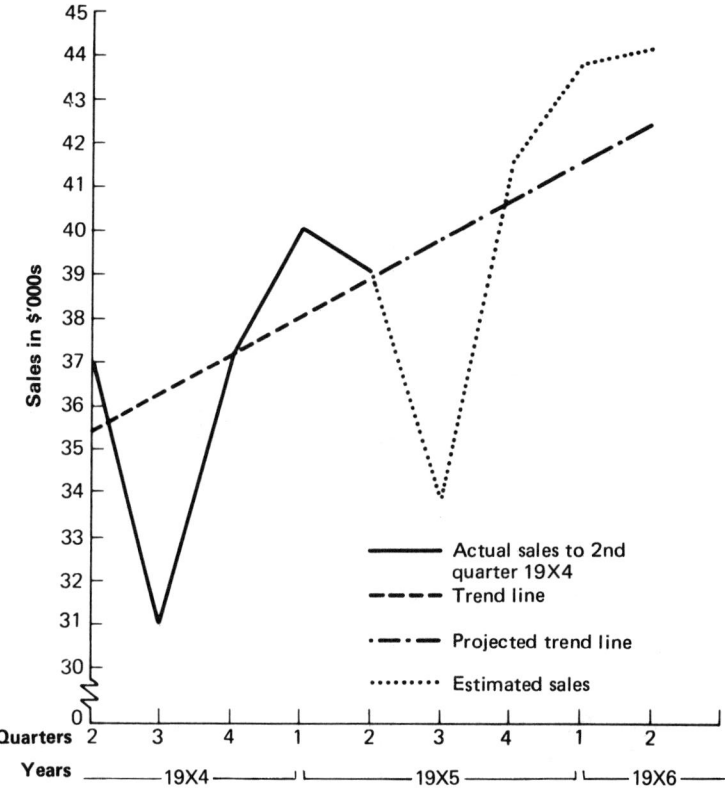

Figure 33. *The seasonally adjusted projected trend line after the mean quarterly seasonal averages have been applied*

The linear equation is:

$$\hat{y} = a + bx$$

where $\hat{y}$ is defined as the best *estimate* of sales corresponding to a given value of x (the Economic Indicator) and a and b are constants to be derived from the data. Using the method of least squares:

$$b = \frac{\Sigma(x_{\text{dev}} y_{\text{dev}})}{\Sigma x_{\text{dev}}^2} = \frac{3533.6}{29056} = 0.1216$$

and

$$a = \bar{y} - bx = 36.8 - (0.1216)(374)$$
$$= -8.7$$

The required equation of linear regression is accordingly:

$$\hat{y} = -8.7 + 0.1216x$$

Fitting the equation:

x	y	$-8.7 + 0.1216x$		$= \hat{y}$
322	25.7	− 8.7	+ 39.15	= 30.45
320	27.7	− 8.7	+ 38.90	= 30.20
311	30.0	− 8.7	+ 37.82	= 29.12
329	33.6	− 8.7	+ 40.00	= 31.30
358	36.9	− 8.7	+ 43.53	= 34.83
363	38.2	− 8.7	+ 44.14	= 35.44
379	39.6	− 8.7	+ 46.08	= 37.38
390	38.6	− 8.7	+ 47.42	= 38.72
430	42.7	− 8.7	+ 52.29	= 43.59
446	43.7	− 8.7	+ 54.23	= 45.53
466	48.1	− 8.7	+ 56.66	= 47.96
4214	404.8*	−95.7	+ 500.22	= 404.52*

* These two totals should agree, but there is a small error caused by the calculation process.

If the basic data is expressed graphically by plotting the relevant pairs, a scatter diagram is evolved. A line of best fit can then be added by picking a value of $\hat{x}$, eg 322, and identifying the corresponding value $\hat{y}$, ie 30.45, and plotting it; in the diagram that is shown as point A. It is then necessary to pick another value of x at the other end of the series, eg 430, together with its corresponding value of $\hat{y}$, ie 43.59, and again plotting it; in the diagram this is shown as point B. Points A and B are then joined, resulting in a line of best fit to the basic data (Figure 26).

It is worthwhile going forward to calculate the 'standard error of the regression'. First find the 'error sum of squares'. This is defined as

$$(1 - r^2)(\Sigma y_{\text{dev}}^2)$$
$$= (1 - 0.945^2)(485.66) = 51.77$$

The 'regression sum of squares' is accordingly

$$485.66 - 51.77 = 433.89$$

The 'analysis of variance' may be illustrated by the familiar

'Pythagoras' diagram as follows:

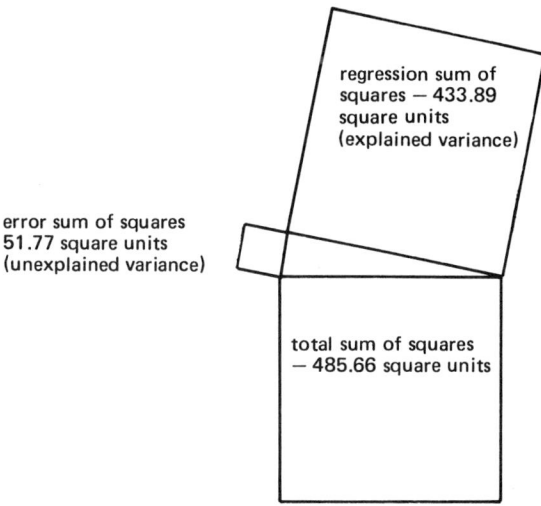

The standard error of the regression equation is then found as

$$\sqrt{\left[\frac{\text{error sum of squares}}{n-2}\right]} = \sqrt{\left[\frac{51.77}{11.2}\right]} = 2.4 \text{ units}$$

The standard error is used in the following way:

If x is, say, 430, the best estimate of y is 43.59 (see table on page 186). But this is an estimate only, subject to a standard error of 2.4 units (distributed normally) and following the convention of 2 standard errors, for a value of x of 430 the value of y lies within the limits of 43.59 plus and minus (2×2.4), ie between 38.79 and 48.39, with approximately 95% probability (the 19 in 20 chance).

Regression — summary

Simple regression

It will be seen from examples on pages 154-168 that simple regression is effected where a linear relationship of the form $y = a + bx$ is assumed and the parameters of a and b are constants (estimated). The factor x can be any variable including time (see page 171) which makes it a time series, or an economic indicator (see page 155) which makes it a causal model. On the other hand, y represents the variable to be forecast, eg sales, costs, profits, market share or some other factor where the outcome depends upon some variation in x.

Multiple regression

By using multiple regression the forecast is based not only on past values of the item being forecast, but on other variables that are thought to have a causal relationship (see multiple correlation on page 166). The multiple regression method determines the existence of some form of functional relationship between a dependent variable such as sales and combinations of a number of independent variables such as gross national product, total consumer expenditure, company advertising expenditure, retail sales, prices, price differentials between own product prices and those of competitors. Multiple regression can handle trend, seasonal or cyclical type data, and can provide confidence intervals, tests of significance and measures of best fit between the forecast values and the data.

Econometric models

Basically, the regression equations needed in the above methods are part of econometrics. An econometric model is a system of simultaneous regression equations which by their nature depend upon each other and therefore their parameters need to be estimated in a simultaneous manner. Thus an econometric model that a company might develop of its industry/market would include several equations to be solved simultaneously. Econometric models are primarily used for forecasting macro-economic series such as gross national product, total consumer expenditure, prices, investment, etc, but they can also be used effectively to forecast the sales of large organizations whose very size influences (to some extent), and is directly influenced by, the activity of a national economy.

The use of probability in forecasting

It is often advisable to calculate the statistical probability of any forecast being correct. But the use of probability linked with the device of sampling is a further statistical sales forecasting tool.

The logic of sampling follows from the law of statistical regularity, which states that a sample group chosen at random from a larger group will tend to have similar characteristics. Sampling is based upon (a) the principle of probability, determining the possible margin of error as to whether the sample is typical of the whole population; (b) the principle of random numbers, that is, to be representative of the whole population the sample must be unbiased and the randomness of the sample ensured; (c) the law of the inertia of large numbers, which shows that the larger the sample the greater the chance of cancelling out errors and minute changes, and thus the average group tends to remain the same.

The tendency to 'normal' distribution

In dealing with consumer populations it must be remembered that, although each individual has his or her own characteristics, perferences and dislikes, there will be, in a large population, a grouping around a central point indicating common opinions or behavior patterns, preferences and dislikes. The tendency for the distribution of certain data to be grouped around a central point gives a regular, bell-like, symmetrical pattern, or frequency distribution curve, that indicates what is termed a 'normal' distribution. In the ideal normal distribution situation the data either side of the central position varies from the actual mean or middle value by chance alone and, therefore, tails off equally on either side. For example, the heights of a group of men chosen at random tend towards the normal frequency curve pattern when set out by height values (Figure 34).

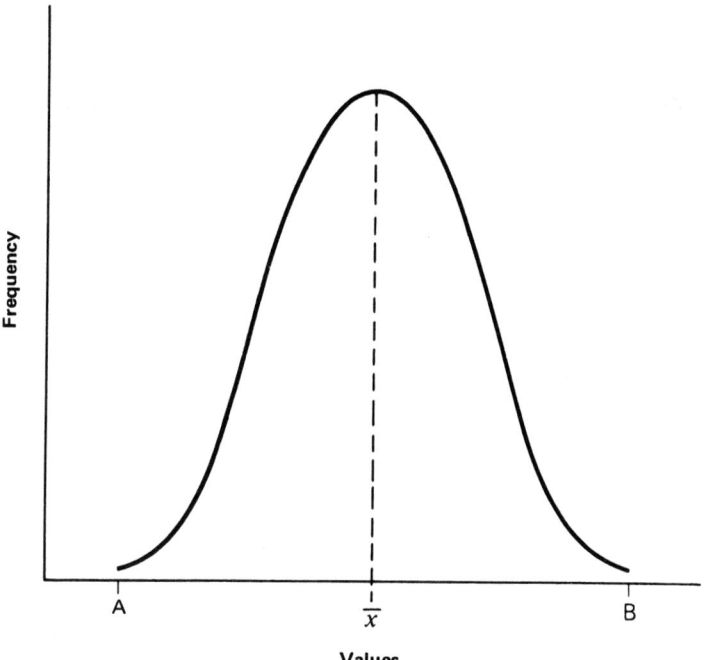

Figure 34. *A hypothetical normal distribution curve*

The vertical axis in Figure 34 shows the frequency at which values occur and on the horizontal axis the values themselves — height, or it could be weight, costs, opinions, survey data, etc. The point of central tendency, giving the peak of the curve, is a particular statistic that represents the middle or central value of a whole series of observations and consequently, due to the intensity or number of the values around this point, dominates the whole series. There are various measures of central tendency — the median, the mode, the geometric mean, the harmonic mean, but the one that is relevant in sampling is the *arithmetic* mean.

The arithmetic mean is the average value ($\bar{x}$) found by dividing the sum total of the values of items by the number of items. It is the most commonly used because it is simple to derive, it is relatively reproducible, it lends itself readily to further mathematical treatment, and represents the most simple arithmetic link between the total of a series of items and the number of items involved. It has the disadvantage that it can be influenced by non-typical extreme items, but in spite of this it is the most useful measure of central tendency for the examination of consumer populations and samples taken from them.

Returning to the normal frequency curve which is an ideal, theoretical distribution, a data series is often assumed to be of this pattern in examining markets when the overall distribution is not known but appears to be influenced by chance factors alone. Alternatively, this assumption may be made when the data series is derived from a number of similar sized but unconnected factors. In both cases the validity of the assumption may be assessed by contrasting the frequency distribution in question with the ideal normal frequency curve. It will be noted that except for the items that fall exactly on the mean ($\bar{x}$) a number of items in decreasing frequencies fall at distances either side, and thus deviate from the mean to form such a curve. On the graph these were contained within the limits of A-B. The scatter of these items about the mean is important — because of their make-up and frequency they may indicate why they are not average. It is also important when considering a market, to know how many persons in the selected population (ie potential customers) are not average and how often they are likely to occur.

The standard deviation and probability

The arithmetic mean has been termed 'a measure of central tendency'. A single statistic describing the scatter of the different items either side of the mean is termed 'the measure of dispersion'. The most commonly used measure of dispersion is the standard deviation indicated by the sign σ (sigma). A particularly useful feature of a normal distribution is that, if its arithmetic mean and the standard deviation are known, it is possible to predict the percentage of that distribution expected to fall between certain limits thereby enabling a forecast to be made (Figure 35).

Objective Methods of Forecasting

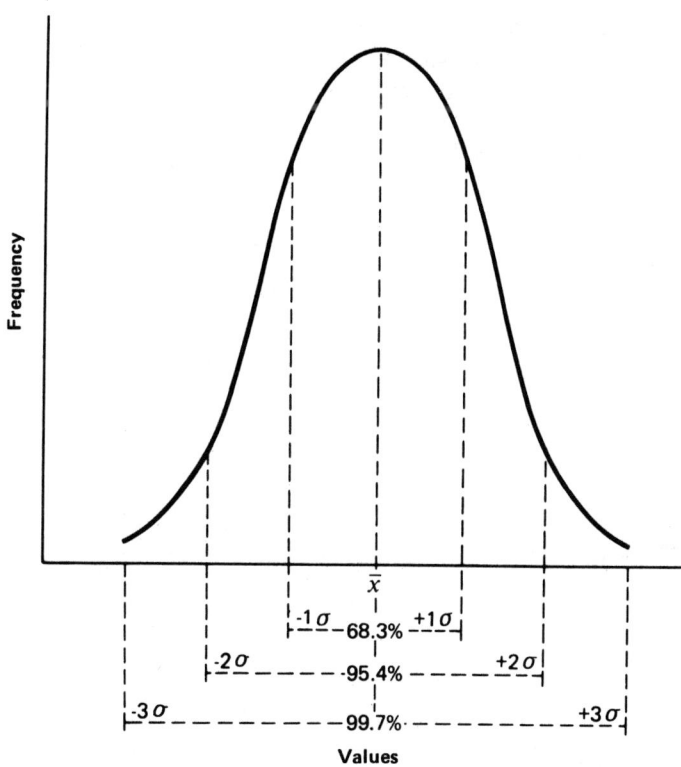

Figure 35. *A hypothetical normal distribution curve analyzed in terms of the dispersion of standard deviation around the mean*

From a normal distribution of the type shown in Figure 35, it can be seen that:

68.3% of the items lie within the range $\pm 1\sigma$ about the mean
95.4% of the items lie within the range $\pm 2\sigma$ about the mean
99.7% of the items lie within the range $\pm 3\sigma$ about the mean

Similarly for an actual sample, if it is truly representative of the whole population, items falling beyond $\pm 1\sigma$ would occur approximately five times in every 100; and items falling outside the $\pm 3\sigma$ limits only three times approximately in every 1,000 items, when projected to cover the whole statistical population.

If the forecaster can build up a sample that is representative of the whole statistical population or universe, it will be possible to make decisions and reach conclusions about the measurements (if it is a continuous series such as the heights of men or sizes of shirts), or the opinions, habits, behavior and reactions of the whole population.

Relevant frequency distributions

A number of samples chosen at random from a particular population will each have its own arithmetic mean, and, if plotted on the same graph, all the sample means will tend to have the normal frequency distribution described above. The three types of frequency distributions with which the examination of markets is concerned in statistical sampling have been summarized[1] as follows:

(a) Universe, the total of all measurements; that is, the total population. Since the frequency distribution of the universe is not known, it is approximated by a

(b) Random sample, which is a small-scale representation of the universe, with characteristics (such as mean, median, or standard deviation) approximately the same as those of the universe. If many random samples are drawn from a given universe, the frequency distribution of the means of all these samples would be a

(b) Distribution of sample means. This distribution tends to be normal, even though the other two are not normally distributed, and it has less dispersion than the other two.

The standard deviation indicates the spread or dispersion of the individual items in a distribution about their mean. The distribution of sample means has a standard deviation of its own which is different from the standard deviation of the universe and the standard deviation of an individual sample. In order to distinguish it from the others, this standard deviation of the sample means is called the standard error. The standard error is used to estimate the probabilities associated with inferences made concerning the universe. These probability statements are based on the known fixed relationships for a normal distribution.

Calculating the standard deviation

However, before considering the standard error in detail it would be useful to examine the standard deviation and its application. The standard deviation is a root-mean-square deviation, that is, it is found by taking the square root of the sum of the squares of the deviations from the mean divided by the number of items.

The standard deviation is given by the formula:

$$\sigma = \sqrt{\left[\frac{\Sigma (x - \bar{x})^2}{n}\right]}$$

where σ = standard deviation
Σ = summation sign (the sum total of)
x = value of the item
$\bar{x}$ = arithmetic mean
n = number of items

---

1. McNair, Brown, Leighton & England *Problems in Marketing* 2nd ed 1957 McGraw-Hill Book Co, USA.

The above formula is precise when the values for the whole population are available. However, when the standard deviation of the population has to be estimated from the frequencies of a sample, the direct application of this formula introduces a bias; then the best estimate of the population standard deviation is derived by using $(n-1)$ as the divisor. Thus the formula would read:

$$\sigma = \sqrt{\left[\frac{\Sigma (x - \bar{x})^2}{n-1}\right]}$$

Where n is less than 30, n and not $n-1$ is used as the divisor. To give a simple example, supposing certain values (heights, sizes, etc), that for the sake of simplicity can be called 1, 2, 3, 4 and 5, were found to occur four times, eight times, 12 times, eight times and four times respectively in a given sample, the data for calculating the standard deviation would be found by setting up a table: Table 19.

x Values	f Frequency	$(x-\bar{x})$ Deviation from mean	$(x-\bar{x})^2$ Deviation squared	$f(x-\bar{x})^2$ Frequency multiplied by deviation squared
1	4	-2	4	16
2	8	-1	1	8
3	12	0		
4	8	1	1	8
5	4	2	4	16
5)15	36			$48 = \Sigma (x-\bar{x})^2$
$3 = \bar{x}$				

Table 19. *An analysis of data to permit the calculation of the standard deviation*

Using the data from Table 19:

$$\sigma = \sqrt{\left[\frac{\Sigma f(x-\bar{x})^2}{n-1}\right]} = \sqrt{\left[\frac{48}{36-1}\right]}$$

$$= \sqrt{\left[\frac{48}{35}\right]} = \sqrt{(1.371)} = 1.2 \text{ approx}$$

Market and Sales Forecasting

If the sample was representative of the population, it will be found that values falling outside the range $\pm 2\sigma$, in this case the arithmetic mean of $3 + (2 \times 1.2)$, ie outside the values of 0.6 and 5.4, are likely to occur only five times in every 100 values observed.

Such a statistical technique is of use in marketing research, forecasting and in marketing generally. It has many applications where the data to be processed is measured in units, lengths, costs, weights, or sizes, etc. For instance, it can be used in forecasting to decide how many of each size of a product to manufacture within a range. For example, it can be used in the manufacture of shirts, so that the range of sizes marketed and the numbers in each size will cover anticipated consumer demand. Further, it can be used in stock control to ensure that the correct proportions of a range of sizes are carried in stock. Also it can be used in complaints analysis and in connection with the expected life of a product in product development analysis, ie to make a prediction for the size of a replacement market, and in many other forecasting areas.

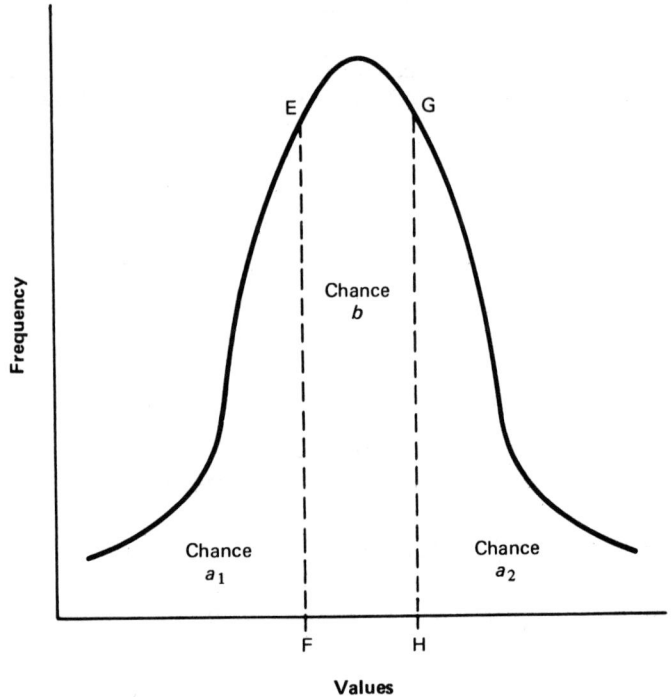

Figure 36. *A normal distribution curve showing the relationships between a_1, a_2, and b values*

The make-up of the normal distribution curve

The normal distribution curve is sometimes referred to as a probability curve because it is possible to calculate from it the probability of obtaining a given number of items within a specified 'values' range in an actual production.

In other words, the area under the whole of the actual frequency or probability curve is considered equal to 1 if working in decimal fractions (or 100% if using percentages), and it is possible to calculate for what probable fraction of the statistical population certain values occur. For example, in the case of a shirt manufacturer, it could be predicted how any of his potential customers would be catered for if he marketed only sizes 15½ to 16½. The technique is to calculate the fractions or parts of the area of the normal frequency curve between the stated limits.

It should be noted that the lines E-F and G-H in Figure 36 are movable inwards towards the mean or outwards away from it, according to the size of the area required. Further, it must be realized that as the lines E-F and G-H are movable, the more they move towards the center (the mean), the smaller chance b will become while chance a_1 and a_2 will become larger, simply because $b + a_1 + a_2 = 1$ or 100%. Normal frequency probability tables have been compiled to indicate the variations in the size of b, a_1, a_2 in relation to the number of standard deviations from the arithmetic mean (Table 22).

In Table 20 T = the number of standard deviations from the arithmetic mean. Chance b = the probability of a value falling between given limits (T standard deviations) either side of the arithmetic mean. Chance a = the probability of a value falling to the right or left of the mean and T standard deviations away or the probability of a value falling outside the chance b limits. It refers to only half the total chance a value as a_1 falls to the left of chance b, and a_2 to the right of it.

It was stated earlier that the measure of dispersion, ie the standard deviation, is measured along the horizontal axis (values). The column in Table 23, shown as T, represents the number of standard deviation from the arithmetic mean, and it should be noticed that parts of it can be considered, as well as whole standard deviations. The column 'Chance a' refers to the measurement of either chance a_1 or a_2 or beyond the number of standard deviations ($T \times \sigma$), away from the mean. The column 'Chance b' represents the probability of a value falling within the area b, ie between the two lines shown on the diagram (E-F and G-H).

With Table 20 the validity of some of the previous statements made can be checked. Previously it was stated that on a normal frequency curve there are, between ± 1 standard deviations away from the mean, 68.3% of the values (ie 34.15% to the left of the mean, and 34.15% of the values to the right of it). Consult the normal frequency

T	Chance a	Chance b
0.0	0.5000	0.0000
0.1	0.4602	0.0798
0.2	0.4207	0.1585
0.3	0.3821	0.2358
0.4	0.3446	0.3108
0.5	0.3085	0.3829
0.6	0.2743	0.4515
0.7	0.2420	0.5161
0.8	0.2119	0.5763
0.9	0.1841	0.6319
1.0	0.1587	0.6827
1.1	0.1357	0.7287
1.2	0.1151	0.7699
1.3	0.0968	0.8064
1.4	0.0808	0.8385
1.5	0.0668	0.8664
1.6	0.0548	0.8904
1.7	0.0446	0.9109
1.8	0.0359	0.9281
1.9	0.0287	0.9426
2.0	0.0228	0.9545
2.1	0.0179	0.9643
2.2	0.0139	0.9722
2.3	0.0107	0.9786
2.4	0.0082	0.9836
2.5	0.0062	0.9876
2.6	0.0047	0.9907
2.7	0.0035	0.9931
2.8	0.0026	0.9949
2.9	0.0019	0.9963
3.0	0.0013	0.9973
3.1	0.0010	0.9981
3.2	0.00069	0.99862
3.3	0.00048	0.99903
3.4	0.00034	0.99933
3.5	0.00023	0.99953
3.6	0.00016	0.99968
3.7	0.00011	0.99978
3.8	0.00007	0.99986
3.9	0.00005	0.99990

Table 20. *Table of normal probability*

Objective Methods of Forecasting

probability tables in column T, where $T = 1$ (ie 1 standard deviation ± the mean), and by reading across to column 'Chance b' the decimal fraction 0.6827; expressed as a percentage this becomes 68.27% and this figure rounded to one decimal place will give a value of 68.3%. Notice that chance b is relevant here (ie the central area of the curve) to show what percentage of the values occur between ± 1 standard deviation about the arithmetic mean.

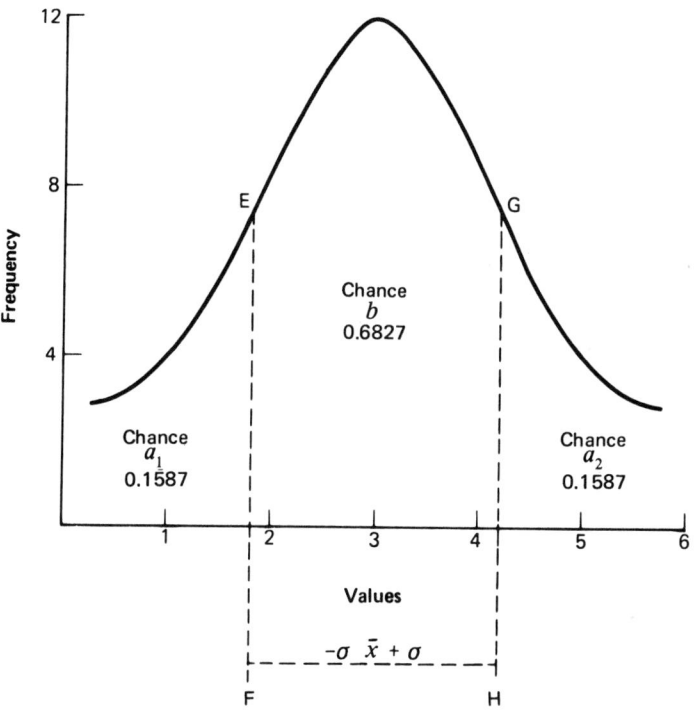

Figure 37. *A normal distribution curve with the chance b value considered as one standard deviation either side of the mean*

Consider the chance a_1, a_2 and b values in Figure 37 and using the data shown earlier in Table 19 which examined the method of finding the standard deviation, the arithmetic mean was the value 3, and a standard deviation of 1.2 was calculated. Measuring along the horizontal 1.2 either side of the mean, the vertical line E-F and G-H in Figure 36 can be inserted. The chance b reading at $T = 1$ is 0.6827, the chance a reading for chance a_1 is 0.1587, and again for chance a_2 0.1587. Therefore, if these values are added the total will equal 1:

Market and Sales Forecasting

$$0.6827$$
$$0.1587$$
$$0.1587$$
$$\overline{1.0001}$$

The odd 1/10,000th above 1 is due to the arithmetical make-up of the tables, and is justifiably small enough to round the overall value off and call it 1.

Forecasting demand using probability

A practical application of this technique could be seen if a possible forecasting problem of a shirt manufacturer is considered; it could apply, however, in any situation where a range of products is involved. The manufacturer may want to know the probability of demand for various sizes of shirts. Suppose he intends marketing a high quality and highly priced shirt. Because of the price, the demand for this type of shirt may be limited, but he has defined a group of potential customers (possibly by income group) to whom he knows this quality product will appeal, discovered possibly through a field survey. Suppose his potential market (total statistical population) is 100,000 men, and having taken a balanced sample of, say, 4,300 he discovers that the mean or average size is 16, and that there is a standard deviation of 0.5 (ie a ½-size in shirts). How many of his potential 100,000 customers will he cater for if he makes only the popular shirt sizes 15½, 16 and 16½? Thus, he will want to discover chance b, as these sizes occur immediately around the mean (16), one ½-size above the mean (16½), and one ½-size below the mean.

The formula required to answer this question is:

$$T = \frac{x}{\sigma}$$

where x is the value away from the arithmetic mean which is being considered

T and σ have already been defined (pages 188 and 195 respectively). Consider first size 16½:

$$T = \frac{16.5 - 16}{0.5} = \frac{0.5}{0.5} = 1$$

On the normal frequency tables it will be seen that where $T=1$, chance b is 0.6827. But sizes 16 to 16½ represent only half the area of the total chance b value (15½, 16, 16½), therefore 0.6827 ÷ 2 = 0.34135.

Similarly, size 15½ also represents 0.34135 by the same calculation, and by adding the two halves the total chance b value is 0.6827 or 68.27%.

It could be concluded that by making sizes 15½, 16 and 16½ the manufacturer will be catering for about 68% of the 100,000, ie 68,000 men.

Situations arise where the chance b values do not fall evenly either side of the mean as above (sizes 15½, 16 and 16½). For example, retaining the same mean size, 16, and the same standard deviation, 0.5, suppose the same shirt manufacturer wanted to know how many more of his potential 100,000 customers he would cater for if, in addition to sizes 15½, 16, 16½, he added size 17 to his marketing range.

Chance b for size 15½ to the mean size 16 has already been calculated as	0.34135
Chance b for the area covered by sizes 16, 16½ and 17 will be:	

$$T = \frac{17-16}{0.5} = \frac{1}{0.5} = 2$$

On the table where $T = 2$, chance $b = 0.9534$. This figure must be divided by 2 as 16 to 17 represents only ½ of the chance b value	0.47725
Total chance b for sizes 15½, 16, 16½ and 17	$\overline{0.81860}$
Thus the size of his potential market when he makes sizes 15½, 16, 16½ and 17 will be 81.06% of 100,000, in other words	81860 men
The size of his potential market (taken from the previous example) when he makes sizes 15½, 16, and 16½ will be 68.27% of 100,000	68270 men
The number of extra potential customers by adding size 17 to his range will be	$\overline{13590 \text{ men}}$

Throughout this and the previous example, four places of decimals have been used and exact conclusions made (eg 13,590 extra potential customers) and this may be seen to give this technique a degree of precision that it would not possess in practice. It has been done to illustrate the method and the use of probability tables, and in the last part of the above example it might be more practical to use rounded values, ie 82,000 minus 68,000 indicates that there will be about 14,000 additional potential customers when the manufacturer adds size 17 to his range. This rounding of values allows for the fact that the practical curve can only approximate to the exact figures for the ideal theoretical normal curve. A further limitation of these hypothetical examples is that neck sizes of shirts are near-normal in their statistical distribution or pattern, whereas many marketing variables are not and therefore need different treatment.

Market and Sales Forecasting 200

Forecasting replacement demand with probability

The use of this technique can be developed further. Consider the situation where a manufacturer is concerned with the life of his product. He may need to forecast a replacement demand, or forecast the frequency at which consumers purchase the product, or assess the size of stocks required (either his own or his wholesalers or retailers). He may also need to consider (in relation to complaints-analyses) whether the number of reports concerning the life duration of the product are within the limits he should expect. The life of a product is often a good selling point, and favorable statistics regarding a product's durability make suitable advertising and sales promotion material. Further, the manufacturer may be concerned with the life of his product in relation to his product development policy. He may be considering improving the quality and consequently the life of the product, or competition may be forcing him to look at the existing product range. The usefulness of the statistical techniques concerning probability, the normal frequency curve and the standard deviation, can be gauged from the following example.

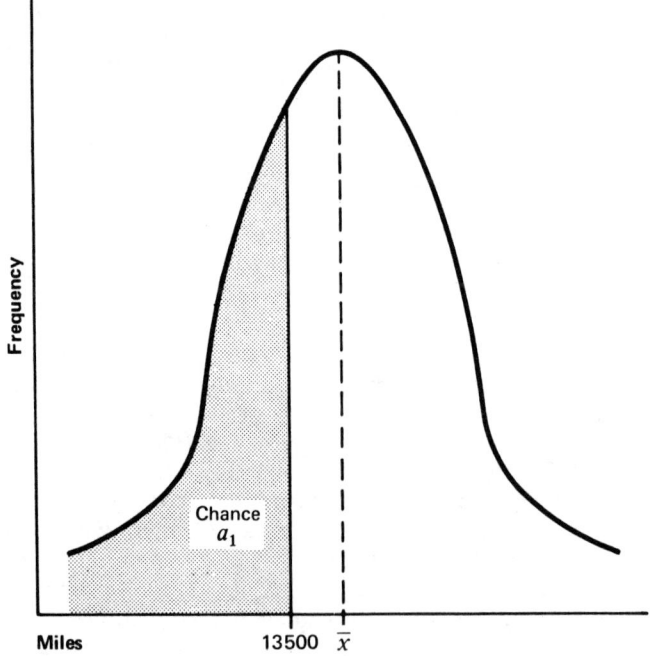

Figure 38. *Distribution curve showing the chance a_1 position on a normal distribution curve relating to the number of tires that will fail before 13,500 miles*

A company manufacturing and marketing car tires expects a mean life per tire of 15,000 miles with a standard deviation of 1,400 miles. Of a batch of 10,000 tires just produced how many can be expected to:

(a) fail before 13,500 miles?
(b) last beyond 17,000 miles?
(c) last between 14,000 and 16,200 miles?

(a) How many fail before 13,500 miles? This will represent a chance a_1 as indicated in Figure 38.

Using the formula $T = \frac{x}{\sigma}$, x is found by calculating how far 13,500 is away for the mean of 15,000, ie 1,500. The standard deviation has already been calculated as 1,400 miles. Therefore,

$$T = \frac{x}{\sigma} = \frac{1500}{1400} = 1.071$$

On consulting the normal frequency tables it can be seen that the value 1.071 does not appear in column T. However, as value 1.071 is between 1.0 and 1.1 it is possible to discover the difference between the two in terms of chance a values, and 0.071 of this figure can be determined.

Where $T = 1.10$ chance $a =$ (according to the tables)	0.1587
Where $T = 1.1$ chance $a =$	0.1357
By subtracting we find the difference	0.0230
Chance a value where $T = 1.0$ has already been found to be	0.1587
The chance a value of 0.071 where the difference between 1.0 and 1.1 is 0.0230, is 0.071 of 0.0230 =	0.0016
Subtract as chance a values are falling between 1.0 and 1.1, and as 1.071 is 0.071 away from 1.0 the answer is bound to be smaller	0.1571

It can be predicted that 0.1571 or 15.71% approximately of the batch of 10,000 tires, ie 1,571 tires, will fail before 13,500 miles.

(b) How many will last beyond 17,000 miles? This will be indicated as chance a_2 in Figure 39.

The value is calculated by determining how far 17,000 is away from the mean of 15,000, ie 2,000. Therefore,

$$T = \frac{x}{\sigma} = \frac{2000}{1400} = 1.428$$

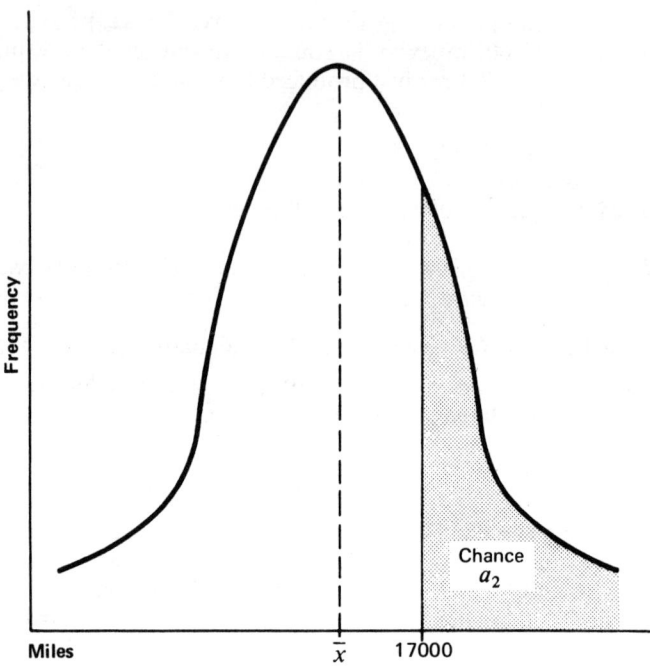

Figure 39. *Distribution curve showing the chance a_1 position on a normal distribution curve relating to the number of tires that could be expected to last beyond 17,000 miles*

Again this value does not appear in column T in the normal frequency probability tables. However, it is between 1.4 and 1.5:

Where $T = 1.4$, chance $a =$	0.0808
Where $T = 1.5$, chance $a =$	0.0668
Difference	0.0140

It has been shown that 1.4 has a chance a value of   0.0808

Further 0.028 of the difference 0.0140 is   0.0004

By subtraction (as the table values are falling) where $T = 1.428$, chance $a =$ 0.0804

It can be predicted that 0.0804 or 8.04% approximately of batch of 10,000 tires, ie roughly 804 tires, will last beyond 17,000 miles

(c) How many tires will last between 14,000 miles and 16,200?

To find this, chance b value is required, that is an area in the center of the normal frequency curve, as indicated in Figure 40. But it will be noticed here that the values 14,000 and 16,200 are spread unevenly either side of the mean of 15,000 miles; and therefore the process will be in three stages. First, find the chance b value for the area to the left of the mean (14,000 to 15,000) and halve it, as it represents the chance b value below the mean only; secondly, find the chance b value for the area to the right of the mean (15,000 to 16,200) and then halve it; and thirdly, add the two halves, so:

(i) $15000 - 14000 = 1,000$. Therefore where $T = \dfrac{x}{\sigma}$

$$T = \dfrac{1000}{1400} = 0.714.$$ This value is between 0.7 and 0.8

Where $T = 0.8$ chance $b = 0.5763$
Where $T = 0.7$ chance $b = 0.5161$
Difference $\overline{0.0602}$

It has been shown that $T = 7$
has a chance b value of 0.5161
Further, 0.014 of the difference 0.0602 will be 0.0008
This time add because chance b values are $\overline{}$
increasing between 0.7 and 0.8 0.5167

However, as the chance b value on one side of the mean only is required, this figure must be halved:

$$\dfrac{0.5169}{2} = 0.2584 \text{ or } 25.84\%$$

(ii) $16200 - 15000 = 1200$, Therefore where $T = \dfrac{x}{\sigma}$

$$T = \dfrac{1200}{1400} = 0.857$$

this value is between 0.8 and 0.9

Where $T = 0.9$ chance $b = 0.6319$
Where $T = 0.8$ chance $b = 0.5763$
Difference $\overline{0.0556}$

It has been shown that $T = 0.8$
has a chance b value of 0.5763
Further 0.057 of the difference 0.0556 will be 0.0031

Add because chance b values are increasing $\overline{}$
between 0.8 and 0.9 0.5794

However, as the chance b value on one side of the mean only is required, this figure must be halved.

$$\dfrac{0.5794}{2} = 0.2897 \text{ or } 28.97\%$$

(iii) Stage three is to add together the results of parts (i) and (ii) above, so:

(i) 25.84%
(ii) 28.97%
      ──────
      54.81%

It can predicted that 54.81% of the batch of 10,000 tires, ie approximately 5481 tires, will last between 14,000 and 16,200 miles.

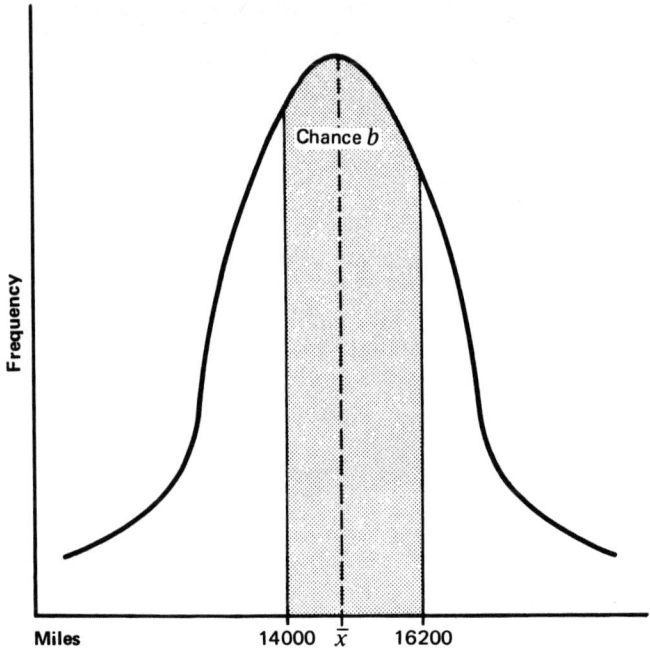

Figure 40. *Distribution curve showing the chance b position on a normal distribution curve relating to the number of tires that could be expected to last between 14,000 and 16,200 miles*

The use of standard error

The usefulness of the measure of dispersion, the standard deviation, has been illustrated in the foregoing examples, but its usefulness is limited for purposes of sampling in marketing research and market and sales forecasting. To extend the usefulness of the standard deviation, the earlier statement regarding the standard error must be considered. It was stated that a number of samples chosen at random from a particular population will each have its own arithmetic mean, and if these means are plotted on the same graph, they will tend to assume the shape and distribution of a normal frequency curve, and will have their own arithmetic mean. This averaging method removes the bias that may be given by extreme items to the arithmetic mean of only one random sample. Obviously, the greater the number of sample means, the more accurately it will reflect the characteristics of the statistical population as a whole. The standard error therefore is the standard deviation of the normal curve obtained from plotting the arithmetic means of a number of sample distributions. The formula used for the calculation of the standard error will depend upon the type of data being considered. One formula will be used for the type of data considered in the foregoing examples, heights of men, sizes of data considered in the foregoing examples, heights of men, sizes of shirts, mileage life of tires, costs, weights, etc, and will be called *measured or continuous data*. Another formula will be used when the data concerned relates to proportions such as opinions and answers to questions, or counts and observations, in field survey work, and this data will be called *enumerated or proportional data*.

Calculating the standard error from measured data

The formula for the standard error (SE) of the distribution of sample means is:

$$SE\ (m) = \frac{\sigma}{\sqrt{n}}$$

Where $SE\ (m)$ = the standard of the distribution of the sample means
σ = the standard deviation of all the items in the population
n = the size of the sample

Often the standard deviation of all the items in the population is not known and in such a case the standard deviation of the individual sample is used as the nearest estimate. Consider a forecasting situation where the height of men was important. Suppose from a large population of men a sample of 100 was taken, and their heights measured. An average height of 70 inches was calculated and the standard deviation was 5 inches.

$$SE\ (m) = \frac{\sigma}{\sqrt{n}} = \frac{5}{\sqrt{(100)}} = \frac{5}{10} = \frac{1}{2}\ \text{inch}$$

If other samples of 100 men and women are taken from *the same population*, their averages would tend to be normally distributed about the mean of the whole population with a standard error of ½ inch. It could be concluded, therefore, that the *sample mean* of 70 inches had a 68.3% chance (see Figure 37) of being within ± ½ inch (one standard error) of the *population mean* and a 68.3% chance that the population mean would be within the range of 69½ inches to 70½ inches (70 ± ½ inch). Further, there would be a 95.4% chance that the population mean would be within the range of 69 inches to 71 inches (ie ± 2 standard errors), and a 99.7% chance that it would be within the range 68½ inches to 71½ inches (ie ± 3 standard errors) or conversely it would be likely to fall outside these latter limits only three times in 1,000 samples.

Calculating the standard error from enumerated data

The previous formula would be of little use where the data to be processed represents a choice of two alternatives as opposed to a series of continuous measurements. Market research techniques are often necessary in forecasting where there is an absence of historic data or where projections from historic data need to be confirmed. For example, in field survey work using questionnaires or observational techniques the collected data will in many cases fit into one of two alternatives. For example, the answers to survey questions may be 'yes' or 'no'; 'I would buy it' or 'I would not buy it'; 'I use it' or 'I don't use it'; 'I use brand X' or 'I use other brands'; 'good' or 'bad', etc. Market research and forecasting is often concerned with proportions or percentages of populations and samples, where those interviewed answer one way or the other. Where the data can only be one of two alternatives, one would be designated as p and the other as q; p indicates the existence of a certain opinion, attribute, action, habit, or characteristics, etc, q indicates the absence of it. The probabilities of getting either answer can be estimated and certain calculations are based on these probability values. Probability can be expressed on a scale 0 to 1 (or 0% to 100%); 0 implying that the event is certain not to occur (or that all the answers to a survey question will be 'no'), and 1 (or 100%) implying that the event is certain to occur (or that all the answers will be 'yes'). Therefore, the formula $p + q = 1$ (or 100%) will apply where a certain number (p) of respondents answer in one way and the remainder (q) answer another way. For example, if the answer to an interviewer's question was either 'yes' or 'no', and 60% of his sample answered 'yes' (p) and 40% answered 'no' (q), 60% plus 40% would equal the total sample, therefore $p + q$ must always equal 1 or 100%.

It was stated earlier that the standard error is the standard deviation of the means of a number of samples, and obviously if the data was assembled from a number of different samples taken from *the same population*, it could not be expected that the proportions would be exactly the same in each case. However, suppose there was a need to forecast product acceptance. A product testing survey was carried out using a sample of 3,000 housewives and 1,800 said they would use the product being tested. Further, if many samples of

Objective Methods of Forecasting

	Percentage answering 'yes'	Frequency (no of times occurred)
mean =	63%	2
	62%	4
	61%	6
	60%	8
	59%	6
	58%	4
	57%	2

Table 21. *The distribution of sample results around their own mean*

3,000 were taken from the same population it would be found that the percentage of the sample answering 'yes' would fluctuate, and the data could be listed as in Table 21.

If the data in Table 21 were plotted on a graph it would be found that it would approximate to the pattern of the normal frequency distribution curve. In fact, the greater the number of times that the population was sampled, the more definite would become the pattern of the normal curve. But to carry out such a great number of samplings would cost much in time and money, and in any case is unnecessary, because by determining the standard error of the sample, the proportions of the sample can be projected to the population as a whole within certain stated limits. It can be seen, therefore, that even when using proportions or percentages, the rules of normal frequency probability will apply because, in practice, random samples will tend to approximate to the normal frequency distribution curve. These rules can be used and applied to the individual case.

The standard error for enumerated or proportional data is given by the following formula:

$$SE\,(p) = \sqrt{\left[\frac{pq}{n}\right]}$$

where $SE\,(p)$ = the standard error of the proportion
p = the proportion of items indicating the existence of a certain opinion, attribute, action, habit, etc
q = the proportion of items where the above characteristics are absent

To illustrate this formula, take a simple situation where there is a total statistical population of 1,000 persons. The forecaster could be

207

interested in these particular people because they have a unique combination of characteristics (age, sex, status, income, etc) which possibly makes them potential customers for a company's product. On making up a representative sample of 180 and interviewing them, 30 answer 'yes' and 150 answer 'no' to a particular question on product use. How many persons in the total population could be expected to say 'yes' and what degree of error is likely?

$$SE(p) = \sqrt{\left[\frac{pq}{n}\right]} = \sqrt{\left[\frac{30 \times 150}{180}\right]} = \sqrt{(25)} = 5$$

If the extreme case is taken and 3 × standard error is calculated, so that it is possible to predict with confidence that in only three cases out of 1,000 will items fall outside these limits (see Figure 35), it will be found that 3 × standard error is 3 × 5 = 15. The number of persons in the sample of 180 who answered 'yes' was 30. As the sample is subject to fluctuation and bias, this must be allowed for by expressing the number as plus or minus 3 × standard error, ie 30 + 15. If 3 × standard error is considered in relation to the population it will be found:

$$\frac{1000 \text{ (ie size of population)}}{180 \text{ (ie size of sample)}} \times 15 \ (\text{ie } 3 \times SE) = 89$$

It could be predicted, therefore, that the number of people in the whole population saying 'yes' would be:

$$\frac{30}{180} \times 1000 = 167 \pm 89$$

Therefore, it could be expected that the number of persons in the population answering 'yes' to the question would be as high as 256 and as low as 78.

An application of the standard error in forecasting

Take a further example of a forecasting situation where a company is product testing a new toothpaste in an area where there are 50,000 housewives (the specialized statistical population). A random sample of 3,000 housewives is taken and they are given free samples which they are asked to use. Out of the sample, 1,800 housewives say they will buy the product. What is the smallest number of housewives in that area likely to buy the product?

$$SE(p) = \sqrt{\left[\frac{pq}{n}\right]} = \sqrt{\left[\frac{1800 \times 1200}{3000}\right]} = \sqrt{(720)} = 26.83$$

ie approximately 27

$$3 \times SE = 3 \times 27 = 81$$

This should be 'grossed up' to cover the whole statistical population, ie

$$\frac{50000 \text{ (ie total population)}}{3000 \text{ (ie sample)}} \times 81 = 1350$$

The value $3 \times SE$ in relation to the population would be:

$$\frac{1800}{3000} \times 50000 = 30000 \pm 1350$$

It therefore follows that it would be possible to say with 99.7% confidence that, providing basic conditions do not alter, the number of housewives likely to buy the product could be as high as 31,350 and as low as 28,650.

Occasions arise in marketing research and forecasting, due to psychological factors, when the results obtained in the last example might not be true, due to consumer bias in answering whether they would buy the toothpaste or not. This might well be due to a subconscious human reaction — having received a gift (the sample), they want to do something in return for their benefactor and so pronounce in favor of the product, but later have no intention of buying it. An unbiased method of testing must, therefore, be found. Further, it might also be desirable to compare the product with those of competitors. Both these points might well be satisfied by a 'blind test', where samples of the new product and those of competing companies are placed in blank containers and lettered for identification. Taking the same sample size as before, 3,000 housewives, it might be found that:

Sample coded X (a competitor's) preferred by 1,000 housewives.
Sample coded Y (our new product) preferred by 1,400 housewives.
Sample coded Z (a competitor's) preferred by 600 housewives.

In which case it would be necessary to calculate, as before, for each sample (there may be more than three), to obtain an unbiased judgement, to determine the strength of competition (at relatively little extra cost) and to obtain the potential maximum and minimum sales in each case, so:

$$X = \sqrt{\left[\frac{1000(Y+Z)}{3000}\right]}$$

$$Y = \sqrt{\left[\frac{1400(X+Z)}{3000}\right]}$$

Market and Sales Forecasting

$$Z = \sqrt{\left[\frac{600\,(X+Y)}{3000}\right]}$$

By carrying through the calculation as in the previous example, it would be possible to determine for each brand the highest and the lowest number of housewives likely to demand it.

Time series analysis and historical analogy

Examination of relationships of variables that make up sales data over a period of time is referred to as time series analysis. A good starting point for company sales forecasting is the plotting of sales data on a time series graph. By doing this the stark mass of figures assume a visual shape; seasonal patterns and general trends can be discerned and consequently deviation from them investigated. For example, the sales history of a particular product could be listed as in Table 22.

Month	19X1	19X2	19X3	10X4
January	120	140	80	50
February	140	170	200	190
March	200	180	170	180
April	280	240	220	200
May	230	280	260	300
June	320	340	360	370
July	380	370	410	410
August	420	460	490	510
September	310	380	420	540
October	270	300	390	560
November	380	420	500	550
December	460	540	620	720

Table 22. *A four-year tabular history of the sales of product A in $000s*

When plotted on a time series graph, the data in Table 22 would assume the graphical shape shown in Figure 41. Unless something happens in the market to change the situation drastically, it could be assumed that a similar sales pattern to that in Figure 41 will emerge in 19X5 and a rough freehand forecast could be made on this alone. However, an examination of the graph will raise certain questions, the answers to which may influence the forecast. For example, why is

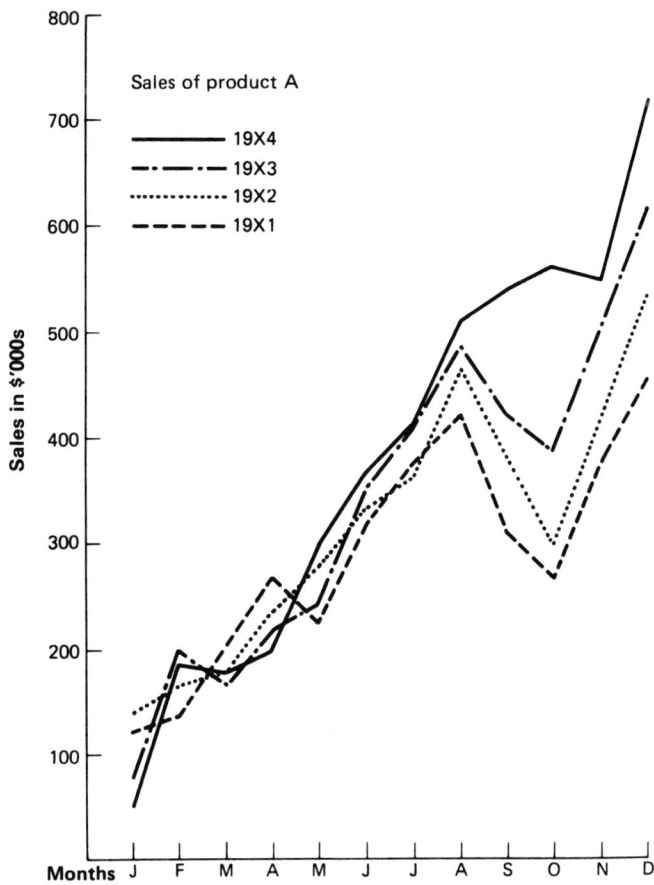

Figure 41. *A four-year graphical history of the sales of product A*

there a tendency over the last two years for the January values to decline but to be preceded by increased December sales figures? What happened to the 'usual' seasonal decline in sales in September and October 19X4? Is the new pattern for these months likely to become permanent? Investigation of unusual factors reveals important indicators for future sales periods.

In the above example, sets of monthly sales data for four years were superimposed, but a further method of graphically presenting time series data is sequentially, ie monthly, quarterly or yearly data can be presented 'end-on' as in Figure 42. Presentation in this way enables trends to be identified and extrapolated through a variety of techniques.

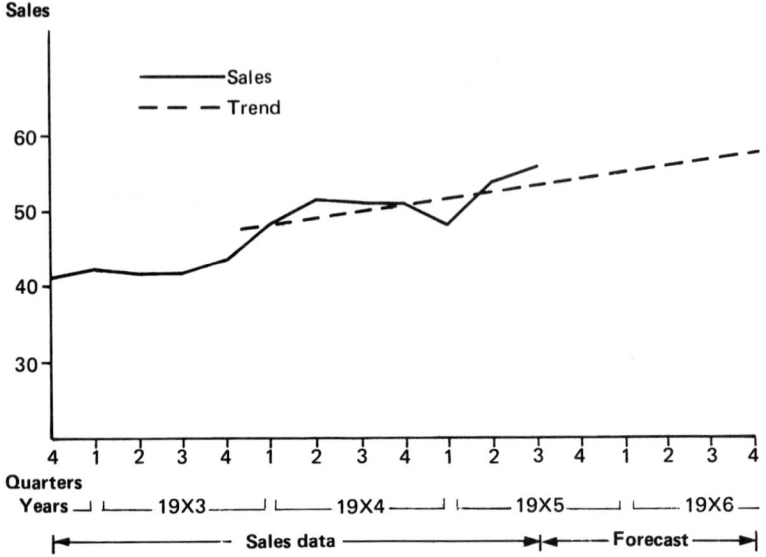

Figure 42. *Time series data presented sequentially together with straightline trend projection forecast*

The old cliché that history repeats itself is often very true in consumer/user demand, in the same sense that certain demand patterns for products and/or services tend to recur from time to time. Some markets are more stable than others and if a recurring demand pattern can be identified its use in forecasting is considerable. Even if a particular month's sales one year may be higher or lower than the same month the previous year, it is possible that its overall seasonal pattern can be relied upon.

To attempt to evolve a new forecast using the 'total sales' approach is one method of using time series data. Others take the form of breaking down the time series data into separate component parts. Then each component part is projected to give a forecast and then all these component forecasts are added in the projected forecast period to give a new 'total' forecast. In this way greater accuracy is often achieved because the influence of the separate individual component parts is allowed for.

One such method of analysis is shown in Figure 43 which 'decomposes' a time series into deseasonalized sales, trend and seasonal variations. Later in the analysis of time series by the moving average

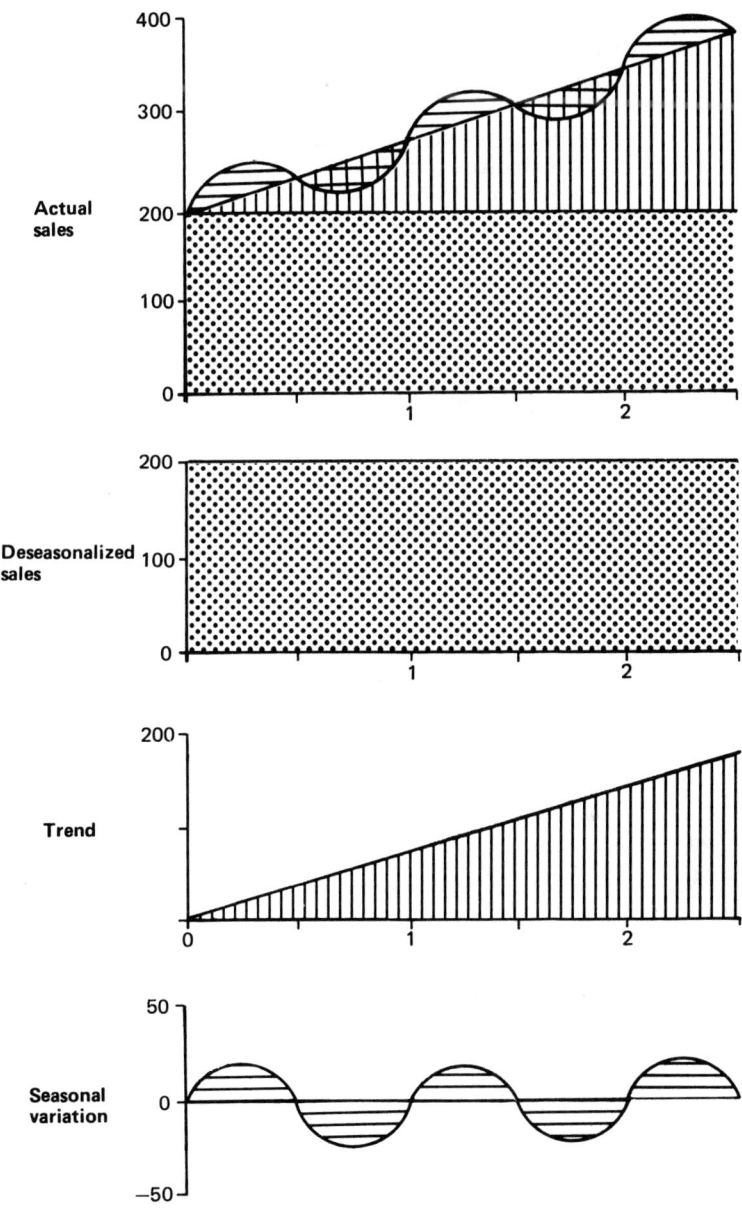

Figure 43. *The 'decomposition' of sales data into the component parts of seasonal variations, trend, deseasonalized sales and random variation*

method (page 242), a further component group is identified; it is that of 'random variations' or the erratic component. These values are relatively small parts of the sales total that cannot be attributed to any of the components mentioned above. They are caused through either the erratic effects on 'once only', non-typical situations or by the very small beginnings of changes in trend or seasonal patterns. Because of their randomness, it is impossible to show them as a pattern in Figure 43. However, they are often considered in time series analysis to permit more accurate forecasting of the various other components. In fact the degree of randomness within this time series data will often affect the forecaster's accuracy in prediction. As a general rule, accurate time series forecasting is possible where there is a low level of randomness and a good, stable, systematic pattern in the other components. The opposite is true where there exists a high degree of randomness (see Figure 44).

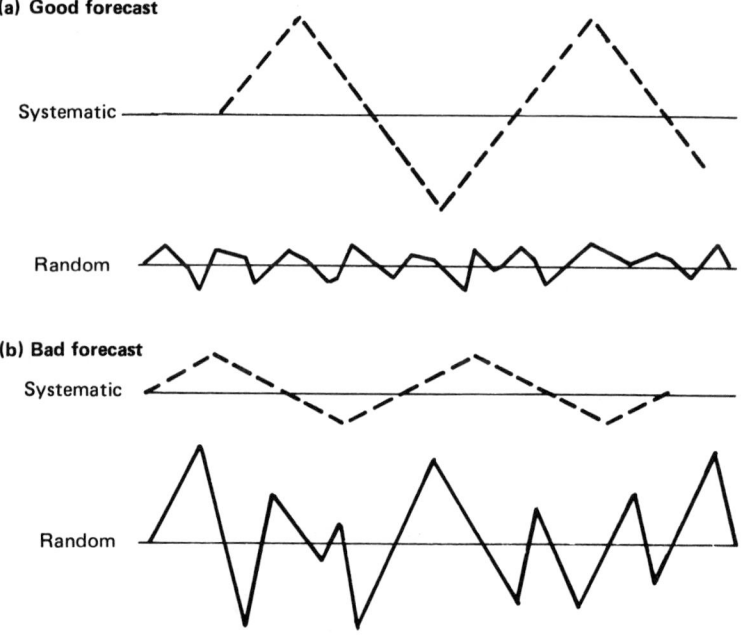

Figure 44. *The impact of the level of randomness on forecasts*

There is a further component part of sales data that is often identified; it is that of the cyclical pattern. This is sometimes referred to as the medium-term business cycle. There are many types of medium-term business cycles; these are demand and related patterns that appear to operate in cycles over a two to five year time span.

One often used for forecasting purposes is the inventory medium-term cycle; the general level of stocks in an industry builds up in one period and then tends to fall in another. For example, the usage of steel indicates a two to three year medium-term cycle. This cycle is found by recording *actual* stocks on a regular basis. Stock figures are obtained by relating tonnage shipments from the steel mills or imports, a plus factor, to the tonnage consumption by steel users, a minus factor. This latter data is obtained from published data on activity in steel-consuming industries. This method is often refined by adding a further factor regarding *normal* inventory and relates to the ideal tonnage of steel that 'consumers' would like to have in stock. This tonnage is roughly a supply of steel sufficient for three months output of manufactured units, and is determined by demand for the manufactured end product. Normal stocks, therefore, have no relationship to steel physically on hand, but are hypothetical; fluctuating with changes in the attitude of business men and in business conditions.

One machine tool company has found that the medium-term business cycle has revolved once every four to five years since the early 1950s in their particular part of the market. This company uses medium-term business cycle data not only for forecasting purposes, but also for the effective launching of new or improved products, which, after allowing for seasonal influences, are launched just before the up-swing of the medium-term cycle.

Compared with seasonal cycles, the medium-term business cycle fluctuates more irregularly in timing and swing (this varies also from industry to industry) but in some cases relatively accurate forecasting can be achieved through it. Whether the medium-term business cycle is easily identifiable or not, some allowance should be made for it in general forecasting.

More effective forecasting through segmentation

When using a time series graph to show the sales of a particular product, it is advisable to research the data in case it reflects the total demand of a multi-segment market. This is particularly necessary when unaccountable movements occur in the sales curve (an up-turn or down-turn), or where the 'normal' pattern is disrupted.

The importance of this can be seen in Figure 45. Obviously it will be easier to forecast in segment A because of the steady growth of sales over a number of periods. Because of the erratic nature of the total sales curve, it will be more difficult to make an effective forecast in total. By identifying the segments of the market and developing individual segment forecasts, a more accurate total forecast is likely to evolve.

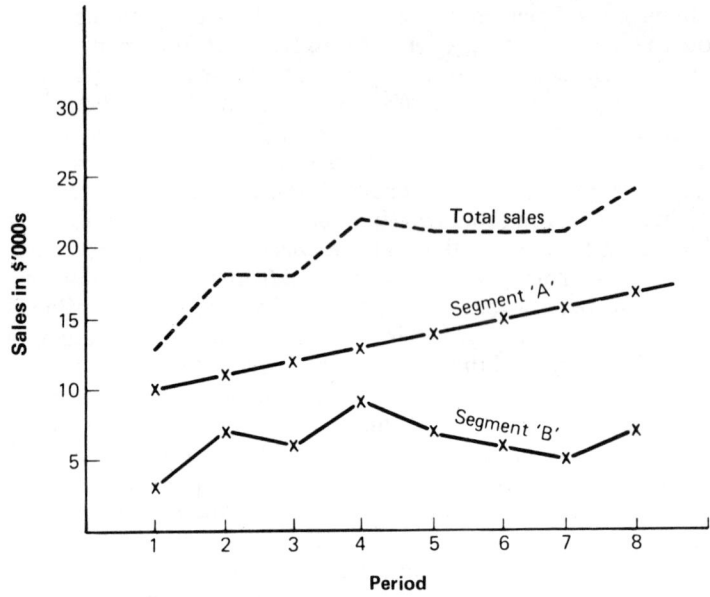

Figure 45. *A total sales curve analyzed in terms of individual market segments to permit more effective product forecasts*

Forecasting by percentage change

One simple method of projecting actual sales data into future sales periods is by the percentage change method, that is if the nature of data permits this. By taking known sales data over a number of past periods and determining the percentage increase or decrease over the previous data item, it may be possible to discern a progressive pattern. A simple example is shown in Table 23.

Sales period	Sales data	Percentage increase/decrease
1	40.0	—
2	42.0	+5%
3	44.5	+6%
4	47.5	+7%
5	51.3	+8%

Table 23. *Sales data and percentage increase/decrease*

In the absence of radical change taking place in the market, it would be logical to assume that a forecast of sales for period No 6 would be approximately 56, ie 51.3 + 9% of 51.3 = 55.917.

Forecasting using index numbers

A similar technique can be applied by converting actual values into index numbers, projecting the index numbers into the forecast period and then converting them back to actual values.

Sales period	Sales data	Index number
1	5020	100
2	5321	106
3		115
4 (forecast)	—	125

Table 24. *Sales data and index numbers*

The index number of 100 is attributed to the sales period No 1. The sales values of periods 2 and 3 are related to this base of 100 giving index numbers of 106 and 115. If the three values (100, 106, 115) are projected forward a forecast index number of 125 is obtained. If this value is related to 5020 = 100 the forecast value of 6275 is obtained.

Simple trend projection allowing for seasonal factors

One of the simplest ways of effectively projecting monthly/quarterly sales data which contains a seasonal element is to deseasonalize the past sales data, project forward the deseasonalized sales trend line into the forecast period and then reseasonalize the projected values. This method is based on the fact that it is often easier to project the straighter line of deseasonalized sales data than the actual sales values containing a seasonal element which makes its pattern more erratic.

The method of calculating an appropriate seasonal factor for each month is to find the monthly average for the last year by totalling all monthly sales data and dividing by 12. The seasonal factor for each month is then calculated, using last year's data, as follows:

$$\frac{\text{sales data for a particular month}}{\text{monthly average for the year}} \% = \frac{\text{January 60 units}}{\text{average 50 units}} \% = 120\%$$

This monthly seasonal factor is then used to deseasonalize last year's monthly sales data and after the deseasonalized data has been projected forward into the forecast period, the forecast values on this line are reseasonalized by multiplying them by the monthly seasonal factor.

A way of calculating a quarterly seasonal factor is shown in Table 17; it is applied to a projected line of best fit in Table 18. Quarterly sales data can be deseasonalized, extrapolated and reseasonalized easily by this method.

Another method is to calculate cumulative quarterly seasonal patterns. This is done by converting monthly sales into quarterly totals for each year and then considering these totals as a percentage of the total for the year (see Table 25).

Quarters	Months	19X2 Sales	%	19X3 Sales	%	19X4 Sales	%
1	Jan Feb Mar	790	16	750	14	720	13
2	Apr May June	1160	23	1140	22	1170	20
3	July Aug Sept	1510	30	1620	30	1760	30
4	Oct Nov Dec	1560	31	1810	34	2130	37
		5020	100	5320	100	5780	100

Table 25. *Calculations for quarterly seasonal sales patterns*

The percentages are then plotted on one of four graphs; one for each quarter as in Figure 46. They are then projected to the point of the forecast year, 19X5, and the projected percentage values read off. Therefore if the total sales forecast for 19X5 were 6358, the predicted trend of the quarterly seasonal pattern would be:

```
19X5 Quarter 1 predicted percentage 12% ie    763
19X5 Quarter 2 predicted percentage 18% ie   1144
19X5 Quarter 3 predicted percentage 30% ie   1908
19X5 Quarter 4 predicted percentage 40% ie   2543
                                             6358
```

Forecasting market share and competitor activity

Many sales forecasting techniques are based on the analysis and projection of trends, based on actual volume (units) and/or value (cash). A further method is to plot past market shares and project the trend; this method brings to light certain influential forecasting factors and underlying trends not revealed by other methods.

Market share should be viewed as a multi-dimensional concept, based on the variety of ways in which markets can be measured.

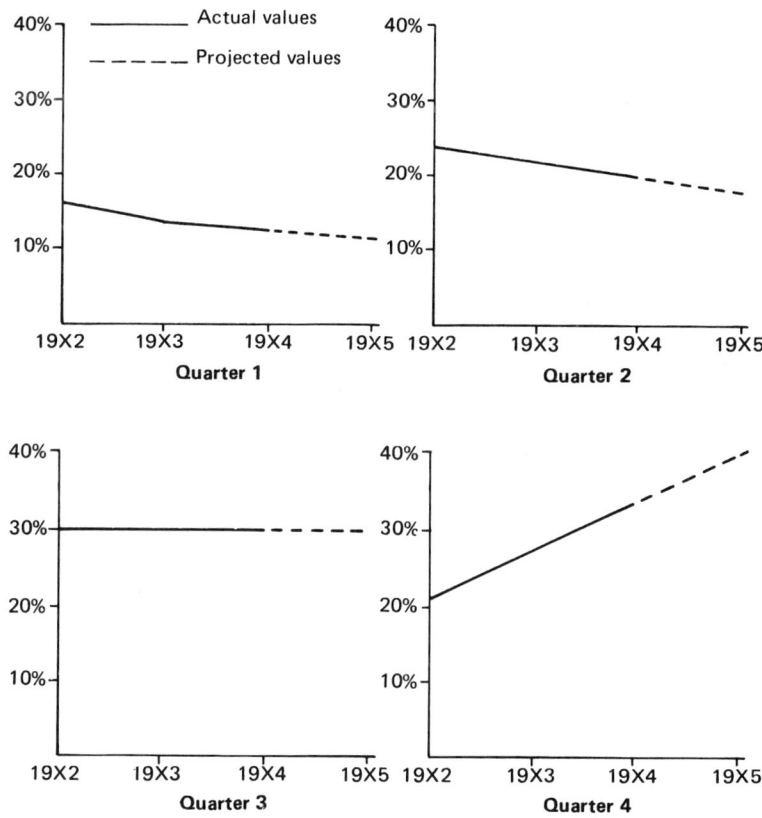

Figure 46. *Cumulative quarterly seasonal graphs — actual and projected values*

Therefore, the first stage is to identify relevant segments of markets, and then identify the company's share of each.

For example, the market for a consumer goods product can be measured and segmented by total volume, by product type, by total market including alternatives, total cash value, consumer profile, (ie age, sex, socio-economic group, occupation, urban/rural dwellers, etc), type of retail outlet, geographic area, size of product unit, etc.

A consumer durable market can be measured in terms of total volume, model type, sterling value, use by men and/or women, total market to include substitutes, consumer profile, buyers versus users (the gift market), type of retail outlet, socio-economic groupings, geographic areas, etc.

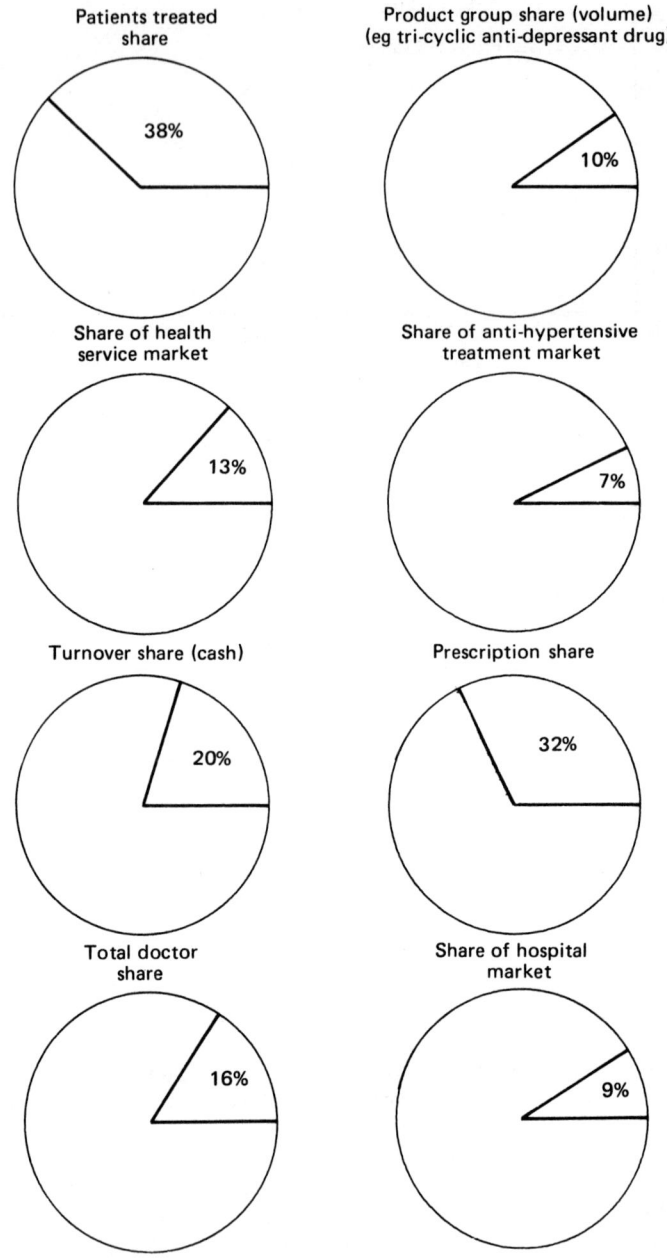

Figure 47. *Eight segments of a market for a pharmaceutical product*

An industrial product market can be measured by total volume, total market to include substitutes, total value, by industry profile (based on Standard Industrial Classification), by user type, geographic area, etc.

In each market segment above, a company's market share can be calculated, analyzed and projected forward as a forecast. If the same procedure is carried out for a number of segments, the speed and influence of various underlying forecasting factors can be identified and the forecast can be weighted accordingly. Also, as the 'residual' market share must be competitors' share, this is an ideal way of monitoring activities and projecting competitive trends.

An example is given in Figure 47 where the market for an antidepressant pharmaceutical product has been measured and segmented in eight different ways. Each of these market segments may be developing at different speeds, and by identifying the company's market share in each segment in recent history a projected forecast may be based on each. It will also be possible to weight certain market segments if it is thought that they have a greater influence on overall sales. Also, the speed of the company's growth/decline in a particular segmented market can be identified and allowed for not only in forecasting but in other aspects of market strategy.

For example, in Figure 47 a 20% of turnover share (cash) compared with a 32% share of the volume (prescription share) could suggest that the product was under-priced. Also a 16% total doctor share compared with a 38% patients' share could indicate that only a relatively small percentage of doctors have been 'converted', but that, once convinced, they become heavy prescribers, or that the medical condition needing this form of treatment is concentrated in certain geographic areas. Whatever the case, it has implications for marketing sales strategy.

If market shares of various market segments can be obtained over recent periods and graphed, a diagram such as Figure 48 will be obtained. The market is segmented by value (cash) and by volume (units) and the market shares are shown for all products in the particular product class. The important thing to recognize is that, no matter how large or small the market is in terms of value/volume, the total amount of product on the market from all suppliers will equal 100%; this percentage market share can be measured on the vertical axis at any point in time. After projections of own company or competitor shares, the forecast needs to be related to an overall product group forecast when converted back into value/volume absolute values.

Forecasting market share and competitor activity can best be done in the following sequence:

1. Determine objectives, what market segments to use, methods of analysis and projection.

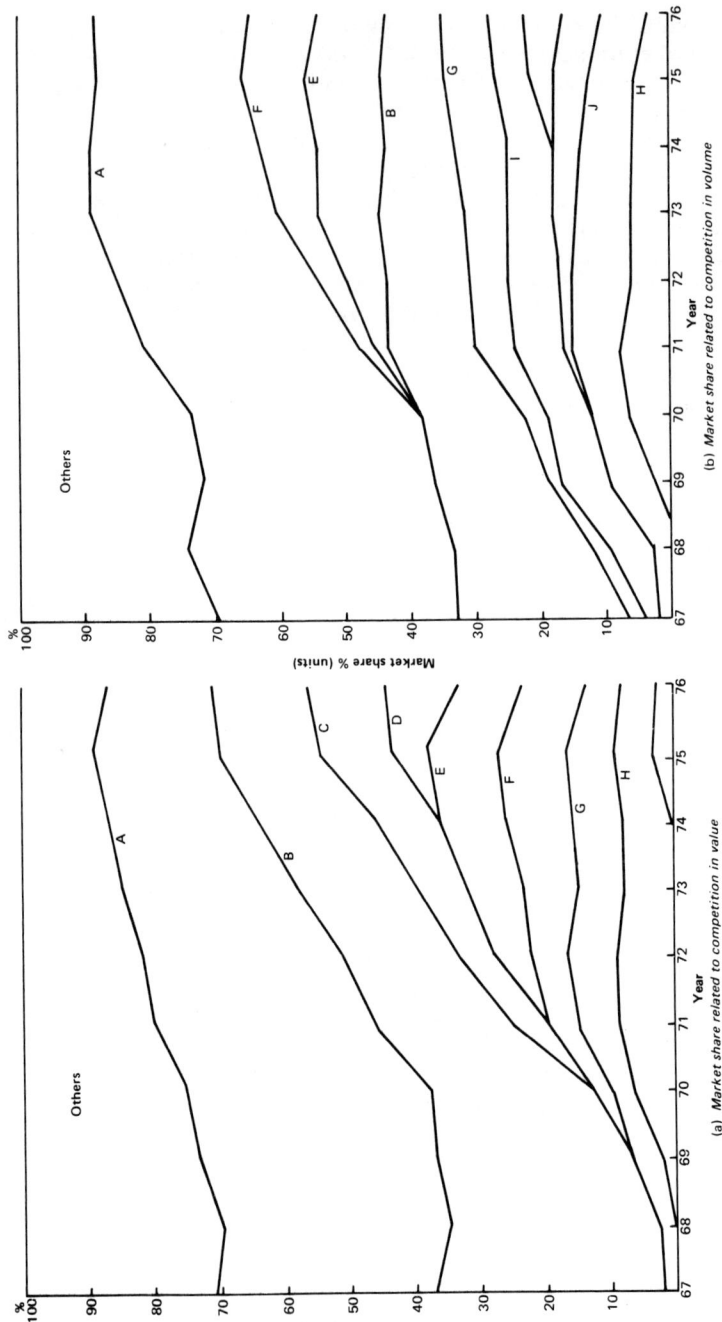

Figure 48. *Market share related to competition in value and volume*

2. Obtain data for a number of relevant market segments for the last five years sales periods, or for any period less than this, for which data is available.
3. Arrange in tabular and/or graph form the data from (2) above and project into the future. This gives a forecast for a number of the market segments defined in a particular way but these may need to be adjusted by the application of human judgement, experience, and intelligence.
4. Collect company sales figures for the last five years within the same market segments as above and relate sales by market segment to the total sales at that time, thereby obtaining a series of market shares. For each market segment project the trend of these market shares into the future. Again these may need adjusting by the application of human judgement, experience and intelligence.
5. Convert all predicted market share values back to actual values eg units, tons, $s etc and make a comparison of these values. Any adjustment to market strategy following market share analysis will need to be allowed for. When variances between them can be explained, use the various segment forecasts to build up a composite forecast.

Percentage take-off graphs

In some markets it is possible to discern a recurring seasonal demand pattern. Even if a particular period's sales one year may be higher or lower than the corresponding period the previous year, it is possible that the overall seasonal pattern can be relied upon.

It is possible, therefore, in some industries to evolve a reliable percentage take-off graph to enable a forecast to be used for production scheduling purposes. This is done by taking the average sales per period over the last three to four years and converting them into a cumulative percentage series as in Table 26. The cumulative percentage is the expression of the cumulative total as a percentage of the total average sales for the period, ie 15 is approximately 1.5% of 965.

From the data in Table 26, two graphs can be drawn. One to show the seasonal pattern, Figure 49, and the other from which can be read the percentage of total sales that can be expected to be sold by a particular time period, Figure 50. This latter percentage can then be applied to the *current* total forecast for the year.

If the sales shown are ex-factory sales, then production controllers can read from the graph, eg 40% of the *current* year's forecast must be produced by the 19th week of the year (ie 9½ bi-weekly periods). If the sales data represents retail sales then an appropriate lead time must be added to allow the product to pass through the channels of distribution. The percentage take-off graph is often used in

Bi-weekly period	Average sales per period over last 3 years $000s	Cumulative total	Cumulative percentage (rounded)
1	15	15	1.5%
2	20	35	3.5%
3	20	55	6.0%
4	20	75	8.0%
5	30	105	10.0%
6	50	155	16.0%
7	75	230	24.0%
8	70	300	31.0%
9	60	360	37.5%
10	50	410	42.5%
11	40	450	48.0%
12	35	485	50.5%
13	20	505	52.5%
14	10	515	53.5%
15	10	525	54.5%
16	15	540	56.0%
17	25	565	59.0%
18	40	605	63.0%
19	60	665	69.0%
20	75	740	77.0%
21	70	810	84.0%
22	65	875	91.0%
23	40	915	95.0%
24	25	940	98.0%
25	15	955	99.5%
26	10	965	100.0%

Table 26. *The analysis of data to permit the development of a percentage take-off graph*

forecasting production scheduling in men's clothing and footwear, but can be used in any situation where the seasonal pattern varies little from year to year.

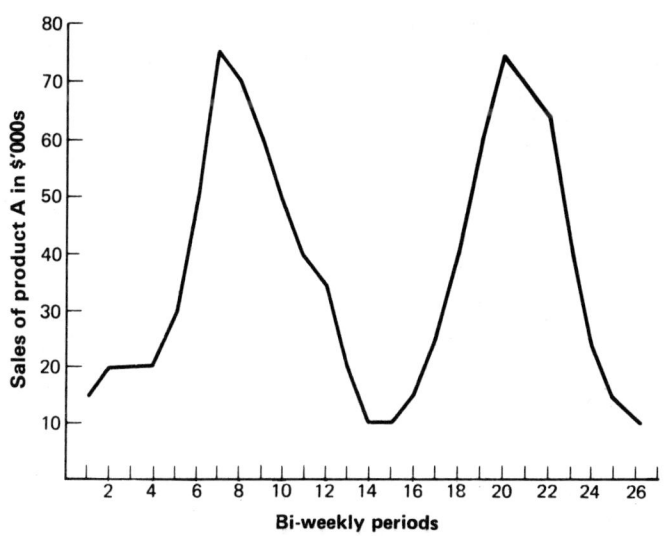

Figure 49. *A time series graph of sales of product A*

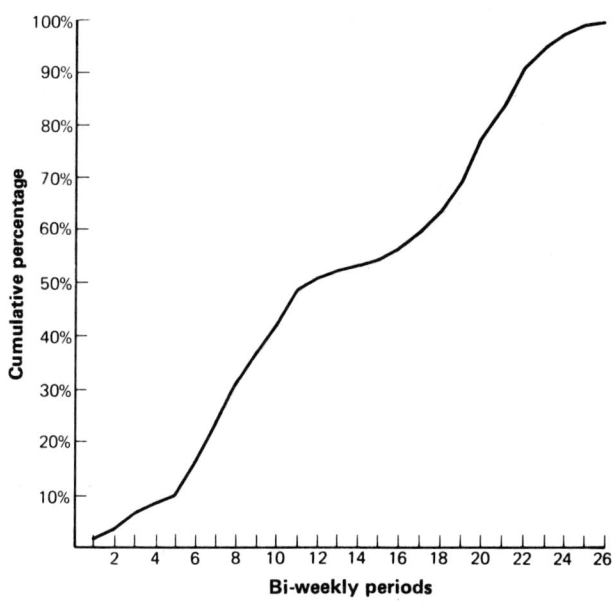

Figure 50. *Percentage take-off graph for sales of product A*

Further, if a reliable total forecast for a particular year can be obtained then the take-off graph will indicate the percentage of this figure that could be expected to be sold at various sales periods (biweekly periods in Figure 50).

Sometimes forecasters are required by management to forecast the sales for the next financial year well ahead of the commencement of that year. For example, where a forecast is required for a financial year commencing 1st January, the forecaster is asked to produce it six months earlier, perhaps in the previous August. The percentage take-off graph enables the forecaster to project sales data to the end of the current year so that with a 'total' sales figure prediction for the current year the forecaster can make a better forecast for the next financial year.

If at the end of the first 12 weeks of the current year, ie six bi-weekly periods on the horizontal axis (Figure 50), it is indicated on the vertical axis that 20% should be sold by the end of that period, then, as there are 5 × 20% = 100%, the actual sales achieved for the first 12 weeks in volume/value is multipled by 5 and this will provide the forecaster with a total forecast for the current year. Thus if the actual sales for the first 12 weeks is $10,000 then the total for the current year, using data in Figure 50, could be expected to be $50,000 (5 × $10,000).

Moving Annual Totals and Moving Quarterly Totals

An organization may record sales in value or volume terms either daily, weekly, monthly or quarterly. Sales thus recorded can show considerable variations and can mask trends. A longer interval tends to show a reduction in variation because time has a 'smoothing' effect. The benefit of the smoothing effect of longer periods can be obtained by identifying a suitable period (day, week, month, quarter, year) and using this on a continuous basis.

A moving total is obtained by adding the value for the most recent day, week, month, etc to the previous total covering the selected period and subtracting the value of the earliest day, week, month, etc, from the total. Alternatively, the difference between the oldest value and the most recent value can be added to or subtracted from the running total.

The example shown in Table 27 can be considered in three parts. The columns 19X3 to 19X6, sales input in $000's, represent monthly sales producing a graphical relationship as shown in Figure 51. Although peaks, troughs and certain peculiarities can be seen, the diagram does not highlight the underlying trend of sales.

The middle part of Table 27 shows the Moving Annual Total (MAT) for each month for the same years 19X3 to 19X6. It will be seen that the total sales for the year 19X3 amounted to 707. The Mov-

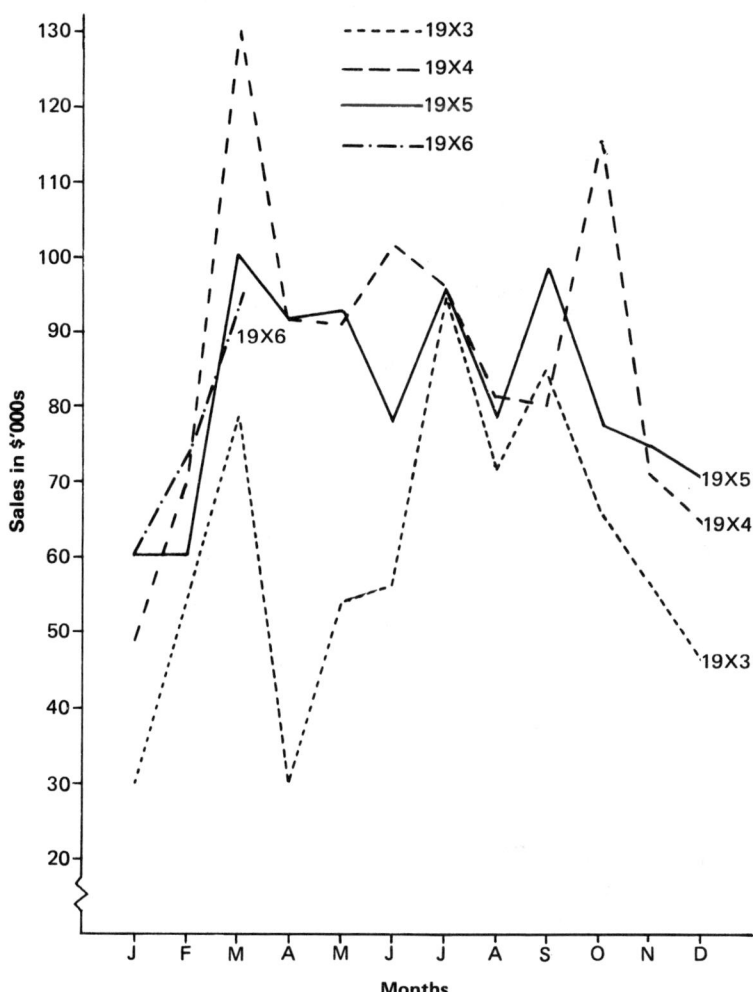

Figure 51. *Monthly sales superimposed annually*

ing Annual Total value for January 19X4 is found by adding the January 19X4 sales input value of 48 to 707 and subtracting the January 19X3 sales input value of 28, giving a new Moving Annual Total value for January 19X4 of 727. This process continues for February 19X4 MAT, ie 727 + 70 (Feb 19X4) − 53 (Feb 19X3) giving 744.

	Sales Input in $000's				Moving Annual Totals in $000's				Moving Quarterly Totals in $000's			
	19X3	19X4	19X5	19X6	19X3	19X4	19X5	19X6	19X3	19X4	19X5	19X6
January	28	48	60	60	–	727	1078	964	–	140	225	202
February	53	70	60	72	–	744	1068	976	–	154	214	201
March	78	129	100	97	–	795	1039	973	159	247	220	229
April	30	92	91	–	–	857	1038	–	161	291	251	–
May	54	90	91	–	–	893	1039	–	162	311	282	–
June	55	101	76	–	–	939	1014	–	139	283	258	–
July	95	96	95	–	–	940	1013	–	204	287	262	–
August	71	80	76	–	–	949	1009	–	221	277	247	–
September	85	79	98	–	–	993	987	–	251	255	269	–
October	66	116	75	–	–	993	987	–	222	275	249	–
November	56	71	73	–	–	1008	989	–	207	266	246	–
December	36	94	69	–	707	1066	964	–	158	281	217	–

Table 27. *Showing sales, Moving Annual and Quarterly Totals*

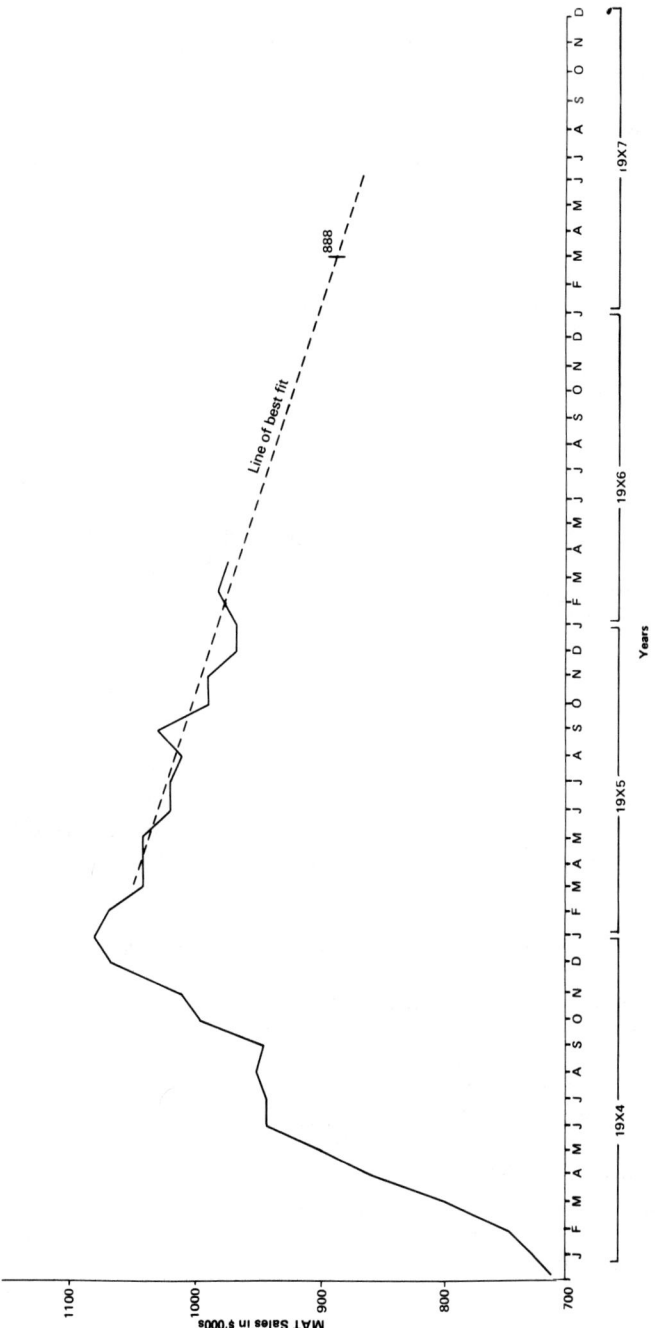

Figure 52. *Moving Annual Totals*

Market and Sales Forecasting

As the process suggests, it is a Moving Annual Total because it moves by incorporating a new month and ejecting the oldest value. In effect the MAT is a value which always contains 12 months sales history. Also by moving forward adding in the latest value and dropping the oldest value, it does not matter whether the year covers January to December or July to June — it will always contain all the seasonal variations in sales.

When all the MAT values have been calculated they can then be plotted on a graph as shown in Figure 52. The continuous line shows that an increasing sales trend line from December 19X3 has changed into a decreasing sales trend line from January 19X5.

When interpreting MAT charts it should be noted that a large upwards swing in one month, eg October 19X4, will cause a downward swing of the MAT sales curve the following year when a more normal level of sales occurs.

Normal seasonal variations in sales will not be indicated because they will be offset by the same seasonal high or low of the previous year.

In Figure 52 a line of best fit (see the least squares method, page 171), has been fitted to the last 13 months MAT values and then projected over the sales period to be predicted. Thus where the last sales input and MAT values are for March 19X6, a 12 months ahead MAT forecast will be 888. This value can be read straight off the projected line because at any point along it it will contain 12 months sales history.

The Moving Quarterly Totals are calculated in a similar way and are shown on the right hand side of Table 27. Being a Moving Quarterly Total the time interval is three months instead of the 12 months for MATs. Because MQT totals cover a shorter period they reflect seasonal changes in sales more readily, and consequently MQT lines will not smooth the sales variations to the same extent as MATs.

The calculations are simply that a total for three months is taken. January, February, March 19X3 values are 28 + 53 + 78 which gives the MQT value of 159 shown in that section against March 19X3. The April 19X3 value is then added and because this then contains four months' values the oldest monthly value is subtracted, ie 159 + 30 − 28, giving the new MQT for April 19X3 as 161. This process is continued for the next MQT value, ie 161 + 54 (May 19X3) − 53 (Feb 19X3), giving a new MQT value of 162.

When all the MQT values have been calculated they can be plotted on a graph as shown in Figure 53. A line of best fit (see the least squares method), ie the dotted line, has been fitted to the last 13 months' MQT values and then projected over the period to be predicted. Thus, where the last sales input and MQT values are for March 19X6 a forecast for four quarters (ie a one year forecast) can be made by

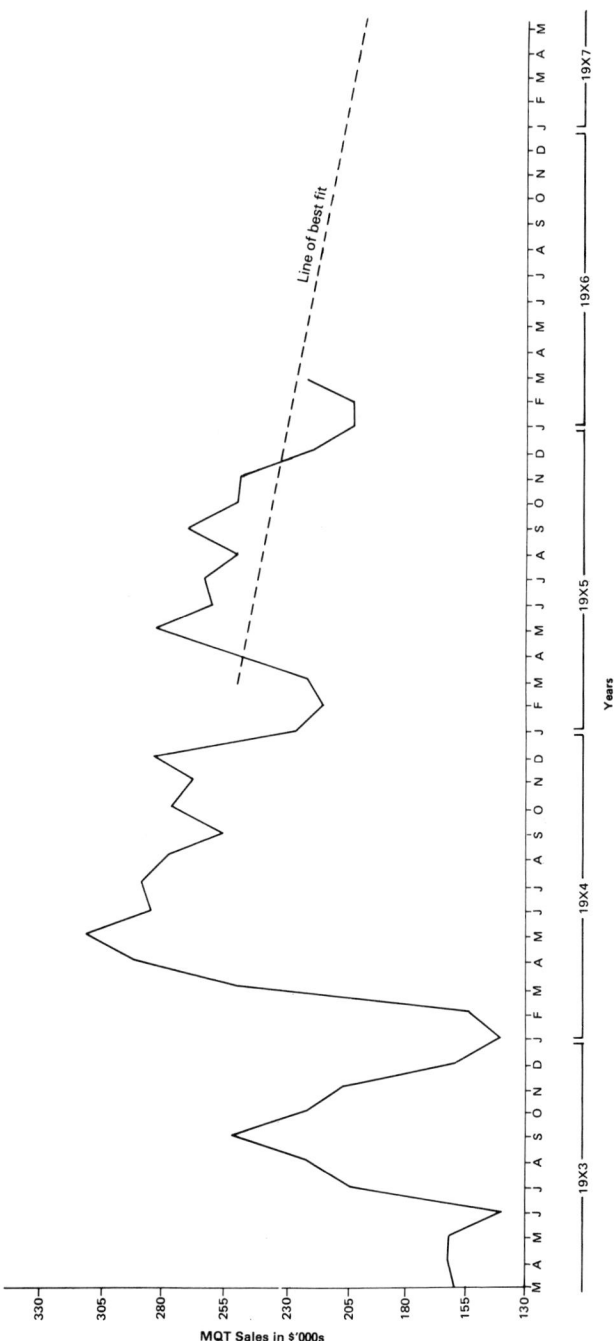

Figure 53. *Moving Quarterly Totals*

identifying the projected line values at June, September, December 19X6 and March 19X7.

```
June 19X6        223
September 19X6   215
December 19X6    210
March 19X7       207
                 ───
                 855 = forecast for year ending March 19X7
```

Conclusion

The extrapolation of the MAT values line indicates a forecast for the 12 months ending March 19X7 as 888. But this would mean an average of 222 for the MQT projected values (ie $4 \times 222 = 888$). This would appear to be difficult to achieve in view of the downwards trend and the fact that three of the last four MQT values before the predictions are below that value.

It would, therefore, appear that a forecast between the two values of 888 (MAT forecast) and 855 might be more appropriate — perhaps 870.

The Z chart

Earlier (page 226) it was suggested that often one of the forecaster's problems is that management requires a forecast for the next financial year well ahead of the commencement of that year, perhaps as much as six months ahead. One technique for projecting current sales to the end of the year to permit a more informed forecast to be made for next year is the percentage take-off graph; another is the Z chart. In fact the Z chart method of short-term forecasting is the combination of the percentage take-off graph (page 225) and the Moving Annual Total (page 229).

The name arises from the fact that the pattern on such a graph forms a rough letter Z. For example, in a situation where the sales volume figures for one product or product group for the first nine months of a particular year are available, it is possible, using the Z chart, to predict the total sales for the year, ie to make a forecast for the next three months. It is assumed that basic trading conditions do not alter, or alter on an anticipated course and that any underlying trends at present being experienced will continue. In addition to the monthly sales totals for the nine months of the current year, the monthly sales figures for the previous year are also required and are shown in Table 28.

From the data in Table 28, another table can be derived and is shown as Table 29.

The first column in Table 29 relates to actual sales; the second to the cumulative total which is found by adding each month's sales to

Month	Year	
	19X1 ($'s)	19X2 ($'s)
January	940	520
February	580	380
March	690	480
April	680	490
May	710	370
June	660	390
July	630	350
August	470	440
September	480	360
October	590	
November	450	
December	430	
Total sales 19X1	7310	

Table 28. *Monthly sales for the first nine months of a particular year together with the monthly sales for the previous year*

the total of preceding sales. Thus, January 520 plus February 380 produces the February cumulative total of 900; the March cumulative total is found by adding the March sales of 480 to the previous cumulative total of 900 and is, therefore, 1,380.

Month 19X2	Actual sales ($'s)	Cumulative total ($'s)	Moving Annual Total ($'s)
January	520	520	6890
February	380	900	6690
March	480	1380	6480
April	490	1870	6290
May	370	2240	5950
June	390	2630	5680
July	350	2980	5400
August	440	3420	5370
September	360	3780	5250

Table 29. *Processed monthly sales data, producing a cumulative total and Moving Annual Total*

The Moving Annual Total is found by adding the sales in the current month to the total of the previous 12 months and then subtracting the corresponding month for last year.

For example, the Moving Annual Total for 19X1 is 7,310 (see Table 28). Add to this the January 19X2 item 520 which totals 7,830, subtract the corresponding month last year, ie the January 19X1 item of 940 and the result is the January 19X2 Moving Annual Total, 6,890.

The Moving Annual Total is a particularly useful device in forecasting because it includes all the seasonal fluctuations in the last 12 months period irrespective of the month from which it is calculated. The year could start in June and end the next July and contain all the seasonal patterns.

The three groups of data, actual sales, cumulative totals and the Moving Annual Totals shown in Table 29 are then plotted on a graph as shown in Figure 54.

In Figure 54 the cumulative data line and the Moving Annual Total line are projected from their September positions (points A and B), along a line that continues their present trend to the end of the year where they meet. The 12 months accumulation of sales figures is bound to meet the Moving Annual Total as they represent different ways of obtaining the same total. In Figure 54 these lines meet at $4,800, indicating the total sales for the year and forming a simple and approximate method of short-term forecasting.

Often the cumulative data line and the Moving Annual Total line are so straight that projection can be effected by using a ruler. However, occasionally it is necessary to superimpose a line of best fit to enable a realistic projection to be made.

Further, there are occasions when the two projected lines do not converge at the 12 months point, either joining before or after that point. This can happen because the data available in, for example, September for the Moving Annual Total contains three months from the previous year and nine months from the current year. The three months data of last year may cause the MAT line to be higher or lower than the cumulative data would indicate because this latter data contains only the nine months relating to the current year. Where the two lines do not converge at the twelfth month point the method is to open or close the projected lines equally until they meet exactly at the twelfth month point thereby indicating a forecast value.

It could be argued that the Z chart is only of use when the MAT line and the cumulative data is over six months into a year. This is based on the need to have an adequate number of data items (perhaps six months) to fit a reliable line of best fit and project it to the end of the year. It would be difficult to obtain a reliable line of best fit on one, two or three pieces of data.

However, to ensure that this technique can be used all the year

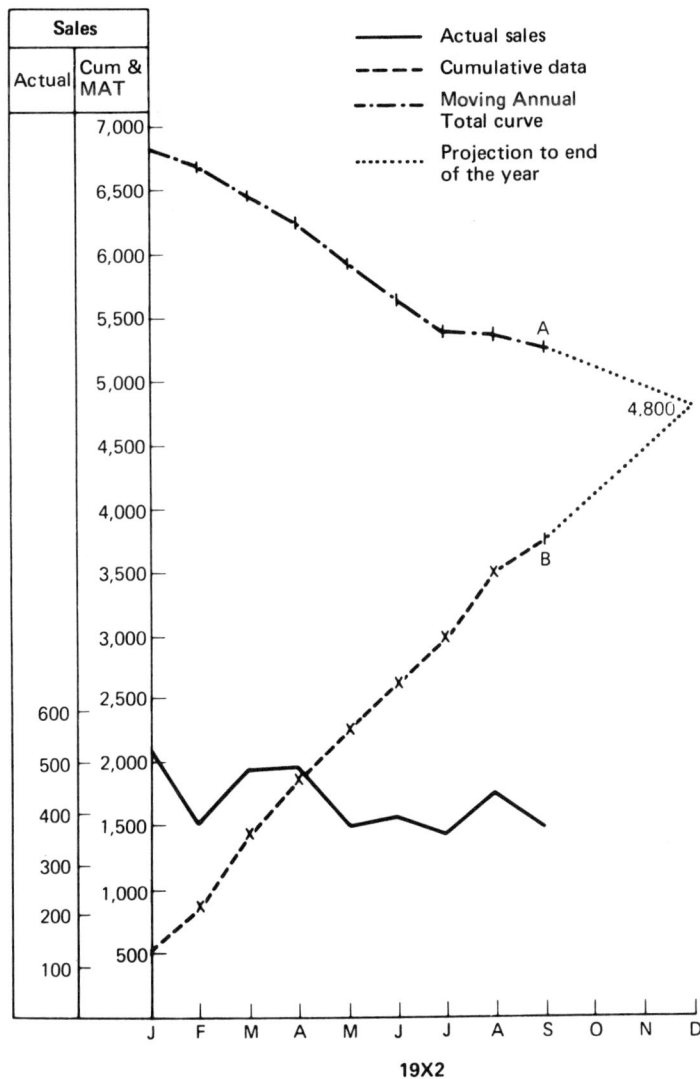

Figure 54. *A Z chart of monthly sales for 19X2*

round the concept of the 'rolling' Z chart has been brought into use. In Figure 54 the Z chart commenced in January with nine months data to September which was then projected to December. A month later it would be possible to carry out another three month projection by starting a new Z chart in February with data to October and projecting it to the end of January in the next year. As each month's sales

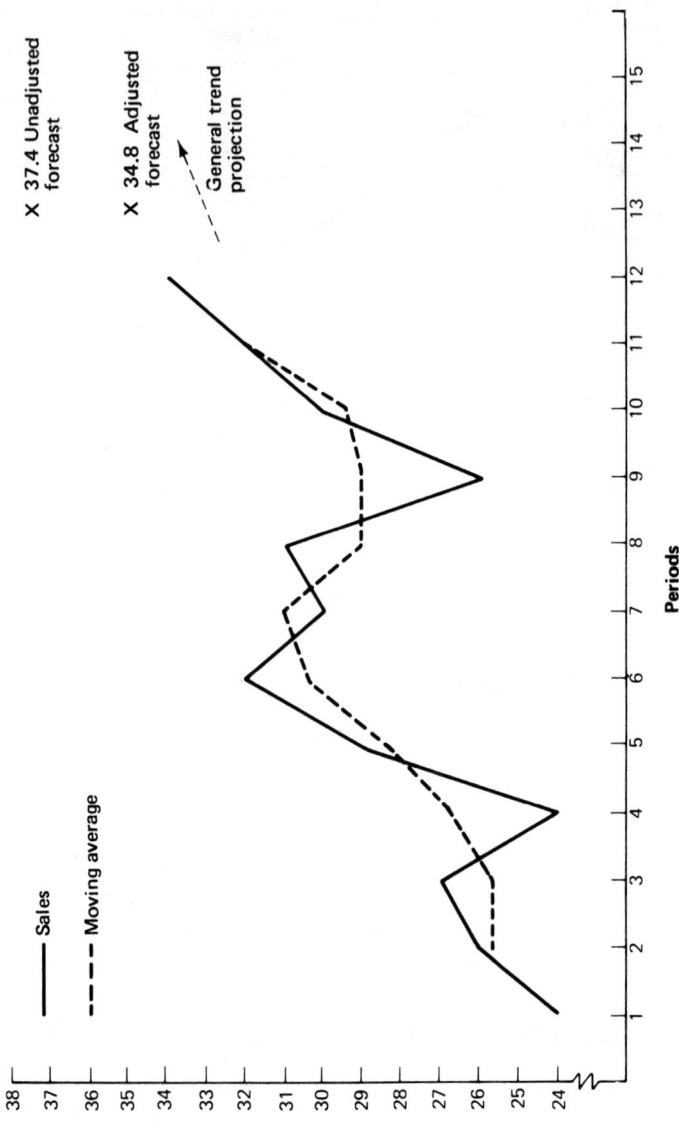

Figure 55. *A three period moving average and projection*

data became available, a new Z chart would be started one month later, thus giving the forecaster a continuous short term forecast.

The Z chart is suggested later (see page 318) as a means of monitoring forecasts and comparing the forecast Z chart value with the previously budgeted figure.

Moving averages

A simple method of forecasting is the use and projection of the moving average. This considers past sales data in tabular and/or graphical form and determines a trend which can be projected into the future.

The moving average method tends not to give a completely straight trend line but smoothes out any wide fluctuations in a sales data curve. For example, a three period moving average could be calculated from monthly sales data as shown in Table 30.

The moving total (column 3 in Table 30) was explained in calculations for the Z chart (see page 232), and the moving average (column 4 in Table 30) is calculated by dividing the moving total by the number of items it includes, in this case three periods $(24 + 26 + 27 = 77 \div 3 = 25.6)$. Trend differences (column 5 in Table 30) are obtained by considering the increase or decrease of the current moving average with the previous moving average.

1 Sales period	2 Sales in $000s	3 3 period moving total	4 3 period moving average	5 Trend difference from last period
1	24	—	—	—
2	26	77	25.6	—
3	27	77	25.6	0
4	24	80	26.6	+1.0
5	29	85	28.3	+1.7
6	32	91	30.3	+2
7	30	93	31.0	+0.7
8	31	87	29.0	−2
9	26	87	29.0	0
10	30	88	29.3	+0.3
11	32	96	32.0	+2.7
12	34	—	—	—
13	*	*	*	*

*Forecast required for this period

Table 30. *Calculation of a three period moving average and trend difference from sales data*

In Table 30 the forecast for period 13 can be obtained by taking the latest moving average and adding twice the value of the latest trend difference, ie

$$32 + (2 \times 2.7) = 37.4$$

Subtraction will be necessary if the trend difference is a negative value. It will be noticed that the moving average and trend difference columns terminate at item 11. It is necessary, therefore, to multiply the latest trend difference by 2 to overcome the lack of information against item 12.

Problems of non-typical items

A weakness in using moving averages lies in the effect of a non-typical item, eg the sales figure of $26,000 in period 9 of Table 30. Mechanical forecasting will not make an allowance for this relatively low value. Often, valuable underlying market information is revealed if, when comparing forecast with actual sales, it can be determined why this occurred. If a non-typical sales value occurred because of some unusual situation, eg a factory strike, temporary raw material shortage, etc, then this value should be adjusted to what would have been a 'normal' level to permit more realistic forecasts to be made in the future. If in Table 31 the low value for period 9 was adjusted to $30,000, the trend difference for the last period (period 12) would be smaller and the data would be as shown in Table 31. Following Table 31, the sales forecast for period 13 would then become

$$32 + (2 \times 1.4) = 34.8$$

Sometimes non-typical, non-recurring items inflate the moving average, and downward adjustments to values can be made to allow for this. A further disadvantage of the moving average method is found when the market situation changes radically and suddenly, eg

Sales period	Sales in $000's	3 period moving total	3 period moving average	Trend difference from last period
7	30	93	31.0	+0.7
8	31	91	30.3	−0.7
9	30 Adj	91	30.3	0
10	30	92	30.6	+0.3
11	32	96	32.0	+1.4
12	34			
13				

Table 31. *Re-calculation of the last part of Table 30 following the adjustment necessary due to a non-typical item*

sales increase by 50%. It will take a number of periods (depending on the base number used in the calculation) before the average comes within an acceptable range of actual sales figures again. It follows, therefore, that this method of forecasting is more effective with gradually increasing or gradually decreasing data.

If forecasts are consistently low or high, allowance should be made by adding or subtracting an appropriate percentage.

Moving average projection

If the moving average trend line is superimposed on the basic sales data, a trend can be discerned and projected into the future as in Figure 55. Notice the inclusion of the forecast for period 13—one adjusted to allow for the appearance of a non-typical item.

Broad trend projections as indicated in Figure 55 are useful for medium- and long-term forecasting. A short-term forecast for the next sales period is best calculated by the tabular method (shown in Tables 30 and 31), or by seasonally adjusting a straight-line projection, described earlier (see page 180).

Moving averages and cyclical trends

In the data shown in Table 30, a cyclical pattern appears to be emerging. In period 4 the upward pattern of the previous periods is reversed and sales dropped 11% from period 3. In period 9 the upward pattern of the previous periods has also reversed and sales dropped 13% from period 8. This type of cyclical reverse would, based on past data, be due to appear again around period 14, and a detailed examination of the underlying factors (seasonal or medium-term) would be necessary to determine the probability of this happening again.

While in the preceding example the moving average is calculated on a three period base, it could be calculated on any number of periods — months, quarters, years, etc, depending upon the data and the requirements of the forecast.

As a general rule a reasonably straight moving average line indicates a recurring cyclical pattern, ie values above the trend line compensate for similar total values below the line. In Figure 55 the fact that the moving average trend line is rather erratic indicates a very weak cyclical pattern on a three period basis.

However, if the same data were used to calculate a five period moving average it would produce Table 31 and Figure 56.

In Figure 56 the relative smoothness of the five period moving average line shows that a cyclical pattern exists, possibly coinciding with seasonal fluctuations or the medium-term business cycle found in many industries. It would be of greater use in forecasting if the straight line projection was adjusted to reflect the cyclical pattern.

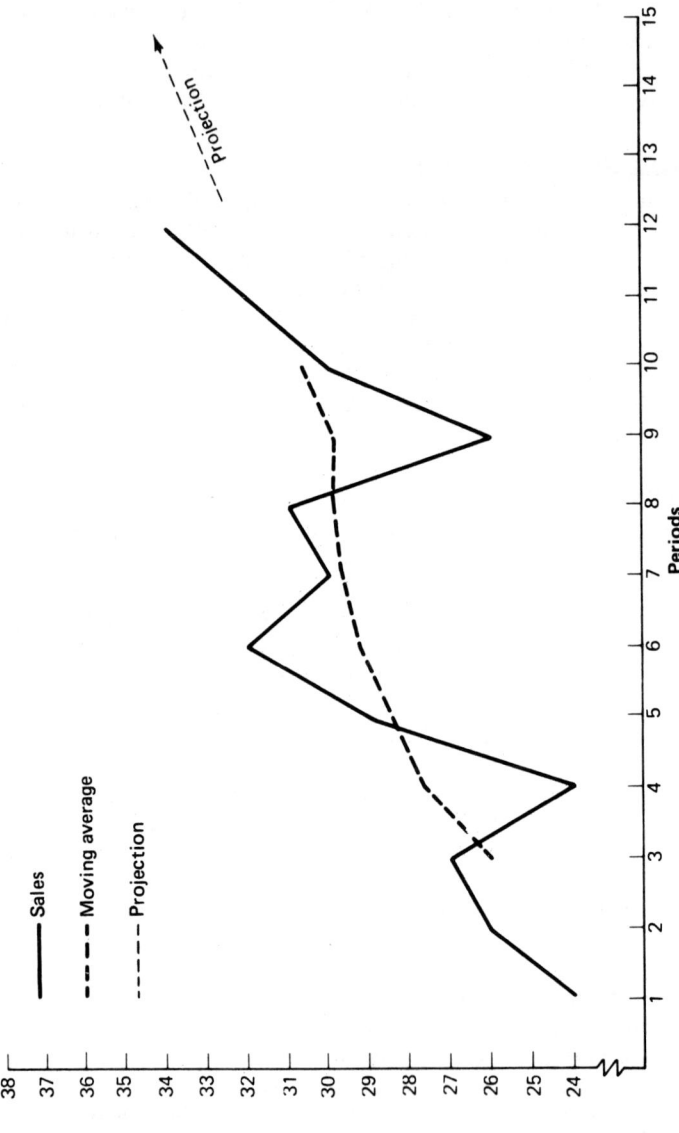

Figure 56. *A five period average and projection*

Sales period	Sales in $000s	Five period moving total	Five period moving average
1	24	—	—
2	26	—	—
3	27	130	26.0
4	24	138	27.6
5	29	142	28.4
6	32	146	29.2
7	30	148	29.6
8	31	149	29.8
9	26	149	29.8
10	30	153	30.6
11	32	—	—
12	34	—	—
13	—	—	—

Table 32. *Calculation of a five period moving average*

In fact, this is one way of determining the length of the medium-term business cycle in a market: take industry sales figures over a 10 year period and experiment with moving averages of differing time periods (3, 5, 7, etc) until a reasonably straight moving average line is found and this time period tends to represent the industry's medium-term business cycle.

Seasonal fluctuations and the moving average

In most industries, while an annual sales total is a good general indicator, it is often not detailed enough for many forecasting requirements, eg production scheduling, and in many cases full use is not made of the data available. Seasonal fluctuations often present quite a problem in sales forecasting and, where possible, the forecaster should make provision for them by dividing the year into months or seasons appropriate to his industry.

If the pattern of sales for a particular year was as shown in Figure 57, then seasons made up of the values for December, January and February followed by March, April, May, etc would highlight the seasonal pattern more than the calendar quarters of January, February and March followed by April, May and June.

Compare:

Calendar quarters	Seasonal quarters
J F M 12	D J F 10
A M J 18	M A M 20
J A S 12	J J A 10
O N D 18	S O N 20

241

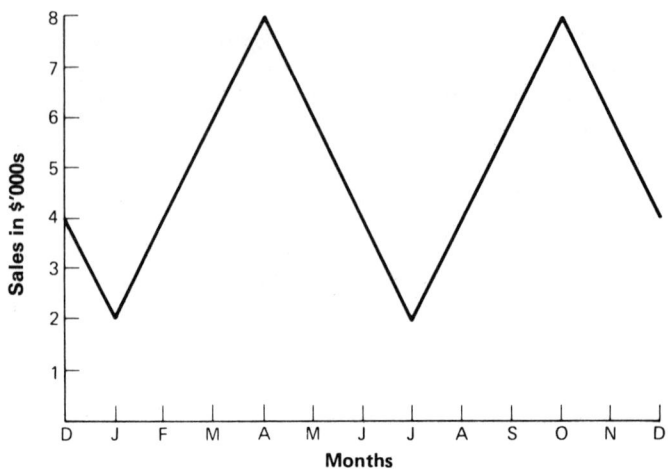

Figure 57. *A seasonal pattern of sales obtained from plotting monthly sales data*

Trend, seasonal and random variation (decomposition) analysis through moving averages

Further, having allowed for a seasonal variation, the forecaster should be able to distinguish more easily between those variations attributable to the seasonal pattern, and those attributable to other random influences. The presence of other random factors would warrant investigation to determine whether they were merely isolated cases or were likely to recur. The moving average method of fitting a trend line to seasonal data and discovering seasonal and random variations could be shown by developing an analysis of the type shown in Table 33. This is known as a decomposition technique (see also page 212 and Figure 43).

In Table 33 the data in columns 1, 2 and 3 refers to the sale of a product per quarter over a period of five years; the same type of analysis could be applied to monthly statistics. The trend has been calculated (column 5) on a four period basis by the moving total and moving average method, eg

19X1, 30 + 29 + 25 + 28 = 112 (MT) ÷ 4 = 28 (MA)

Because of the absence of a middle item in a group of four the moving total and moving average have been placed against the third item in each case, ie 112 (MT) and 28 (MA) against the third quarter of 19X1. The advantage of a four period MT and MA is that all seasons of a year are included in each calculation no matter which quarter starts the year.

1	2	3	4	5	6	7	8	9
Year	Quarter	Sales in $000s	4 period moving total	Trend 4 period moving average	Sales deviation from trend (3−5)	Average quarterly seasonal deviation	Quarterly figures corrected for season (3−7)	Random variation (8−5)
19X1	1	30	—	—	—	—	—	—
	2	29	—	—	—	—	—	—
	3	25	112	28	−3	−3.6	28.6	0.6
	4	28	111	27.75	0.25	1	27	−0.76
19X2	1	29	111	27.75	1.25	2.125	26.875	−0.875
	2	29	113	28.25	0.75	1.562	27.438	−0.812
	3	27	117	29.25	−2.25	−3.6	30.6	1.35
	4	32	122	30.5	1.5	1	31	0.5
	1	34	127	31.75	2.25	2.125	31.875	0.125
	2	34	129	32.25	1.75	1.562	32.438	0.188
	3	29	132	33	−4	−3.6	32.6	−0.4
	4	35	134	33.5	1.5	1	34	0.5
	1	36	137	34.25	1.75	2.125	33.875	−0.375
	2	37	139	34.75	2.25	1.562	35.438	0.688
	3	31	141	35.25	−4.25	−3.6	34.6	−0.65
	4	37	145	36.25	0.75	1	36	−0.25
	1	40	147	36.75	3.25	2.125	37.875	1.125
	2	39	150	37.5	1.5	1.562	37.438	−0.062
	3	34	154	38.5	−4.5	−3.6	37.6	−0.9
	4	41	—	—	—	—	—	—

Table 33. *The development of a 4 period moving average trend, seasonal weighting, seasonally adjusted sales figures and the identification of random variations from basic monthly sales figures*

Market and Sales Forecasting

The purpose of columns 6 to 9 in Table 33 is to analyze the sales figure for each quarter, dividing it into its component parts: (a) normal trend, (b) the mean seasonal variation, and (c) random variations.

Data in column 6 is found by subtracting the individual trend items in column 5 from the actual sales items in column 3. The data in column 7 is calculated by taking all the deviations-from-trend items (column 6) according to quarters, adding them, and then dividing by the appropriate number of items. Thus, from the data in column 6 the average quarterly deviation can be calculated for all first quarters in this way:

19X2 quarter 1	1.25
19X3 quarter 1	2.25
19X4 quarter 1	1.75
19X5 quarter 1	3.25
	$8.50 \div 4 = 2.125$

Therefore, in column 7 against all first quarters the value of 2.125 is shown. This process is repeated for the other quarters.

In column 8 in Table 33 the actual sales figures (column 3) are then seasonally adjusted by subtracting the average quarterly deviation (column 7) from them. Then by subtracting the trend (column 5) from the seasonally corrected quarterly figures (in column 8), the residue indicates the extent of the other influences present. The sales figure of a particular quarter can be analyzed as in Table 34.

	19X5 quarter 2
(a) The normal trend	37.5
(b) The average quarterly seasonal variation	1.562
(c) Other random variations	− 0.062
Original sales figure	39.0

Table 34. *Component parts of a sales figure*

The analysis in Table 34 enables attention to be focused on the random variations after the trend and the seasonal effects have been eliminated. The forecaster must then ask to what causes these random variations can be attributed, ie why should the sales figure for the first quarter of 19X5 be $1,125 above the seasonally adjusted trend? Often the variations from the trend are converted to percentages to allow proportional assessment.

On investigation it may be found that random variations have been caused by the beginning of a new trend, eg increased product

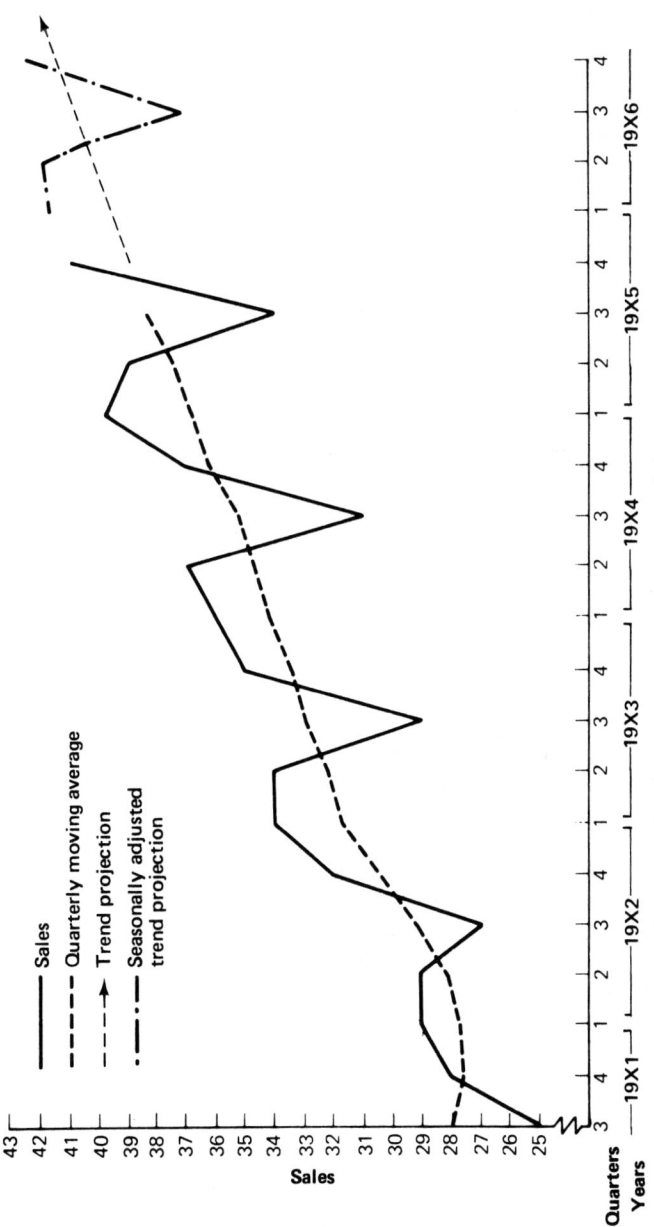

Figure 58. *Sales data and quarterly moving average and projection*

usage, a new application, appeal to a new market segment, etc; in which case the forecaster can allow for this in the future forecasting activities. Alternatively, the random variations may have been caused by an ad hoc factor that is unlikely or cannot be guaranteed to happen again, ie a once-only special order, a strike at a competitor's factory, etc. In such a case the unusual sales item can be withdrawn from the total sales volume figure for the period, otherwise it will affect future moving averages and other trend calculations adversely.

The sales data and the trend can be shown on a graph and the general slope of the latter projected into the future (see Figure 58). The general trend obtained can be used for medium- and long-term trend prediction.

Table 33 represents an analysis of the quarterly sales data, but a sales forecast for the next period, Q1 19X6, could be made based on the method described earlier when calculating the three period moving average (see Table 30). The method would be to take the latest moving average value available in Table 33, ie 38.5, and add twice the difference between it and the previous moving average, ie 37.5. Therefore,

$$38.5 + (2 \times 1) = 40.5$$

plus the average quarterly seasonal deviation (see column 7, Table 33) for all quarter 1 values. The forecast for quarter 1 of 19X6 would be

$$40.5 + 2.125 = 42.625$$

or $42,000 rounded.

One method of projection forecasting would be to plot on separate graphs the trend, seasonal pattern and deseasonalized sales. In each case these would be projected forward and finally all the component parts added together at a particular point in the future to form a total forecast. Alternatively, a forecast for the next year (four quarters) based on the current trend indicated in Figure 58, could be obtained by taking the projected trend values for each quarter and adding or subtracting the appropriate average quarterly seasonal deviation, as in Table 35. The seasonally adjusted forecast is shown graphically in Figure 58.

Other decomposition methods

In the last example each quarterly sales figure was 'decomposed' into its component parts of trend, mean seasonal average, deseasonalized sales and random variations or residual error.

The so-called *classical decomposition method* of forecasting not only analyzes sales values in this way but also makes a forecast by predicting each of the components separately and then combining

Year	Projected trend value obtained from graph	Average quarterly seasonal deviation	Forecast
19X6			
Quarter 1	39.6	2.125	41.725
Quarter 2	40.4	1.562	41.962
Quarter 3	41.0	−3.6	37.4
Quarter 4	41.6	1.0	42.6

Table 35. *A seasonally adjusted forecast based on Figure 58*

them to make a total forecast for the next time period(s).

A more sophisticated decomposition method is known as *Census II*; it provides statistical credibility for the results and uses empirically proven methods of estimation. The Census II procedure has been described as primarily consisting of

'several smoothing operations carried out by applying moving averages of varying weightings and orders to the data converted into percentage ratio to trend index numbers. When an initial estimate of the seasonal-irregular component has been obtained, irregular fluctuations are removed by using two-standard deviation control limits[1] and replacing extreme values by averages of surrounding values. In the same ways, values at the beginning and end of the series, which are lost through the moving average procedure, are replaced. The data is then centered for each year and, by smoothing the columns of individual months (or quarters), estimates of preliminary seasonal factors are obtained, again by replacing end-values by an averaging procedure. These preliminary estimates are then used to remove some of the seasonality from the original observations and the smoothed residual is applied to obtain a second or intermediate estimate of the seasonal component. This, in turn, is then smoothed, irregularities are removed and such values, together with end observations, are replaced. The series is centered and by once more smoothing the columns of individual months, estimates of the final seasonal factors are obtained. This series can then be used to finally adjust the original observations for seasonality and by further suitable smoothing and replacing, final estimates of the irregular, cyclical and trend components can be identified.'[2]

A decomposition technique that can be used as a causal model on top of a time series is called the *Foran System*. It decomposes a set of

1. See page 180
2. G Briscoe & M Hirst *Long Range Planning* Sept 1973, p 79

Market and Sales Forecasting 248

data (both dependent and independent variables) into each of its component parts (mentioned above) and then provides a forecast for each of the variables using a number of smoothing methods. At the same time it provides a measure of accuracy of each of the forecasts, thus helping the forecaster to choose the most appropriate method. Ideally, the independent variable should be a leading indicator of the lagging dependent one so that a turning point can be predicted.

Weighted moving averages

One of the problems in using moving averages is that this method gives equal weight to all items, whereas the circumstances that helped to form the sales volume in the most recent period will influence actual sales to a greater extent than those operating a number of periods ago; this is particularly relevant in yearly moving averages.

One method used in forecasting is that of giving more weight to more recent periods. Consider the last four periods of Table 30 (page 237) recalculated on a four period moving average basis and shown in Table 36.

In fact, the same moving average could be obtained by calculating:

$$\frac{1}{4} \times 26 = 6.5$$
$$\frac{1}{4} \times 30 = 7.5$$
$$\frac{1}{4} \times 32 = 8.0$$
$$\frac{1}{4} \times 34 = 8.5$$
$$\overline{1} \qquad \overline{30.5}$$

Additional weight could therefore be given to more recent periods by increasing the fraction, ie

$$\frac{1}{10} \times 26 = 2.6$$

$$\frac{2}{10} \times 30 = 6.0$$

$$\frac{3}{10} \times 32 = 9.6$$

$$\frac{4}{10} \times 34 = 13.6$$

$$\overline{1} \qquad \overline{13.8} = \text{weighted moving average}$$

Quarter	Sales in $000s	4 period moving total	4 period moving average
9	26		
10	30		
11	32		
12	34	122 ÷ 4 =	30.5

Table 36. *Calculation of a four period moving average*

The effect of this weighting on forecasts can be seen by comparing forecasts based on unweighted and weighted moving averages developed in Table 37.

In this case, by giving more weight to more recent periods, the weighted moving average produced a higher forecast. Depending on the values of recent periods it would be possible to obtain a weighted forecast that was lower.

Period	Sales $000s	4 period unweighted moving average	Difference between current and last moving average	4 period weighted moving average	Difference between current and last moving average
8	31	–	–	–	–
9	26	–	–	–	–
10	30	29.75	–	30.1	–
11	32	30.5	0.75	31.8	1.7
12	34	–	–	–	–
13	–	–	–	–	–

Forecast for period 13 using unweighted moving average
= 30.5 + (2 × 0.75) = 32

Forecast for period 13 using weighted moving average
= 31.8 + (2 × 1.7) = 34.2

Table 37. *A comparison of unweighted and weighted moving averages*

Exponential smoothing

When calculating weighted moving averages in the previous example more weight was given to more recent periods. In fact, the weighting declined by a constant quantity value, ie by the value of 1/10th on each item, 4/10th, 3/10th, 2/10th, 1/10th. Another method is to reduce the weighting by a constant percentage or ratio, eg perhaps by halving the weighting 1/2, 1/4, 1/8th, 1/16th, 1/32nd, 1/64th. This produces a geometric progression and, when graphed, smooths the raw sales data into an exponential curve; the method is therefore referred to as *exponential smoothing or weighting*.

It is a simple but highly reliable weighted moving average technique. Its main advantages are that relatively few past observations are required, it is easy to use and is highly reliable in the short term. Its usefulness to the forecaster is that it highlights the effects of current

Period 7	$\frac{1}{32} \times 30 =$	0.937
Period 8	$\frac{1}{32} \times 31 =$	0.968
Period 9	$\frac{1}{16} \times 26 =$	1.625
Period 10	$\frac{1}{8} \times 30 =$	3.75
Period 11	$\frac{1}{4} \times 32 =$	8.0
Period 12	$\frac{1}{2} \times 34 =$	17.0
	1	32.280

Table 38. *The make-up of an exponentially weighted moving average*

trends and seasonal patterns and diminishes the effect that past forecasts which have failed (perhaps because of sharp non-typical fluctuations) will have on the current forecast. Also, it gives greater weight to more recent periods and tends to give more accurate forecasts.

Using the same data as in the earlier weighted moving average example (Table 37) an exponentially weighted moving average could be calculated as shown in Table 38.

The reducing exponential weights could go on for ever with ever-decreasing fractions, but in practice when the value becomes relatively insignificant (eg where it produced 0.937 in Table 38) it is wise to terminate the series. A useful device is to repeat the same fraction, ie 1/32nd against periods 7 and 8. If this is not done the sum of the fractions will not equal 1, and, therefore, the exponentially weighted moving average will be fractionally low.

When the exponentially weighted moving average has been calculated for the last two periods, a forecast can be made by the same method used with the unweighted and weighted moving averages.

Period	Sales in $'000s	Exponentially weighted moving average
6	32	
7	30	
8	31	
9	26	30.624
10	30	32.280
11	32	
12	34	
13	—	

Table 39. *A method of obtaining an exponentially weighted moving average to form the basis of making a sales forecast*

The difference between two exponentially weighted moving averages is 1.656. The forecast for period 13 is therefore 32.280 + (3 × 1.656) = 37.248.

The main disadvantage with this method is that a greater number of items are used to form the average: six in this case (because of the fractions required to make the value of 1) compared with four in the weighted moving average (Table 37). Because of this, there are no moving averages against periods 11 and 12, and therefore the difference between the last two moving averages had to be multiplied by three to produce a forecast for period 13.

A second method of exponential smoothing for forecasting

A more useful approach to forecasting through exponential smoothing is to determine the constant ratio factor by examining past data and then use it to forecast the next period.

For example, where $\hat{y}$ = the prediction to be made for the next period, p = sales in past periods ($p_1\ p_2\ p_3$ etc) and A = the constant ratio factor.

$$\text{Let } \hat{y} = p_1 + p_2(A) + p_3(A^2) + p_4(A^3)$$

In the last example (Table 39) consider how the sales in period 12, ie $34,000, would be arrived at by using this formula.

$$34 = 32 + 30(A) + 26(A^2) + 31(A^3)$$

The factor (A) is found by completing the formula mathematically or by working through various values to find one that completes the formula. This latter method can be tedious initially but in the ensuing periods the factor will vary only slightly when updated. Inserting the factor

$$34 = 32 + 30(0.0634) + 26(0.0634^2) + 31(0.0634^3)$$
$$= (32 + 1.902 + 0.104 + 0.008)$$

Using the same formula and the above factor to predict sales for period 13

$$\hat{y} = 34 + 32(0.0634) + 30(0.0634^2) + 26(0.0634^3)$$
$$= 34 + 2.029 + 0.120 + 0.006 = 36.155$$

or, rounded to the nearest $100, $36,100 which is the forecast for period 13.

Alternatively, factor A (the constant ratio factor) can be found by completing the formula mathematically as follows using the same basic formula and the same data as used above:

Period	Sales
8	31
9	26
10	30
11	32
12	34

What is the best estimate for period 13 using the formula:

$$\hat{y} = p_1 + p_2(A) + p_3(A^2) + p_4(A^3)$$
$$34 = 32 + 30(A) + 26(A^2) + 31(A^3)$$

Using the formula

$$ax^2 + bx + x = 0, \text{ ie } 26(A^2) + 30(A) - 2 = 0$$

Objective Methods of Forecasting

To solve the equation using formula

$$x = \frac{-b \pm \sqrt{(b^2 - 4ac)}}{2a}$$

insert appropriate figures:

$$A = \frac{-30 \pm \sqrt{[30^2 - (4 \times 26 \times (-2))]}}{(2 \times 26)}$$

$$= \frac{-30 \pm \sqrt{(900 + 208)}}{52}$$

$$= \frac{-30 \pm \sqrt{(1108)}}{52} = \frac{-30 + 33.29}{52}$$

$$= \frac{3.29}{52} = 0.06327$$

To forecast the sales ($\hat{y}$) for period 13

$$\hat{y} = 34 + 32(A) + 30(A^2) + 26(A^3) + 31(A^4)$$

= 34	34.0000
+ 32 (0.06327)	2.0204
+ 30 (0.06327²)	0.1200
+ 26 (0.06327³)	0.0066
+ 31 (0.06327⁴)	0.0005
	36.1511

Best estimate of sales for period 13 = $36,151.

Exponential smoothing forecast using deseasonalized data

Another approach to exponential smoothing is one that modifies the value of the previous forecast according to the value of the resulting sales performance. As actual sales data becomes available for a particular sales period, the forecast for that past period is updated by a part of the difference between the two values. The resulting value then becomes the forecast for the next period. The formula is:

$$\hat{y} = F_{-1} + A(S_{-1} - F_{-1})$$

Where y = forecast for next period
              A = the alpha factor or smoothing constant
              F_{-1} = forecast for last period
              S_{-2} = actual sales for last period

Sales period	Volume forecast (000s)	Actual sales (000s)	% Variance forecast related to sales
1	118	124	−4.8
2	118 + 0.6(124 − 118) = 122	126	−3.1
3	122 + 0.6(126 − 122) = 124	122	+1.6
4	124 + 0.6(122 − 124) = 123	125	−1.6
5	124 + 0.6(125 − 124) = 124	127	−2.36
6	126 + 0.6(127 − 124) = 126	124	+1.6
7	126 + 0.6(124 − 126) = 124		

Table 40. *A forecasting flow for the next six sales periods*

Table 40 illustrates a hypothetical forecasting flow for the next six sales periods. The sale of the product experiences period-to-period variations but the 0.6 smoothing constant adjusts the forecast according to the most recent forecasting 'error'. The size of the smoothing constant can be initially set by experience of variations in the market or by the previously described method of exponential smoothing or even arbitrarily. Any value between 0 and 1 may be used, but the larger the value of the constant, the greater will be the influence of the most recent period. The smoothing constant can be adjusted should basic conditions in the market change.

In the above table the value of 118 at the commencement of the series could either represent a 'guesstimate' of the sales of a new product to be launched into the market or could be obtained by another forecasting method to start the series. This is important as there must be a forecast and an actual sales performance figure to determine the error. It is upon the adjustment of the error that the method works.

Thus, in period 2 the previous forecast is taken (118) and 0.6 of the error between the forecast and actual is added, giving a forecast of 122 for period 3.

In period 4, as the forecast is higher than the sales achieved, the error is negative (122 − 124); 0.6 of this negative error is, therefore, subtracted from the previous forecast value of 124.

The method is more effective with a stable time series and, should seasonality be a major factor, sales will need to be deseasonalized before being subjected to this method. After being exponentially smoothed and projected, the ensuing values can be reseasonalized (see page 183) to give a seasonally adjusted sales forecast.

The main advantage of this method of forecasting is that it needs little data (forecast and actual) to calculate a forecast; contrast this with the amount of data needed to calculate a 13 period moving average. Also it is based upon the most recently known sales period, whereas the middle point of a 13 period moving average which forms the trend is six months back.

Seasonally weighted exponential smoothing

The exponential smoothing method can be adapted for use with seasonal data (monthly, quarterly, etc).

Year	Quarters	Sales ($'000s)
19X4	4	37
19X5	1	40
	2	39
	3	34
	4	41

Table 41. *Part of the quarterly sales data taken from Table 33*

If the data for the last five quarters from Table 33 are used the exponential smoothing factor can be determined in this case by again using the formula

$$\hat{y} = p_1 + p_2(a) + p_3(a^2) + p_4(a^3)$$
$$41 = 34 + 39(0.153) + 40(0.153^2) + 37(0.153^3)$$

The factor in this case has been found by working through various values to find the one that fits the formula. In the above case the prediction actually equals 41.033 but this was the nearest obtainable and has been rounded for convenience.

The forecast for quarter 1 of 19X6 can now be calculated using the same formula and constant ratio factor:

$$\begin{aligned}\hat{y} &= 41 + 34(0.153) + 39(0.153^2) + 40(0.153^3) \\ &= 41 + 5.202 + 0.9226 + 0.1433 \\ &= 47.2679 \text{ or rounded to } \$47{,}250\end{aligned}$$

However, using the exponential smoothing technique in this way does not allow for seasonal difference with individual quarterly predictions, although values for all four seasons are present in the four quarters moving average. Therefore, certain data in the current example can be extracted, rearranged, and developed to show a moving average, a trend, a forecast and seasonally adjusted forecast, thereby making the fullest use of available data — this is shown in Table 45. As the sales data becomes available each month, the constant ratio factor used above, 0.153, can be applied or recalculated and a continuous sales forecast can be evolved.

In Table 45 the year, quarters and actual sales are shown in columns 1 and 2. In column 3 the previous average sales value, 36.75, (see trend value quarter 1, 19X5 in Table 33) is multiplied by 0.847, that is 1 minus the constant (A) 0.153, and then added to the current quarter's sales (in column 2) multiplied by the constant; for example, in quarter 1,

$$36.75 \times 0.847 + (40 \times 0.153)$$

which indicates the new average sales value of 37.24.

The actual difference shown in column 4 of Table 42, is found by subtracting the previous month's average sales from the current month's average sales. For example, in quarter 2,

$$37.50 - 37.24 = 0.26$$

The difference trend (column 5) is found by taking its values in the previous month and multiplying it by 1 minus the constant, ie 0.847, to which is added the actual difference (column 4) for the current month multiplied by the constant 0.153. For example, for quarter 4,

$$0.35 \times 0.847 + (0.61 \times 0.153) = 0.38$$

In column 6 the current difference trend is multiplied by 1 minus the constant divided by the constant and added to the average sales figure in column 3. For example, for quarter 1,

$$0.49 \times \frac{0.847}{0.153} + 37.24 = 39.94$$

In column 7 the mean quarterly seasonal deviations are extracted from Table 33 column 8 and listed, and in column 8 of this table these weightings are added to or subtracted from the values shown in column 6. Using this method, the forecast for quarter 1 of 19X6 is, therefore, 41,795, or $41,800 approximately.

Exponential smoothing — more sophisticated techniques

It will be seen from the above examples that exponential smoothing is very similar to the moving average approach but does not use a constant set of weights for the n most recent observations. In fact, an exponentially decreasing set of weights is used so that the more recent

1	2	3	4	5	6	7	8
Quarters	Actual sales in $000s	Average sales based upon trend value = 36.75	Actual difference	Difference trend	Straight forecast for the next quarter	Mean quarterly seasonal deviation (col 8 in previous table)	Seasonally adjusted forecast for the next quarter
19X5 1	40	37.24	+0.49	+0.49	39.94	1.562	41.502
2	39	37.50	+0.26	+0.45	39.98	−3.6	36.38
3	34	36.96	−0.54	+0.35	38.98	1.0	39.89
4	41	37.57	+0.61	+0.38	39.67	2.125	41.795

Table 42. *The calculation of a seasonally weighted exponential moving average and forecast*

values receive more weight than older values.

Exponential smoothing in its 'pure' form (as originally suggested by C C Holt) should only be used by itself for stationary, non-seasonal time series. The methods on pages 251 and 253 are examples.

Many time series are in practice both seasonal and non-stationary. But such time series can be converted into non-seasonal and stationary series by appropriate deseasonalizing. The series can then be extrapolated exponentially and the trend and seasonal pattern then added to the projected values; such a method was suggested on page 217. However, methods have been developed which integrate these stages and which take into account the seasonal pattern; one such method is one suggested by Brown (see example on page 255).

The *Holt-Winters exponential smoothing* method handles time series and allows for both trend and seasonal variations, both of which are updated by exponential smoothing.

Auto-Regressive Integrated Moving Average (ARIMA) techniques are the most sophisticated of the single time-series approaches to forecasting. Basically they follow the same philosophy as the methods mentioned previously but use a different procedure for determining how many of the past observations should be included in preparing the forecast and in determining the appropriate weight values to be applied to those observations.

A series of techniques that fall into the ARIMA category are *adaptive filtering techniques* which can be used for any type of data whether seasonal, cyclical or trend. They are similar to other smoothing techniques in the sense that they weight past observations in such a way that the error between actual and forecast value is minimal. They are called adaptive filtering because, in the process of minimizing the error, they 'filter' the 'disturbances' out of the data.

The most commonly used ARIMA method is the procedure developed by Box and Jenkins. Like adaptive filtering this method assigns varying weights to past observations until an optimal set of weights is discovered. In fact they differ only in the way the weight values and the terms to be included are determined. The *Box Jenkins method* is more sophisticated than adaptive filtering methods because it can handle more than two variables and because it makes use of the statistical properties of estimation to test the appropriateness/quality of the model being used and its significance. It is based on the assumption that successive observations of economic/industry/market series are correlated. Further, it tries to discover and make use of such autocorrelations to obtain accurate predictions about the future.

	Advertising expenditure last year $	Percentage of last year's advertising %	Sales last year $	Percentage of last year's sales %
January	3,100	7.3	50,000	5.8
February	3,400	7.9	62,000	7.4
March	3,800	8.8	68,000	8.0
April	4,200	9.8	76,000	8.9
May	3,600	8.4	84,000	9.9
June	3,150	7.3	72,000	8.5
July	2,600	6.0	63,000	7.4
August	3,050	7.1	52,000	6.1
September	3,850	8.9	61,000	7.2
October	4,350	10.1	77,000	9.1
November	4,900	11.4	87,000	10.2
December	3,000	7.0	98,000	11.5
	43,000	100.0	850,000	100.0

Table 43. *A comparison of advertising expenditure and sales over a 12 month period*

Forecasting sales by the assessment of advertising

An analysis of advertising expenditure related to sales is often a good indicator of future sales. But it would be wrong to assume that to increase or decrease advertising expenditure will automatically increase or decrease sales. Normally, sales are not only a function of advertising but also of other factors such as price, performance and function of product, seasonality of demand, effectiveness of the sales force, competitive effects and distribution. Also increased expenditure on, or increased quantity of, advertising does not necessarily mean improved quality. But it is important to recognize that advertising affects sales by influencing consumer/user knowledge, opinions, reactions or attitudes towards a product or service.

Comparisons of advertising expenditure and sales

As long as the limitations are recognized, the amount spent on advertising could be used to indicate future sales based on past expenditure and results. An elementary way of doing this is shown in Table 43.

From Table 43 indications of the likely effects of changes in advertising expenditure could be examined. In Table 43 there appears to be a lead/lag relationship of advertising expenditure to sales: increases in advertising appear to have an effect on sales in the following month. Also, seasonal patterns have been allowed for in advertising expenditure.

A graph of the advertising expenditure and sales percentages can also indicate that a company is missing marketing opportunities if the two plot lines do not run together in similar patterns. Advertising may be appearing too early or too late to do the best possible marketing job.

Sales leads as a basis for forecasting

In some cases companies can directly determine future sales. This situation is found where companies use advertising to get sales leads, ie where the advertisement includes a form to be completed and forwarded to the company. This may request literature or a demonstration of the product or a visit by an engineer to discuss particular problems. For example, this method is used to sell vending machines to factories and central heating installations to householders.

The company gears its advertising to the number of sales it wishes to achieve. From past experience the company determines the number of replies it will receive from various newspapers, magazines or trade journals. As in central heating installation marketing, ratios can be established between the number of replies to initial visits by engineers, to quotations submitted, to orders finally received. Thus, by increasing advertising in the correct advertising medium, predicted sales are not only achieved but can also be measured.

Share of advertising expenditure versus share of the market

Another approach that is particularly useful during the launch of a new product is to analyze data that compares the attained market

Product	Attained share of sales	Average share of advertising during the introductory period
A	39	47
B	19	33
C	13	32
D	12	30
E	6	13
F	4	8

Table 44. *The effect of share of advertising expenditure on share of the market*

share with the average share of advertising during the introductory period.

Table 44 shows that with six household products the level of advertising expenditure had a marked effect upon the share of market attained.

By analyzing past market share and advertising expenditures as in Table 44, sales forecasting can be made more effective.

The percentage increase/decrease method

A further advertising/sales technique is that of comparing the annual percentage increase or decrease in market share with the annual percentage increase or decrease in a company's share of all advertising expenditure (see Table 45).

Product	Annual increase/decrease in market share	Annual increase/decrease in share of all advertising expenditure
A	+ 4%	+ 13½%
B	+ ¾%	+ 5½%
C	+ 2½%	+ 2½%
D	− 1¼%	− 3¾%
E	− 4½%	− 8½%

Table 45. *Relating increase/decrease of share of all advertising expenditure with increase/decrease in market share*

It has been said that the market share of a product will tend to increase/decrease in direct proportion to the difference between its market share and its share of total advertising in the market.

Naive correlations between advertising expenditure and sales are not reliable in effective sales forecasting because of the possible effects of other variables of the marketing mix and the market place. But the device of historical analogy (history repeating itself) causes forecasters to look at past data to consider the effects of changes in advertising expenditure upon sales or market share.

Model building and forecasting

Models have become popular marketing management devices in

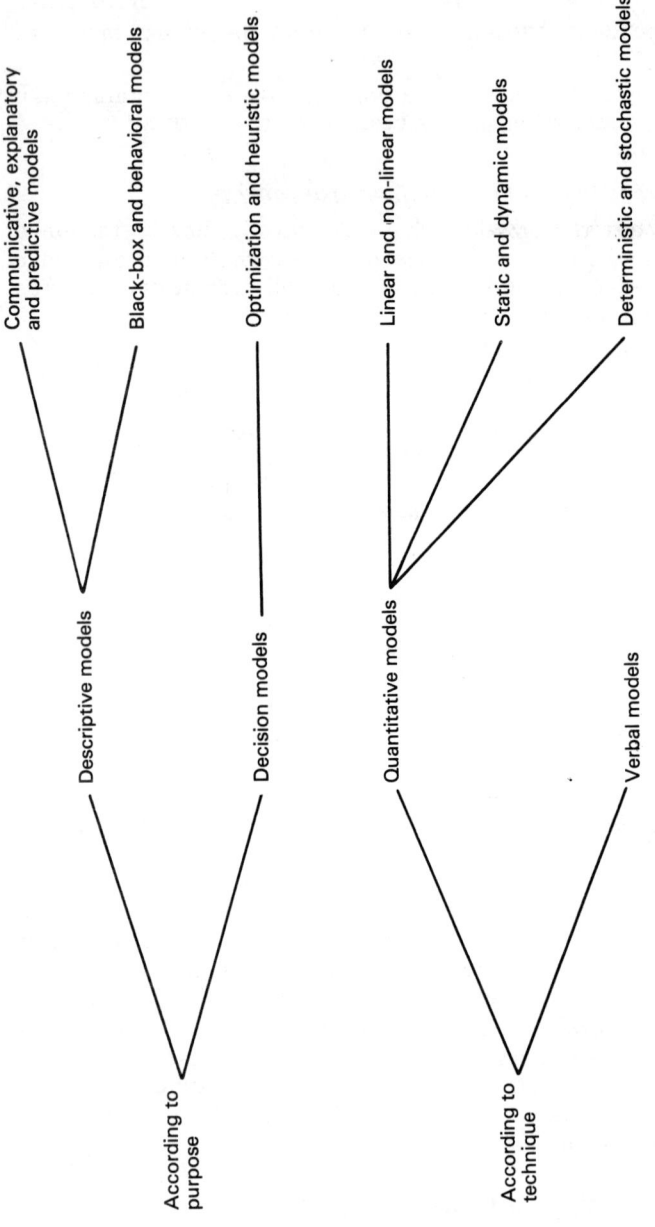

Figure 59. *The relationship of the various types of models as expressed by Kotler*

some organizations, but every operating rule in marketing could be defined broadly as a model: for example, where company reaction or response to a change in a particular variable is laid down. This could apply where courses of action are pre-determined to deal with changes in consumer response to advertising, or in a competitor's strategy or in the effectiveness of certain channels of distribution. In model building the marketer evolves rules and/or equations which express the relationship of certain variable and non-variable factors in the marketing system and uses them to predict the effect of the changes on the system. Models can be used to explain, select, optimize and predict markets and marketing sub-systems.

The variety of model types has been classified by P Kotler[1] and is shown in Figure 59.

Some of the types of models shown in Figure 59 are more relevant to forecasting needs than others. Also, a number of the elementary forms of model building have already been explained in earlier sections and can be used to explain the basic principles of each group.

'Black box' models[2] were examined qualitatively in the section dealing with sociological and consumer behavioral change, by showing that certain patterns of group or individual behavior were inputs into the marketing system and the outcome was a pattern of sales, eg the trend towards increased leisure and its effect on demand for recreation and leisure products (page 131 *et seq*).

Behavioral models seek to explain what happens between the input and the output of the 'black box', eg the qualitative and descriptive examination of individual behavior on page 132.

The input/output method described on page 135 is a model of the national economy reflecting interrelationships with the various component industries. It examines the inputs into each industry and the resulting outputs, but does not seek to explain how the result was arrived at within the 'black box'.

The methods of least squares (page 171) and exponential smoothing (page 252) could also be described as quantitative 'black box' models. They are based on equations

$$\hat{y} = a + bx$$
and
$$\hat{y} = p^1 + p^2(A) + p^3(A^2)$$

---

1. P Kotler p 222 *Marketing Management* Prentice-Hall, New Jersey, USA, 1967.

2. The concept of the 'black box' was examined by P Kotler in the *Journal of Marketing,* Vol 29 (October 1865, p 37). 'The buyer is subject to many influences which trace a complex course through his psyche and lead eventually to overt purchasing responses...The buyer's psyche is a 'black box' whose workings can be only partially deduced. The marketing strategist's challenge to the behavioral scientist is to construct a more specific model of the mechanism in the 'black box'.'

respectively, that are set up to describe a particular system or situation and the relationships of the inputs and outputs without analyzing why the variables changed or why the outcome has happened.

The equation $\hat{y} = a + bx$ used in the least squares method (page 203) illustrates the input/ouput mechanism. Consider a situation where sales data and advertising expenditure for three years were as in Table 46.

Year	Sales $000s	Advertising expenditure $000s
19X1	86	2.0
19X2	122	4.0
19X3	113	3.5

Table 46. *Sales volume and advertising expenditure over a three-year period*

The equation $\hat{y} = a + bx$ becomes

$$\text{sales} = 50 + 18x$$

This means that for every extra $1,000 of advertising expenditure an increase of $18,000 in sales would be expected and that with no advertising at all, sales of $50,000 could be expected. A simple, though perhaps naive, 'black box' model.

Decision models

Decision models usually incorporate factors that permit analysis and assessment of the various courses of action and/or suggest optimum strategies to management. Within the overall decision making theory area, one of the most useful aspects for forecasting is that of the expected value concept. Examples of expected value in two of its forms as used in forecasting are shown on pages 286 and 291.

Effective use of the expected value concept for forecasting depends on the ability of the forecaster and/or company executives to identify the various business environmental conditions that affect sales and the situations likely to prevail in changing situations. It also depends on their ability to provide realistic probability factors and potential outcome values (eg profits at various levels of activity) for each.

Closely linked with the expected value concept is Bayesian decision theory, which combines objective and subjective probabilities with revised data and information derived from such sources as the field sales force, research, economic and political fact situations. An example of an application of part of Bayesian decision theory is shown on page 287.

Linear models

An example of a linear model has already been shown to illustrate its role as a different type of model of the 'black box' category: it is the equation $\hat{y} = a + bx$ or as it was re-stated, sales $= 50 + 18x$. Such an equation establishes a linear or straight-line trend suggesting that continued increments of \$1,000 spent on advertising would on each occasion increase sales by \$18,000 *ad infinitum*. In practice, returns on advertising would begin to level out after a particular point and eventually decline. Regression analysis and the least squares method (pages 154 and 171) are also examples of linear models.

Models based on learned behavior

Purchasing/consumption in many cases is a form of learned behavior. This is particularly true of consumer goods and services but also occurs in industrial markets. Preferences are developed and purchasing habits develop and consumer/users tend to repeat their past purchasing/consumption activities/decisions. Consumer/users do not objectively evaluate and compare competing/alternative product/service 'deals' every time they make a purchasing decision. There is often a measurable degree of 'brand loyalty' that exists at varying levels of intensity until some 'cue' (eg a change in price, quality, availability, etc) causes consumer/users to reconsider and possibly change their brand or product loyalty.

Market share models

Obviously the fewer the number of companies competing in a market the easier it will be to develop a market share model, but even when a number are competing it is possible to consider the companies with major market shares and group all others together. The sales of a particular company are often dependent upon its actual/relative/perceived market position with regard to its competitors. Because of brand/product loyalties there is a tendency for competitors to share a market with each other at a relatively constant rate. Although changes in market shares take place, the percentage market share held in one sales period is a good indicator of the starting point for market shares in the next period.

As a prerequisite for market share forecasting it is normal for the market to be segmented; both segmentation (page 215) and forecasting using market share and competitor activity (page 218) were considered earlier.

Brand-switching models

Another quantitative model useful in forecasting is the brand-switching model. In many areas of marketing, effective forecasting will depend on the ability of the forecaster to seek explanations for and/or measure the tendency of consumers to be loyal to a brand, or to switch to another. The importance of brand-switching models to forecasting in certain areas of marketing is obvious, as it is concerned with the measurement of repeat purchases and the switching-in and switching-out rate for each brand. As Kotler says:[1]

'The attitude of marketing executives toward brand-switching is quite simple: the switching-out rate must be slowed down, and the switching-in rate must be increased. The factors affecting brand choice must be analyzed, and this knowledge applied where possible in order to alter existing brand-switching rates.'

These activities will affect sales and, therefore, forecasts. The forecaster will be able to determine product sales patterns over a period of time, whether the switching rates are constant or are changing in a predictable direction.

It is usual to construct brand-switching models concurrently with models concerning price/supply situations, and models relating to competitive response. Which competitors will have or already have the resources to react, and what will be the nature and timing of counter activities and their effect on sales?

The primary model for brand-switching analysis is the Markov process which is concerned with the consumer's preference for a particular brand. But the consumer's preference may change from time to time, and he may switch brands. In a total market, brand-switching by groups can be aggregated and expressed as a probability.

Consider an elementary application of the Markov process to illustrate the principle involved: a situation with three brands, A, B and C which have 20%, 30% and 50% shares of the market respectively. A 'transition matrix' can be evolved that will express the probabilities of the various types of brand-switching that can occur. These probabilities could be derived from panels of expert opinion, or from past market behavior (historical analogy) or from a survey of buyer's intentions, etc. Such a transition matrix based on the above data is shown in Table 47.

After the formation of Table 47, the next step is to apply the probabilities to the existing brand shares. This is shown in Table 48.

The calculation of the new brand share values for A in Table 48 is based on the expectation that it will retain 0.5 of its existing 20% share of the market, ie 10%, *plus* a brand switch of 0.4 of B's existing market share of 30%, ie 12%, *plus* a brand switch of 0.3 of C's

---

1. Philip Kotler *Marketing Management* Prentice-Hall, New Jersey, USA.

market share of 50% of the current market, ie 15%: a total of 37% of the anticipated market in the next period.

In turn, the probabilities can be applied to the new brand shares. This process can be repeated a number of times to produce a forecast pattern of demand for the three brands for any number of future periods.

This method assumes that the probabilities remain constant or will change at a predictable rate. At some later point they may have to be adjusted if new information becomes available.

	A	B	C
A	stay 0.5	change 0.3	change 0.2
B	change 0.4	stay 0.4	change 0.2
C	change 0.3	change 0.3	stay 0.4

Table 47. *Probability that consumers will switch brands*

Preference analysis

This is a progression from the Markov and other brand-switching models which have a number of disadvantages as well as a number of advantages for direct forecasting applications. The main disadvantages of many brand-switching models are that they do not take account of once-only brand purchases or the buying of several brands

				New brand shares anticipated
A	0.5 of 20% = 10%	0.4 of 30% = + 12%	0.3 of 50% = + 15%	= 37%
B	0.4 of 30% = 12%	0.3 of 20% = + 6%	0.3 of 50% = + 15%	= 33%
C	0.4 of 50% = 20%	0.2 of 20% = + 4%	0.2 of 30% = + 6%	= 30%

Table 48. *The application of probabilities to the existing brand shares to determine the post-switch market shares*

at the same time and that they are unable to cope with variations in pack size and price. However, methods for measuring market response to promotional activity can be built into some more advanced brand-switching models.

Preference analysis is designed to show the short-term effects of advertising, sales promotion and product change on all the brands being offered in the market.

The information input for the preference analysis model is obtained weekly from a regionally and socially representative sample of 5,000 households reporting their household purchases by brand, price, shop and special offer. From this data, brand loyalty, brand switching and the effects of sales promotion can be estimated. The interpretation of the data is important. What may appear to be loyalty to a brand may, in fact, be loyalty to a particular retail outlet that stocks only one brand, or to changes in stocking patterns by retailers, rather than a change in consumer preference.

Preference analysis allows for sub-preferences within households perhaps due to the presence of more than one purchaser, or because the purchaser is relatively indifferent to the choice of brand available or because different products in the same product field are complementary or are substitutes.

Product life cycle models

Product life cycles were considered in depth in Chapter 2 and as such the characteristics of each stage of the life cycle and the appropriate marketing strategy responses have already been considered. However, the fact that the rate of change in sales revenue/units differs throughout the life of the product/service may have a significant effect on forecasts, especially those covering the medium and long terms. Depending on the product/service type being considered the length of life cycles will differ, but in modelling terms can be considered either as historic fact to be projected forward by trend analysis or in terms of a predictive model based on historical analogy, ie that history will repeat itself.

Other models

Other models linked with learned behavior can relate to the effect of advertising and promotional activities and changes in them (see page 259). There is an obvious link between the sales forecast and the ability of advertising and sales promotion to influence sales. In this area, media planning models have developed and, through the technique of linear programming, consider a variety of viable combinations of how much time and/or space to buy in general and in specific media and at what frequency of interval, to achieve a particular market objective.

Various marketing-mix models have been evolved by companies. These attempt to measure the effect of different combinations of the various sub-functions of marketing (marketing research, advertising, direct selling, distribution, etc) and marketing strategies, on sales.

Simulation models

Models have been constructed to simulate the market and marketing situations facing a company; particular variables are then changed and a prediction made of how the other variables will react. Simulation can be defined as a general method of studying the behavior of a real system or phenomenon; the method usually involves the following features:

1. devising a model, or set of mathematical and logical relations, which represents the essential features of the system;
2. carrying out step-by-step computations with these relations which imitate the manner in which the real system might perform in real time.

Because of the increasing complexity of a number of the models mentioned, particularly those involving simulation and the need to cut calculation time, the development and use of computers has led to an increased awareness of the use of models in forecasting.

Examples of market simulation models are 'market correlation with economic indicators' (page 155), correlation and company sales (page 157), and multiple correlation (page 168). However, all these methods operate with a small number of variable factors, whereas it is possible, using a computer, to increase the number of variables and analyze the system created by their interrelationships, using them as a series of interacting factors. As certain key variables are changed, the effect upon the other factors can be assessed. These methods are often referred to as market/business throughput systems and are developed as mathematical models.

A further development of this is the concept of a simulation model forecasting the immediate period ahead and then continuing to move on through the ensuing periods; the model is moved on artificially through time.

Computers and forecasting

The development of electronic computers has presented the forecaster/marketing executive with a more effective method of processing information, and has also provided a problem-solving tool. This is particularly so in the area of forecasting, where computers can be used to handle highly complex problems that would otherwise be impossible or too costly to solve. But they can also be used to handle many of the traditional types of statistical forecasting techniques. On a computer, many of the statistical types of forecasting already mentioned could be more quickly obtained, in greater detail, with a variety of breakdowns, using far fewer man-hours.

The computer is not a separate forecasting technique, but merely a means of making some techniques possible to use, of making others more effective in their application, and of making the results of some techniques more readily available because of time and cost considerations.

One of the main uses of the computer in forecasting is to maintain past and present records of purchasing patterns and other relevant facts that can be used to make computerized or manual forecasting more effective. It can analyze demand history and break down past patterns of sales into trend, seasonal, cyclical and random variation values.

It is also used to search for factors outside the company that have a degree of correlation with the level of sales, eg bank advances, gross national product, hire purchase debt, the employment position, etc. The computer's ability to handle a large number of variables often makes it the best way, and sometimes the only way, of using multiple correlation techniques.

It is possible to simulate many market situations on a computer and, by changing the size of one or more variables (eg price), to assess and quantify the effect this will have on sales volume in a particular market.

Computers can be used to assess and improve the 'machinery' of forecasting by examining basic patterns of demand and applying and testing various techniques (ie moving averages, least squares analysis, etc) and their variations (ie weighted moving averages, seasonally adjusted least squares analysis) so as to identify the most suitable combinations of forecasting techniques.

Storage and retrieval of appropriate forecasting data, together with the actual forecasting calculation, its probability and the comparison of various forecasts, can all be carried out by a computer at high speed at an increased frequency interval. It must be appreciated, however, that the computer is merely a forecasting tool developing a series of quantified relationships between sales and a variety of variables, because the forecast evolved by a computer is only as good as the data put in. Further, it must also be appreciated that computer forecasts must be 'humanized' by being subjected to human intelligence and judgement.

A further application of the computer is the auditing of forecasts: monitoring the accuracy of the forecast by comparing it regularly with actual sales. Built-in warning systems can be arranged to indicate when actual sales fall outside the acceptable probability limits, so that action can be taken.

In fact, the computer can be used to carry out a wide range of forecasting activities that concern most objective and statistical techniques.

Which method to use?

In a later chapter ('Controlling the Forecast') one of the controls suggested is to 'audit the machinery of forecasting' (ie the methods used). In this way, by comparing actual sales with forecasts, the most effective methods of forecasting for a particular company can be identified.

Often the forecaster wants to know which methods to use *before* the forecast is made and therefore before an 'audit' can be carried out. One method is to take data for the last five sales periods and apply various techniques to the first four pieces of data and then compare the resultant forecasts with the sales that were actually achieved in the fifth period. Those methods which give the closest forecasts to the actual sales figures can then be used to make some real forecasts for the next period, ie period six.

CHAPTER 8
Subjective Methods of Forecasting

'Persons pretending to forecast the future shall be considered disorderly.'
New York Crime Code

Subjective methods of forecasting
Subjective methods of forecasting tend to be intuitive techniques that are the application of experience, intelligence and judgement to the forecasting situation; in fact they tend to be based on deduced conclusions. Some methods included in this section are wholly subjective, basically representing an averaging of a variety of opinions, eg a survey of consumer/user intentions. Others, although derived subjectively, can be made more useful by the application of an objective method, eg the addition of probability values to panel forecasting.

Indicator assessment method
The indicator assessment or 'balance the facts' method again makes use of economic indicators. An assessment is made of the general factors which are likely to be operating, and will affect the company, in the next sales period.

Where particular economic data have been found to reflect the economic climate in a particular industry, the appropriate economic indicators are listed in two columns. One column will show all those indicators that are favorable towards an expansion of trade, and the other column those that indicate a contraction of trade. The strength and effect of these indicators is assessed and a final conclusion formed and written up. To illustrate this technique, take a hypothetical case where a forecaster is endeavoring to determine the extent of future business activity in the economy related to a particular company's markets (see Figure 60). Actual figures and graphs for each indicator have been omitted but these would be necessary for a clear assessment.

Unfavorable factors	Favorable factors
1. *Employment.* Allowing for high seasonal peaks, unemployment has increased especially in certain capital goods industries.	1. *Machine tool orders.* Following a decline in the early part of the year, there has been a steady increase in orders from July onwards.
2. *Government spending.* This has been curtailed in the last four months due to signs of inflation in the economy.	2. *Factory building approvals.* There has been a slow but steady upward trend throughout the year.
3. *Industrial production* has levelled out again in the last part of the year.	3. *Bank advances* are rising strongly.
4. *Home building starts* are again levelling out.	4. *Terms of trade.* These were steady in the early part of the past year but turned in our favor from August onwards.

ASSESSMENT

Business activity in the coming year will tend to level out. Although government spending has been temporarily curtailed, it can be expected to increase again and introduce a boost to the economy if the present decline in employment continues. The machine tool orders and factory building starts indicate confidence in the present situation by business men generally. This is encouraged by the fact that bank advances are rising strongly, and this will have a good effect upon the ability of consumers to purchase durable products.

Favorable terms of trade indicate that import prices have become cheaper relative to export prices and this should help to increase consumer spending power without increasing the present inflationary tendencies when terms of trade advantages are reflected in retail prices.

The conclusion is, therefore, that, although business activity will tend to level out, total national disposable income will continue to rise, but not at the same rate of growth as last year.

Figure 60. *An assessment of appropriate economic indicators*

A variation of this method is to identify various appropriate indicators and send recent past data and current data to three or four interested company executives asking them to 'sort' the items into currently 'favorable' or 'unfavorable' columns. A further refinement is to ask the executives to rank the favorable and unfavorable factors in order of their importance to the company/product range.

Sometimes one executive may place an indicator in the opposite column to the others. In such a case the economy/market is being assessed taking different influences into account; it is important for the forecaster to investigate these differences.

The indicator assessment or 'balance the facts' method can be used either to give some indication of anticipated business activity, or to gauge the effect of various economic indicators upon the sales of a

Influence/impact factors	Rank in order of importance	IMPACT							
		Considerable (5)	Some (4)	Average (3)	Little (2)	None (1)	Favorable	Adverse	Neither
1) International factors a) b) c) d)									
2) Economic factors a) b) c) d)									
3) Industry factors a) b) c) d)									
4) Market factors a) b) c) d)									
5) Company factors a) b) c) d)									
6) Consumer/user a) b) c) d)									
7) Competition factors a) b) c) d)									
8) Environmental a) b) c) d)									
9) Psychological factors a) b)									

etc

Figure 61. *Subjective factor assessment form*

product or range of products. It is a balancing technique, where the statistical/data approach is counter-balanced by experience and judgement.

Subjective factor assessment

Earlier it was suggested that no matter whether an objective/mechanical method of forecasting was simple or highly sophisticated, its prediction should always be subjected to human judgement, intelligence, reasoning and logic; is the projected forecast feasible within what is known of the total situation?

The forecaster and/or the expert being consulted is being asked for an opinion as to the credibility of the forecast and if and how he would adjust it. The effectiveness of this approach will depend upon the breadth of the expert's knowledge and experience, his ability to identify relevant factors and their trends, his ability to quantify and measure the factors' impact on the forecast. Many good experience-based forecasts are made by 'experts' not apparently wholly aware of the stages through which they should proceed if their ultimate forecast is to be more than an unrelated guess. It may help therefore to get them to formalize their approach by asking them to complete such a form as in Figure 61; the factors included would be necessarily different for each company.

Experts are asked to identify influencing/impact factors under each heading, to rank them in order of importance, to grade according to anticipated impact and then to indicate whether they consider it to be favorable or unfavorable. By assigning rank and weight to factors a quantitative dimension is given to a qualitative (judgemental) opinion. The expert can now be asked to modify a 'mechanical' forecast in the light of the weight of his opinion; it also permits quantitative comparison to be made between periods.

The Delphi method

This method eliminates the committee activity seen in some types of subjective forecasting in favor of a program of questionnaires designed on a sequential basis. It attempts to make more effective use of informed intuitive judgement. It is based on personal expectations of individuals and therefore may take into account forecasting and influencing factors not considered by other people or included in the calculation of statistical forecasts.

A panel of experts is selected and the first questionnaire which asks a series of questions on the likelihood of some particular event/situation/phenomenon happening is put to them. It attempts to establish median values of the particular variable. This is summarized and, together with extreme values, is passed back to the members of the panel. The members are then asked to reconsider their previous answers and modify them if they think appropriate; those who made extreme estimates are asked to explain why such estimates were made. The procedure continues in this manner until a consensus is reached.

The questionnaires usually contain a means of indicating whether individual members of a panel consider themselves ill-equipped to respond to a question in a particular area. Some examples of Delphi type questions are as follows:

A. In what year do you forecast with 100% probability the first specific legislation on population control?
Year....
Expertness –   Yes   No
Comments –

B. In what year do you forecast that vegetable sources will provide 25% of the human protein consumption now obtainable from animal sources?
with 20% probability Year......
with 80% probability Year......
Expertness –   Yes   No
Comments –

C. By what percentage do you forecast the present telephone network based on cable being superseded by a network based on radio waves by 1990, with 50% probability?
.....%
Expertness –   Yes   No
Comments –

D. What % probability do you give to the forecast that the issue of motor vehicle licences will be selective by a defined system of priorities in the year 1990?
Probability .....%
Expertness –   Yes   No
Comments –

E. What percentage of private motor cars do you forecast will be propelled by the following in the years stated, each at 50% probability?

	Year	
	1990 %	2000 %
Internal combustion		
Steam		
Gas turbine		
Electric		
Other		

Expertness — Yes   No
Comments —

Survey of consumer/user purchasing intentions

A simple and direct method of forecasting sales is to ask customers and potential customers what they are planning to purchase. In consumer goods markets, where sheer numbers make it impossible to interview everyone, an appropriate representative sample must be approached if the eventual forecast is to be meaningful. It may involve a sample survey at two levels: the consumer's intention to buy a particular product or brand, and the wholesaler/retailer intention to stock and promote it.

With industrial products the number of customers and/or potential customers may be relatively few, and sampling may not be necessary. The main problem will be to persuade customers to make such a prediction or to give enough reliable information regarding future production, plans, future expenditure, manufacturing capacity, new product development policy, existing stocks, etc, so that a forecast can be made.

Various aspects of surveys were considered earlier in the sections dealing with the collection of data and original field research. Survey results should not be used alone for forecasting but in conjunction with other methods. Executives of customer companies may think that in forecasting for a supplier they cannot be held responsible as in their own organization, and an arbitrary guess rather than a considered estimate may result. Further, it will be difficult to gauge changes in policy matters within a customer company (eg the possibility of a change in the size of stock holding), or genuine market reaction (eg the effect of their or your competitors' activities), or the effect of changes in price and/or discount policy. Despite these problems, a good estimate by a 'buyer' will provide forecasting information regarding how 'buyers' feel *at the moment.* Over a period of time a pattern of reliability will be established regarding various 'buyers'.

The forecaster may modify the survey results by his own interpretation of anticipated future events in the economy, market or company.

Panels of executive opinion

Whereas the previous method concerned a prediction of the market from the customer's point of view, this technique obtains a forecast, short-, medium- or long-term, based on the facts and the considered opinion of key executives within the company's own organization. Executive forecasts are evaluated, combined and averaged, and through discussion a single forecast emerges. Executives should appreciate the need for forward planning and will realize that this is based ultimately on the number of items that can be sold. If executives can be encouraged to obtain forecasting data and opinions from within their own functional areas and make a considered forecast of these, this method is in effect the distilled forecasting thinking of the company. Company policy will be known and the panel fed with basic economic and market information and assumptions.

The various marketing executives (marketing research, new product development, advertising and sales promotion, sales, and distribution) are obvious members for such a panel. But so are production, purchasing, finance and personnel executives, not only because the best mental resources within a company are being brought to bear on the forecasting problem, but also because their forecasts will be influenced by their own specialized areas of operation and the distilled forecast of their particular business environment. Executives have an interest in the continued existence of the company and often have very definite views of the future under existing policies and how these could be improved.

One use of a panel of executive opinion is that of assessing and adjusting other forecasts based on mathematical and mechanical projection. Specialized human judgement and intelligence are used to check the credibility of objective techniques.

Panels of executive opinion can also be used in the final stages of the development of a forecast. Where forecasts have been obtained from various sources, there is a need to assess and evaluate each one before adopting an actual forecast. A panel of executive opinion is one way of achieving this.

'Prudent manager' forecasting

A variation of the previous method is where a small panel of specialists from all parts of a company is set up. They are asked to assume the role of members of the purchasing decision making unit *in a customer company*. They are asked to evaluate the supplying company's total sales proposition and to forecast the sales of various products. They are asked to do this from a customer's point of view, prudently assessing the facts that are available, and to produce purchasing requirements that customers would be likely to want in the conditions prevailing in a market.

Composite forecasts of the sales force

The term 'grass-roots' has been used to describe the relationship of the salesman, area or regional managers and sales managers to the customer. The close proximity of the sales force to the roots of demand (the customer) is the justification for its use in many cases to carry out research and forecasting functions.

This type of forecast can be used as a prediction technique in its own right, particularly if statistical data from other sources limits the amount of forecasting that can be done by other methods. It can also be used as a practical check on more mechanical methods of forecasting.

Ideally, the salesman should be given some basic tuition in elementary forecasting. Also he may be given historic data on past sales over an appropriate period of time or may be expected to derive this information from his own records. The ensuing forecasts are totalled to give an overall sales forecast for the company. Special forecasting forms to be completed by the salesman can be arranged in such a way as to produce not only a total sales forecast but one analyzed in terms of product group and/or sub-group size or value, by area or type of customer or industrial classification. The main justification for this type of forecasting is that it is presumed that salesmen have a detailed knowledge of their own areas of a market. One of the main disadvantages claimed for this method is that of bias by members of the sales force. One type of salesman may deliberately undervalue his forecast because he thinks that it may become the basis of his sales target; by setting it lower it becomes easier to achieve. But, although this may be a problem initially, after a small number of sales forecasting periods a salesman's method of operating soon becomes apparent. It is possible to discover an average percentage, eg salesman A's sales always tend to be 5% up on his forecast: salesman B tends to be 12½% down on forecast. There will always be differences due to external forces, but the pattern of bias will be indicated fairly clearly.

Other disadvantages claimed are that forecasts by salesmen are influenced by recent successes or failures rather than by future sales opportunities.

An additional use of obtaining forecasts from salesmen is as a motivational device. Forecasts by salesman are made and then discussed with sales executives and agreement is reached eventually on the forecast which then becomes the basis of the salesman's target. The salesman feels that he has had a part in calculating his target, and he has been consulted. This in turn often makes him more enthusiastic in his attempts to achieve the target, and he will, therefore, be more likely to reach and pass the agreed sales value than if the target figure had been arbitrarily imposed from above.

A refinement of the above technique is where, in addition to salesmen making forecasts, area, regional and national sales managers can be asked to produce forecasts for their own appropriate areas of responsibility. At each level these can be totalled and a sales forecast obtained. Further, comparisons can be made between the sum total of salesmen's forecasts in each area with the area manager's forecast and the variance between the two figures analyzed, eg why is the salesmen's composite forecast 15% above the area manager's forecast? What factor has the area manager taken into account that has not been considered by the sales force or vice versa?

In addition to bias, it is said that this method is a costly way of obtaining information, is unreliable because of lack of forecasting training for salesmen and uses valuable selling time. On the other hand, the salesman can produce the necessary data fairly easily in many marketing situations, appreciates technical considerations in industrial marketing situations, is already known to the customer, has his confidence, and also tends to discover market intelligence additional to the forecasting data.

Surveys of expert opinion

This approach can range from buying in forecasts from consultants to running a panel made up of experts from within the company (marketing researchers, salesmen, etc) and specialists from outside, ie economists, marketing experts, specialist psychologists, typical customers, etc. Further, the method can be of the kind where each panel member makes a forecast and never meets the other members, or where they meet as a committee and, through discussion, arrive at a composite forecast. In the former case the variations in the different forecasts can be analyzed and an eventual forecast obtained (sometimes by the simple device of averaging); but in the latter case the role of forecasting has been delegated to the committee.

The main danger of such composite forecasts is that they may contain a number of judgements or arbitrary forecasts, and their validity may be dubious. It is difficult for the forecaster to know whether such forecasts are soundly based, and, therefore, difficult later to determine and analyze why the forecast varies from actual sales. Further, with the individual parts of composite forecasts it is impossible to distinguish between what is optimistically desirable and what is realistically possible.

In spite of these difficulties the survey of expert opinion is a useful forecasting tool, because the individual component part forecasts suggest the range of possibilities and by averaging them a 'middle of the road' forecast can be obtained.

Uncertainty and probability in subjective forecasting

One of the biggest problems in top management decision making today is how to cope with the uncertainty in information regarding the organization's external environment.

Many capital budgeting policies and their input forecasting procedures require only one-number forecasts/estimates, thus neglecting the problem of uncertainty completely. For example, two experts may forecast 1750 units, but one may be 95% certain of his forecast and the other only 50% certain.

Misinterpretations and ambiguities occur simply because judgements about uncertainty are difficult to transmit to others, and also because forecasts/estimates from subordinates can be biased and because the capacity for risk-taking differs among individuals.

Suppose an expert forecasts/estimates that there is a 'good' chance that sales will exceed 200,000 or a 'fair' chance that sales could be as high as 300,000. Or there is a 'reasonable' chance that Competitor X will introduce a new product next year that will adversely affect sales. What do these statements mean? Does 'fair' mean that the chances are two out of 10, or four out of 10? Does 'reasonable' mean five out of 10 or perhaps seven out of 10?

A number of companies require 'optimistic', 'pessimistic' and 'best estimate' forecasts from various experts. These supposedly widely understood terms open up the possibility of very different interpretations and to some extent may even encourage 'political' manipulation because of their ambiguity.

For example, even the range from the optimistic to the pessimistic level could vary widely between two 'information specialists' even though they both guess the actual uncertainty to be about the same.

Much staff and analytical effort goes into estimating the 'single-number' forecast, whether it is the sales to an individual company or the overall sales of a particular product or product type. The manager either has to accept the expert's forecast/estimate about the future or make a compensating judgement. However, if compensation is made at a number of levels or points, the true position will become blurred, as the uncertainty underlying the eventual forecast is not visible.

In some companies information experts are more concerned with attaining their own personal rewards than they are with choosing estimates that reflect their best estimates of future sales. In practice

Market and Sales Forecasting

some companies tend to reward information experts when sales performance exceeds their original forecast, penalize them when performance falls below forecast, and do neither when they are 'spot-on'. In such circumstances the expert has little to gain by reporting an impersonal, objective forecast, and much to gain by estimating conservatively or even by under-forecasting and over-achieving.

Making uncertainty visible

There are several ways of presenting uncertainty in a visible and precise manner.

Cumulative Probability	Maximum sales expected
1.00	1200
0.95	900
0.75	700
0.50	600
0.25	500
0.05	300
0.00	0

Table 49. *Probability judgements*

(a) Probability judgements. Probabilities are given by the forecaster to various levels of sales as in Table 49. This table shows, for instance, that the chances are only one out of four (or 0.25) that sales will be less than 500; or conversely, the chances are three out of four (0.75) that sales will be greater than 500. Similarly, the chances are 50/50 that sales will exceed 600, and three out of four that they will be less than 700. The chances also are 50/50 that sales will fall within the 500 to 700 range. Identifying the uncertainty in this manner provides a more comprehensive view of a forecast figure.

(b) Visual probability range displays. Figure 62 shows the information expert's judgements regarding the underlying uncertainty in a visual manner. The probabilities on the vertical scale show the chances of actual sales falling within a particular range. For example, the chances are one out of 10 that sales will fall in the 300 to 400 range, and one out of 10 that they will fall in the 400 to 500 range.

(c) Uncertainty index. Often for the purpose of simplifying the subsequent financial evaluation and for implementing planning and control objectives, a 'single-number' forecast eventually has to be

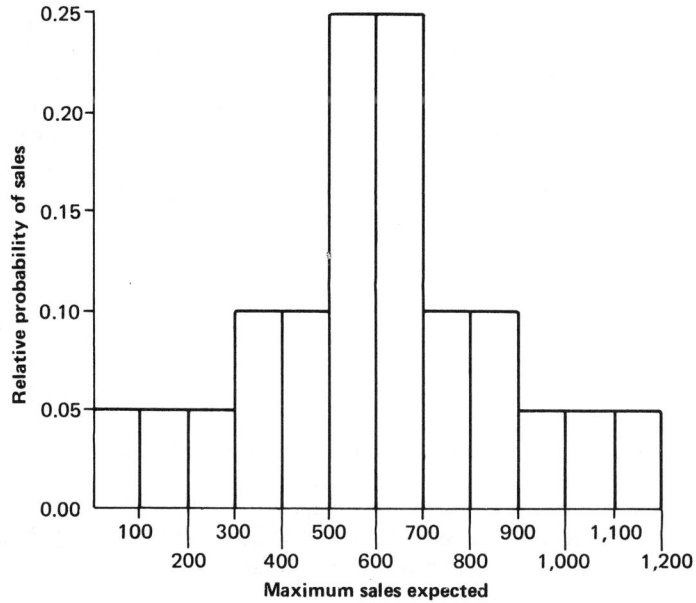

Figure 62. *Visual probability range display*

decided upon. In Figure 63, the uncertainty index shows the probability of sales falling below the forecast. Thus the index indicates that for a forecast of 500 the chances are only one in four that actual sales will be below this level.

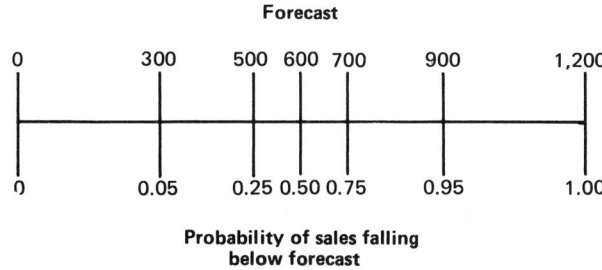

Figure 63. *An uncertainty index*

Market and Sales Forecasting

Presenting forecasting information in these various ways does not prevent the top-level manager from applying his own judgements to a situation, but, before he does, he has a better idea of what experts and information specialists were actually thinking when they made their forecast/estimate. But even where experts are expected to produce a 'single-number' forecast/estimate, they will tend to produce more effective and objective forecasts/estimates if they 'think probabilistically'.

Probability and forecasting by composite opinion

In the previous section it was suggested that experts who were asked to make subjective forecasts should be required to give not only their best estimate/forecast but also their most optimistic and their most pessimistic. There is an analogy between this and the least squares (line of best fit) method on page 185, where the best estimate could be construed to be the projected trend line and the most pessimistic and the most optimistic forecasts could be likened to the control lines set two standard deviations above and below the trend line.

In fact the range between the most pessimistic and the most optimistic forecasts can be used to 'adjust' the best estimate forecast and also calculate the probability of its being within certain limits. This can be done when asking one expert or when asking a panel of experts to forecast subjectively (although part of the forecast may be based upon facts/experience). This will add a quantitative 'sharpening up' of a qualitative (judgemental) forecast.

For example one 'expert' (perhaps a product manager, salesman, etc) is asked for his highest (most optimistic), best estimate (expected) and lowest (most pessimistic) forecasts of a particular product's sales in a specified time period. He gives the following information:

Lowest: 99 units
Best estimate: 110 units
Highest: 112 units

First a weighted average method is applied; weighted because if a value is really what he expects (his best estimate), it should be given more weight than the two 'outsiders' (highest and lowest).

$$\text{weighted average} = \frac{\text{lowest} + (4 \times \text{expected}) + \text{highest}}{N}$$

The weighting of 4 has been given to the 'expected' but the size of this weight depends purely on the subjective judgement of the forecaster. In this case the divisor is 6 because 4 (expected) + highest + lowest are six items. Therefore:

$$\text{weighted average} = \frac{99 + 440 + 112}{6} = 108 \text{ adjusted forecast}$$

Probability around this adjusted figure can be determined by first calculating the 'degree of uncertainty' (D) with the formula:

$$D = \frac{(H - L)^2}{6^2} = \frac{(112 - 99)^2}{36} = 4.69$$

The standard deviation can be found by calculating the square root of the 'degree of uncertainty' (D), i.e.

$$\sqrt{(4.69)} = 2 \text{ (approximately)} = \text{standard deviations}$$

To obtain 99% certainty 2.5 standard deviations are needed (to be exact, 2.5 standard deviations give 98.7% certainty, see page 196); therefore the probability will be:

$$2.5 \times \text{standard deviation} = 2.5 \times 2 = 5$$

Therefore, using the adjusted forecast of 108, there is:

a) 99% chance of sales being not less than $108 - 5 = 103$
b) 99% chance of sales being not more than $108 + 5 = 113$

Suppose this method is now applied to some of the panel situations described earlier in this chapter, our expert above being one of four experts consulted. Each expert is asked for his best estimate forecast and his highest and lowest, assuming no change in present policy. Each forecast should be given without consultation and should be supported by the individual's reasoning.

	Lowest	Best estimate	Highest
Panel expert 1	99	110	112
Panel expert 2	90	95	104
Panel expert 3	97	100	102
Panel expert 4	80	90	95

Calculate for each set of figures:

a) $\text{weighted average} = \dfrac{\text{lowest} + (4 \times \text{expected}) + \text{highest}}{6}$

b) $\text{degree of uncertainty} = D = \dfrac{(H - L)^2}{6^2}$

	Weighted average	Degree of uncertainty
Panel expert 1	108	4.69
Panel expert 2	96	5.5
Panel expert 3	100	0.6
Panel expert 4	89	6.25

Calculate the average mean figure:

$$\frac{108 + 96 + 100 + 89}{4} = 98$$

$$\text{average } D = \frac{4.69 + 5.5 + 0.6 + 6.25}{4} = 4.26$$

$$\text{standard deviation} = \sqrt{(4.26)} = 2.06$$

$$2.5 \times \text{standard deviation} = 2.5 \times 2.06 = 5 \text{ approx}$$

Circulate the results as follows:

Average forecast 98;
with 99% chance of sales being not less than $98 - 5 = 93$
with 99% chance of sales being not more than $98 + 5 = 103$

Ask experts to give reasons for high/low forecasts, request revised forecasts, repeat exercise and establish agreed forecast and levels of certainty.

Probability and expected values

A further forecasting application of probability is with the concept of expected values. In some subjective/probability forecasting methods it is possible to incorporate factors that permit analysis and assessment of the various courses of action or choice open to management. For example, a company considering two alternative product projects, A and B, and wanting to forecast the profit outcome, could, by using a model based on market share, net outcome and the probability of achieving particular market shares, calculate the expected values of the two alternatives and forecast which would be the best alternative to take. An example is given in Table 50.

In Table 50 for simplicity only three levels of market share have been considered; a wider range of market share calculations is possible in a practical marketing situation.

If the market shares indicated were achieved, it has been calculated that the profits that would be achieved (net financial outcome) would be as shown for project /markets A and B. If the best current judgement of the likelihood of these market shares being ob-

1 Market share %	2 Net financial outcome	3 Probability project A	4 Expected value of A	5 Probability project B	6 Expected value of B
0 to 30	−$10,000	0.3	−$3,000	0.2	−$2,000
31 to 60	+$3,000	0.5	+$1,500	0.7	+$2,100
61 and over	+$40,000	0.0	+$8,000	0.1	+$4,000
		1.0	+$6,500	1.0	+$4,100

Table 50. *Showing the expected value of two alternative product projects*

tained is then expressed as a subjective probability (columns 3 and 5), the expected values are found by multiplying the net financial outcome (column 2) by the appropriate pobability.

In the example shown in Table 50, the forecast 'best' project/market would be A as the expected value for it is $6,500 as against $4,100 for B.

A forecasting application of Bayesian decision theory

Closely linked with the expected value concept is Bayesian decision theory, which combines objective and subjective probabilities with revised probabilities. Revised probabilities are influenced by relevant updated data and information derived from such sources as the field sales force, research, economic and political fact situations.

The key element in using Bayesian decision theory is the development of decision trees. A decision tree is a network of lines showing the outcome of each considered decision alternative, the expected values and the associated probabilities. A decision tree is constructed from left to right by sequentially sub-dividing the major decision alternatives into their component parts. An application of part of Bayesian decision theory appropriate to sales forecasting is shown in Figure 64.

In Figure 64 the company had originally intended to re-launch an existing product with an additional size, a new pack and an updated promotional/product image. However, following market rumors (confirmed by marketing research) that a competitor was intending to launch an improved version of the product, the company has a decision to make from three alternatives:

(a) launch a new generic product, or
(b) launch an improved version of existing product, or
(c) continue with plan to re-launch the existing product.

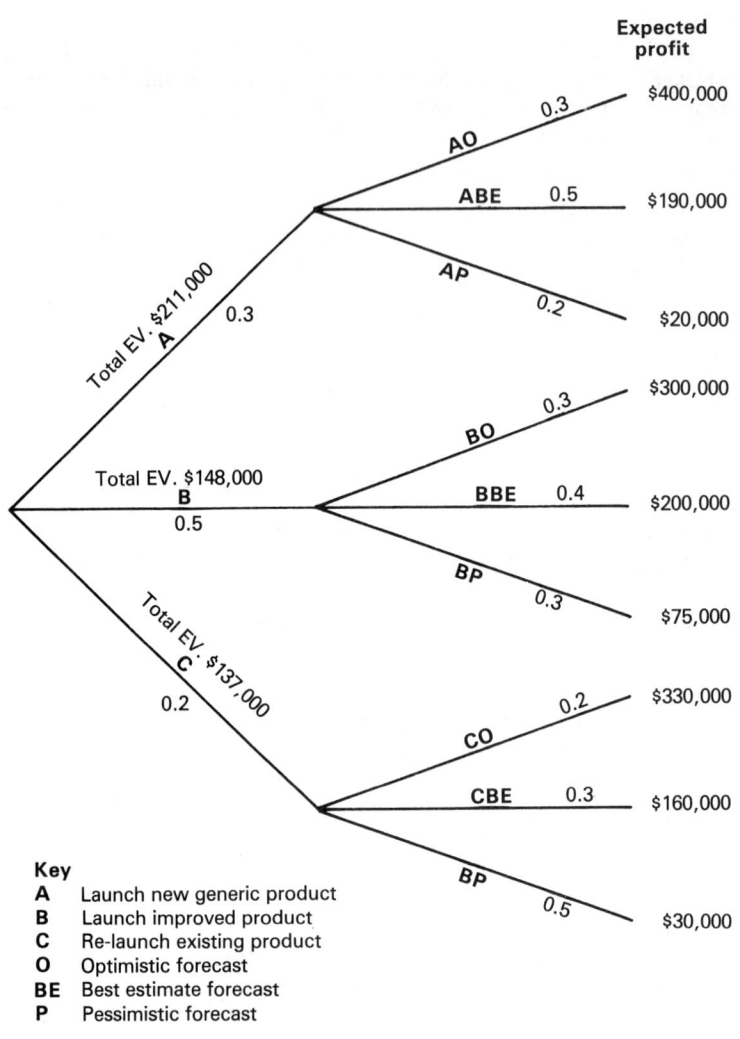

Figure 64. *A decision tree relating to alternative choices of action with probabilities of achieving forecasts and expected profits against forecast*

For each of these alternative courses of action, the company obtained an optimistic and a best estimate and a pessimistic forecast; it also obtained the probabilities associated with each. It was decided to consider the optimistic and best estimates forecast as viable for any

288

course of action.

The expected profit on each forecast is shown to the right of Figure 64. The expected value should now be calculated for each forecast and then totalled for each alternative course of action.

Action	Probability of forecast	Expected profit	Expected value
A. Launch new generic product			
Launch	0.3	$400,000	$120,000
Launch	0.5	$190,000	$95,000
Abandon	0.2	−$20,000	−$4,000
Total EV for this alternative			$211,000
B. Launch improved product			
Launch	0.3	$300,000	$90,000
Launch	0.4	$200,000	$80,000
Abandon	0.3	−$75,000	−$22,000
Total EV for this alternative			$148,000
C. Re-launch existing product			
Launch	0.2	$330,000	$66,000
Launch	0.5	$160,000	$80,000
Abandon	0.3	−$30,000	−$9,000
Total EV for this alternative			$137,000

It would appear that to launch the new generic product is the best alternative (A) and even to launch an improved version of the existing product is better than to re-launch the existing product itself.

Such analysis is only a guide for the forecaster/executive decision maker and there are obviously other factors that would have to be taken into account, eg cash flow implications, financial position of company, the opportunity cost of not following other alternatives and even whether it would be worth spending more money on marketing research to obtain more or better information. Market forces and/or management style may also play a part as to the choice of alternative that has the least likelihood of failure or that poses the greatest risk of failure.

Probability forecasting with large contracts or 'lumpy' items

Many forecasting techniques require continuous data (weekly, monthly, quarterly sales) to enable trend, seasonal and cyclical patterns to be identified and projected. But some sales situations relate to non-continuous data; single, large, multiple item contracts (eg a pharmaceutical manufacturing company bidding for a foreign government contract for antibiotics) or a potential order for a single high value item (eg a large scale earth moving machine). In such cases it is not possible to 'trend' historic data and although regression analysis and correlation using economic indicators may be able to forecast the total market value/volume it will not help the individual company in determining whether its individual bid or group of bids will succeed. Some forecasters are confronted with a situation where the company, having made a number of bids, requires a forecast of sales for this part of its potential sales revenue. It may be possible for the forecaster to divide the forecast into two stages; one when the bid is first made, ie possible sales, and secondly when negotiations and discussions have taken or are taking place and some of the contenders for the business have dropped out or have been 'eliminated' by the purchasing company, ie these contracts could be described as 'probables'. By analyzing past success/failure rates the forecaster could

Possibles		Probables	
Company	Bid	Company	Bid
Acme Manufacturing	$15,000	T James Inc	$17,000
A Williams Inc	$19,000	M Hobbs & Sons Inc	$16,000
Sutton Publishing Inc	$14,000	Guardian Pharmaceuticals	$46,000
Quostaphortune Inc	$58,000	GB Enterprises Inc	$32,000
GJB Corporation	$25,000	Durability Manufacturing	$58,000
Otley Group	$31,000		$169,000
T White Inc	$23,000	Discount @ 25%	$42,000
Queenie Bee Manufacturing	$48,000		
Coldharbour Production	$33,000		$127,000
	$266,000		
Discount @ 75%	$199,500		
	$66,500		

Total contract forecast based on past probabilities, $66,500 + $127,000 = $193,500.

Table 51. *Possible/probable contract forecasting*

come to the conclusion that in the past the company has been successful in obtaining the 'possible' contracts in one out of four bidding situations; therefore, assuming this will continue, there is a 25% probability of success. The forecaster may also come to the conclusion that in the past the company has been successful in obtaining 'probable' contracts in three out of four bidding situations; therefore, assuming this will continue, there is a 75% probability of success. Table 51 illustrates this method of achieving a multi-contract forecast.

With regard to the single 'lumpy' item bid, one forecasting method is that of ranking particular purchasing decision factors in order of importance, then rating the company's product advantage for each purchasing decision factor using the base of 100. This process is carried out for the company's own bid and, if the information is available, for each known competing bid. A subjective judgement is then made as to the possible success of the company's bid based on the assembled information. Table 51 shows this method.

Factor	Rank in order of importance in this bid	Product advantage (using base of 100)
Price Performance Design Delivery Product image Company image Technical service After sales service Spares availability etc		

Table 52. *Factors influencing purchasing decisions*

Success forecasting in a competitive bidding situation

In a competitive bidding situation it is obvious that an abnormally high bid price will tend to result in a very good sales revenue/profit return but would carry with it a relatively low success probability. Alternatively, if the bid price quoted is particularly low (with comparable quality and/or performance), it may almost certainly ensure that the bid will be accepted by the purchasing company but at an unacceptable level of sales revenue/profit return for the supplying company. These two extreme situations will both lead to low or no sales revenue/profit return but at some price point on the spectrum between them is a position which optimizes the level of sales revenue/profit and the success probability.

The main objective of any bidding analysis therefore is to identify a contract bid price which maximizes the sales revenue/profit pay-off. At the same time there is a need to determine the probability of success and to calculate the potential marginal loss (or penalty) which will be incurred if the contract is not awarded to a particular bidding company.

The first stage is to estimate the chance of being awarded a contract over a range of bid prices and to calculate the profit percentage and what this means in terms of money; from this can be calculated the net worth of bidding at a particular price which optimizes the situation for the supplier.

Subjective certainty of getting contract	Bid price	Profit percentage at bid price	Actual profit	Net worth (probability ×profit)
90%	$2,000	0	0	0
80%	$4,000	5%	$200	$160
70%	$6,000	10%	$600	$420
60%	$8,000	15%	$1,200	$720
50%	$10,000	20%	$2,000	$1,000
40%	$12,000	25%	$3,000	$1,200
30%	$14,000	30%	$4,200	$1,260
20%	$16,000	35%	$5,600	$1,120
10%	$18,000	40%	$7,200	$720
0%	$20,000	45%	$9,000	0

Table 53. *The calculation of net worth values of contracts over a range of bid prices*

The net worth is calculated by multiplying the various levels of profit by the probability of being awarded the contract at a particular bid price. Thus at a bid price of $6,000 the net worth is $600 × 70% = $420. It will be seen in the situation depicted in Table 53 that the highest net worth value is $1,260 and therefore the contract bid price which optimizes sales revenue/profit return and the probability of success is $14,000.

In many sales/marketing situations, price is not the only purchasing factor; the question of the customer-perceived market position of a supplying company's product/service, the company/product/service image, past relationships and experiences, etc, all have an influence on the final decision whether or not to award a contract. Many of these factors are qualitative and add up to a bias for or against a supplier. Because of the multi-aspect nature of this bias, the degree of impact can only be arrived at subjectively. Its application is carried through by considering what the chance would be for the contract to be awarded if there was an exact match in the bid price between a company and its competitors. If it was considered that the company/customer relations were very favorable, it might be estimated that the company could expect a 60%/70% chance of being given the contract in the event of an exact match of bid price with a competitor.

Where there are wide differences in product specifications wide differences in bid prices will emerge, although the purchasing company may have very specific objectives for product performance. There is therefore an element of 'appropriateness' of the company's 'total deal' (product, service, etc), which must be estimated, perhaps as in the method described on page 291. The concept of a total deal rather than simply aspects of a product is important as it could relate to the advantages of before and after sales service, availability of spares, credit and/or financing facilities, etc.

However, there are usually several factors to be considered in price differential situations. Where there is little product difference and price differentials are nominal, an estimate of 'favorable/adverse relations' bias mentioned above will normally be enough to cover this. But where major bid price differences are expected between a company and its competitors, then several questions need to be asked and judgements made. For example, how much higher (in percentage terms) would the company's bid price have to be for this to outweigh any bias in favor of the company? Conversely, how much lower (in percentage terms) would the company's bid price have to be, compared with competitors to be certain to be awarded the contract? For example, it could be estimated that there is an 80% chance of the purchase decision being based on a small/medium/large price differential. Conversely, this implies that there is a 20% chance that a small/medium/large price differential will not be the deciding purchasing decision factor.

Further, it should be possible for a company to estimate, on a 'spread' of expected bid prices, the relationship of the company's prices to those of a competitor, and consequently the 'certainty' of getting a contract at a particular price and the 'certainty' of not getting it at another.

Thus in Table 54 it is estimated that the company has a 50/50 chance of being awarded the contract at $10,000 and (not taking into account whether the potential customer is for or against the company) a 60/40 chance that it would be awarded to a competitor bidding the same price. The table also implies that at $4,000 the company

Bid prices	Company cumulative probability relating to bid prices	Competitor cumulative probability relating to bid prices
$4,000	1.0	
$6,000	0.8	1.0
$8,000	0.6	0.8
$10,000	0.5	0.6
$12,000	0.4	0.4
$14,000	0.2	0.2
$16,000	0.1	0
$18,000	0	

Table 54. *Cumulative probability for a company over a range of bid prices compared with a major competitor*

would be certain to get the contract and at $16,000 it has only a 10% chance and at $18,000 the company will definitely not get the contract.

This is based on the concept of cumulative probability. For example, in the situation in Table 54 there is certainty that there will be no bids below $4,000 or above $18,000; so all the probabilities will be contained within the limits set by these two values. Further, all the probability values within this range must total 1.0, ie 100%. Just as there is a 50/50 chance of the company getting the contract at $10,000, there is a 60% certainty but still a 40% uncertainty of getting the contract at $8,000.

Further, if there were just two competitors there is a 0.5 chance (ie 50/50 chance) of one of them quoting above or below the middle value bid price, ie $10,000. The chance of them both quoting above or below the middle value bid price is $0.5 \times 0.5 = 0.25$ chance. As a general indicator it could be said that with more than 4 or 5 competitors it becomes very unlikely that the contract will be awarded above the middle value bid price.

If a company's bid price is consistently higher than those of competitors, an investigation of how fixed/overhead costs are allocated in comparison with competitors should be carried out (if this is possible). It could be that the contracts concerned are carrying an undue fixed/overhead cost in relation to the opportunity cost which, in real terms, they afford the company.

A further consideration in determining the value of the optimum price will be the degree of risk involved. The larger the risk and the greater the marginal loss/penalty incurred if the contract is lost, the more aggressive will be the bidding and value of bids; lower than 'normal' bid prices tending to emerge. Thus, if a company and/or its competitors are more dependent on bid contracts than on 'normal' continuous sales, the more aggressive will be the bidding. Contrast the situation where a company's business is divided into 80% from normal continuous sales and 20% from contracts, with the converse situation of only 20% from 'normal' continuous business and 80% from contracts; more aggressive bidding can be expected in the latter case. A weighting factor therefore needs to be estimated for the company and each of its competitors; how important is the contract to them and how aggressive (price cutting, cutting of profit margins, increased discounts, favorable trade-in prices, etc) are they likely to be in bidding?

Another influencing factor that follows on from the division of the type of business done (contracts or 'normal' continuous sales), is that of the penalty on under-utilized production (or other) capacity if a contract is not received. Thus it may be more desirable to quote a lower price in an effort to increase the certainty of getting a contract than to risk losing it if under-utilized production/plant or other capacity exists. In such a case, as long as the variable costs involved are covered, any revenue in excess of this is at least a contribution to fixed/overhead costs and profit. A weighting value for the risk or penalty factor needs to be built into the bid price considerations.

Conclusion

Success forecasting in a competitive bidding situation is a highly subjective process and assumes the use of the best managerial forecasting judgement available based upon well informed knowledge of the industry, market, competition, customers, etc. The process can be summarized as follows:

1. Obtain the net worth to the bidding company of obtaining a contract at a certain bid price; this is calculated by identifying a range of prices, and profit at these prices, which is then multiplied by the subjective certainty value of obtaining the contract at these prices.
2. Estimate the 'bias' probability factor (favorable or adverse) which is expected to be effective in the event of an exact match or tie of prices with competitors.
3. Identify the 'appropriateness' of the product/service 'deal' being offered by the company compared with competitors and in the light of the purchasing company's specific needs.
4. Estimate the probabilities of obtaining the contract in the case of small/medium/large price differentials.
5. Calculate the range of cumulative probabilities of the company and its competitors over the range of possible bid prices.
6. Calculate the probabilities of competitors making bid prices at

various levels above and below the expected middle value bid price.
7. Consider recalculating the allocation of fixed/overhead costs if the company's bids are consistently high.
8. Calculate the risk factor and/or the marginal loss/penalty incurred if the contract is not obtained, with special consideration of:
    (a) the emphasis of the company and competitors' dependence on contract business, ie an 'aggressive bid' allowance.
    (b) the amount of under-utilized production (and other) resources that exist in relation to the company and its competitors, ie a further 'aggressive bid' allowance.
9. Carry out a basic calculation to determine over a range of bid prices the ideal 'true net value'; this is:

(Bid price × probability of getting contract) — (marginal loss/penalty × probability of not getting contract)

Even though this method is based on many subjective/judgement factors it does provide the forecaster/company with a considered forecast of the likelihood of being awarded a particular contract.

Major customer forecasting

Earlier (pages 215 and 218 *et seq*) it was suggested that greater forecasting accuracy could be achieved and the forecasting role made easier by segmenting markets.

Similarly, more accurate forecasting can usually be achieved by forecasting the separate product-groups that make up total company sales. The well known management 80/20 rule often applies, ie companies tend to obtain 80% of their sales/profits etc from 20% of their products. This applies particularly to companies with a large product range. If time availability of computer capacity is not available to carry out forecasting on, say, 3,000 different products, then priorities must be established. This is done by identifying those products/product groups that are most critical/important to the company's sales/profits contribution, ie the 20% of products that make up the 80% of sales/profits. The sales of these critical/important products could be forecast individually (or at least in sub-groups) while the remaining 80% of the product range which contributes 20% of the sales/profits could be put together in sub-groups and forecasts made for them, perhaps using market indicator factors obtained for the 'critical' products forecasts.

The same rule sometimes applies to customers; where a company obtains 80% of its business from 20% of its customers. For example, one metal components company obtained 62% of its business from four customers. One specialist trade journal obtains 42% of its advertising from three advertisers. Sometimes the same principles can be applied to individual salesmen's territories, where a relatively small number of active accounts provide most of the sales/profits from that territory. Obviously the identification of these major customers and the establishment of precise sales forecasts/objectives for them individually is crucial to the overall forecast for the company.

Because so much sales/profit performance depends upon these major customers, more time is often given to them and more details considered about them than is the case with the large number of customers who make relatively little contribution to the sales/profits total.

It is normal, for example, for the forecaster/salesman/sales manager to research a fairly detailed customer profile covering home address, type of business, know-how, resources, experience, sales/market area, reputation, image, whether a subsidiary, industry/national/international connections, estimated number of employees, estimated sales/profits, product lines supplied, their quality, range, suitability, market position, price relativity, cost-effectiveness, etc.

This is usually followed by an analysis of the business done generally by the major customer and the business done specifically with the forecasting company. For example, what is the major customer's management philosophy — is it to rationalize, expand, maintain the status quo, retrench, re-invest, diversify, etc? Is its general business remaining stationary, expanding or declining? What has been its overall purchasing 'spend' over the last few years and particularly last year, and what is its intention for the coming budget period? How much of this purchasing 'spend' comes to the forecasting company and how much in absolute terms as a percentage went to the forecasting company's competitors?

A list of pre-forecasting factors that have to be considered is then compiled before a subjective prediction can be made. These would include the historic trend of recent sales with the major customer, the seasonal/purchasing pattern of sales, the company's strengths and weaknesses regarding this account, an estimate of possible business and probable sales, possibly related to outstanding quotations/bids etc; how much repeat business can be expected and how much business would be possible if given additional sales/marketing/public relations support, what new market business is desirable/feasible, what action/reaction can be expected from traditional and/or new competitors?

At the same time as the major customer profile, analysis, pre-forecasting factors and forecast is carried out, some companies also require their salesmen/sales managers to indicate an action plan with specific objectives, showing their strategies and/or tactics as to how the forecast will be achieved.

CHAPTER 9
Sales Forecasting for New Products

'To seek out the best....we must resort to other information, which, from the best of men, acting disinterestedly and with the purest motives, is sometimes incorrect.'
Thomas Jefferson

The major difference between forecasting sales of an existing product and a new product is the lack of historical data: there is no past performance pattern to consider. Because of this absence of hard facts, there is a tendency for forecasting methods to be subjective rather than objective and the use of intuition and the crystal ball is readily rationalized. But because of the increased degree of uncertainty and the high level of investment risk, effective new product forecasting is essential.

Some forecasting techniques that have particular relevance to the new products are:

- The historical analogy approach
- The marketing research approach
- The test market approach
- The life cycle approach
- The substitute approach
- The composite forecasts of salesmen and sales executives

The historical analogy approach

Often the sales of a new product will follow the pattern already set by an existing product in the same or similar type of consumer or industrial goods market. Many types of household appliances have followed a similar product life cycle curve, although it is important to define product similarities clearly in terms of potential consumer appeal in particular market segments. The product benefits, logical or psychological, may not appeal to all social or economic consumer groups. Alternatively, an analogy may be found from past history in another country. It will be necessary to allow for the differences in environment that exist in these other countries, eg the standard of living, incomes, national characteristics; but a sales pattern may be identified that will enable the forecaster to make a better than arbitrary guess.

The marketing research approach

This can take two forms: a survey of a sample of potential customers for the new product which is then multiplied to give a picture of total market demand, or a survey of the channels of distribution (wholesalers, distributors, retailers) to obtain their view as to whether their customers will buy the new product and to what extent. The main problem with the first form is that if the new product is fairly revolutionary the potential consumer may not be able totally to comprehend the new concept or be able to identify himself with its use. And with the second form the forecast depicted by the enthusiasm of middle-men because of product profitability may not be matched by consumer enthusiasm for the real benefits the new product may offer. Alternatively, a negative attitude from middle-men because of such factors as stocks of existing products, increased investment required, etc, may produce a lower forecast than the new product warrants. Obviously, this latter method should be used only to supplement or confirm other forecasts. See page 125 *et seq* for marketing research methods applicable to forecasting.

The test market approach

In the absence of historical data for the demand of a new product, it is possible to gauge consumer reaction by test marketing the new product. This can be done on a limited scale, ie to sell the product from one shop or get one industrial customer to use it. Obviously, they would have to be 'typical' outlets, although samples of one are highly dangerous. Alternatively, a test town, test industry or test area would reveal more of the sales potential for the product. At this stage it might be necessary to ensure that the product had adequate general acceptance, in terms of performance, size, color, taste, price, etc, before proceeding to forecast sales. In the case of consumer products where the effectiveness of advertising and sales promotional media can affect demand considerably, a test area might be more appropriate. In this case an area is chosen (such as television area) and the same amount of promotional expenditure per head of population is used as is envisaged for the national launch of the new product, and the sales reaction is measured. Finally, allowing for regional differences, the test area sales are projected on to a national scale to become a forecast.

The life cycle approach

The forecast is obtained by considering the new product as a further logical stage in the life cycle of some overall customer satisfaction market, the sales of which will continue to grow at an anticipated rate. Thus in the home laundry market the sales growth of detergents continued and extended directly from soap powder, and in industrial machine tool situations numerical control devices have evolved directly out of the demand for manual control machines.

The substitute approach

Where a new product replaces an existing one, a straight continuation and possible extension of demand may be able to be predicted for the new product. For example, in the packaging industry an aerosol container or plastic sachet may be substituted for a bottle. But it is not simply a case of considering the existing demand level being transferred to the demand for the new product, but also the length of the transition period must be estimated. Also, a prediction should be made of the proportion of this it will be possible to capture. Further consideration should be given to the extent of consumer reaction to the new product. For example, if a substitute packaging material has a high convenience factor, the sales of the product it contains may increase.

The composite forecasts of salesmen and sales executives

This method was mentioned earlier as a viable method of general forecasting, but it has also been used effectively in the special situation relating to new products, particularly in industrial markets. In some cases the combination of the salesman's technical knowledge of the product together with his personal knowledge of customers, their purchasing methods and their own marketing requirements, enables him to give an informed estimate of the future sales potential of the new product, or at least to predict reaction to it, and even to interpret customer reaction to the new product concept when confronted by it.

Combinations of the above techniques are often used to forecast the sales of new products, but such predictions should always be accompanied by the assumptions made about the new product and the market, stating as clearly as possible the risks involved.

CHAPTER 10

The Application of the Forecast

'There are no such things as applied sciences, only applications of science'

L Pasteur

Market and sales forecasting was considered as a company marketing planning and targeting tool in Chapter 3, as a predictive device for both market volume and company sales in Chapters 5, 6, 7, 8 and 9 and will be examined as a control mechanism in Chapter 11. In the current chapter the use of the forecast by management and its application to various operational areas of a company is examined.

The forecast as a decision-making tool

The completed sales forecast presents the management of a company with a prediction on which several decisions must be made, eg whether to go ahead with production to meet the predicted demand or not. This is a typical management go/no-go decision. Also, there is the decision of how to apply the forecast to company functions (production, the sales force, etc) and/or to consider it in terms of external factors such as the choice between various alternative channels of distribution.

There will be a market size and/or market share below which it will not be profitable (in the short, medium or long term depending on the company objectives) to consider producing or purchasing. Such a decision is linked with the pattern and climate of competition, the optimum size of operation and the structure of the actual market (size and location of customers, etc), in fact with the total environment in which the company hopes to operate profitably. At this stage the sales forecast could be used to determine which markets or segments of markets to enter, or whether company resources could be used more profitably in alternative markets.

Break-even analysis

A major technique in the go/no-go decision-making process is break-even analysis.

This type of analysis (broadly used in Chapter 2, page 46) considered the cost-volume-profit relationship of producing and marketing. It produces a break-even percentage value which indicates at which level of activity or production total cost will equal total revenue.

Break-even analysis shows the position of the forecast in relation to the break-even point and indicates whether it would be profitable for the company should the forecast demand be achieved. It indicates whether or not profits would be made, but whether it is an acceptable level of profit is a management decision.

The break-even point can be calculated as follows. With a particular product a company has an annual fixed cost of \$5,000; at 100% capacity/activity its variable costs are \$20,000 and its sales revenue \$30,000.

$$\text{total cost} = \$5000 + \frac{x}{100} \times 20000 = 5000 + 200x$$

$$\text{total sales} = \frac{x}{100} \times \$30000 = 300x$$

The break-even point ($x\%$) is where total cost equals total sales, therefore:

$$5000 + 200x = 300x$$
$$5000 = 100x$$

$$= \frac{5000}{100} = 50\%$$

This data is shown graphically in Figure 65.

If a forecast is considered as a point on the total revenue line in Figure 65, then a forecast below 30,000 units, or \$15,000 sales revenue, is clearly not profitable. However, the product may still be made if it is in a developing market, or if as a complementary product it is to be used to help sell more profitable products. Any forecast or sales above the 50% break-even point would be profitable, but the degree of profitability may or may not be acceptable. A forecast beyond 60,000 units or \$30,000 sales revenue (ie 100% capacity) is not possible to achieve with existing equipment unless some new factor such as shift working is introduced, but it does present a marketing opportunity and it must be considered whether to add another machine or production unit. This will depend on a comparison of the short-term and the medium-term forecasts, ie to deter-

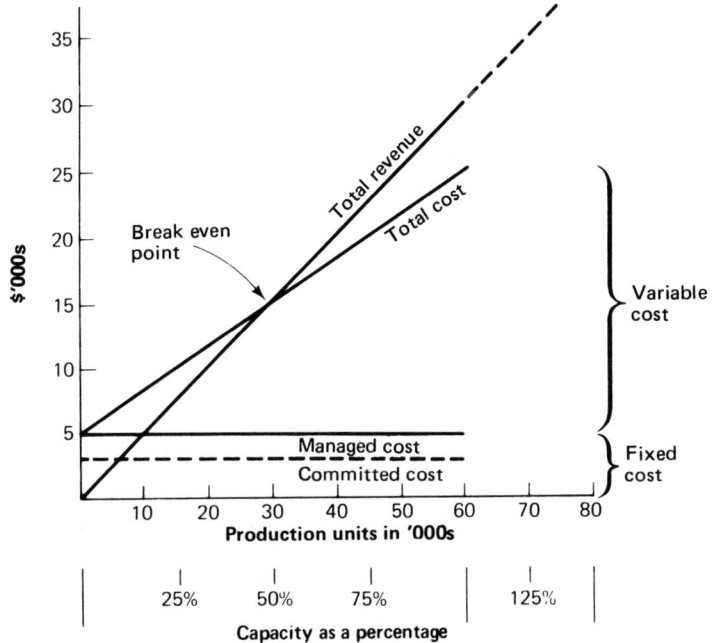

Figure 65. *A break-even diagram showing the point in production and sales where a product moves from a position of loss to one of profit*

mine if the higher level of demand is to continue in the more distant future.

Alternatively, the excess demand indicated by the sales forecast could be met by sub-contracting or obtaining 'private label' goods from other sources. Adding another increment of production will have the effect of increasing committed cost, thereby lifting up the total cost line and cutting profitability at lower volumes. In capital goods industries companies often sell the extra products with an ever lengthening order book.

Committed and managed costs

An unprofitable situation indicated by the sales forecast and break-even analysis may be made profitable in several ways, for example, if sales volume can be enlarged by a less than proportionate increase in the cost of an expenditure variable such as advertising or sales promotion. A more profitable situation may follow from increasing or decreasing the price, although this may in turn affect volume. A reduction in the variable cost per unit and the 'appropriation' of managed cost will increase profitability. Managed costs are those costs that do not vary with production and while necessary in an ideal situation, they could be avoided if the profit situation required it. For example, the making of films for TV commercials, once completed, becomes a committed cost, but the cost of exhibiting on TV is a managed cost. The managed cost must be budgeted for but could be avoided by cancelling the television time purchased to show the commercials up to eight weeks before the showing date. The effect of 'appropriating' $1,000 of managed costs can be seen on the break-even chart in Figure 66.

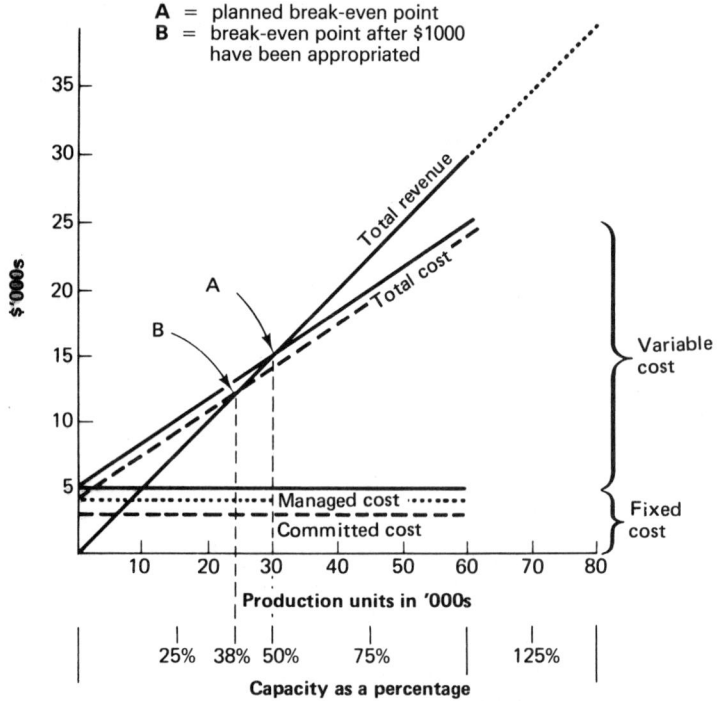

Figure 66. *The effect of 'appropriating' $1,000 of managed cost upon total cost and the break-even point*

In Figure 66 fixed costs have been reduced by $1,000 to $4,000 by appropriating $1,000, thereby increasing profitability by the same amount. But the most significant factor is that the break-even point is now at 38% capacity instead of 50%, and profits can be made after 22,000 units or $11,000 sales revenue. The appropriation of managed cost will sometimes make a forecast level of sales profitable, but if the planned expenditure was justified and then does not take place, the company will lose some benefit in the short, medium or long term.

Product mix and ratio analysis

Other methods in the go/no-go decision-making process of applying a sales forecast include product mix and ratio analysis. In multi-product companies the total sales forecast should be refined by breaking down the forecast in terms of profit, contribution to profit, sales volume, assets used, etc, applied to individual product groups, salesmen's areas, industry groups, and immediate and ultimate customer types.

The forecast is applied to production by the allocation of the various product requirements to production facilities and, in fact, the forecast should form the basis of all production budgets. The total forecast could be achieved by a variety of combinations of product sizes, models, colors, types, etc. Therefore, before applying the forecast to production facilities, the optimum product mix must be considered. From this a decision can be made as to which combination of products, and the variety within each product line, will be most profitable.

Product-range mix analysis was mentioned in Chapter 1 as one of the stages of an operational marketing plan (Figure 2). It assumes that an optimum profit can be obtained by selling the various product lines in a certain ratio, perhaps

A B C D
7 : 4 : 3 : 1

If a total forecast has been given, it should be applied to products in this most profitable ratio pattern. Product mix analysis should relate profits to the sales needed to make them, and the assets used. A sales/profits/assets analysis matrix is shown in Table 55. Here, if B is

Product	Sales	Profits	Assets
A	40%	30%	20%
B	10%	10%	30%
C	20%	25%	10%
D	30%	35%	40%

Table 55. *A sales/profits/assets analysis matrix*

a declining product and its resources can be applied to product C, then this transfer should take place if the forecast indicates an appropriate level of demand in the C market.

The use of these two devices at this stage of forecasting enables predicted sales of individual products to be related to the profitability of various combinations of products. The application of the forecast in this way permits the best possible product mix to be chosen in situations of limited company resources.

Application of forecasts to profit centers
Another variation of the application of the forecast is to apply it to the various 'profit centers' throughout a company. The profit center concept treats the various functional parts of a company (production, purchasing, marketing, and subdivisions such as selling and distribution), as separate centers that should each show a profit from the raw materials it buys after costs of its own operation have been met and the materials 'resold' to production. Application of the forecast to profit centers permits a more effective profit target to be set for each center.

Application of forecasts to sales territories
The sales forecast should also be applied to sales territories and where this is done it can form the basis of sales targets for salesmen. The sales potential of each area should be calculated to ensure that an appropriate target is set in relation to a company's expected share of a market.

Application of the forecast in industrial markets
In industrial markets user industries can be classified (using Standard Industrial Classification definitions and numbers), the size of these industries determined, and the percentage of business they each generate calculated. The share of business each company in an industry accounts for can be determined by taking the total sales of an industry and allocating them to companies on a basis of percentage of the total of the number of employees or the value of assets used. For example:

>Total sales in industry $10m
>Total employees in industry 10,000
>Therefore every employee = approximately $1,000 of sales turnover

Application of the forecast in consumer goods markets
In consumer goods industries, area potential can be calculated on a basis of the pattern of population spread, related to the type of consumer expected to purchase the product. It may be company marketing strategy to use TV areas as a basis for area planning. Data is published by specialized information sources, the TV companies and others, giving a breakdown of population in terms of age, sex, socio-economic grouping, location, etc.

From data of the kind in these tables it is possible for the forecaster to determine a pattern by which the forecast should be applied over the country, and/or the priority in developing national coverage region by region. This approach to applying the forecast will not only permit the setting of sales targets for individual members of the sales force, but can also be used to set area goals that can be used later to compare performance with forecast in a region.

But the share of the sales potential that a company can expect in any area must be determined before the sales forecast is finally applied. The sales target set for a salesman must be realistic as well as desirable. A guide can be obtained from past records; what was the territory potential in past periods and what share of the market did the company achieve? Allowances must then be made for any changes in local external factors (eg a new competitor) and internal factors within the company (eg an increase in advertising expenditure).

Application of the forecast by distribution channels

Another approach to applying the forecast is by means of detailed analysis of the profitability of using various types or sizes of retail outlets, individually or in combination. In many companies the bulk of the contribution to overheads and profit (ie the sales revenue minus direct costs) is produced by relatively few outlets. Often as much as 75/80% of the contribution comes from 20/25% of the number of retail outlets (by size or type). However, because the cost of marketing in general, and selling and distribution in particular, is broadly proportionate to the number of outlets used, a large part of total cost is generating a relatively small part of the contribution. For example, in a particular sales period the situation shown in Table 56 could arise.

Outlet type or size	Percentage of total outlets %	Sales ($)	Contribution to overheads and profit ($) (%)		Marketing costs ($)	Profit/ loss ($)
A	40	1,000	500	50	650	−150
B	30	2,000	800	40	500	300
C	20	4,000	1,200	30	400	800
D	10	13,000	2,600	20	350	2,250
	100	20,000	5,100	25.5	1,850	3,200

Table 56. *The cost of dealing with outlet types related to contribution-to-overheads and, therefore, to profit*

In the situation depicted in Table 56, the cost of dealing with outlet type A is more than the contribution produced. If the sales through the other outlet types (particularly D) can be increased by $1,000, it

Market and Sales Forecasting 308

may be desirable and, indeed, more profitable, to cease distribution through outlet type A.

In consumer goods industries the pattern of application of forecasts by specialized retail outlets can be determined from data of the kind shown in Tables 57 and 58.

Table 57 shows the total US grocery store trends by store type; Table 58 shows per capita buying income and retail grocery sales by US region.

An apportionment of a sales forecast in the food/grocery area on a basis of retail outlets or turnover, plus the pattern of past company experience in a region/outlet type, will make a more reliable predictor of sales.

Other sources of retail/wholesale distribution data are listed on page 111.

	ANNUAL SALES % Change vs. year ago					BIMONTHLY SALES			
Total	14	10	8	7	11	10	9	10	
Chain		11	9	9	11	10	10	10	
Large independents		11	11	9	12	11	9	11	
Remaining		5	−3	−2	7	9	9		
Total $	116.80	128.43	138.23	147.99	163.99	29.98	28.04	29.93	
○ Chain	69.62	77.16	84.42	91.62	101.84	18.81	17.70	18.49	*
○ Large independents	25.67	28.59	31.82	34.80	39.05	7.16	6.60	11.44	**
Remaining	21.51	22.68	21.99	21.57	23.09	4.01	3.75		
					% Share of sales				
Chain	59.7	60.1	61.1	6.19	62.0	62.8	63.1	61.8	*
Large independents	22.0	22.3	23.0	23.5	23.9	23.9	23.5	38.2	**
Remaining	18.3	17.6	15.9	14.6	14.1	13.3	13.4		
	1974	'75	'76	'77	'78	DJ '79	FM	AM	

* Chains with annual vol. of $1 million or over
**Remaining includes chains under $1 million and all sizes of independents
Source: *44th Neilsen Review of Retail Grocery Trends* p 83.

Table 57. *Total US grocery store trends by store type*

	Per capita grocery store sales ($)		Share of income spent in grocery stores (%)	
	1977	1978	1977	1978
US	689	757	11.5	11.6
New England	696	763	11.3	11.2
New York	642	693	9.1	9.2
Middle Atlantic	703	765	11.3	11.4
East Central	702	754	11.7	11.6
Chicago	641	689	8.8	9.0
West Central	642	711	11.1	11.2
Southeast	683	763	13.2	13.5
Southwest	701	780	12.8	12.8
Los Angeles	747	806	10.9	10.6
Remaining Pacific	737	820	12.0	11.9

Source: *44th Annual Neilsen Review of Grocery Trends*, p 87.

Table 58. *Per capita effective buying income and retail grocery sales*

In industrial markets the forecast can also be applied in terms of profitability of dealing direct with industrial users or through industrial wholesalers, factors or distributors.

This method of analysis applied by industrial product companies operating in a variety of industries (eg a range of pumps may have applications in many industries) could mean that unless there was future potential in certain user industries, a supplying company may find it more profitable not to actively market or sell to such industries.

The forecast as a basis for budgeting and control

By applying the forecast in the various areas described above, specific sales targets can be set, and the sales forecast can become the basis of all budgets in the company, ie production, finance, marketing, plant and equipment, raw materials, manpower, etc. In fact, all budgets in a company are based eventually on how many items the company anticipates selling. Further, from the sales forecasting data available, controllable operational plans can be evolved with appropriate strategies and tactics.

Not only is the total sales forecast attributed to various areas, outlets, salesmen, etc, who are responsible for achieving various levels of sales and profit and performance, but conversely it is attributed to production, purchasing and distribution functions to ensure that products and/or services are available in the right quantities and at the right time.

Combined objective/subjective forecast plan

Throughout this book a combined objective/subjective approach has been advocated. In the sections dealing with objective (statistical) methods, the application of human judgement, experience and intelligence to modify 'mechanical' methods has been recommended. In the sections on subjective (intuition, conclusions, 'gut feel') methods, some objective methods (eg weighted averages, probability) have been suggested to 'sharpen up' the subjective approach. In getting the forecaster/product manager/sales manager to calculate a forecast both approaches need to be brought together. Also, such personnel must obviously turn the forecast (after it has been costed and accepted) into an action plan (being responsible for the sales performance) and as such can make the forecast happen or at least influence it. Therefore it will be necessary to take into account any activities such personnel (and others) intend to carry out that will improve the organization's standing in the market place, and therefore influence sales.

One approach is to summarize (perhaps on one sheet of paper) the main components of a forecast/action plan; it would include the following sections.

1. General identification data — product/service group; market covered; year and forecast period(s), date of forecast.
2. Relevant economic data and forecasts — growth or decline trends, money supply, interest rates, government policies.
3. Relevant industry data and forecasts — growth or decline trends, changing methods, new materials and/or applications, substitute industries, etc.
4. Appropriate competitor data — identification of direct and indirect competition, estimated competitor shares, whether these are (slowly or rapidly) increasing, static or declining, key product/service changes.
5. Factors that influence purchasing/using decisions, weighted and ranked in order of importance, eg quality, price, delivery, design, image (product and company), performance, perceived market position, technical services, spares availability (if appropriate) and before and after sales service.
6. Present situation — totals for previous sales periods, value of quotation submitted and active, partly completed contracts, etc.
7. Forecasts
    (a) Strategy — either global forecast broken down into component parts, or the component parts added together to make a total forecast. Identifications of purpose/aims of forecast.
    (b) Objective forecasts using appropriate techniques from those examined earlier, where possible giving

The Application of the Forecast

maximum/minimum values as well as best forecast. This should be done for the market as a whole, the product group generally, and for specific products in the context of short-, medium- and long-term forecasts. Forecast market potential, market share, and probable forecast.
(c) Subjective forecasts using appropriate techniques from those examined earlier, giving most optimistic, pessimistic and best estimate values. Also applying subjective judgement to the mechanical method forecasts in 7(b).
8. Action/activities by company and/or individuals that will affect (favorably/adversely) company standing/competitiveness/image in the market place. These actions/activities should be described, a date fixed for implementation, their duration and their expected effect identified and whether this will be an immediate, short-, medium- or long-term effect. Contingency plans if forecasts are not being achieved. Rules for re-forecasting or updating.

The format of such a forecast/action plan will vary from company to company and not all the above factors will be appropriate, desirable or feasible in all cases. However, such an approach will ensure that all relevant factors are taken into account in making a forecast, that a range of techniques is used to ensure a balanced approach and that the anticipated effect of proposed action/activities during the forecast period is allowed for in the forecast.

CHAPTER 11
Controlling Forecasting and the Forecast

'I claim not to have controlled events, but confess plainly that events have controlled me.'

Abraham Lincoln

Scope of control

Effective control requires the measurement of performance against pre-determined objectives and standards, and the interpretation of trends and results. It also implies knowing where, when and how to take corrective action on time. A further aspect of control is recording performance data for use as a guide in planning future operations and to highlight marketing opportunities.

These aspects of control apply to effective forecasting and take the form of comparing, evaluating, interpreting and auditing the performance of the economy, the market, the market segment and the company's sales with the various forecasts. Then remedial action can be taken if necessary to update the forecast or change the methods used.

In fact, in many organizations it is normal to have several updates of a forecast during a sales period, eg one year. Further, 12 or 18 months ahead rolling forecasts are often made at predetermined points during the year. This is done to ensure that company strategy is reacting quickly to market/economic forces, to ensure continuity of forecasting and to confirm that the cash flow position will be as predicted.

It is also important to recognize that a sales revenue performance in any time/sales period is the result of a number of market forces all moving at different speeds or having different degrees of influence at different times. The control activity is to identify the factors that were of a different intensity/magnitude at the time the sales were made compared with what was anticipated in the forecast. Activity in this stage of the forecasting process can be classified into three main areas:

(a) The running audit which makes daily, weekly, monthly or quarterly comparisons of economic data, company sales and/or market performance against forecast.

(b) The annual audit which makes an assessment and comparison of forecasts over a longer period and in greater detail.
(c) The audit of the 'machinery' of forecasting within the company in terms of the objectives, policies, and the methods used; some forecasting techniques are more effective in certain market circumstances than others.

Within these three areas, forecasting can be made more effective by obtaining more or improved information for techniques at present in use or by developing methods, and by improving existing techniques or replacing ineffective forecasting devices.

Forecasts versus actual sales

There are various approaches to assessing forecasts against actual sales; they include:

1. Comparison between sterling and unit forecasts and sales in absolute terms.
2. Sales related to sterling and unit forecasts as a percentage achieved figure (eg 95% of forecast).
3. Sales related to forecast on a cumulative basis of 'the year to date' and the percentage achieved.
4. Percentage increase/decrease over last year.
5. Measurement of difference in timing or pace of sales as planned in the forecast compared with actual performance.

However, these assessments merely indicate deviations from the anticipated situation, and it further requires a curious and analytical approach to discover why, when and how they occurred, which factors were involved, and the likelihood of the situation occurring again. This is necessary to determine whether the forecast should be amended or whether other action should be taken, ie a change in marketing strategy or a change in forecasting techniques.

The degree of sophistication of assessment depends on marketing needs and/or what is economical for the company.

Variance analysis

The simplest approach is to graph the forecast and sales values. A visual examination will indicate any lead or lag effects and also highlight the magnitude of the differences between the two sets of values.

It will often show where short-term method forecasting has been correct but the outcome has been influenced by medium- and/or long-term factors. This will be indicated on the control graph by the sales performance pattern horizontally matching the forecast pattern but its level being higher or lower, the outcome being a poor forecast (see page 261). It then becomes a matter of priority to identify, take account of, measure and predict the forces causing the difference in the sales performance level.

Another approach is to make a comparison between forecast and sales values in absolute terms and to obtain a ± variance. For example:

        Sales   210
        Forecast 200
        ± Variance 10 units

It is useful to list the variances month by month (or by other appropriate time periods), and to convert them into percentages. When plotted on a graph a pattern of percentage variance, either by season or product or forecasting method, etc, is often indicated. Investigation will show the reasons for the pattern and either the methods of forecasting can be changed or the anticipated degree of variance allowed for.

Ranking variances

An alternative method of listing is to rank all the variances in their order of magnitude, ie starting with the largest positive variance through to the largest negative variance. If plotted on a graph this data should form a normal distribution curve, which indicates that there should be, over a period of time, just as many positive variances as negative variances, and the same magnitude of forecasting error. If the distribution is shown and there tends to be a greater number of variances in one direction, or the magnitude of errors is greater in one direction, then investigation into long-term bias is necessary.

Ratios

It is possible to calculate the ratio of the period sales to forecast, allowing for seasonal and medium-term cyclical factors, and to obtain an adjusted ratio. Acceptable levels of ratios can be established; they can also be graphed to permit comparison over a period of time.

The sum of forecasting errors

A further monitoring method is to take the sum of the forecasting errors over a period and divide by the mean absolute deviation. As sales emerge and a comparison is made, it is possible to detect where the forecast is not in line with the anticipated actual sales pattern.

The standard error as a monitoring device

At the end of each sales period the difference between the forecast and actual sales is calculated, these differences are squared and the squared values for all items are totalled (Σ). This total is then divided by the number of sales periods, and finally the square root is calculated. The result is the standard error and the calculation can be expressed:

$$\text{standard error} = \sqrt{\left[\frac{\Sigma(\text{actual sales} - \text{forecast value})^2}{\text{number of sales periods}}\right]}$$

where Σ = sum over all sales periods

The forecasting method giving the lowest standard error is therefore the most efficient method during the period under consideration. As this method is calculated by using 'differences', it affords a method of comparison of the efficiency of various methods where different units of measure are used, eg dollars, weight, bulk barrels, metres, boxes, etc. An objective of all forecasters is to minimize the standard error with any forecasting method.

Investigation of variances

In comparing actual sales with forecast, the important factor is not only the variance itself, but why it occurred. Analysis will indicate whether an aspect of forecasting was at fault or whether some new sales factor has emerged. The ± variance may have been caused by the beginning of a new trend, eg increased product usage, a new application, an appeal to a new market segment, etc, in which case the forecaster can allow for the new factor in future forecasting activities.

Alternatively, the variance may be caused by an ad hoc factor that is unlikely to occur again or cannot be guaranteed to happen again, eg a once-only special order, a strike at a competitor's factory, etc. In such a case the unusual sales item could be adjusted to a more normal level for the period, otherwise it will affect future forecasting, ie it will unduly weight moving averages and other trend calculations.

Levels of accuracy

Acceptable levels of accuracy of forecast depend largely on the company and market situations. A market that experiences wide fluctuation from one period to the next can obviously expect a greater average error than an industry where sales are relatively stable. Thus, while an 8% error may be acceptable in one market, a 4% error may be considered too high in another. There appears to be a correlation between the degree of accuracy and nearness to the eventual customer. Thus, as a general rule, consumer goods manufacturers are able to produce more accurate forecasts than component goods

Sales forecast control sheet   **Month ending** ―――――

Product, type size or model	This month			Year to date			Sales last year to date	Percentage increase/decrease over last year
	Actual sales	Forecast	% Achieved	Actual sales	Forecast	% Achieved		
Totals								

Figure 67. *A format for comparative assessment of sales and forecasts*

Forecast control sheet		Jan	Feb	Mar	Apr	May	Jun	Jul	Aug	Product: Sep	Oct	Nov	Dec
Month		Jan	Feb	Mar	Apr	May	Jun	Jul	Aug	Sep	Oct	Nov	Dec
Last year actuals	Units												
	Revenue												
Forecast Jan 1	Units												
	Revenue												
March reforecast	Units												
	Revenue												
July reforecast	Units												
	Revenue												
Actuals	Units												
	Revenue												
Actuals	Units												
	Revenue												
JAN	Units												
	Revenue												
FEB	Units												
	Revenue												
MAR	Units												
	Revenue												
APRIL	Units												
	Revenue												
MAY	Units												
	Revenue												
JUNE	Units												
	Revenue												
JULY	Units												
	Revenue												
AUG	Units												
	Revenue												
SEPT	Units												
	Revenue												
OCT	Units												
	Revenue												
NOV	Units												
	Revenue												
DEC	Units												
	Revenue												

Figure 68. *Forecast control sheet*

Market and Sales Forecasting 318

manufacturers who are several stages removed from the customer. There also appears to be a correlation between the accuracy of the forecast and the amount of money and number of techniques used to obtain it. Thus, in industries where forecasting is not considered too important or where sophisticated methods cannot be afforded, the level of accuracy tends to decrease. This does assume that a high degree of accuracy is necessary. In some industries a less sophisticated system meets the forecasting needs.

Formats for comparative assessment

A useful format for a combination of some of the forecast assessment methods mentioned above is one that permits a running audit and also produces the data to enable an annual audit to be made later.

The format used in Figure 67 would permit easy analysis and comparison of data and immediately highlight important variances.

A further simple format is, in each time period and for each product or product group, to lay out

— the cumulative forecast
— the cumulative actual sales
— the cumulative variance
— the cumulative variance as a percentage

Another format is shown in Figure 68. This is a forecast control sheet which shows last year's actual sales in each period and the forecasts of 12 sales periods commencing January of the year in question; this was possibly calculated three to six months before the beginning of the forecast year. It follows therefore that, in a dynamic market situation, it may be necessary to re-forecast in March (ie perhaps six to nine months after the original forecast was made) and again in July (which would be half way through the year), so these re-forecasts are shown. Under these, the actual sales values are inserted as they occur.

A three months rolling analysis of actual sales is then shown; this helps to highlight seasonal patterns, where sales expected in one period are carried over to the next, and also helps in the two re-forecasts.

All these calculations are shown in both volume (units) and in value (revenue) but, if appropriate, could be analyzed also in any other sub-divisions.

The Z chart as an auditing device

Another method for auditing forecasts is the use of the Z chart; this type of chart has already been discussed as a forecasting tool (page 232), but it can also be used for making graphical comparison of actual sales and forecasts.

Figure 69 shows a format that enables data to be collected relating

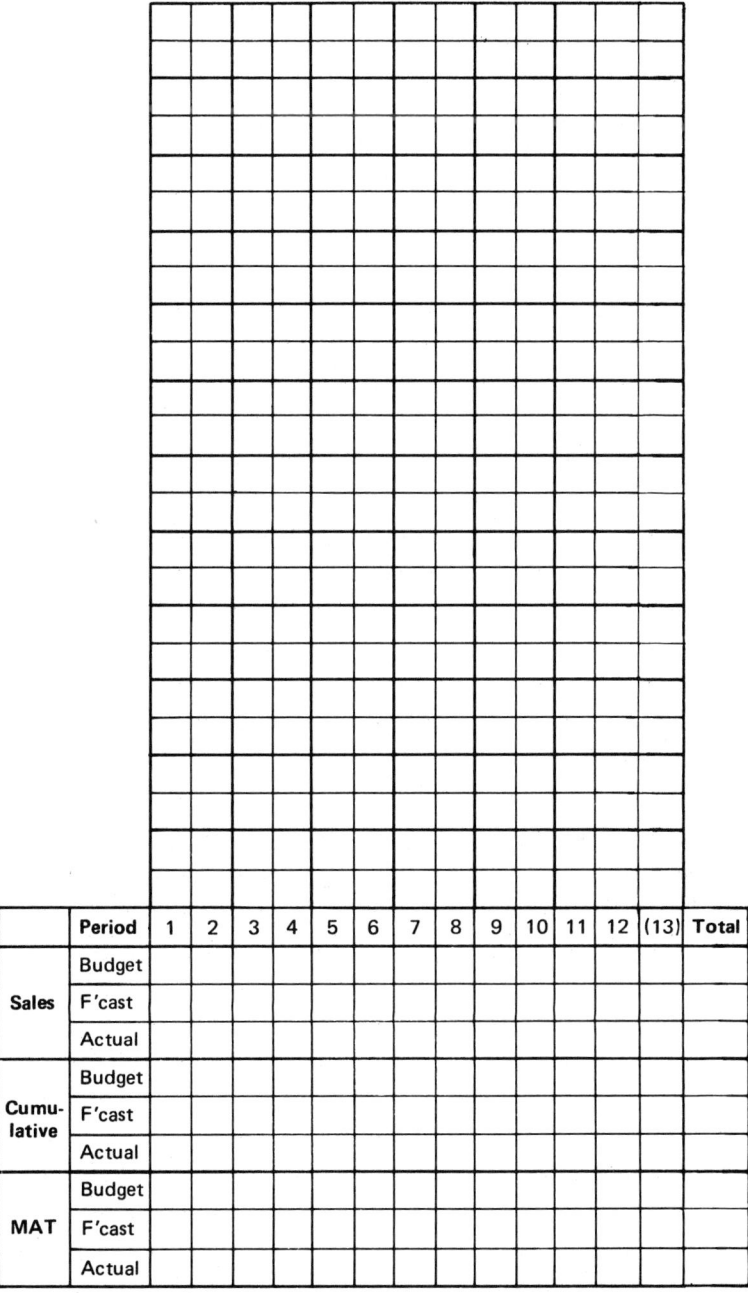

Figure 69. *The collection of budget forecast and actual sales as the basis for forming a Z chart to use as a control device*

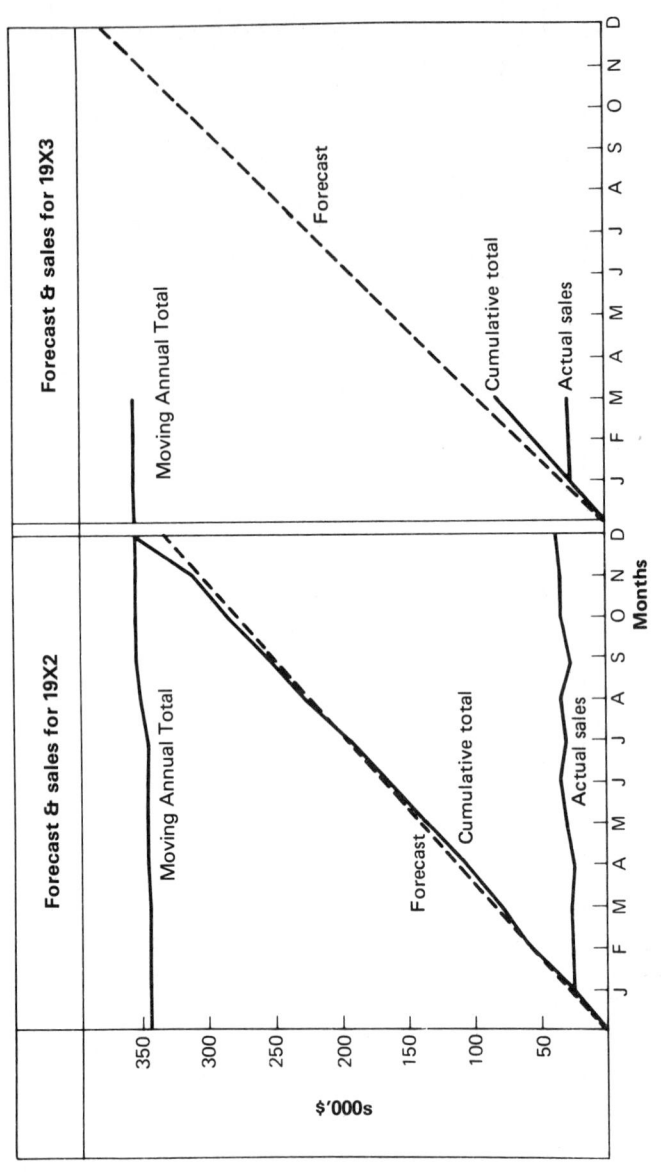

Figure 70. *The Z chart as an auditing tool — sales compared with forecast by months*

to the original forecast, the budget which is the forecast figure after it has been adjusted following management's examination of the financial implications of such a forecast, and the actual sales which are entered as they occur. These three measures are entered as actual sales values, cumulative values (the new values are added to the previous totals as they occur, see page 223) and as Moving Annual Totals, (see page 226).

Figure 69 could provide three Z charts, budget, forecast and actual sales; the former two acting as predictive devices (as on page 232) and the latter, actual sales, acting as a control device as in the following example.

The Z emerges as sales figures become available. In Table 59 a hypothetical sales situation is developed and the data shown can be expressed as a Z chart, see Figure 70.

In Figure 70 the Moving Annual Total and the cumulative total are calculated as shown earlier when the Z chart was used as a forecasting tool (Tables 28 and 29). The forecast is shown as a straight dotted line.

Month Year 19X2	Actual sales	Cumulative total	Moving Annual Total
January	25	25	346
February	26	51	346
March	28	79	347
April	25	104	348
May	30	134	349
June	32	166	349
July	30	196	349
August	32	228	350
September	28	256	352
October	31	287	353
November	33	320	354
December	35	355	355

The forecast for 19X2 was $330,000. The total sales figure for the previous year, 19X1, was $345,000.

Year 19X3	Actual sales	Cumulative total	Moving Annual Total
January	26	26	356
February	27	53	357
March	29	82	358

The forecast for 19X3 is $380,000.

Table 59. *Historic sales data and forecasts used to develop a Z chart for auditing purposes*

Market and Sales Forecasting

The situation shown in Figure 70 poses a number of questions when considering forecast and sales performance. For example, why was the forecast for 19X2 set at $330,000 when the total sales figure for 19X1 was $345,000; were there indications that the market would decline? Why were sales below the forecast line for the first half of 19X2 and above for the latter half? Was this due to seasonal fluctuations or are there other reasons? What were the reasons for increasing the sales forecast to $380,000 in 19X3 in what appears to be a relatively static sales situation? Is the market expanding or is some extra marketing effort being expended to achieve the higher figure? With regard to 19X3, it can be seen that, although the actual sales are higher each month compared with 19X2, total sales are proportionately further below the forecast line. This situation would indicate a need to re-examine all the factors involved, to determine whether the market and environment had changed radically and whether the forecast should be amended.

As sales performance figures become available they can be plotted on the second graph and a continuous comparison can be made.

The management accounting approach to auditing the forecast

An adaptation of accounting methods is useful where the sales forecast assessment is complicated during the forecasting period by changes in sales by units, price changes, dollar value changes, and perhaps by changes in the product mix. Further, in the previous chapter when the forecast was applied to product types, areas, and channels of distribution, profits influenced decisions. Therefore, a comparison of the effects of profit, sales and price performance against forecast is an important part of the total forecasting process. These relationships can be illustrated by the company situation depicted in Table 60.

Actual sales made during April 19X5 were:

Product X	3,000 units sold for	$6,500
Product Y	7,500 units sold for	$7,200
Product Z	9,400 units sold for	$4,200

It will be seen that a true assessment must take into account three possible variances, price, volume and product mix.

1. *Sales price variance* — comparing budget price and actual price obtained. This indicates the effect of changes in price made during the period, perhaps the result of special deals, increased discounts, etc.

Product	Budget price	Actual unit sales	Actual sales at standard price	Revenue obtained	Variance
X	$2.00	3,000	$6,000	$6,500	+$500
Y	$1.00	7,500	$7,500	$7,200	−$300
Z	$0.50	9,400	$4,700	$4,200	−$500
			Overall sales price variance		−$300

2. *Sales volume variance* — relating the volume of sales to profit or loss.

Product	Budgeted sales volume	Actual sales at standard prices	Variance	Profit margin	Profit margin × variance
X	$8,000	$6,000	−$2,000	40%	−$800
Y	$7,000	$7,500	+$500	30%	+$150
Z	$5,000	$4,700	−$300	20%	−$60
				Overall volume variance	−$710

3. *Product mix variance* — comparing the budgeted pattern or mix of products within the total budgeted sales with the actual pattern during the period.

Product	Units sold	Budgeted price	Actual sales at standard prices
X	3,000 @	$2.00	$6,000
Y	7,500 @	$1.00	$7,500
Z	9,400 @	$0.50	$4,700
	Total actual sales @ standard price		$18,200

In Table 60 the mix or pattern of sales in the budget is $8,000 of X, to $7,000 of Y, to $5,000 of Z; ie, 40%, 35% and 25% respectively of total budgeted sales at standard prices ($20,000). If actual sales had been made on this pattern the sales mix variance related to profit or loss would be as shown in Table 61.

Table 61 shows how sales of individual products deviated from the pattern or mix laid down in the budget and the consequent effect on profits. However, within the pattern laid down in the budget it is

Sales unit forecast	Product X 4,000		Product Y 7,000		Product Z 10,000		Total
	Each		Each		Each		
Sales at standard selling prices	$2.00	$8,000	$1.00	$7,000	$0.50	$5,000	$20,000
Standard cost of sales	$1.20	$4,800	$0.70	$4,900	$0.40	$4,000	$13,700
Standard profit on forecasted sales	$0.80	$3,200	$0.30	$2,100	$0.10	$1,000	$6,300

Table 60. *The sales budget and forecast of XYZ Inc for the month of April, 19X5*

Product	Budget pattern	Total actual sales at budget prices	Actual sales on budget pattern	Actual sales @ SP	Variance	Profit margin	Profit or loss
X	40% of	$18,200	$7,280	$6,000	−$1,280 ×	40%	−$512
Y	35% of	$18,200	$6,370	$7,500	+$1,130 ×	30%	+$339
Z	25% of	$18,200	$4,550	$4,700	+$150 ×	20%	+$30
					Total variance		−$143

Table 61. *Profit/loss of XYZ Inc if sales had been made on budgeted pattern giving a profit/loss variance*

possible for variances to occur within the sales mix. This can be seen by comparing budgeted sales with actual sales on the budget pattern as in Table 62.

1	2	3	4	5	6
Product	Budgeted sales volume	Actual sales on budget pattern	Variance (3 − 2)	Profit margin	Profit variance (4 × 5)
X	$8,000	$7,280	− $720	40%	− $288
Y	$7,000	$6,370	− $630	30%	− $189
Z	$5,000	$4,550	− $450	20%	− $90
				Quantity	− $567
			Total sales mix variance from Table 61		− $143
				Overall volume variance	− $710

Table 62. *A comparison of budgeted sales with actual sales on budget pattern*

The type of analysis shown in Tables 58, 59 and 60 clearly indicates where sales, revenue and profit are not according to forecast, and, therefore, where action should be taken.

Using probability in control of the forecast

Probability was used on a number of occasions in Chapter 7. Of particular application in auditing forecasts is the use of the probability control lines set two standard errors either side of a projected value. The graph from the earlier example is used to illustrate the usefulness of this device in Figure 71.

In Figure 71 a least squares trend line and control lines (two standard errors either side of it) were calculated on the original sales data available to the end of July, see Table 15 (page 178). The control lines have been projected to the end of the year, and the later sales values have been marked with an X.

The main use of this device is to indicate acceptable deviations away from the trend line. Thus the August, September, October and December values are within the acceptable limits. The November value, being just outside the lower limit line, would warrant investigation but not necessarily action. As two standard errors have been used there is a possibility that in five cases out of 100 the sales

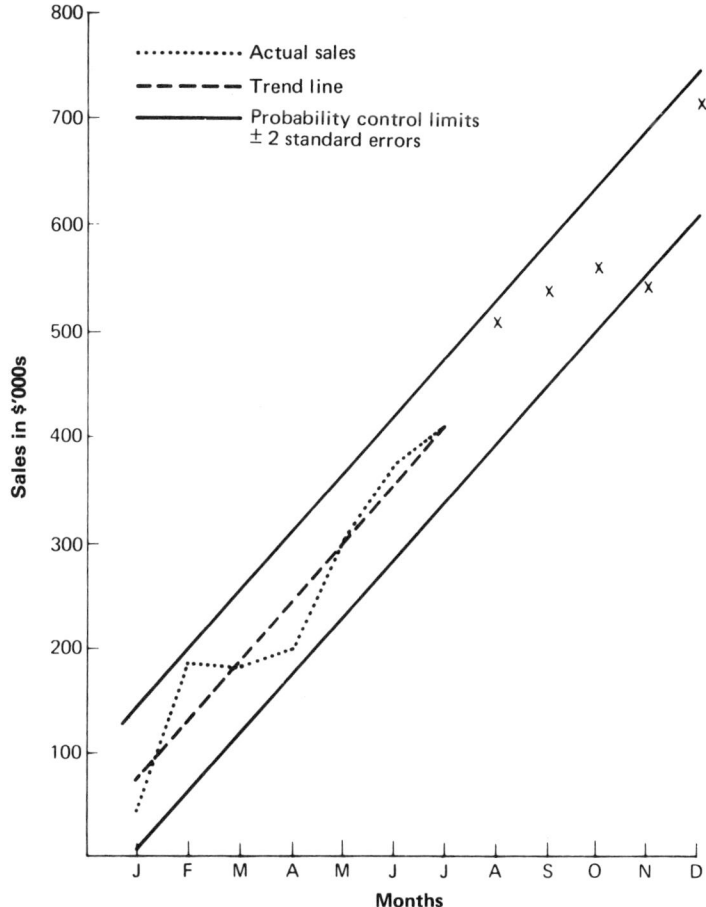

Figure 71. *A graph of monthly sales, a least squares trend line and confidence limits set two standard errors either side of the trend and projected into the future. The actual sales figures for later months are marked as X*

volume achieved will fall outside the limits. However, if the December value had also fallen below, this would increase the probability that there had been a fundamental change in the variables affecting the market place, although it could still be a matter of sheer chance. Investigation and action would need to follow; the result could be the amendment of the forecast.

Another use of this control method is that it affords comparisons to be made between different forecasts. Where the control lines are more narrowly placed in one case compared with another, it indicates that a greater degree of accuracy, and conversely a lower magnitude of variation in forecasting, could be expected. Where this is not the case, investigation as to the cause should be made and in many cases new factors, or the increased magnitude of some influencing factors, will be found.

By using probability (as shown in the section dealing with correlation – page 163) it would be possible to calculate the chance of obtaining a particular sales performance by sheer chance. If in a particular case the odds are very high against an achieved sales value being obtained by sheer chance, then it must be determined which new variables are present.

Quantitative assessments and measurement values
In Chapter 5 (page 111) it was shown that there were various quantitative assessment values to which a forecast could be related.

In addition to these quantitative assessments there are also measurement values that imply relationships between the various quantities and these are necessary yardsticks by which to measure the effectiveness of the forecast or the company's performance in a market. Three that are widely used are:

1. Market segmentation
This indicates the number of special segments the market has been divided into. When a new generic product concept is introduced there is no market segmentation initially, but, as the market develops and special consumer needs are identified and satisfied, the market becomes increasingly fragmented. Degrees of segmentation are possible either by using a scale of subjective values, ie a market can be seen to be 'highly segmented' or by quantifying. Quantification is possible by considering the number of special uses and/or applications, or by considering the use by socio-economic groupings, user industries, sex, age, location, etc.

2. Market saturation
This measurement term is usually expressed as a percentage, indicating the relationship of actual market volume to market potential. A market segment is saturated when actual market volume equals market potential (100%) and degrees of saturation are expressed as percentages. The degree of saturation is useful to the forecaster as an unsaturated market indicates marketing opportunity.

3. Market penetration
This measuring device relates company actual market share and sales

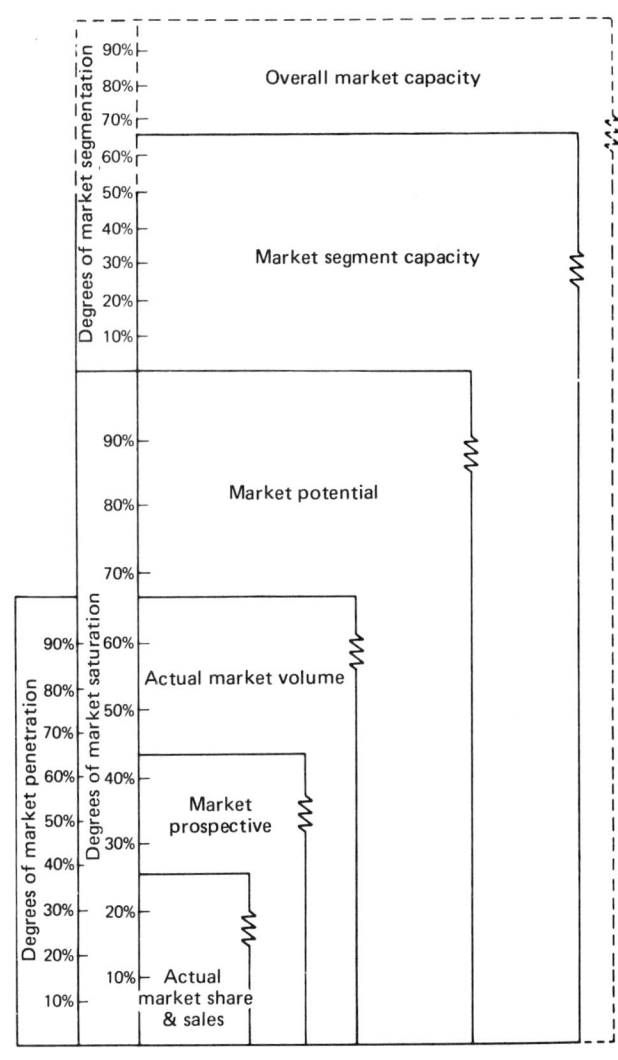

Figure 72. *Relationships between quantitative assessment and measurement values*

to actual market volume. Degrees of market penetration can be expressed as a percentage and can be used to assess the effectiveness of past marketing strategies and tactics, and also to set targets for the future, eg to increase market penetration from 10% to 15% in the next year.

The relationship between the various assessment terms, and between them and the measurement devices, can be seen in Figure 72.

Forecasts are made on assumed levels of segmentation, saturation and penetration. In the auditing process of forecasting, an assessment of actual sales compared with forecast in the light of these three factors may reveal that they have not progressed according to the anticipated pattern. Therefore, it may not be the machinery of a company forecast that is at fault but rather the assumptions and information on which the forecast was based.

Auditing the 'machinery' of forecasting

Earlier, it was stated that there should be a multi-technique approach to forecasting. From this a general pattern of forecasts will emerge and should there be any great difference between forecasts it will be a valuable exercise to discover why. Within the limitations of time, cost, availability of information, need, etc, as many techniques as possible should be used to build a composite forecast. The component forecasts can be used in total as a control device. They should be listed, compared with actual sales achieved, and the variances expressed as a percentage. The degree of accuracy between techniques is revealed, and over a number of periods a pattern of degrees of accuracy for each component forecast can be established. These degrees of accuracy will indicate the degree of reliability that can be placed on some methods of forecasting in the individual company situation, compared with others. Its reliable performance in the past must not cause unqualified acceptance of a forecast from a particular technique. All forecasts should be exposed to critical human judgement and intelligence, and assessed for credibility.

Further, an examination of the make-up of the various component forecasts in relation to their degrees of accuracy will often indicate the most important variables that are common to several forecasts. It might then be possible to improve the forecasting system by concentrating on methods that are dominated by these high priority variables.

Accuracy of forecasting methods

Listing the accuracy of the various forecasts also serves another purpose: it can be used as the basis for an audit of the techniques of forecasting. Some techniques that are relatively accurate during one part of the life of a product may become ineffective as the market situation changes. A forecasting method that has been relatively accurate and suddenly becomes less reliable should be investigated for the emergence of a new influencing factor in the market. Unless a forecasting method that is widely inaccurate over a period can be improved it should be dropped and an alternative found.

The life-cycle approach to choice of techniques

A life-cycle approach should be made to determine the combination of the various techniques that could be used. At the beginning of the life-cycle for a new generic product it will be impossible to use statistical techniques based on historic data, as none exists. In such a case it will be necessary to use basic marketing research methods, historical analogy, and subjective methods such as panels of experts or panels of executive opinion. As the life-cycle progresses, adjustments to techniques will have to be made, eg the alpha factor used in exponential smoothing may have to be radically changed. As the life-cycle levels out, the constant percentage increase method will become less effective, but segmentation analysis becomes more effective. However, basic methods of forecasting the economy or an individual market will tend to apply throughout the life-cycle.

The forecasting control cycle

Any system of control of forecasting depends upon the quality of feedback information, the effective analysis and interpretation of it, and the ability to make decisions regarding the need to change the forecast or the machinery of forecasting.

The stages of the cycle for the control of forecasts will vary with the needs of the various market situations, but ideally should include the stages shown in Figure 73.

In Figure 73 a logical starting point from which to consider the forecasting control cycle would be the information inputs. Although in practice there will be no starting point, the results of the previous output will provide part of the information of the new input, and the whole process can be seen to be continuous.

If the information input is considered it will be seen to be based on the reaction (a) by management through changes in the marketing plan, (b) by the market, and (c) by competitors, all within the context of environmental change. Together with data from monitoring and auditing the current market and sales forecast, this data will form the feedback information. Linked with new data it will provide the information input.

An appraisal of whether the techniques of forecasting need to be adjusted should be made in relation to their past performance as good predictors and the objectives of the forecast, by the forecaster or the forecasting committee.

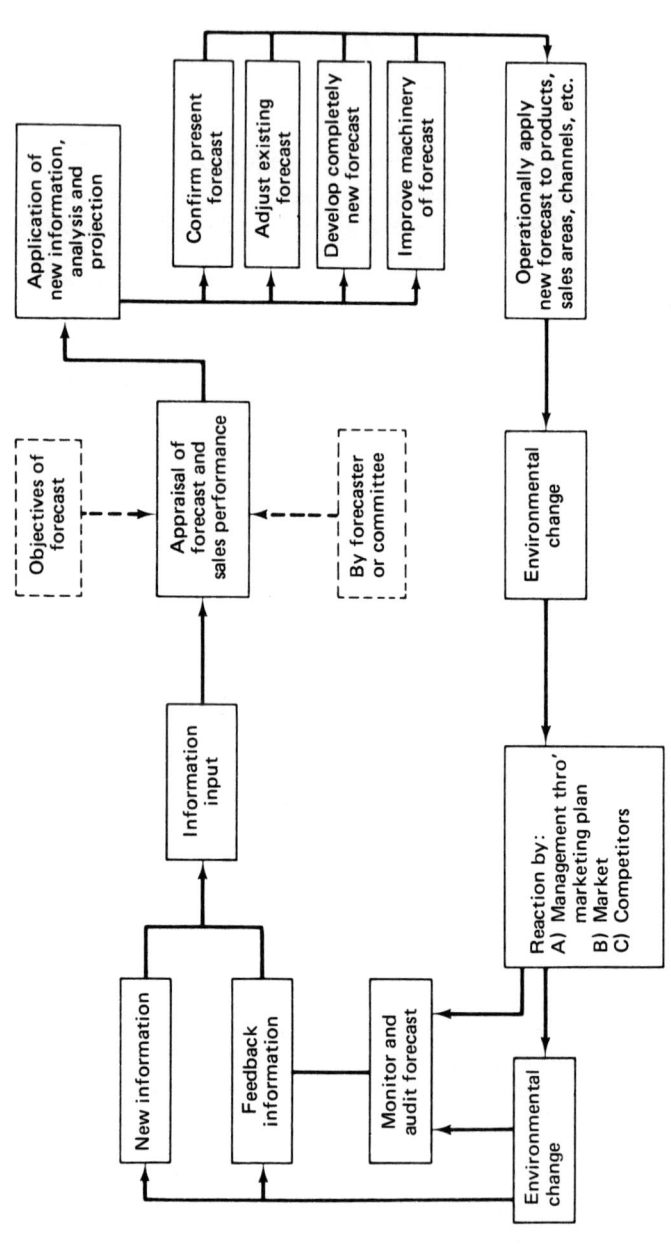

Figure 73. *Control of forecasts — a flow diagram of the forecasting control cycle*

The various techniques of forecasting are then applied to the new information input, and analysis and projection of the data are carried out to produce a series of forecasts. The variances between the various forecasts obtained through different techniques should be investigated and eventually reconciled.

The application of human intelligence and judgement should then be carried out on forecasts obtained by individual techniques and on the final overall composite forecast.

The integrated forecast (which may be for a total market, market segment, product range, or individual product type) is then either confirmed, adjusted, or a completely new forecast is evolved. Where existing techniques do not give forecasts in which the forecaster has a high degree of confidence, new techniques may have to be introduced or existing techniques modified.

Taking remedial action

The process of control involves not only the measurement of sales performance against a forecast but also taking remedial action on time.

The control flow process suggested in Figure 73 should take place on a continuous short-term basis (ie as sales figures become available) and also on a long-term ad hoc basis (perhaps an overall assessment once each year).

Just as the time periods for forecasting techniques (weekly, monthly, quarterly, yearly, etc) vary according to company needs, so will the time periods allowed before some adjustment is made to a forecast that is not proving to be relatively accurate. Weekly or monthly returns of information may indicate that sales performance is significantly different from the forecast, but a longer period should be allowed to elapse before the actual forecast is adjusted to the 'new pattern' of sales. But even when forecasts are adequate on a quarterly basis, the monitoring of weekly or monthly results will give an early indication of the need for possible change.

Re-forecasting

The time to re-forecast will be indicated when the acknowledged forecasting objectives are not being met and performance data are falling outside acceptable error limits or probability limits for that particular market. As a general rule this would not be done on a sample of one sales period unless it was obvious that the forecast was fundamentally poor. Usually, re-forecasting action will be taken after investigation and perhaps confirmation of a new emergent pattern through the results of further periods. The exception would be where factors change that are fundamental to the whole forecast, eg where a credit squeeze is imposed, thereby affecting the sales of products that

Market and Sales Forecasting

have to be financed, or where a new competitor enters a market having achieved a technological breakthrough in a particular product area, etc.

The facts that emerge from auditing forecasts (already mentioned in this chapter) may also indicate the basis for a revised forecast. For example, an in-depth investigation and analysis of the variance between sales and forecast may indicate the need to change the forecasting objectives or to amend the policies and/or programs by which the objectives are achieved. It may also indicate the need to develop new techniques that are more appropriate to the proposed revised forecast and show the need to re-train personnel involved in any change. It may even indicate the need to completely reorganize the forecasting function of a company.

By taking corrective action and revising the forecast, the forecaster is in effect setting new objectives, thereby starting the whole cycle (see Figure 73) again.

Setting forecasting objectives, standards and goals not only makes possible the development of policies and programs to achieve them, but also permits the measurement of every piece of relevant environmental and sales performance data. Effective forecasting control is not imposed simply to discover how good or bad forecasts have been in the past, but also to determine what action to take *today* to improve forecasting results *tomorrow*.

'This is not the end. It is not even the beginning of the end. But it is perhaps the end of the beginning...'
                                                                Winston Churchill

Index

accounting ratios, 94
actual market volume, 111, 113
adaptive filtering techniques, 264
advertising, 22, 26, 85, 104
    forecasting sales by assessment of, 259-61
    expenditure and sales, comparisons of, 259-60
    expenditure versus share of the market, share of, 259-60
applications engineering, 23
ARIMA, *see* Auto-Regressive Integrated Moving Average
aspirational groups, 132
assessment terms, 111-12
auditing of forecasting, 312ff
Auto-Regressive Integrated Moving Average, 258

Bayesian decision theory, 264-5, 287-90
'black box' models, 263-4
Box Jenkins method, 258
brainstorming, 143-4
brand life cycle, 36-64
brand management, 31-3
brand-switching models, 266-7
break-even analysis, 302-3
budgets, 29, 30, 31, 81-2, 84, 86, 309
business cycles, 75-9, 214-15
buying motives, 61-2
    general, 61
    industrial, 61-2

Census II, 247
channels sales volume, 92-3
classical decomposition methods, 246-8
co-efficient of correlation, 160-71
collection of data, 90-110

335

committed costs, 303-4
commodity units, 114
company market share/sales, 112
company resources, 20-21
comparative assessment formats, 318
comparative marketing, 140
competitive bidding situation, success
    forecasting in, 291-6
competitive elements, 20-21
competitive patterns, 57-60
competitor activity, forecasting of,
    218ff
competitors as sources of data, 101,
    105
composite forecasts of sales force,
    279-80
composite opinion, probability and
    forecasting by, 284-6
computers, 269-71
conferences, 29, 30
constant or base year price sales
    volume data, 112
consumer income levels, 45-6
consumer markets, 33-4
consumer sales data, 54-6
consumer satisfaction environment,
    72-3
consumer/user behavior
    change in, 130-5
    during life cycle, 60-2
consumer/user purchasing intentions,
    survey of, 277-8
continuous data, 205-6
correlation, 154-71
    co-efficient of, 160-71
    and company sales, 157-62
    with economic indicators, 155-7
    inverse or negative, 164-8
    multiple, 168-71
    and regression analysis, 154-5
critical path and network scheduling,
    29, 30
cultures and sub-cultures, 130-1
current price sales volume data, 112

decision models, 264-5
decline stage, 38-9, 44-6, 49, 58-9
'decomposition' of sales data, 212-14,
    246-8
Delphi approach, 144, 276-8
demand analysis, 116-19
    and elasticity and price, 116-19
demography, 130
derived demand and tied indicators,
    151
deseasonalized sales data, 217-18

desk research,
   into internal records, 91-5
   into secondary sources of
      information, 95-103
direct extrapolation, 145
directories as sources of data, 100
dissociative groups, 132
distribution, 27-8, 85, 92-3, 104,
   307-9
   system, change in, 123-30

econometric models, 188
economic indicators, 122-3, 124-7,
   155ff
   and market correlation, 155-7
economies of scale, 50-52
enumerated data, 205, 206-8
envelope curve extrapolation, 146-7
ex-factory sales data, 54-6
expansion demand, 43
expected value concept, 264
   probability and, 286-7
experimental marketing, 108-9
expert opinion, surveys of, 280-1
exploitation stage, 38-9, 41, 49, 58-9
exponential smoothing or weighting,
   250-9, 263-4
   forecast using deseasonalized
      data, 253-4
   seasonally weighted, 255-6
   sophisticated techniques of, 256-8
external influences, 21

face-to-face groups, 132
field inspections, 29, 30
field research, 103-5
   use of in forecasting, 109-110
Foran System, 247-8
forecasting control cycle, 331-3
forecasting errors, sum of, 314
forecasting objectives, 81-6
   and finance, 84-5
   and marketing, 84-8
   and personnel, 84
   and production, 83
   and purchasing, 83
   and research and development, 83
forecasts,
   application of, 301-11
      in consumer goods markets,
         306-7
      by distribution channels, 307-9
      in industrial markets, 306
      to profit centers, 306
      to sales territories, 306

as a basis for budgeting and control, 309
collection of data for, 90-110
company-wide uses of, 86, 87-8
controlling of, 312-34
as decision-making tools, 301
long-term, 74, 76-7
medium-term, 74, 75-6
planning role of, 67
short-term, 74-5
as targets, 67-8
versus actual sales, 313
frequency distributions, 192

government controls, 21
government sources of data, 96-9

historical analogy, 210-15, 298-9
Holt-Winters exponential smoothing method, 258

indicator assessment method, 272-5
industrial change, 135-9
industrial markets, 33-4, 104
industry or market environment, 72-3
input/output tables, 135-9
internal influences, 22
international change, 139-41
international environment, 72-3
international sources of data, 102
introduction stage, 38-9, 40, 49, 57-8
inverse correlation, 162-6
investment, 22

job description, 29, 30

large contracts, probability forecasting with, 290-1
lead and lag techniques, 151-4
chain reaction in, 153-4
lead/coincident and lag method, 152-3
learned behavior, models based on, 265
learning theories, 133-5
least squares method, 171ff, 264-5
with confidence limits, 176-8
with even number of items, 175-6
using non-time-constrained data, 184-7
life cycle approach, 300
to choice of techniques, 331
life cycle stage recognition, 60
linear models, 265
line of best fit approach, 146
long/short-term performance graph, 147-8

major customer forecasting, 296-7
managed costs, 303-4
   appropriation of, 304
management accounting approach to
   auditing forecast, 322-6
market and sales forecasting, 26
   67ff, & *passim*
market development stage, 38-9, 40-1,
   49, 57-9
market economy, 18
market forces, 73-4
marketing audits, 29, 30
marketing cost data, 93
marketing, definition of, 17
marketing executive 29, 31
marketing mix, 21, 22-9, 32
marketing research, 22, 23, 300
marketing strategy, life cycle effect
   on, 63
market intelligence, 23
market orientation, 19
market penetration, 328-30
market potential, 111, 113
market prospective, 111-2, 113
market saturation, 328
market segmentation, 328
market segment capacity, 111, 113
market share,
   forecasting of, 218ff
   models, 265
Markov process, 266
MAT, *see* Moving Annual Totals
maturation stage, 38-9, 41-3, 49, 58-9
measured data, 205-6
measurement of change, 122-49
measurement values, 328-30
membership groups, 132
merchandising, 104
metamarketing, 17
model building, 261-4
morphological research, 141-2
motivation research, 108
Moving Annual Totals, 226-32
   232-6
moving averages, 237ff
   and cyclical trends, 239-40
   problems of non-typical items,
     236-9
   projection, 239
   and seasonal fluctuations, 241
   trend, seasonal and random
     variation (decomposition)
     analysis through, 242-6
   weighted, 248-9
Moving Quarterly Totals, 226-32
MQT, *see* Moving Quarterly Totals
multiple correlation, 168-71

multiple regression, 188
multi-product companies, life cycles in, 56-7
multi-technique approach, 120-1
multivariate analysis, 168-71

national economy environment, 72-3
negative correlation, 164-8
new products, sales forecasting for, 298-300
non-government sources of data, 99-100
'normal' distribution, 189-90
    curve, 195-7
normative relevance tree techniques, 142-3

objective methods of forecasting, 150-271
objective/subjective forecast plan, 310-11
observational methods of data-gathering, 108
operational marketing plan, 29, 30
order size statistics, 93
overall market capacity, 111, 113

packaging, 25, 27, 85, 104
panel of executive opinion, 278
panel or audit methods of data-gathering, 107-8
percentage change method, 216-8
percentage increase/decrease method, 261
percentage take-off graphs, 223-6
performance appraisal, 29, 30
postal surveys, 107
preference analysis, 267-8
pre-forecasting considerations, 68
press sources of data, 100
pricing policy, 25
pricing studies and income, 119-20
'private-labelling', 52
probability, 188ff
    and expected values, 286-7
    and forecasting by composite opinion, 284-6
    forecasting demand using, 198-9
    forecasting with large contracts, 290-1
    forecasting replacement demand with, 200-4
    and uncertainty in subjective forecasting, 281-2
    judgements, 282

range displays, visual, 282
  using in control of forecasts, 326-8
product group management, 31-3
production 'blocks', 48-50
production economy, 46-8
product life cycle, 21, 36-64
  models, 268
product mix, 56-7
  and ratio analysis, 305
  variance, 323
product orientation, 19
product/service development, 25
product/service planning, 52-3
product support group, 28
profit centers,
  application of forecasts to, 306
  concept of, 29, 30
profit gap analysis, 70
profit planning, 53-4
proportional data, 205, 206-8
'prudent manager' forecasting, 278-9
public relations, 22, 26

quantitative assessments, 328-30

ranking variances, 314
ratio analysis, 29, 30
  and product mix, 305
ratio of period sales to forecast, 314
reference groups, 132-3
re-forecasting, 333-4
regression analysis, 154-5
remedial action, 334
repeat demand, 43
replacement demand, 43
research and development, 22, 37-40, 49, 58, 83

sales and cost analysis, 29, 30
sales 'curves', 48-50
sales force, 27, 85
  composite forecasts of, 279-80, 300
  as information sources, 105-6
  statistics, 94
sales forecasting definitions, 79-82
sales leads as a basis for forecasting, 261
sales potential, 93
sales price variance, 322-3
sales promotion, 27, 104
sales service, 28

sales volume,
    as data for forecasting, 91-3
    variance, 323
saturation stage, 38-9, 43-4, 49, 58-9
scenario writing approach, 144-5
'S' curve trend comparison, 147
seasonal adjustments to straight line trends, 180-4
segmentation, 215, 216
short- and long-term comparisons, 173-5
SIC, *see* Standard Industrial Classification
simple regression, 187
simulation models, 269
social/socio-economic classes, 131-2
sociological change, 130-5
standard deviation, 190ff
standard error,
    application of, in forecasting, 208-10
    calculating from enumerated data, 206-8
    calculating from measured data, 205-6
    as a monitoring device, 314-15
    use of, 204-51
Standard Industrial Classification, 92-3
stock control data, 94
subjective factor assessment, 275
subjective methods of forecasting, 272-7
subscription and consultancy services, 101
substitute approach, 300
systems analysis, 142

taxes, local, state or federal, 115
technological change/forecasting, 141-9
technological trend extrapolation, 145-9
telephone surveys, 107
test market approach, 299
tied indicators and derived demand, 151
time series analysis, 210-14

uncertainty,
    index, 282-3
    made visible, 282-3
    and probability in subjective forecasting, 282-3

value satisfactions, 19
variance analysis, 313-14, 315
vector approach, 145
visual probability range displays, 282

weighted moving averages, 248-9

Z chart, 232-7
    as an auditing device, 318-22

NOW . . . ANNOUNCING THESE OTHER FINE BOOKS FROM SPECTRUM

DO IT NOW: How To Stop Procrastinating, Dr. William J. Knaus. In *Do It Now*, the author explains how you can stop putting things off by breaking the procrastination habit. Dr. Knaus shows how to recognize and overcome the bad habits that cause you to delay and postpone. Included are simple techniques for stimulating a person into action.
☐ $5.95 paperback (216606)   ☐ $11.95 hardback (216614)

QUALITY CIRCLES MASTER GUIDE: Increasing Productivity with People Power, Sud Ingle. This book shows exactly how the productivity techniques used so effectively in Japan can be applied to Western technology to improve performance and productivity on the job. This guide explains step by step the methods used to create a harmonious feeling among workers, improve morale, produce higher-quality products without increasing costs, and get started on a quality drive without having to make a large investment. A must book for managers.
☐ $14.95 paperback (745000)   ☐ $24.95 hardback (745018)

THINK ON YOUR FEET: The Art of Thinking and Speaking Under Pressure, Kenneth Wydro. For anyone who must speak in front of a large group of people, here's a book that reveals dozens of exercises, examples, and insights into the creative process of quick thinking. *Think on Your Feet* shows how to relax and free the creative mind instantly, how to take command of any situation, how to develop confidence, and much more.
☐ $4.95 paperback (917807)   ☐ $11.95 hardback (917815)

To order any of these books, please complete the form below.

Please send me the books I've checked above. Enclosed is my check or money order for	
_____ Yes, please send me the Spectrum Catalog of all your fine books. Please add 50¢ per book for postage and handling.	___.50 _____
TOTAL	_____
Name _____	
Address _____	
City _____ State _____ Zip _____	
Cut out and mail this form to: Prentice-Hall, Inc. Spectrum Books Att: C. Moffa Englewood Cliffs, New Jersey 07632	
Prices subject to change without notice. Please allow 4 weeks for delivery.	